The Skillful Leader II

Confronting Conditions That Undermine Learning

The Skillful Leader II

Confronting Conditions That Undermine Learning

Alexander D. Platt, Ed.D.

Caroline E. Tripp, Ed.D.

Robert G. Fraser, Ed.D., J.D.

James R. Warnock, M.Ed.

Rachel E. Curtis, M.Ed.

READY ABOUT PRESS
Distributed by Research for Better Teaching
Acton, Massachusetts

Cover and text design: Catherine Hawkes
Composition: Jessica Phillips
Production Management: Post Publishing Services
Developmental and copy editing: Merry B. Post

Contents

We dedicate this book, with love and hope, to a future generation of learners—to Deven, Nora, Maggie, Brady, Will, Nate, Isabel, Ava, Alex, Kosmo, Namid, Sophie, Ben, and all their schoolmates for years to come.

Preface

It's not fair!" children often say. We agree. American schools are still not fair. Whether you attend school in the wealthiest suburb or the poorest urban or rural setting, your chances are low of being consistently assigned and able to rely upon a teacher who cares about you, a teacher who knows you individually and knows the course content deeply, a teacher who expects great performance and demands that you rise to meet that challenge. Despite more than 15 years of sustained educational reform, what you get to learn and how you get to learn it in America still depends. . . It depends in large measure on how much mediocrity your school, your school district, and your individual teachers have learned to tolerate and have accidentally or deliberately come to protect.

We wrote volume I of *The Skillful Leader* because we were moved by the plight of children consigned to classrooms where no real learning took place and by the pain of teachers and administrators who knew what was happening and felt powerless to stop it. We believed then, and still do, that one good teacher can make an extraordinary difference in the life of a child. But one good teacher is not enough. For learners to have a fair shot in American schools and classrooms, the quality of their education cannot depend on luck or privilege. It cannot depend on the presence of dedicated individuals who may briefly give children access to a scarce commodity. Schools have to be full of expert practitioners; districts have to be full of schools that demand and produce high-quality learning. Somehow we have to solve what Richard Elmore (2005) calls the problem of scale. We need to influence positively, and permanently, the caliber of every single exchange between those who teach and those who learn. The task is a daunting one.

Since we first reported leaders' dilemmas in 2000, we have watched with great interest as a series of policies, procedures and whole-school initiatives have been aimed at solving the "teacher quality" challenge. The opportunities to confront mediocrity—and the interventions designed to take advantage of those opportunities—seem to fall into four basic categories:

- *Externally imposed mandates, policies, systems, and structures* such as those found in the No Child Left Behind regulations that are designed to raise teacher quality across the board
- *Institutionally controlled systems and procedures*, from curriculum revision to supervision and evaluation, that are intended to influence practice at the local district level
- *School-based practices* designed to build shared conviction, and sometimes competence, in the adults most directly responsible for student learning
- *Supervisory skills, strategies, and structures* meant to address individual cases of mediocre performance

Underlying each of these new efforts to ensure that every child has access to expert instruction are quite different assumptions about what the problem is, who "owns" the problem, and what the solutions might be.

District- and school-based interventions attempt to influence the contexts in which people operate. They share an assumption that some of the blame for mediocre student and adult learning can be placed on local conditions: politics, policies, practices, structures, lack of rigor, and low expectations that block improvement efforts. Much of our new work focuses on what leaders can do to change the district and school contexts that support and sustain mediocrity. Specifically, we see the potential value of mobilizing people into high-performing professional communities capable of bringing about genuine improvement. We also see the current dilemmas of group work gone awry:

- Adults caught in a ferocious whirlwind of activities for activities' sake
- Exercises in compliance that meet the institution's need for superficial indicators of progress but produce little or no substantive learning
- Opportunities lost and ideas buried because the toxicity of the exchanges between colleagues or the deadening impact of ineffectual leadership silences individuals who are quietly pursuing excellence

These pages are a compilation of what we have learned by listening and looking, exchanging ideas with colleagues, and analyzing what happens when administrators and teachers try to spread new knowledge and improved instruction from one narrow arena to an entire school. Chapters are organized to consider multiple entry points for confronting the conditions that undermine learning.

Chapter 1, "Conditions Worth Changing," presents three portraits of instructional improvement that has been encapsulated and blocked from spreading. These cases introduce the potential power of effective professional communities and the ways in which leaders overlook or tolerate "unprofessional" communities, failure to collaborate, and adults who are no longer learning. Chapter 2, "Confronting Blocks to Organizational Learning," describes the symptoms of five conditions, ranging from Broken

Lens Syndrome and Organizational Attention Deficit Disorder to Feedback Failure, that have a negative affect on a district's ability to spread improvement from one part of the organization to another. It suggests ways that leaders can check for the presence of these conditions and actions they can take to change them.

Chapters 3 through 6 focus on the role of professional communities in bringing about school-wide gains in student learning. To help leaders analyze the behavior of different subgroups within their schools, "Professional Communities and Mediocre Learning" (Chapter 3) describes community function as a continuum that includes five different professional cultures: toxic, laissez-faire, congenial, collaborative, and accountable. This chapter also examines the capacities (Conviction, Competence, and Control) that high-functioning professional groups need to tackle student learning problems effectively. "Community Building 101: Setting the Stage" (Chapter 4) is full of practical strategies for helping groups develop their Conviction, Competence, and Control. Chapter 5 "Challenging and Changing Malfunctioning Groups" focuses on cases of low-functioning schools and groups whose failure to collaborate affects learning opportunities for students. Ineffective and effective strategies for intervening with such groups follow each case. Readers who are dealing with schools characterized by inconsistent adult learning and ineffective teams or departments may want to start with this chapter. Chapter 6 "Moving Communities from Collaborative to Accountable" presents a serial case study of an improving school that is temporarily stuck and trying to move from excellent learning for some to excellent learning for all. Here we examine a number of different potential stretch points superintendents and principals can use, including the development and nurture of teacher leaders.

Chapters 7 through 13 are resource chapters to help readers with practical strategies for ongoing challenges and everyday tasks. "Collecting and Using Data: Vehicles" (Chapter 7) presents many different structures for gathering data in order to use it in learning focused supervision, learning focused evaluation, and collaborative problem solving. In Chapter 8 "Collecting and Using Data: Sources," we explore the same applications, but this time we focus on selecting sources of data for supervision and evaluation and for identifying obstacles to student learning. School leaders need skill in confronting individuals who ruin groups. Chapter 9 "Confronting Individuals Who Undermine Learning" contains eight profiles of typical "underminers" organized in three categories: Teachers Who Actively Undermine Team Functioning, Teachers Who Detract from Group Competence, and Leaders Who Do Not Lead. Each profile is accompanied by an analysis of ineffective versus skillful approaches to intervening with the individual in order to bring about a change in performance. Chapter 10 "Improving Hiring, Induction, and Tenure Decisions" examines the Conviction, Competence, and Controls necessary to staff our schools with high-functioning teachers and collaborators. Chapter 11 "Principal Development and Support" offers practical, field-tested approaches for recruiting and developing high-performing school leaders. No matter what their skills and background, all leaders eventually face the need to respond to unmet expectations and unprofessional behavior in the workplace. Thus Chapter 12 "Responding to Behaviors That Undermine Learning" offers a range of ways to communicate stop-start messages and models for escalating the response if the first effort is unsuccessful. Chapter 13 "Influencing Contracts and Collective Bargaining" examines the impact of certain legal obligations on a leader's ability to staff each classroom with the best possible teacher available.

This book, like a baby elephant, had a long gestation. During the 22 or so months it was taking shape, other ideas, advice from wonderful colleagues, and nuggets from reading and research found their way onto a list of things to consider. When it became clear that this was an expanding elephant, we had to begin cutting. Hence the Epilogue in which we offer some of those ideas as hopes to sustain the leaders we admire as they pursue their commitment to confronting mediocrity.

Acknowledgments

This is the scariest part of a book to write. We want to remember and acknowledge everyone, and we know that we will not be successful on our first attempt. Moreover, if we were to cite all the people who have shaped our thinking, enriched our understanding, and listened to our bellyaching as we wrote, the list might be as long as the book itself! We have been truly fortunate to have extraordinary colleagues who have given selflessly of their time and insights. First, thanks go to all of the members of Research for Better Teaching and particularly to: Jon Saphier our respected guide and mentor who has influenced us in so many ways over the years, Mary Ann Haley-Speca and Deb Reed who trained us, Sandra Spooner who coached and encouraged us along the deadline-ridden road, Kathy Spencer and Ned Paulsen who assisted us greatly with case studies and early drafts, and Maxine Minkoff and Greg Ciardi who kept us focused on indicators of student learning and places with great expectations. Ken Chapman's contributions of written models and a process for documenting poor performance were invaluable. Ruth Sernak bravely went team-building in difficult places and reported what she learned. Nancy Love generously gave us crash courses and critical feedback on using data. Ann Stern, the queen of shared resources, taught us about standards and criteria—and tries to keep us honest and laughing. Elizabeth Imende Cooney and Laura Porter inspire us daily with their energy and innovative teaching. Marcia Booth skillfully transforms our initially vague ideas into workable strategies, and Fran Prolman-Zimmerman excels at modeling courage and conducting difficult conferences. We would be lost without the incomparable RBT home team of Ivy Schutt, Carole Fiorentino, Penny Kudirka, and Bill Moonan whose enviable grace under fire and unfailing support pick us up and set us back on course again and again.

We are especially grateful for those individuals who invited us into their schools and classrooms or shared stories of their learning as we gathered data for this book. These include: Paul Bambrick-Santoyo, Andrew Bott, Laura Bott, Karen Daniels, Mary Driscoll, Jose Duarte, Dana Lee Platt

Feingold, Suzanne Federspiel, Michael Fung, Alyssa Goodrich, Elizabeth Goettls, Cathy Guy, William Henderson, Carrie Hickey, Linda Hunt, Richard Kelley, Aimee Morgan, Mairead Nolan, Janie Ortega, Tina Penna, Shana Pyatt, Vera Rowsey, Richard Schaye, Mary Skipper, Cindy Tucker, Sandy Weist, and Anne Zeman.

A number of leaders deserve immense gratitude for inviting us to do sustained work with their administrative teams, study their district initiatives, and collect data intermittently over several years. Gary Cohn, Superintendent, and Michelle Reid of the Port Angeles (WA) School district and the entire Port Angeles administrative team reacted to early drafts. Patricia Grey, Principal of Balboa High School, San Francisco, helped us think about how to build powerful high school learning communities. Phyllis Harrington, Superintendent, Laura Seinfeld, Assistant Superintendent, Dennis O'Hara, High School Principal, Allyson Brown, Laura Keenan, Pat Murray, Tom Lynch, Jen Etline and the entire administrative team from Oyster Bay East Norwich School District (NY) provided a laboratory to pilot learning focused supervision.

Dozens of colleagues in the Center for Skillful Teaching and throughout the Montgomery County Public Schools helped us to understand what a sustained commitment to adult growth and learning and to workforce excellence looks like and can accomplish. We thank Darlene Merry, former Associate Superintendent for Organizational Development; Bonnie Cullison, President of the Montgomery County Education Association; Dr. Rebecca Newman, President of the Montgomery County Association of Administrative and Supervisory Personnel; Peg Donnellon, Director of the Center for Skillful Teaching, and Larry Bowers, Chief Operating Officer. Their shared vision of what collaboration could accomplish and their high expectations have been transformative.

Margarita Muñiz, Jen Moghaddam, and Melanie Livingston of the Hernandez School, Boston, were helpful in piloting student-focused data conferences. The vision and skill of Eliot Stern, Principal, Edison Middle School, Boston, strongly influenced our thinking about teacher leadership and instructional leadership teams. Paul Dakin, Superintendent, and Ann Marie Costa, Assistant Superintendent, of the Revere (MA) Public Schools provided us with concrete images of high-functioning administrative teams and leaders who stay the course to produce results. Mike Hanson, currently superintendent of Fresno Unified, as Associate Superintendent in Elk Grove pushed our thinking about instructional leadership. We are indebted to Dr. Thomas Levine of the University of Connecticut who contributed valuable insights, leader alerts, and helpful notes about community building based on his recent research at Stanford.

Our team also included critical friends. For reading and critiquing early chapter drafts and for their wise counsel we thank: Irwin Blumer, Research Professor, Educational Administration and Higher Education, Boston College; Judy Boroschek, Former Director of Curriculum and Instruction for the Wellesley (MA) Public Schools; Diane Rispoli Canino, Clinical Professor of Educational Leadership, Syracuse University; Liz City; Peter Dillon, Executive Director of Policy, Office of Portfolio Development, New York

City Department of Education; Tim Knowles, Executive Director of the Center for Urban School Improvement, University of Chicago; Peter Mello, Director, Castleton College Center for Schools, Castleton, VT; Michelle Reid, Asssistant Superintendent, Port Angeles (WA); Henry Scipione, Superintendent, York (ME) Public Schools, Lee Teitel Lecturer on Education and Director of the Executive Leadership Program for Educators at Harvard University; Holden Waterman, Superintendent, Lamoille South Supervisory Union, VT. Pam Posey and Diane Dillon gave critical feedback on cover choices, and Shirley Stiles assisted in designing walks.

Special, heartfelt thanks go to the following sustaining members of our "stick it out and do it right" team: the late Ellen Cunniff, a superb principal and our esteemed colleague, helped us to truly understand the attributes of high-quality supervision. Judy Boroschek and Lanea Tripp applied their eagle eyes and incisive intelligence to early research and did a thorough final review of the manuscript; they helped us make sense of what we had tried to say.

Carolyn Platt cheerfully read and proofread, and edited and read again, and Kate Bowers counseled on overcoming writer's block and meeting deadlines. Patty Fraser, Ray Tripp, Carol Gibson Warnock, and all the offspring, in-laws, and "grands" patiently endured several years worth of lost evenings and weekends, book meetings in corners, moaning monologues, and absent-minded encounters. They helped us stay centered and sane.

Finally, we are most fortunate to have worked with Merry Post, a most skillful and tolerant project manager and editor who never lost her sense of humor. Merry's hand and head are everywhere in this book.

About the Authors

Alexander D. Platt, Ed.D.

Andy Platt is a founding and senior consultant with Boston-based consulting firm Research for Better Teaching (RBT). In 2000 he founded Ready About Consulting, dedicated to working with leaders of underperforming schools. He specializes in coaching urban principals on raising the quality of instruction through supervision and has presented at many national conferences and institutes including the Harvard Institute for School Leaders and the Association of California School Administrators (ACSA). He has taught long-term supervision and evaluation courses to over two thousand administrators in the United States, and to administrators in Europe and Japan. Dr. Platt has been an Assistant Superintendent for Curriculum in the Wayland (MA) Public Schools, a leadership consultant to NESDEC (New England School Development Council), and has served as President of the Massachusetts Association for Supervision and Curriculum Development (MASCD). He is the lead author on the best-selling book, *The Skillful Leader: Confronting Mediocre Teaching*.

Caroline E. Tripp, Ed.D.

Caroline Tripp is a consultant with Research for Better Teaching (RBT) and a member of the faculty of the Boston Principal Fellows program. She specializes in helping districts build effective administration teams, designing and implementing supervision and evaluation systems for teachers and administrators, and supporting the development of new administrators. For the past nine years, Dr. Tripp has been the director of curriculum and training for RBT's joint project on workplace excellence with the Montgomery County (MD) Public Schools. Caroline is a former lecturer at the Harvard Graduate School of Education and Assistant Superintendent of the Shrewsbury, MA, Public Schools. She has presented nationally on a wide range of topics related to teacher quality and leadership development and is a co-author of *The Skillful Leader: Confronting Mediocre Teaching*.

Robert Fraser, Ed.D., J.D.

Bob Fraser is an attorney and former Assistant Superintendent for Personnel with more than 32 years' experience as a labor negotiator. His primary areas of expertise are personnel administration, labor law, negotiations, and education law, including special education. Dr. Fraser has been a member of the Massachusetts and American Associations for School Personnel Administrators. He is a partner at the Boston law firm of Stoneman, Chandler and Miller, and he has been an instructor at Boston University and Harvard School of Education.

James R. Warnock, M.Ed.

Jim Warnock is a consultant with the Boston-based consulting firm Research for Better Teaching and has 30 years' experience in education. His consulting work centers on instructional leadership, teacher training, supporting districts in developing standards-based supervision and evaluation systems, and working with principals of underperforming schools. Jim also directs the Sino-American Seminar on Educational Leadership for the University of Vermont's Asian Studies Outreach Program and has traveled and worked extensively throughout China. He has provided technical assistance to schools in Russia as part of a U.S. Department of State Community Connections program and has conducted teacher training in Australia. Jim was Assistant Superintendent of Schools for the city of Burlington, VT, and also served as a secondary principal, K-12 staff developer, and teacher.

Rachel E. Curtis, M.Ed.

Rachel has 20 years' experience working in and with urban school districts and has taught at the early childhood and graduate levels and provided student support at the secondary level. Rachel most recently served as the Assistant Superintendent for Teaching and Learning in the Boston Public Schools. During her decade of work in Boston, her accomplishments included: devising the instructional coaching model that is currently used district-wide for literacy and math coaching; founding the Boston Principal Fellowship and supporting the creation of the Boston Teacher Residency, nationally recognized, district-based principal and teacher certification programs; and developing teaching standards and a new teacher induction program and evaluation system aligned to the standards. Rachel now consults with school systems, foundations, higher education, and the policy sector on human capital strategies for urban schools.

The Skillful Leader II

Confronting Conditions
That Undermine Learning

 # Conditions Worth Changing

This is a test. It does not claim to be high stakes or scientific, but take it all the same. Imagine that you are an educational leader, in either a teaching or an administrative position, and you are contemplating three different schools that must improve student achievement. To pass this test you'll have to choose the right course of action for each case school, but first you will have to decide what the problem is.

CASE 1.1 **Mid-Balkans High School**

Without exception, the teaching in the English department at Mid-Balkans is excellent. Student achievement scores have risen significantly in each of the last five years for all subgroups. The number of minority students successfully completing AP and college level courses in English has doubled in the last three years. The department is the poster child of reform for the Central Office, which regularly parades visitors through its classes. However, no other department produces such results, and all the positive attention to English has engendered resentment among faculty members. Stung by cynical comments about how they are "mollycoddlers" and "bleeding hearts," half the English teachers say they are no longer willing to spend time arguing the merits of the strategies they use. They keep to their own wing unless there is a required school-wide meeting.

By contrast, mathematics achievement at MBHS reached an all-time low two years ago. The superintendent attributed the poor performance to weak departmental leadership, and she and the principal "restructured" the high school administration in response. They moved the former math department head to a district curriculum job and recruited Marla W, an assistant principal from Tech High with an outstanding math background. Charged with leading "a school-wide effort to improve mathematics achievement," Ms. W quickly introduced the same textbook series that Tech High had been successfully using and organized a series of voluntary workshops that were sparsely attended and much ridiculed. Failure rates in the 9th and 10th grade soared, and teachers blamed the new materials. By the end of the second year, most of the juniors who wanted to take calculus were being told they were ineligible because of their sophomore grades. In response, the Mid-Balkans principal diverted funds that were supposed to go to science textbooks and another assistant football coach to provide after-school test preparation and tutoring for math. That decision caused two newly hired science teachers to request transfers to Tech High. They will be leaving at the end of the year, as will Marla. She says she is "fed up with faculty resistance to any kind of change" and with the math department's apparent hostility toward students who need even modest support or modification of instruction.

With more budget cuts likely, remaining department heads are lobbying for funds and trying to protect their programs from further inroads to support math. Marla's two veteran colleagues report that they are hearing more complaints than usual and that staff morale is low. At a meeting on curriculum rigor, a new social studies teacher's proposal to reinstate Economics as a way of beefing up program offerings was greeted with scorn by math department members. They pointed out that "kids who can't pass Algebra II probably won't get Economics either." Although several English teachers told her she was right when they met her in the parking lot later, the social studies teacher said that she had learned her lesson and wouldn't open her mouth again.

CASE 1.2 **Miraculous Middle School**

Thanks to the extraordinary work of teacher leaders and teacher teams, strong Central Office support, and a dedicated group of administrators, this once-threatened school has all but transformed itself over the last five years. Only the 8th grade is a hold-out from the "bad old days." As 6th and 7th grade student performance has risen dramatically in all subjects, the drop-off in 8th grade results has become more obvious and acute. Both school and Central Office administration think the primary difference is the performance and capability of teams at the different grades: 6th and 7th grade teams collaborate effectively and have identified and eliminated a number of key obstacles to student learning. The faculty who teach 8th grade have never been able to act in concert on any significant instructional improvement. They have continued to do what they have always done even as students and curriculum requirements changed.

This year there were three openings in 8th grade. To "keep them from being infected by the predominant culture," administration put all three newcomers into 8 Platinum. The beginners are struggling to figure out the curriculum pacing and handle the disproportionate share of special needs students, but at least they're getting along well with one another. The other two "teams" are really loose collections of genuinely excellent teachers and difficult-to-work-with people who have, over time, intimidated others into giving them the working conditions and student loads that make their teaching life easy and predictable. No one really knows how anyone else's students do. The 8th grade experts cherish their autonomy and have thus adopted a live-and-let-live approach to colleagues. In fact, the 8 Silver and 8 Gold teams come together only in opposition to administrators' requests. Recently they were asked to collaborate and design new schedule configurations that would provide built-in opportunities for re-teaching any concept that 30 percent of their students had not mastered. That request provoked a scathing "open letter" to parents and the community authored by two of the self-appointed deans of the 8 Gold team. The letter claimed to represent many other faculty members and warned readers that the quality of their children's education was being sacrificed to meet the needs of a few "limited ability" students. Two of the most effective 8th grade teachers already provide such time; privately they disagree with colleagues, but neither was willing to speak up in a public meeting.

What do these two schools have in common? They are not really case studies in widespread mediocrity, i.e., places full of teachers whose performance is not good enough to get the job done and not bad enough to fire. Individual teachers and groups within these schools have been successful in helping their students overcome obstacles to achievement and make academic progress. We might, instead, describe Mid-Balkans and Miraculous Middle as places that have problems distributing learning and guaranteeing high-quality instruction across an entire school. The gains in understanding and performance accomplished by some members of the organization are not shared or used by others. The rate of improvement has stalled, and the degree of improvement is insufficient.

The students at Mid-Balkans and the 8th graders at Miraculous Middle need help. This is still a test. If you were one of the administrators or teacher leaders, what would you do? And why should you do it? For advanced credit, be prepared to consider the costs and benefits of each option below.

Option A: Get out of the way of the gifted teachers whenever possible. Celebrate and protect the exemplars of excellence—the kind of instructors you want for every child. Ignore the petty jealousies of others who do not have the passion or conviction to get the job done. Send members of the latter group to observe high performers and have high performers provide professional development for those who are not yet able to help their students meet important learning goals.

Option B: Use formal tools and authority. Supervise, evaluate, or challenge individuals who are not getting the job done. Uphold the standards for adult collegiality and interaction by "writing up" those who don't share ideas or behave professionally with others.

Option C: Think and act positively. Concentrate on building morale and vision, on motivating everyone else to be as good as your best practitioners. Build the self-esteem of individual faculty who are showing promise and help them create their own initiatives so that they too will get resources and will feel less antagonistic and competitive towards the high flyers and successful departments or teams.

Option D: Transfer or reassign troublemakers, loners, and folks who disrupt the harmony of the school. Encourage those who want to "do their own thing" to apply for specialist positions, find a school that will respect their individual talents and autonomy, or perhaps consider administration. Break up ineffective groups and/or lard them with skilled folks who are new to the building and do not buy into some of the old patterns of behavior.

Option E: Focus on how the school is spreading learning about what helps students from one professional community to another. Determine why some groups have the conviction, competence, and resources to help all of their students make progress while others do not. Stop tolerating the malfunctioning groups. Start interventions that give them the message their non-performance is unacceptable. Determine what it will take to make the whole organization and all the professional communities within it, behave more intelligently and capably.

In some ways this looks like a real test. Certainly all of the situations are real; we simply borrowed them from people who have described their dilemmas to us. If we have been successful in "item design," more than one option in A-D should attract you by its pragmatism or familiarity.

Then there is Option E. The different wording and strategic position gives it away to savvy test-takers; it's clearly the answer on our minds. A few years ago, however, Option E might not have made our list. Over the last several hundred conversations, strategizing sessions, and visits to schools, we have come to understand that "fixing" a challenging individual whose teaching is mediocre or a team that is not getting the job done may be a critical short-term goal. But fixing one case doesn't always help a leader address what is happening for large numbers of other children in the school. It won't make the school or grade level group any more capable of helping children learn, and it won't take on the nonproductive behaviors getting in the way of adult development for the rest of the faculty. Taking on cases one at a time is not guaranteed to make a dent in what really matters.

Equity and opportunity matter. Spreading the best of what we know and are able to do across an *entire* institution, not just a few teams, schools, departments, or single practitioners matters. If we care about all the learning of all the students at Mid-Balkans or the 8th graders at Miraculous, we need to create what Perkins (2003) calls "smart organizations," places where all the adults "pool mental effort" as well as physical effort to make a difference for children.

Now, just for a moment, consider one more case: Edgeland Elementary where "everything is beautiful," but the tests don't know it or show it.

CASE 1.3 **Edgeland Elementary School**

Edgeland Elementary sits on a lovely plot of land in a once-solid family neighborhood whose population has changed dramatically over the last six years. Its principal, Marvin R, grew up in the city and knows everyone who's anyone in both local politics and the school department. Marvin says Edgeland is like a "big, loving extended family; once you're part of it you don't need anyone else." Many of his staff are sons and daughters of old (or new) friends; his assistant principal is a former student, his cousin is the guidance counselor, and his aunt runs Food Services. Staff stay for years; everyone knows everyone else's personal business, and, until recently, everyone knew the students' families and stories.

Because of his connections, Marvin can pick up the phone, call in a favor, and get almost anything done. Newly appointed principals, particularly if they have been hired from within the district, tend to see Marvin as an informal mentor. He puts himself out to welcome them, tell them the inside scoop and the way things run, and introduce them around to the various board and department heads in city hall. In return they support his positions with the "know-nothings and eggheads" in the district office. Marvin's response to requests for change or new initiatives sets the tone for his staff and his mentees alike. He tends to support the status quo, which he believes has worked well for him. Staff learn, and teach newcomers, that it is best not to "make waves"; rarely does anyone bring up difficult topics.

For years Edgeland's scores teetered at or just below state average. Even when other elementary schools in the district began to have scores noticeably above that average, Marvin was never worried. Kids were different now, he said. He declined invitations to see what others were doing across the district or to go to conferences. Because Marvin was pleasant and politically connected, district leadership left Edgeland alone. Then two years ago, student achievement scores in both literacy and mathematics went down precipitously; the school has been unable to make AYP since then. In response Marvin has initiated a whirlwind of requests and activities: he demanded that the Central Office find funds for new books and programs; he wanted extra special education staff, more testing of individual students, more outside placements, and some big-name speakers to motivate his staff. He announced that his problem was not like anyone else's and that he was too busy to come to district meetings that were all theory and had nothing to do with his problem. Lately, he's always late to required events; he skips important grade level and curriculum meetings without apology or excuse. Other members of the administrative team are irritated and beginning to imitate him in (they say) self-defense.

So what does Edgeland have in common with our two earlier cases? True, it's another school in trouble. If you're hardhearted, you might say its troubles are its leader's own fault. Unlike our other two cases, however, we may need to look at a different starting place than the behavior of groups within the school. Edgeland's troubles, we think, can best be understand by looking at the institutional conditions that allowed it to become a mediocre performer and to stay that way long after other schools within the district had begun to change. Thus we might examine who got hired (and how), the process of induction, the belief systems that have governed decision-making and actions, and the role (or lack) of district leadership teams and of district expectations and culture.

FIGURE 1.1 Sources of mediocre teaching.

In *The Skillful Leader: Confronting Mediocre Teaching*, we suggested that the problem of mediocre instruction is a nested or multi-layered one whose sources are represented by Figure 1.1.

Deciding where to place blame or who should take ownership of the problem is not easy. Behind individual cases of second-rate instruction, for example, we could identify the supervisory shortcomings and the institutional norms, beliefs, and practices that had allowed those cases to exist. To take on cases of mediocre performance, we proposed a mixed approach: go after the unpromising practices and debilitating beliefs that support mediocrity at the institutional level and help supervisors learn how to address its varied and challenging individual faces in buildings and departments.

Keep that image of nested causes for mediocrity, but focus on the adult and organizational learning that ultimately affects the opportunities available for students. Consider our three cases. In each school, a few individual adults have successfully tackled and solved problems that were blocking students' achievement. Even more important, some groups of adults have shared knowledge, pored over data, experimented, and coached one another to achieve significant results. They now know what it is like to be part of a high-functioning professional community and how to collaborate when the next unfamiliar challenge appears. But the collaborative behavior of these groups and their new knowledge about improving student learning has not spread. It is as if there were impermeable barriers between one department and another, between one team and another, or between one school and the rest of the district. There is no significant transfer of practice.

Mediocre teaching may be an individual problem. However, mediocre student and adult learning are team, department, or grade-level problems, school-wide problems, and district ones. Mediocre learning results when school districts do not provide the structural resources, the vision and tenacity, or the skill development necessary to help leaders confront poor performance. Mediocre learning results when adults in schools cannot or will not collaborate to tackle obstacles to achievement. It happens when people choose to organize their time and effort in service of their own comfort rather than students' needs and when adults who know better look the other way to preserve relationships, harmony, or the illusion of peace. Finally, learning is undermined or blocked when leaders and teachers resign themselves to surviving in environments made toxic by the inappropriate behavior of other adults.

Five key assumptions have shaped our thinking about conditions worth changing in schools and the ways in which we might help skillful leaders transform struggling schools or jump start those that are stuck:

1. Strong groups who commit to continuous improvement of practice in response to students' learning needs can affect both student achievement and the performance of individual teachers in their classrooms.

2. Even successful schools or school districts have great variation in the effectiveness of their component working groups. High-performing, accountable professional communities are the exception rather than the norm.

3. Good role models and programs for team development are rare in most districts.

4. Just as they need to tackle cases of sub-par teaching, leaders must know how to confront and seek improvement from malfunctioning groups.

5. Group problems are almost always caused by individuals, but the solutions are rarely found by confronting individuals alone. When a professional community malfunctions, it is the problem of that community collectively.

FIGURE 1.2 Group malfunction as a source of mediocrity.

Given these assumptions, confronting the conditions that undermine learning requires that we add a new circle to our nested sources of mediocrity. As Figure 1.2 illustrates, we must also examine the characteristics, behaviors, and competencies of groups of adults who work in schools.

To change practices that are not working and expand our understanding of those that are working, we need every teacher engaged in the push. We believe the effort requires the same multi-pronged approach that helped us confront mediocre teaching: the 3 C's of Conviction, Competence, and Control defined below and represented in Figure 1.3.

Conviction: Holding and consistently acting on a set of beliefs or stances that move the school or institution closer to its mission of making sure children learn and achieve at high levels.

Competence: Using a repertoire of skills and substantive knowledge about effective teamwork and adult interaction and

FIGURE 1.3 Confronting the sources of mediocrity.

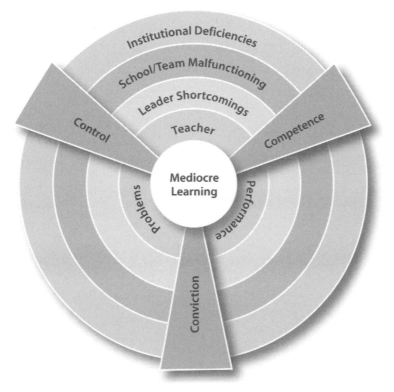

using problem-solving skills to address student learning needs.

Control: Adequate structures, processes, and resources to support groups charged with improving student achievement and carrying out the mission of the school.

In the following chapters, we will explore the ways in which skillful leaders use these three capacities to break down invisible barriers and allow learning to spread.

$\overset{2}{\diamond}$ Confronting Blocks to Organizational Learning

Most of *Skillful Leader II* focuses on the challenges leaders face as they try to mobilize groups of people to pool their intelligence, collaborate effectively, and improve student learning. However, student learning is not the only focus of this book. Adult learning is also important; it affects the opportunities available to students and the likelihood that they will be able to seize those opportunities.

The most significant improvements for children are likely to happen at the classroom and school level. However, as Figure 1.1 shows, organizational capacity and the organizational context in which schools operate affect what they are able to accomplish. Mediocrity at the institutional level can block the spread of improvements beyond the single school or classroom in which they occur. To identify the conditions that affect adult (and eventually student) learning, we need to look at an organization's capacity to identify and solve what Heifetz and Linsky call adaptive challenges, i.e., problems for which there is no currently known solution, as well as technical ones that require people to apply the know-how they already have (14-15). We need to examine how the organization helps its members process and productively use information from instructional innovations and mistakes, and how it helps members to acquire new tools to help students. Before we start to consider the symptoms of mediocre organizational learning or non-learning, however, we should acknowledge three key assumptions.

1. **Organizational or institutional learning is a means to a goal, not an end.** Acquiring new tools, processing knowledge, analyzing the impact of decisions, spreading effective practice from one part of the school system to another—all of these outward learning behaviors must lead to intelligent actions that significantly improve teaching and learning.

2. **An emphasis on organizational learning is only useful if it helps skillful leaders scale up improvement efforts** to affect, in some posi-

tive way, more young people in more classrooms.

3. **By _leaders_ we mean everyone with a recurring opportunity to affect the caliber of learning in schools and classrooms.** At the institutional level, that might mean everyone from curriculum and program directors/coordinators, human resource and staff development personnel, and business and technology managers, to community/cluster superintendents, deputy or assistant superintendents, superintendents, headmasters, heads of schools, and CEO's.

Although their daily worries may focus on their own immediate arenas, many teachers, curriculum leaders, principals, coaches, specialists, and support staff take their long-term cues from what they deduce that the broader organization cares about and actively supports. They watch the designated leadership to determine what the organization tolerates or ignores. They note what it takes on or seeks to eliminate. Consider this recent comment from a K-12 director:

> Why should I kill myself to make sure our at-risk kids have mastered this technology? Do you see any of the higher ups making this a priority even after we showed the board the potential impact on test scores? Have you heard anyone talking about keeping the buildings—or _even one lab_—open so kids without computers can work after school? Nah, no one's going to divert resources to this. They have other more important fish to fry—getting funding for the indoor track and protecting the elementary music program. Not to say those aren't important, but I've got the message. My kids don't have a constituency, so they don't count.

or this observation from a staff development specialist in a large county district:

> Dr. X has made it clear—really clear let me tell you—that closing the minority achievement gap is what we're all about, and everything's got to be linked to that until we get some progress going. The unions are on board. That's what the clusters talked about in their meetings; that's what our unit is going to be doing. And you better not be standing up at any meeting and saying why you can't do it.

For our current purposes, it is not important to worry about whether these speakers are correct in their assessment of the institution's intent. It is important to acknowledge that they and their colleagues are constantly looking for signals of which problems a school district cares about and is genuinely trying to solve. Such signals will shape what they expect of themselves as leaders and learners, and what they expect of others. In this chapter we'll look at some of the potential obstacles to organizational learning, the institutional behaviors that reveal such obstacles are present, the data sources that help leaders take stock of their own surroundings and performance, and strategies skillful leaders can use to confront what they uncover.

Conditions That Undermine Organizational Learning

Because they represent just the opposite of what organizational development experts extol, we selected five common conditions that block organizational learning and adult growth for closer consideration. They are:

1. Broken, clouded, or cockeyed lenses
2. Organizational ADD
3. Operating by the law of the jungle
4. Knowing/doing gap
5. Feedback failure

Though we need to examine each condition separately to understand how it affects the performance of individuals and communities, keep in mind that these are not isolated phenomena. They interact to reinforce negative patterns. Confronting one condition may uncover another; improving and changing one may have a positive effect on another. We expect that no one school district will be able to find an exact specimen of each condition, but that many reflective leaders will find recognizable variations.

Condition 1: Broken, Clouded, or Cockeyed Lenses

The importance of having and pursuing a clear and compelling vision peppers the literature on leadership. It is hard to imagine how a leader might create a sense of hope and urgency, a sense of forward movement and worthwhile goals without drawing upon a powerful image of a better, or perhaps simply a very different, future. Without that image, how does a leader recognize disparities in current achievement and name problems to be solved? Vision is a good place to begin looking for conditions that undermine organizational learning. We can characterize organizational vision problems in three ways:

1. Leaders' failure to define and articulate a coherent, deeply desired *personal* image of what future school success would look like for students—or of what they personally hope the institution will be able to accomplish for children
2. Leaders' inability to make a realistic assessment of what the organization currently values and how it currently behaves in contrast to the desired vision
3. Leaders' inability to mobilize others by developing what Senge calls "shared images of the future they seek to create and the principles and guiding practices by which they hope to get there" (7).

When we think of broken lens syndrome, we think of leaders whose "visions," if they offer any at all, are narrow, fragmented, and full of blind spots. The focus of their communication is utilitarian (i.e., "Let's get the state off our backs" or "Let's not complicate matters by probing too deeply"), and the presentation is rarely deeply felt or deeply motivating. Because they cannot summon or communicate a picture of substantive learning, these leaders often focus on a small concrete piece of the future. They speak as if that specific step toward a goal were the goal itself:

A computer for every child (versus every graduate mastering and being critical consumer of modern technology)

Getting the workshop model into every literacy block in middle school (versus all our students able to read and interpret college-level content selections by the time they graduate from high school)

Smaller class sizes (versus a school where every child connects with a significant adult)

Specific targets are useful for taking action. They are appealing to the groups who support them. However, because they emphasize compliance and one-size-fits all approaches, they rarely conjure up an image that is encompassing enough to mobilize multiple parts of the organization to a common purpose. More is required.

Leaders with broken lenses may be able to "see" (i.e., name, enumerate, and identify as problems-to-be-solved) only their present realities. Instead of creating a guiding image of what it would look like if those present realities were to be significantly improved, they expend effort highlighting the contrast between present and past states of affairs:

"This used to be a community that cared about education; now it's a community of retirees who don't want to spend a dime on anything."

"My teachers are totally demoralized by the board's stance on class sizes. Their advice has been rejected. How am I going to attract and keep good people?"

"At one time we would have had 500 people for a back-to-school night, but now we do all this work for a few motivated parents who already know what their children are doing in school."

The issue in all the preceding examples is not the truth of the statement or the validity of the perception. All the problems are real and difficult. The issue is the missing second half of the message. There is no future image to accompany the present lament. These leaders do not imagine aloud a time when teachers and parents will interact in small community gatherings or when school people will go to parents in places where they congregate. They do not seek and communicate data about what the district has accomplished with smaller class sizes and how those desired outcomes should be pursued in other ways. Thus the ability to see only the broken part of the picture drains the conviction of those who look to these leaders for hope.

Clouded lens syndrome occurs when leaders' visions of a possible future are colored by debilitating beliefs, parochialism, or limited education and experience. All responses to problems begin with the assumption that "my reality is your reality, and there is no other possible explanation for what I see:"

> "Those of us who grew up in this town are proud of it and we get what the school needs; we don't need outsiders to tell us what to do. We don't have fancy notions of who we are."

> "I know there's been a lot of talk about creating a support system for the Hispanic students, but I don't think this is the time. There's too much riding on the funding vote, and people here don't take kindly to singling out any one group for special privileges."

> "People, let's get real here. I didn't take calculus. Most of us here didn't have much college math, and we're doing just fine, thank you very much. Not every district needs to compete with colleges."

Lacking outside role models, exemplars of high-quality practice, or experiences that test traditional assumptions and stereotypes, such leaders' outlook is diminished. We know a number of school districts led by hard-working "home-grown talent" who choose to use high-impact strategies from the world beyond their doors. However, other schools and districts are led by individuals whose whole value system and sense of the possibility has been shaped by a single place, a small set of similarly minded colleagues, and few encounters with the larger world. What happens in those schools mirrors such limitations. When leaders allow their organizations or themselves to become deeply inbred, suspicious of outsiders, dismissive of research and academia, unaware of the knowledge and skill of colleagues in similar roles throughout the state, defined by old-boy or old-girl networks, or governed by truths learned when the leaders themselves attended junior high school in the town, they open the door to mediocrity.

Finally, *cockeyed lens syndrome* describes what sometimes happen when leaders have been whacked by politics or circumstance so that all future choices or problem-solving options are defined by a small set of acceptable responses: placating unions and the public after a strike, damage control in response to group opposition to a policy or program, avoiding the appearance of impropriety after a scandal, limiting a budget increase, making budget cuts, or holding onto one's job and mandate when a board is split. In the real world of schools and of district leadership, all of these are time- and energy-consuming dilemmas that skew one's perspective. They hamper a leader's ability to look ahead and to evaluate present actions and opportunities in light of a vision of the future.

Organizational vision problems can result in low standards and expectations across the board for all but the few most talented students and teachers. They can result in a relentless pursuit of fads and quick fixes that drains energy, a sort of cheerful celebration of being forever average, or a cavalier write-off of large segments of the student population. Good individual schools with politically savvy leadership can usually survive in an organization that lacks vision at the top. However, only a small proportion of the dis-

TABLE 2.1 Conducting a Vision Check

Sources of Data	Sample Indicators of Intact Vision
Formal Speeches and Presentations	• Offer compelling positive images of children's learning and achievement and of graduates' future opportunities and future contributions • Judiciously balance warnings or lists of deficits and disappointments with pictures of the ways in which the organization and its members are resilient, resourceful, and driven by high goals for students • Contain references to knowledge, capacities, or approaches to problems created outside of the organization and available for use • Cite the ways in which schools and groups within schools are tackling problems and creating new solutions the district can use • Present a realistic, positive agenda communicated without jargon and using stories and images that hold meaning for the audience
Informal Exchanges	• Contain more proactive questions and speculations than reactive ones • Invite others to share stories, images, and evidence of progress • Are characterized by a tone of inquiry and experimentation as opposed to blame or unleavened lament • Repeatedly connect present decisions to short and long-term learning goals, desired progress, and potential implications for learners • Acknowledge and cheer on people's efforts to apply new ideas to persistent challenges, question practice, and spread learning • Seek feedback on ideas or actions that others perceive to be counter to the long-term goals
Staff Commentary to Both Insiders and Outsiders	• Contains phrases and images that suggest a strong sense of moral purpose and conviction about the contribution the organization can make to children • Offers stories, metaphors, and pieces of evidence that are shared across all levels of the organization • Includes questions that provoke others to reflect and invitations to share information from level to level • Contains specific, verbatim references to organizational and building goals • Balances worries and lists of present concerns about outside forces with evidence that such forces have been successfully tackled in the past—or with statements of optimism about the future

trict's children will benefit from what that successful school is able to do, and no one at other schools will learn from the successful school's efforts.

Finding and Fixing Vision Problems

- **Focus daily/weekly/monthly attention on the future that staff are creating for students.** It is always a great temptation to tackle the matter of creating a clear, shared vision by convening a large committee, collecting lots of data about people's hopes and aspirations, and laboriously crafting paragraphs, lists, or sometimes just phrases that attempt to capture these ideas. Such a strategy has advantages: it builds at least temporary awareness and ownership among participants, many of whom may come from outside the school district, and it signals that the district stands for something important. This strategy yields nothing more than fancy window dressing, however, unless everyone makes the resulting document a reference point for ongoing discussions and decisions.

- **Conduct a vision check to see what messages top leadership is sending.** It is certainly possible for reflective and committed leaders to conduct their own vision check using documents, meeting notes, and unvarnished recollections of exchanges, but it may be difficult to get a variety of honest opinions. If all members of the organization feel totally comfortable being honest and open with the superintendent, board members, or other Central Office administrators and are capable of providing focused feedback about the district vision, that vision is probably in good shape already. Using some clear criteria and indicators and asking insiders to assess the messages in different kinds of interactions can help with self-assessment (see Table 2.1). It may also be useful to ask an outsider or two to conduct that check.

- **Collaborate with visual thinkers and unleash the power of metaphor.** Skillful leaders look for ways to build on their own strengths and to compensate for weaknesses. If your natural preference is for the practical and the concrete, collaborate with others who like to think and talk in images or stories. From time to time, have teams work with activity structures that force them to create symbols for complex ideas or to make analogies. Activities such as synectics or brainstorming allow individuals who may typically contribute less to a practical discussion to show what they can do. They give leaders important data about how a team is analyzing a problem or making sense of a charge.

- **Ask teachers to help with stories and analogies that, in their opinion, capture the spirit of what the district is trying to achieve.** Vision is of little use if it never gets translated into actions that stretch learning and transform lives for the better. Letting it be known that you are collecting anecdotes, stories, and pictures that teachers think are great examples of vision being realized in action both engages others in keeping vision alive and allows a leader to determine which parts of a particular set of goals are actually meaningful to the people who have to pursue them.

- **Listen for and challenge debilitating beliefs.** Vision turns into empty rhetoric quickly if the people who have to carry it out do not believe that students and adults can get smarter, the district can get smarter and more capable, children and adults deserve the best possible goals and outcomes, and that many problems are solvable.

Condition 2: Organizational ADD (Attention Deficit Disorder)

Staying focused on solving large adaptive problems amidst clamoring priorities takes both significant skill and genuine conviction. Currently schools are supposed to be (among other charges):

Extraordinarily responsive to numerous constituent groups with widely varying agendas

Ready responders to state and federal audits, inquiries, report requests, surveys, and RFP's

"Logical places" to get a hearing and air time for everything from bike safety to local history

Safe, warm, welcoming, wise, and able to chase and chastise while producing world-class scholars

Given even this small sample of demands from the outside, it seems inevitable that we would see such well-known symptoms of organizational attention deficit disorder as:

- **"Drop everything and do this" urgencies of the week** that require administrators and teachers to fill out forms, answer emails, complete reports, assemble data, or compose an elaborate proposal that will have little or no positive impact on immediate or long-term learning—but that help other people check things off their "to-do lists."
- **Fads of the year** (e.g., the Year of Gifted and Talented, followed by the Year of Differentiated Instruction, followed by the Year of Project-Based Learning) intended to show that the district is "on the cutting edge" or able to have what all the neighbors have.
- **Activity for activity's sake** (We're doing curriculum audits; we're doing strategic planning; we're restructuring the whole school; we're implementing portfolios) that confuses means with desired ends.
- **Initiative overload** that results when multiple competing priorities emanate downward from the Central Office. (This year, *before December* we want you to revise grading, do more geometry, create departmental assessments, collaborate for interdisciplinary curriculum, write rubrics, create challenge projects, etc.)
- **Wasted effort** that shows itself in large amounts of energy spent on initiatives that have little or no effect on helping students reach

important academic targets (e.g., acting out Paul Revere's ride, doing a school-wide peach blossom festival, raising funds for the playground committee, recreating a medieval tournament.)

Note that few of the specific curriculum or activity examples above are bad per se. Many of these initiatives might benefit children if they were part of a coherent, in-depth plan to reach some clear learning goals.

What causes organizational ADD? One possibility, of course, is the lack of clear vision and the accompanying ability to set priorities based on that vision. Without guiding vision, decision-making looks as if it is a matter of stimulus-twitch response: the last, loudest, nastiest, or most influential person to lobby the leader gets his or her wish. Leaders' apparent lack of conviction about sticking with identified vision and priorities when they find themselves under pressure from competing demands is a second, related explanation. It is hard to believe in the long-term value of investments and to allocate large amounts of time to an ongoing initiative in the face of the short attention spans and slightly hysterical environment leaders regularly face. "Responsiveness" (to community concerns or media attacks for example) begins to trump tenacity as a quality to be appreciated and cultivated.

Organizational ADD can also result from unstable leadership: a high rate of superintendent or Central Office turnover, multiple principals in a short period of time, or highly politicized governing boards and unions that routinely introduce new agendas and diverting pressures. If new leaders are driven by ego, i.e. a need to assert their own identity and preferences, then schools can find themselves careening wildly from one transformative initiative to another over short periods of time. If superintendents or principals find themselves under fire from boards that are also driven by ego rather than data, they may balance staying on course against protecting their own jobs.

Outside forces contribute to the distractions, irritability and lack of focus that are the hallmarks of organizational ADD. Leaders cannot prevent economic downturns, new state and federal mandates, natural disasters or personnel scandals from off-the-job behavior. They can only manage the districts' responses either by allowing attention to swing from one bit of miserable news to the next or by keeping everyone's eyes on the target as much as humanly possible.

Finally, organizational ADD can be caused by leaders' lack of skill in:

- Identifying the right problems to solve
- Mobilizing people to collaborate effectively to solve important problems
- Monitoring implementation and learning from mistakes
- Handling conflict

Organizational ADD means that school and district personnel are unable to determine which problems are the truly significant ones to take on. It means staff are unable to persist with an effort long enough to correct initial mistakes, fine tune practices, and see the results of their hard work. In essence, no one stays with anything long enough to develop a degree of expertise or in-depth knowledge; no one gets any smarter at the school and classroom level and no one in Central Office gets the benefit of studying a sustained, successful initiative to determine what characteristics can be reproduced to support further improvement.

Organizational ADD pulls effort off instructional improvement and confuses teachers. It also provokes a variety of survival responses that then contribute to blocking adult learning. It can make skilled, caring, and committed people fretful, anxious, and seemingly resistant to any more new ideas, no matter how valid they might be. It may promote a culture of glibness and gloss where the ability to spout the latest jargon or put a good spin on very

TABLE 2.2   Checking for Organizational ADD

Focus of Data Collection	Sample Questions to Ask
Volume of new program initiation	• How was the need for a new program or change of direction identified? (What data justified the need?) • How many other initiatives across the district were in their first 2 years of implementation at the time? • How many initiatives in their first two years of implementation affected the same target population?
Student learning goals that provoked new initiatives	• What explicit, unmet student achievement goals provoked the new initiatives? • What data was used—and how was it used—to identify unmet learning goals? • What evidence indicated that existing initiatives could not be modified or strengthened to meet these goals?
Speed of direction change or new program initiation	• How much lead-time did the district provide before the change? • Who was involved in identifying and sharing information about the problem? • How much time was allocated to develop competence in implementing the change effectively?
Number and type of rationales for program initiation or significant direction change e.g., new leader, need to update, demographic change, economics, got a grant, state made us	• How many reasons could be directly linked to the preferences of powerful individuals or small groups vs. student learning needs supported by compelling data analysis? • How many rationales had little or no connection to established district or school priorities? • How many rationales had only "window dressing" links to district or school vision and priorities?
Anticipated and unanticipated outcomes	• How much competition for resources has been created by new program initiation over the last 3 years? • What unanticipated problems did we create as a result of new program initiation this year?

little accomplishment replaces any substantive thinking or questioning. Or, it can cause both excellent and mediocre leaders and teachers to retreat into their shells by closing building and classroom doors and minimizing contact with outsiders.

Finding and Fighting Organizational ADD

Get regular check-ups, particularly before setting off in a new direction. Like a vision check, a bi-annual examination of behavior that reveals the organization's ability to focus can help skillful leaders diagnose problems. If trusted implementers report distress, overwhelm, loss of focus, or the feeling of being pulled in too many directions all of the time, it is worth investigating the reasons for those feelings. They may be normal responses to significant change, a signal that the district is grappling with serious adaptive challenges—or they may be indicators of organizational ADD. Table 2.2 suggests some worthwhile questions to investigate.

Beyond the vision check-up, leaders who want to combat organizational ADD should:

- **Use data-driven decision-making.** Skillful leaders can help members of the organization learn how to shift decision-making so that it is based on substantive analysis of student need and prior program results rather than being driven by personal influence, perceptions of crisis, or ego. Asking for the data as a habit of practice can reduce the effects of frequent turnover or outside politics.

- **Create a strong district-level instructional leadership team.** Fragmentation of energy and effort occurs partly because of decentralized decision-making. Schools, teams and departments need the ability to make choices that help their students, but all those choices made at different levels of the organization fall on the same set of classroom teachers. To keep from feeling overwhelmed and unsuccessful, faculties need to see how initiatives are connected to one another and to the larger good the district is trying to achieve for its students. A representative group of instructional leaders can help determine whether newly proposed programs clearly match district goals and how they are linked to one another. It can also help communicate these connections to members who were not involved in decision-making.

- **Determine performance-based criteria for program success.** Although it seems an obvious step, many schools and districts never define what they will consider acceptable evidence that an initiative is successful. Or, they substitute indicators of popularity or acceptance for evidence that a program has actually had a positive impact on student learning. Thus a pilot of reading materials is "successful" if teachers say they like it or an after school enrichment program is considered effective if parents enroll their children. Clear, performance-based criteria for success help to explain why particular initiatives are supported or why some programs are not continued.

- **Use problem-identification protocols.** Knowing what problem they are really solving (as opposed to jumping from one short-term fix for a symptom to the next) helps skillful leaders conserve energy and invest time wisely. Never let administrative teams, design groups, or curriculum committees jump to solutions before they have spent time identifying the nature of the challenge they are trying to tackle.

- **Seek and speak about connections.** It is hard to understand the "big picture" of district initiatives when you are in the midst of taking care of your own particular piece. Skillful leaders do not assume that others automatically see or understand how programs fit together. Thus they consciously and repetitively point out the credible links between cherished existing programs and new efforts.

- **Use visuals to predict and summarize.** Just as road maps with highlighted routes help travelers, charts, maps, diagrams and other tools that capture relationships between programs and district goals can help members of the organization stay focused. Consider mapping out the potential impact of a new effort on different parts of an organization, as system dynamics experts do. That process can help a leadership team anticipate where overload or unnecessary distraction might occur and determine whether the timing and pace of proposed changes are appropriate.

Condition 3: Operating by the Law of the Jungle

The possibility of wide-scale adult learning that will help improve instruction for students is deeply compromised when superintendents, school boards, or principals themselves make the environment in which leaders are operating so high-risk and so dangerously competitive that individuals must focus most of their attention on survival. Attending to the basics of keeping one's job diverts crucial energy and strategizing away from improving student learning and onto "making things look good" and "covering your ass."

Living by the law of the jungle gets established in different ways. Sometimes it is a deliberate strategy on the part of top leadership. For example, a powerful superintendent of a large district with frequent turnover and thus frequent opportunities to shuffle administrators says he intentionally creates a sense of vulnerability and danger by pitting principals against one another and by repeated warnings that "everyone is replaceable on a moment's notice." He believes the natural urge to survive "gets the competitive juices flowing," causes an individual's adrenaline to rise, and eventually results in improved school performance. The theory is that the principal will conduct that pressure downward to the staff, and the staff will apply it to the students.

Finding and Changing Jungle-Like Cultures

We think the more likely explanations for the existence of a jungle-like culture in some organizations have to do with limitations in leadership such as:

1. Inability to create and nurture high-functioning teams

2. Lack of personal experience with effective collaboration

3. Violation of existing norms or agreed-upon processes

4. Inability to demonstrate being open to feedback and able to hear difficult information without becoming defensive

5. Lack of confidence or competence in dealing with difficult individuals and conflicts

6. Poor communications skills

7. Vision problems

8. Accidental messages

9. Well-intentioned actions being misinterpreted by others

The kinds of progressive interactions that help an organization solve problems and improve learning for students rely on leaders' integrity, conviction about the benefits of collaboration, and knowledge and skill. Individuals who have never been part of a high-functioning collaboration or an environment characterized by mutual respect and accountability often have difficulty creating it without some outside help. Fortunately, once organizational leaders make a commitment to building powerful professional communities and act on that commitment consistently, the skills to fix the first five limitations on our list are all learnable. Observing models, using print and web resources, providing formal training, creating leader study groups, getting coaching, and using self-assessments and reflection on action can all be used to confront and change a jungle-like culture.

Replacing a high-risk competitive culture with a more collaborative one also requires building trust: not trust that nothing will go wrong but rather that others have the best interests of the school system in mind and will act accordingly. Skilled superintendents and building principals know that giving in to prima donnas is terribly tempting and guaranteed to have long-term negative consequences. If they allow gifted but difficult underlings to break rules, run roughshod over others in meetings, throw scenes, or engage in political backstabbing to get their own way, they undermine the trust and confidence of the remaining players on the team. Learning and using the skills to confront unprofessional behavior, broken promises, or unmet expectations is crucial.[1]

Items 6 through 9 on our list of potential explanations for jungle-like cultures require different types of interventions. We have already discussed vision problems. "Poor communication skills" can sometimes refer to a leader's difficulty in writing or speaking clearly. However, it is more often a catch-all phrase people use to describe everything from a leader's introverted personality or taciturn style to his/her tendency to move rapidly, communicate in cryptic sound bites, and not check for audience understanding. It can mean the individual barks first and inquires later or that s/he is deliber-

---

[1]For resources to help see Patterson et al., *Crucial Confrontations: Tools for Resolving Broken Promises, Violated Expectations, and Bad Behavior*, New York: McGraw-Hill, 2005.

ately vague and noncommittal in response to any query requiring a decision. Frequently it is the term that teachers and administrators use to describe a district level leader who is secretive and rarely explains how decisions are made, what might happen next, or what the district expects of its personnel. Poor communication intensifies the tendency to assume that the law of the jungle is in effect. In the absence of clear information or the ability to clarify understanding easily, teachers and administrators either make their own meaning and rules or pull back into their protective armor and "safe" inaction.

Leaders who have recognized that communication is a problem, or that their communications produce messages they did not intend, need to find and regularly use trusted "sounding boards." These are colleagues who are expert communicators, willing to be open and honest with their feedback, and able to edit and coach. Their job is not to shape the vision but rather to determine whether the amount and quality of communication supports what the leader is trying to accomplish. Sounding boards serve best when they have an opportunity to help a leader think through the potential consequences of a piece of communication, imagine how it might be heard and interpreted by others, and plan strategies to ensure that the communication works in the ways the leader wants it to.

Condition 4: The Knowing-Doing Gap

Pfeffer and Sutton describe a kind of inertia that sometimes afflicts organizations as knowing a great deal but not acting on that knowledge. They call the phenomenon the "knowing-doing" gap and trace its origins back to a "basic human propensity: the willingness to let talk substitute for action. When confronted with a problem, people act as though discussing it, formulating decisions, and hashing out plans for action are the same as actually fixing it" (21).

Being aware of and ready to confront the knowing-doing gap becomes particularly important for school districts that are deeply enmeshed in strategic planning, vision setting, school improvement planning and other kinds of potentially valuable but time-consuming future-oriented activities. This gap between smart-sounding talk and actions that improve instruction is also a danger in districts where leaders are avid consumers of the latest research and newest methods. There, jargon, strings of abstract assertions, or fault finding based on theory can be offered up as evidence that the district is moving forward when in fact little of direct benefit to students has happened.

Finding and Closing the Knowing-Doing Gap

Leaders of companies that avoid the knowing-doing gap, Pfeffer and Sutton note, share five key characteristics. They:

1. Get to know the practical demands of the work within their organization by doing it personally alongside their employees

2. Use plain talk and understandable concepts to communicate plans and focus their efforts on a small number of priorities

3. Ask "How do we solve the problems you just described?" whenever they encounter people who can only list reasons for not taking action

4. Hold people accountable for reporting on the actions that were taken as a result of a decision or a round of talk

5. Value learning by experience and encourage people to jump into action, experiment, and refine their thinking in successive rounds of learning (33-41)

How do these findings translate to schools? In subsequent chapters, we offer a number of different strategies to help skillful leaders nurture and support effective collaboration. Many of them, like the capacity-building ideas in Chapters 4 and 6 or the data-gathering vehicles in Chapter 7, encourage teams to learn through the process of tackling and solving student achievement problems. Talking about these strategies or sending people to workshops to learn about them cannot be substituted for actually using them effectively in the field. From a distance with only secondhand reports, it is difficult to assess where knowledge is not translated into action. To determine whether a particular part of the organization or the organization as a whole suffers from an inability to get to action, skillful leaders need to spend substantial time working on real issues with teams of teachers and administrators. Some Central Office staff assign themselves to a particular school, department, or committee and dive into action with that group for three months to a year. Some principals become members of ineffective grade level teams or struggling job-alike groups to find out what exactly is impeding their function and how they can be helped.

Beyond learning the real challenges a district faces by immersing oneself in a particular aspect of the work, leaders can monitor their own talk and ask an outsider to observe the meetings they run for evidence of jargon, excessively complicated presentations and explanations, or preferential treatment for those who "talk a good game" over those who quietly get the work done.

Finally, leaders can demonstrate the organization's commitment to powerful action that moves it toward its goals, as opposed to name dropping and fast talking, by:

*   Making concrete, commonsense discussion of how top priorities are pursued a regular part of supervisory and administrative team interactions

*   Making time on meeting agendas to share experiments

*   Visiting classrooms to observe program implementation several times a year

*   Spending meeting time teaching one another a practical technique

*   Campaigning against convoluted explanations and "edubabble" in

public communications

All these activities and many others come under the heading of "walking the talk" and help the leader focus the organization on making its efforts count.

Condition 5: Feedback Failure

In thinking about feedback, we find it helpful to adopt (and slightly adapt) Grant Wiggins's definition: "Feedback is information about how a person did in light of what he or she attempted—intent versus effect, actual versus ideal performance. . . . The best feedback is highly specific, directly revealing or highly descriptive of what actually resulted, clear to the performer, and available or offered in terms of specific targets and standards" (46). Wiggins, of course, was originally talking about feedback to students, but we think his concept is relevant for adult learners and organizations as well. Implicit in this definition is the idea that if individuals know and understand the consequences of their choices, they can make informed decisions about what to do next. Otherwise they are likely to expend their time and energy on effort that accomplishes little.

Faced with adaptive problems and the need to discover approaches that are not currently in their repertoire, teachers and schools must be free to experiment. They must be able to take risks and to do business in atypical ways. And they must be able to determine how well those experiments are working so that they can make another round of intelligent decisions. Ulrich and Smallwood note that "Effective learners are feedback junkies—they always want to know how their work is viewed by others and the effect it has on others. They ask what worked and what didn't so that they can adapt and improve their work. . . . They do not make the same mistake over and over" (70).

Feedback failure means individual learners and teams do not use relevant information about the success or failure of their endeavors to shape their next actions. It means the organization repeats its mistakes and continues to act in ways that do not benefit student learning. Often it means that individuals at all levels are unable to convince anyone that a difficult adaptive problem exists and that "business as usual" will never solve it.[2]

Reasons for this condition vary. Some may be technical. For example, the school or district's pool of useful data about how well students are currently doing in meeting benchmarks or performance targets can be poor or nonexistent. Perhaps there has been no push to develop or consistently use common assessments that would provide that information. Perhaps people are not currently skilled enough or committed enough to create those assessments. Or if the problem is one of vision, it may be that no one in the district cares whether such information is available. If lenses are broken or clouded, all eyes may simply be focused on end-of-the-year testing, and little attention may be paid to students' current progress and needs.

---

[2]See Heifetz and Linsky's compelling description of the difficulty that lies at the heart of convincing people to take on an adaptive challenge (9-30).

Even when the district has common assessments or a range of midyear measures in place, structural limitations may prevent easy access to the results. Too few computers, too little workspace, outmoded equipment and software, cumbersome, time-consuming data analysis programs, a lack of personnel to provide technical support, or arbitrarily tight restrictions on access to information can all hinder teachers' and administrators' ability to use feedback to make sense of what they have tried. When such technical problems result in feedback failure, it is always tempting to blame outside forces: no money, no support from the board, no time for professional development, and staff cuts. But vision and focus affect feedback as well. If collecting and analyzing data to provide teams, schools, and individuals with information about how they are doing is not really important to top leadership, then it will not be assigned resources from whatever pool exists.

Feedback can take many forms, and not all feedback requires money. Teachers who care about how their actions are affecting their students and what students are thinking about, ask students to give them that information in a variety of ways from simple paragraphs or self-assessment prompts to more elaborate surveys. Feedback failure can also happen because districts lack similar conviction. For example, there may be no enforced or monitored requirement that teachers and administrators use data to modify instruction, improve programs, or change practice. Rhetoric about data use does not count. Statements in plans that claim data use do not count. Only actions, verified through observations, conversations, documents, and results count. In districts where feedback failure is a common condition, leaders think it is "too embarrassing" or "too threatening" to ask a teacher whether what she did actually worked for students or why students didn't learn something. Superintendents do not ask principals for data about program success before approving budget requests. Principals do not ask teachers for feedback on their meetings or on current programs. In meetings, people assert "facts" but rarely are asked to provide supporting evidence. The cliché applies too often. In districts with feedback failure few people practice what they preach.

Finding and Stopping Feedback Failure

Some of the antidotes to feedback failure are self-evident. Chapters 7 and 8 lay out dozens of data sources and vehicles for collecting and analyzing information about the consequences of actions and next intentions. They answer the question of what individuals and teams committed to taking a hard look at their practice might do—and how they might do it. More than any other intervention, however, we think top leadership's behavior sets the direction for the rest of the organization. If the central administration never asks for feedback or does not use feedback from other levels of the organization, why should principals feel impelled to seek information about how well they are doing from their faculties, parents, and students? If supervisors do not provide clear, highly detailed feedback about how a teacher is doing in relation to a performance target and a learning outcome, why should the teacher provide that information for students?

Like vision checks or focus checks, leaders can submit themselves and other members of the organization to a feedback check-up. Diagnostic prompts for writing or discussion might include:

- Name the most helpful piece of feedback you have received in the last month. Explain how you got the feedback, what you did with it, and what happened as a result.

- Name a circumstance in which you wished you could receive more feedback and explain why.

- How would you rate this organization's commitment to getting and using feedback? What are the indicators you use to make that rating?

- Name a circumstance when you know feedback should have been used and was not. Keep the description general rather than naming names, and focus on the consequences you saw from feedback not being used.

- What do you see as the biggest impediments to using feedback in this district?

- Who is your role model or mentor for feedback use? Why?

- How much consistency do you think there is between our talk about feedback and what we actually do?

- How well do you think people respond to feedback in this district? What is the evidence on which you are basing your rating?

- Cite an example of this organization using feedback effectively to improve something it did.

These discussion starters are meant to elicit information about how well individuals understand the purpose of feedback and the nature of effective feedback, how they perceive the organization's ability to collect and learn from feedback, and what messages about the value of feedback people are reading in the behavior of leaders. The check-up points are not meant to be a comprehensive list. Nor do we suggest that you ask all of your staff to respond to all of them. Pick a small selection that you think are particularly relevant to your own setting. Experiment with allowing teams or individuals to do some quiet writing and reflection followed by discussion or use several of the prompts in a supervisory conference. Finally, look at how meeting time and administrative retreat time is spent. If there are never opportunities to give and receive feedback, the message about its importance at the center of improvement is probably clear.

Professional Communities and Mediocre Learning

Seeking to spread teaching expertise and opportunities for high-quality learning across all classrooms, school leaders have increasingly turned to teacher group (or team) work—and with reason. Literature now links the building of professional or Teacher Learning Communities with positive impact on student learning. Schmoker (1999, 2001), Dufour (1998, 2004), McLaughlin and Talbert (2006), and others cite case studies describing the transformative potential of adult collective work. These findings buttress our conviction that collaboration focused on solving student learning problems is an essential ingredient in raising achievement.

As we observe groups in action and listen to leaders who are trying to transform their schools and districts, however, it is not hard to note the gap between the promise of adult collaboration and the current reality. High-performing, learning-focused professional groups or communities are the exceptions to the norm. Too often what we see are newly created "teams" or renamed configurations of adults going about mediocre business as usual—but together rather than separately. Individuals complain, criticize, dance around difficult topics, divert the agenda from serious to superficial concerns, attend meetings sporadically, listen little, or pontificate often. In schools, marginally functioning groups frequently "share" strategies without ever connecting them to student learning needs, or they comply with newly mandated protocols for looking at student work without ever making changes in instruction. At the district level, members angle for individual benefits, protect turf, tune out discussions about anything not in their immediate domain, or fail to follow through on group agreements. In the worst scenarios, groups at all levels agree that "others" (students, parents, administrators, teachers, politicians, or unions) are the root of all problems and settle comfortably into paralysis. Often the well-meaning and skilled members of such barely evolved groups are as frustrated as the leaders who encouraged them to collaborate.

For adult collaboration to generate productive solutions to persistent learning and teaching problems, we must have groups that:

- Have a common understanding of the indicators of high quality learning
- Share a common commitment to high quality learning for every student
- Are capable of acting on that commitment efficiently and effectively
- Receive and use appropriate data and feedback to monitor their own performance and adjust their efforts

"Pooling mental effort," Perkins (2003) notes, creates smarter organizations; however, pooling mental effort is both difficult to do and not well understood. Thus we need an image of excellence against which we can judge collaborative efforts and a common language and concept system for naming what is not going well. In this chapter, we propose a continuum of community function and adult learning that ranges from toxic, or actively blocking, to accountable, or highly likely to produce significant improvements in student achievement over a sustained period.

FIGURE 3.1 Continuum of community function.

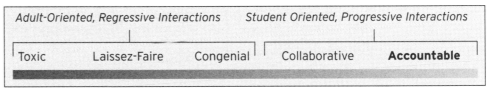

Here we use the term *community* to mean both the informally and formally constituted groups or clusters of associated players one can find in a school or school district who serve as filters and channels for improvement efforts. Thus a community might be an official unit such as all the elementary principals associated with a particular cluster or sub-district, a K-12 or high school department, an elementary grade level in a particular school, a house or freshman academy, a curriculum committee, a middle school team, or all the K-4 reading tutors. However, a community can also be an informal group of similarly inclined or bonded individuals who have some regular mechanism of association: all the people who teach World Civilization, the veterans who have eaten lunch at a certain time and table in the teachers' cafeteria for years, the gang that plays basketball together on Friday afternoons, the group that meets for coffee or walks together before school, the people who have always inhabited a particular part of a particular hall—or, as in one district we know, all the people who started their career with and were shaped by a particularly forceful principal. Finally, formally designated communities have subgroups within them that are informally established but nonetheless potent.

Communities that Undermine Learning

Many different groups want to call themselves professional communities these days, and some do indeed fulfill the promise of professional learning set forth by DuFour and others. Lest we fall into the trap of proclaiming success where none exists, we need a mechanism to distinguish between communities that pool their mental effort to develop organizational intelligence in the service of greater student learning, i.e., Collaborative and Accountable Communities, and those groups whose interactions intentionally or unintentionally block improvement and protect mediocre performance by both students and adults. In the latter category, we propose three prototypes drawn from our reading and experiences: the Toxic Community, the Laissez-Faire Community, and the Congenial Community. All three share certain attributes. As collective entities they:

- Accept or tolerate low performance, inertia, or lack of contribution from their own members

- Expect and accept low performance from groups of students who have somehow been labeled as less worthy or less capable

- Attribute poor student achievement to external factors like family background, lack of financial support for schools, or community conditions

- Have abandoned hope for their own ability to overcome the effects of external factors

- Derive benefit from, and therefore exert effort to sustain, conditions that favor adult comfort or convenience over student needs

- Have little or no collective experience with, or models for, effective problem-solving skills and strategies

- Have been historically protected or excluded from focused, honest exchanges about student performance data

Finally, in each of these groups, conversations and interactions are what Perkins terms *regressive* (21); that is, they are largely ineffective in improving learning and teaching because information is either not shared productively with a focus toward achieving genuine learning gains for students or because information is shared in "narrow, confused, and cautious ways" that limit the group's ability to arrive at good decisions.

Real schools are full of such groups, and in subsequent chapters we'll consider how to challenge and change them. First, we need get a sense of who they are and contrast their characteristics to those of Accountable Communities. Keep in mind that each prototype is a starting point intended to help skillful leaders analyze what is taking place in their own schools. By necessity such composite profiles cannot fully capture what researcher Tom

Levine calls "the contradictions and nuances" of actual communities whose behavior may straddle several types (2006).

The Toxic Community

As their name implies, toxic groups are distinguished by their "negative take" on almost all aspects of schooling and by their real or perceived ability to stifle initiative, punish heretics (anyone who takes a leader's side on an issue), derail emerging solutions to problems, and blame everyone but themselves for mediocre student or adult learning. Sarcastic humor and weary cynicism bind vocal members together in an "us versus them" or "this too shall pass" stance that serves to protect members from external demands and to drive non-subscribers to silence or to the safety of other spaces. Toxicity may result from—or be fueled by—a number of factors:

- A pattern of district bungling or lack of supervision and feedback
- Prior experience with manipulative, punitive, or ineffective administrators
- Lingering resentments over past injuries like strikes or destructive bargaining sessions or over past disappointments and unfulfilled promises, e.g., promotions that never came, program support withdrawn, or changed assignments
- Emotional exhaustion resulting from external challenges, e.g., life-threatening illnesses, death of family members, divorce, fiscal difficulties
- Physical or emotional exhaustion from years of "initiative overload" and unsupported effort
- The continual stirring of a few "ringleaders" who derive gratification and a sense of purpose from being aggrieved

By nature guarded and suspicious, toxic groups do pay attention to what the organization wants from them and to the ways in which organizational goals or changes in practice might affect their traditional rights and privileges. They often use the union contract to defend the status quo. Rather than embracing promising ideas on their merits or supporting leaders who want to find ways of trying out new practices within the framework of the contract, Toxic Communities vote for and encourage union leaders who take a tough, protective stance. Finally, the information Toxic Communities share and the way in which they share it focuses on why things should not be done, cannot work, or are a problem for something that already exists. Thus members most often present themselves as blockers to improvement efforts and as individuals whose job is to sort, select, and label both children and other adults.

The Laissez-Faire Community

While Toxic Communities are often bonded by their sense of injury or by a common vision of "the other" as enemy, groups we have designated *laissez faire* share little beyond a desire or belief in their right to be left alone to "do their own thing." In Laissez-Faire Communities, teachers or administrators co-exist pleasantly but are disconnected from institutional goals and from each other's work and work concerns. Members are largely motivated by personal needs either for comfort and convenience or for instructional autonomy; no shared purpose or vision drives their interaction. If Toxic Communities snarl and snort in response to requests for collaborative problem solving, laissez-faire ones sniff and sigh with martyred resignation. Time spent in team or group work is seen as time drained away from more important endeavors or perhaps simply time wasted tilting at windmills. The school's designated goals don't appear to have immediate relevance or utility. Rather than adversarial as in Toxic Communities, relationships with leaders are often collusive: i.e., "You scratch my back, I'll scratch yours." Laissez-Faire Communities frequently evolve in heavily decentralized districts or schools and in the absence of strong leadership. They also develop when leadership defines its role as protection of cooperative members and motivation through favors and deals. These communities tend to support mediocre learning because they see it as an inevitable result of student limitations and because examining and subsequently changing one's core practice would violate the fundamental value of autonomy.

The Congenial Community

Congenial Communities are "happy" or "nurturing" places to work. Members know and usually trust one another. Considerable energy and effort go into activities to build and maintain adult relationships and comfort—and correspondingly to circumvent or dilute any demand that might strain the careful balance. Garmston and Wellman describe these groups as "counterfeit communities [where] getting along with one another is the primary goal" (185)—the stage of extensive politeness. Unlike Toxic or Laissez-Faire Communities, congenial ones have no difficulty with requests to collaborate. Members usually enjoy one another's company and have positive or neutral relationships with the leaders who make such requests. Mediocrity is sustained because members are unwilling or sometimes unable to challenge one another's ideas and practices in service of better student learning. Such groups, Garmston and Wellman note, "confuse comfort with safety" and thus "sacrifice productive tension for the ease of conviviality." Problems are quickly reduced to simplistic statements and solutions, and no real effort is made to get at the core practices that are no longer serving children's needs.

Like their regressive counterparts, Congenial Communities can be direct byproducts of supervisory shortcomings. In their recognition of the important role that good relationships and trust play in effective teams, administrators often focus their sights on creating congeniality and thus send signals to their working groups about what should be of paramount importance. Such leaders describe their departments or schools as "one big happy family," see themselves as being responsible for keeping peace and harmony, and worry that any attempt to press for genuine changes in practice will "undermine school morale" without producing results. Thus everyone understands that naming an ineffective practice or "telling truth to power" goes against established cultural norms, and difficult questions about poor student or adult performance are swept under the rug.

Communities that Sustain Adult and Student Learning

Collaborative and Accountable Communities are both characterized by what Perkins calls *progressive interactions*: that is, they "exchange information and ideas in ways that foster astute decisions, good solutions and farseeing plans" (20). Unlike participation in Toxic or Laissez-Faire Communities, such interactions leave members "feeling good about working together and looking forward to doing more together" (Perkins 20). Both communities are student- rather than adult-oriented, and both exert effort and reinvest mental energy in their teaching (Bereiter and Scardamalia). They are high-functioning groups because they can, and do, have significant impact on students' opportunities to learn. However, both are not equally evolved.

FIGURE 3.2 Communities that sustain learning.

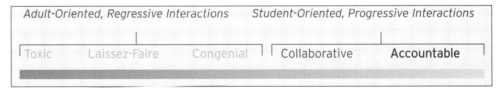

The Collaborative Community

Collaborative Communities have moved beyond the simple or superficial compliance with administrative mandates that is the hallmark of toxic or laissez-faire groups, and they define their success in very different ways from Congenial Communities. Members of Collaborative Communities share clear objectives for student learning, and most express a commitment to helping all young people succeed. They use meetings productively to develop common units and assessments, to resolve questions about resources and directions, and to define and address gaps in student achievement. Individuals derive benefits from the instructional improvements that their membership in the community helps them to bring about and from the results that those changes frequently generate. Congeniality is a valued commodity. Meetings may include "checks ins" allowing the team to stay connected with member's personal lives, but the group does not allow this activity to become an end in itself.

Beyond the shared objectives, trust is the glue that holds the Collaborative Community together. It grows, and is reinforced, perhaps through affection and history, but more important through respect for one another's demonstrated competence and reliability over time. Often, Collaborative Communities emerge and are successful because they are made up of individuals with a predisposition to work well with others or because they contain one or more members who are skilled facilitators. These groups depend upon the good will of each person in getting the job done as required or on the willingness of some members to "cover for" others, i.e., to carry a larger share of the load and pitch in more often without complaint. However, unlike Accountable Communities, Collaborative Communities do not expect or hold themselves responsible for self-assessment and self-policing. Moreover, they lack mechanisms for responding to something that might threaten trust: individuals who violate norms, low expectations for student performance or mediocre student work, promises not met, data that suggest students are receiving insufficient or ineffective instruction in a particular area, or the persistence of actions and approaches the group has agreed to abandon. In such cases, the mere "doing" of something together or the appearance of collaboration begins to become more important than taking on the problematic data and risking a difficult interaction or threatening a good relationship. Elephants start to sit unnamed and unacknowledged in every meeting.

Finally, because they derive their greatest sense of success from working together and taking steps that will have immediate impact on their own students, we think Collaborative Communities are most effective when they are facing what Heifetz and Linsky would call technical challenges: i.e., problems for which they have some repertoire and some known solutions that can serve as starting points.

Accountable Communities

Accountable Communities are the much desired but rarely achieved ideal; they are demanding and sometimes uncomfortable places to work. Members place student learning and achievement over adult needs and preferences. They take direct responsibility for their own actions and for calling others on behaviors and stances that are not helpful to the mission or to the group. Accountable Communities differ from Collaborative Communities in their:

- Ability to acknowledge and deal with the "brutal facts of their current reality" (Collins 2001)

- Willingness (1) to move beyond the most obvious solutions and responses to problems to seek other explanations and opportunities and (2) to let go of treasured approaches when faced with data indicating their lack of success

- "Process smarts," i.e., their trust and skill in raising controversial issues, debating options, giving one another feedback when norms are being violated, and reconciling competing needs
- Explanations of and responses to initial failure, repeated difficulty, or threats
- Ability to monitor their work and to deal with members who are not meeting their obligations rather than to wait for external authorities

FIGURE 3.3 Confronting conditions that undermine learning.

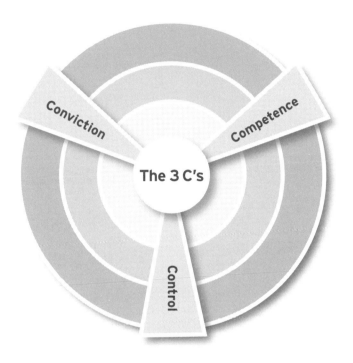

The 3 C's

What is involved in helping groups push themselves towards this vision of an Accountable Community? We think skillful professional communities that confront mediocre learning need the same 3 C's as the leaders who confront mediocre teaching: Conviction, Competence, and Control. Conviction shapes responses to challenge; it governs the kinds of decisions individuals and teams make when faced with hard-to-tackle learning problems or initial lack of success. Conviction also allows individuals to (1) expose conflict and deal with it productively rather than driving it under the table and (2) admit to and struggle through the feelings that arise when one is asked to subsume one's preferences or style to meet greater necessities identified by the group. Competence saves groups from drowning under the weight of the workload or the turmoil of emotions generated by people who are trying to face and make difficult changes. Competence can be the difference between endless, ineffective group activities undertaken for activities' sake and meetings that move the agenda forward and leave members full of hope and urgency. Finally, we're categorizing all the structures, processes, and resources that enable people to get the job done once they have identified it and committed to it as the third capacity, Control. Those who have tried to work collaboratively at great distances, without technological support, without time, or with no agreed-upon process for tackling challenges probably recognize the value of this category.

Conviction

Conviction is the spirit and drive that keeps groups moving in the face of discouraging results or seemingly insurmountable obstacles. Paying attention to conviction does not mean mounting mind reform or re-education campaigns or even trying to change people's beliefs by talking, haranguing, or mandating. It does mean that skillful leaders must:

- Recognize the role beliefs play and address the outward manifestations of those beliefs: i.e., the choices and actions that become impediments to student learning or to the efficacy of the group

- Build and nurture climates that support those who are willing to suspend their doubts and take action and that encapsulate those who will not do so

- Make sure that all their own actions and words send clear, consistent messages about their own hope and positive vision

Ability to Learn

Of all the different points of Conviction groups need, the belief that one can grow, get smarter, or somehow change one's present level of performance to something better is perhaps the most critical. High-performing communities of teachers are bonded by the public stance that effective effort rather than sheer innate ability accounts for a great deal of students' performance in meeting academic standards and intellectual challenges. Therefore they assume that their ability to motivate and engage students and to uncover the secrets and strategies of good academic performance can make a difference. That does not mean that individual members do not have doubts about individual students or about whether schools have adequate time and resources to overcome major obstacles. Adult discussions may include the role of natural talent or a predisposition to excel in a particular area. However, innate ability becomes one of a set of significant variables to be harnessed, or planned for, not an excuse for no action to be taken. Talk is about "not yet reaching standard" not "can't reach the standard." Teachers reward both improvement and academic learning.[1]

---

[1] Corbett, Wilson, and Williams highlighted a key attribute of schools that succeeded in closing the achievement gap. "Thus using good instructional practice does not separate the 'Its my job'/'No excuses' teachers from the others. Adhering to the belief that teachers are responsible for student success does" (133).

FIGURE 3.4 Conviction.

Conviction: Holding and consistently acting on a set of beliefs or stances
that move the school or institution closer to its mission of making sure children learn and achieve at high levels.

Conviction includes a constellation of beliefs or stances that fall into categories
such as:

- **Ability to Learn**
  Students and teachers can "get smarter." Intelligent behavior can be developed through hard work, use of strategies, and investment of time.
  If we work together effectively, we are likely to be smarter than if we struggle
  alone.

- **Development of Expertise**
  Each of us is individually responsible for engaging in productive problem-solving, for contributing to group knowledge and understanding, and for making
  our voices and opinions heard within the professional community.

- **Need for Autonomy versus Collective Commitments**
  Once we have jointly committed to a group strategy to benefit students, none
  of us has the right to ignore or go against that decision when the classroom
  door is shut or when the going gets rough.

- **Ownership and Responsibility for Results**
  It's my job, it's our job, to do whatever it takes to help students master difficult
  concepts and meet rigorous intellectual challenges independently and effectively. When students do not learn, we have the responsibility to figure out
  why and to take action to remedy situations we can influence.

- **Urgency and Hope**
  The situation is urgent; we cannot wait for other times and other days. There
  are no children to waste. They have only this time with us, and every minute
  counts. We have the moral and ethical obligation to hold onto hope even when
  causes seem lost.

High-performing communities of administrators hold the same confidence about their own and other adults' ability to learn and change to
improve student learning.

Development of Expertise

Rhetoric suggesting that "the older one gets, the easier it gets" or "once
you've seen one, you've seen them all" can be common in lower performing
communities. It is rare in accountable ones. The more evolved and responsible a group gets, the more it begins to understand that expertise is not a fixed
entity but something constructed and changed by regular stabs at improvement. Bereiter and Scardamlia note that experts, as opposed to what they
term "experienced non-experts," routinely reinvest mental energy in their

teaching and engage in progressive problem-solving rather than in problem reduction. Negative beliefs or mental models about expertise and the acquisition of expertise become important if they (1) cause individuals to attempt to shift ownership for improvement to some "other" outside entity ("They haven't given us any training. How do they expect us to do this?") or (2) result in efforts to reduce complex situations to fit known procedures (reverting to paper and pencil drills rather than allowing students to use a mix of manipulatives, calculators, and visuals to tackle problems). "If it ain't broke, don't even look at it" or "If it's what I like to do, then leave it alone" might be apt slogans for toxic and laissez-faire groups; the message is don't make extra work. Certainly in the real world not all members of Accountable Communities may enjoy tinkering or be delighted by the chance to fine-tune something that appears to be effective for many students. Nonetheless, most recognize that progressive problem finding and problem solving is an essential response if the group is to reach those students who do not yet "get it," cannot yet meet performance standards, or do not believe they can learn.

Need for Autonomy versus Collective Commitments

Although they suffer the same time pressures and the same temptations to just "close the door and do whatever," members of Accountable Communities place considerable confidence in the power of their collective effort. They believe that they can draw upon group expertise or can jointly develop approaches that will help everyone on a team to be successful. As members experience the satisfaction of effective problem solving, they begin to be increasingly willing to take on shared challenges. This stance contrasts sharply with less developed "professional communities" where a request for collaborative consideration of a learning issue becomes either a drain on other members' energy and optimism or an imposition to be squelched.

Accountable Communities also accept and live by the covenant that collective decisions trump individual autonomy. Once the group has decided on a course of action, individuals do not have the right to ignore that decision in their classrooms. Members expend time and energy in defining a learning problem, understanding the options, and devising strategies to address it; once that work is done, everyone is expected to use the strategy as consistently and substantively as possible.

Ownership and Responsibility for Results

Perhaps the single most distinguishing dimension of Accountable Communities is where they place responsibility for results and what they do when initial efforts fail. Low-performing groups attribute lack of success to outside variables—to not having the right students or to conditions in students' lives that are assumed to limit likely achievement. Accountable Communities look inside first, using a number of different tools and lenses to see if they can craft a better understanding of the problem to be solved. Accountability rests with the team as well as individuals. If students are not successfully answering open-ended questions, this becomes a team problem with a team solution. All members then hold each other responsible for implementing agreements. If an individual is violating a norm or failing to take actions the team has identified as important to student success, it is the team that gives feedback, not the principal.

Urgency and Hope

In Accountable Communities there is a shared sense of urgency: the kids can't wait; they need our best skill and effort now. Time is of the essence. Everything we do with our students should make a difference. If something does not work, we need to support each other and try it again immediately. Urgency is tied to rigor and challenge (Saphier 2005; Schlecty 2001). The outward manifestation of a shared sense of urgency is not a desperate, scattershot pursuit but rather effective effort focused on the right things, on important problems that impact student learning. Put another way, Accountable Communities are results oriented, not activity oriented (Schmoker 2002).

Hope must accompany urgency. Writing about the role that hope plays in sustaining leadership through difficult times and reminding people of the moral purpose that brought them into education in the first place, Michael Fullan offers the words of Vaclav Havel:

> Hope . . . is not the conviction that something will turn out well, but the certainty that something makes sense, regardless of how it turns out. It is hope, above all, that gives us strength to live and to continually try new things, even in conditions that seem hopeless. (qtd. in Fullan)

Hope, in this sense, seems to be the antidote to burnout: one's willingness to keep the faith and return for yet another beating is fed not necessarily by success but rather by the sense that one's goal is worthy and merits significant effort. In Accountable Communities, enough members have this certainty to keep group energy alive or to at least rotate the role of torch bearer when the going gets tough. By contrast, members of Toxic, Laissez-Faire, and Congenial Communities have often given up hope. Citing overwhelming external forces or other greater goods, they determine that it is "more realistic"— that is, less time consuming, less stressful on head and heartstrings, and less work—to simply give up hope and go home when the final bell rings or the contract permits.

Competence

Conviction and Competence are interdependent. Conviction can turn into empty rhetoric if groups do not have the skills to take action productively and effectively. But providing training on the requisite skills to developing group and/or organizational competence can be an empty exercise if the fundamental beliefs that underlie those skills are missing. Figure 3.5 offers a sampling of the kinds of skills that group members and groups as a whole need.

FIGURE 3.5 Competence.

Competence: Having and using a repertoire of skills and substantive knowledge about effective collaboration and adult interaction; having and using problem-solving skills to address student learning needs.

Skills for group competence can be divided into rough sets:

- **Taking on the Tough Stuff**
  Dealing with conflict
  Confronting the "elephants" (unpromising practices and "brutal facts")
  Communicating in difficult situations

- **Developing Problem-Solving and Decision-Making Skills**
  Helping the group get smarter (making conversations progressive)
  Knowing and using problem-solving processes to arrive at collective action
  Knowing and using "step-back" or checking strategies

- **Anchoring the Work**
  Using standards and data
  Establishing and enforcing norms

- **Sustaining Transparency**
  Making practice public
  Examining one's practice with curiosity and vulnerability

Skill Set I: Taking on The Tough Stuff

Dealing with Conflict   Leaders who want to help groups develop the capacity to work effectively need to check their own beliefs and skill and those of others in dealing with conflict (Goleman, Boyatzis and McKee). Laissez-Faire, Congenial, and Collaborative Communities are most often discomfited by conflict. They attempt to suppress it, ignore it, or deal with it in endless parking lot conversations, often with unfortunate consequences for both students and adults. Interestingly, we think, communities at either end of our spectrum are neither afraid of nor feel themselves condemned by the presence of conflict. Toxic groups use disagreement and push back—sometimes at ideas and sometimes at individuals—to help define their stances and divert attention from having to meet expectations for performance. Accountable Communities understand that conflict is a healthy and manageable by-product of a rigorous effort to define problems, assess alternatives, and develop common agreements. In fact, Garmston and Wellman note that a "[high-performing] community cannot exist without conflict" (186). High-performing groups accept and agree to work through the inevitable tension that occurs when the desire for individual autonomy conflicts with the need to uphold collective decisions. Part of group competence is the ability to surface disagreements openly, keep discussion focused on issues rather than personalities, and call one another on behavior that violates norms of respect.

Confronting Unpromising Practices and "Brutal Facts"   Jim Collins in his book *Good to Great: Why Some Companies Make the Leap ... and Others Don't* details how great companies "confront the brutal facts of their current reality" in order to improve that reality (2001 13). Toxic, Laissez-Faire and Congenial Communities tend to regard any attempt to consider facts about the present success of strategies and programs or their own performance as a group as an indictment of individual members, an attack, or a straw man to be challenged. Consequently, they expend considerable effort denying or rationalizing difficult information rather than dealing with it and with its implications. Leaders or group members who attempt to surface such information and handle it honestly either find themselves ignored, shouted down, or labeled as "not nice" or "not helpful to group morale." By contrast, high-performing groups do not avoid bad news and what Barth calls the "undiscussables." Accountable Communities are proud of dropping practices that are not working and make dropping these practices a regular agenda item for discussion. They expose failures. They create a "stop doing list, and systematically unplug anything extraneous." (Collins 2001 124).

LEADER ALERT ───

Make Your Deeds Match Your Words   Because so many people in schools have been socialized to believe that open conflict is unhealthy and/or inefficient, they often suppress information that might help the group make a better decision. Many believe that surfacing genuine concerns or asking probing questions is tantamount to "nay saying" or that doing so will result in recriminations from an administrator. Be conscious of the messages you send both in word and deed; avoid cutting off debate that might lead to a better understanding of an issue or silencing healthy skepticism without identifying any way to check the speaker's point against data. Structure meetings so that opposing points of view can be surfaced safely, and be worried when an initiative that should genuinely change people's practice sparks no debate at all.

───

Communicating in Difficult Situations   One of the major dysfunctions of teams, Patrick Lencioni notes, is "the unwillingness of team members to tolerate the interpersonal discomfort that accompanies calling a peer on his or her behavior and the more general tendency to avoid difficult conversations" (2002 212). Skills for progressive interactions and effective collaboration such as those listed above are useful when the group work is proceeding effectively or with a minimum of disruption. In the real world, however, conditions change. New members arrive with different value systems and different understandings of their roles and responsibilities. Under pressure to meet targets or when resources are strained and people are tired, old bad habits can reemerge or abilities to "push one another's hot buttons" can assert themselves and strain relationships. Members may respect one another's skills and dedication but not like one another particularly or be so close that they fear jeopardizing friendship. One characteristic that distinguishes Accountable from Collaborative Communities is members' ability to respond to situations that challenge equilibrium—to openly name and deal with what is going wrong, reestablish productive interactions, and move on. Resources such as Stone, Patton, and Heen's *Difficult Conversations* or Patterson et al.'s *Crucial Conversations* can help groups identify and practice the skills that they need.

Skill Set 2: Problem-Solving and Decision-Making

Making Group Conversations Progressive   Examine groups that perform well and you are likely to find that members have acquired and consciously practice certain skills that facilitate their interactions. The exchange of information is progressive; it moves the problem-solving along and makes members feel that their conversations are productive, worth the time spent, and likely to advance the group's knowledge and understanding. Garmston and Wellman include the following as essential to helping the process of problem-solving:

- Pausing
- Paraphrasing
- Probing for specificity
- Putting ideas on the table
- Paying attention to self and others
- Presuming presuppositions
- Pursuing a balance between advocacy and inquiry

Another skill is giving data-based, nonjudgmental feedback so that conversations focus more on data than on impressions.

Using Problem-Solving Processes to Arrive at Collective Action   High-performing communities not only share a commitment to collective action on group agreements, they also learn and use a variety of skills and protocols that allow them to reach agreements that are understood and owned by all. The sense of the collective subsumes individual autonomy. Training in (or study of) effective problem-finding, ways to evaluate potential solutions, and ways to set goals and action plans helps such groups to balance individual ideas and goals with those that define the larger interest. Knowing where and how to begin in order to postpone a rush to judgment or blame— or settling for easy (and often already ineffective) "solutions" is important.

Using "Step-Back" or Checking Strategies Making sure that an approach is genuinely working to produce what it was intended to produce becomes important when groups are caught up in either the excitement or pain of trying changes in practice. Along with learning and applying techniques for data collection, Accountable Communities develop the habit of taking stock of their own understandings, their own degree of comfort, or their own ability to implement something. To do so, they need to learn processes that keep the room safe while individuals are putting work and partial understandings on the line. The same structured approach to checking for understanding, summarizing, or examining student work against established criteria that teachers use in a classroom can be used by groups. These processes ensure that effort is effective and wisely spent.

Skill Set 3: Anchoring the Work

Using Standards and Data Accountable Communities at the school level use curriculum or academic standards and data about students' present performance in relation to those standards as the foundation for their work. They use standards to set goals for and to assess students' learning and to identify gaps between present and desired performance. At the district level, performance standards and definitions of excellence (organizational expectations) have "life and clout" for students but also for teachers and administrators. "Life" means that standards are not just located in dusty documents but are readily referenced in conversation and decision making. "Clout" means that, when necessary, they serve as accountability tools for evaluation of students, teachers, and administrators.

Gaps in achieving standards are viewed as opportunities for growth. In some cases they are celebrated as worthwhile targets finally made concrete and therefore attainable. Toxic Communities can use data sporadically and selectively to buttress arguments for resistance or to justify discrimination; Laissez-Faire and Congenial Communities often rely on perceptions and fragmented information. Collaborative and Accountable Communities have learned to seek and to analyze data that will help them take stock and make good decisions, e.g., data about how well initiatives are working, about students' responses to different strategies intended to help them overcome obstacles, or about parts of the curriculum that are neither well understood nor well retained. They have also learned how to thread the needle between too little concrete information at all and data obsession or "paralysis by analysis." Though Collaborative Communities often use data in their joint work but not individual work, Accountable Communities expect one another to engage in systematic examination of data in the classroom and to bring insights to their joint work (Saphier 2005).

Finally, when communities are accountable, teachers can react to external demands more convincingly and effectively because they have routinely collected and considered alternative data. If individuals at all levels of the institution regularly use multiple qualitative and quantitative sources of data to assess student performance, teaching performance, and leadership performance, work is aligned and thus feels logical, coherent, and meaningful.

Norms High-performing groups are governed by mutually determined, published, and readily referenced norms: that is, rules, guidelines, or standards governing group interaction. Norms define expected, not just ideal, behavior. They can cite specific skills to be used during discussion such as pausing, paraphrasing, and probing for specificity (Garmston and Wellman 37). Norms also focus on cultural values such as celebration and caring or honest, open communication, or systematic examination of data (Saphier 2005 32). The goal is to institutionalize skills and values so that they become an organizing structure with a specified set of processes that will govern interaction. "A skill (or a value) becomes a norm if it is the 'normal' behavior in the group" (Garmston and Wellman 37). For example, to guide the way in which they work and the focus of their efforts, groups might generate statements such as the following:

> We will focus our meetings and work time on openly examining our classroom practice and its impact on student learning.

> Agendas and conversations will allocate the majority of time and attention to important matters of teaching and learning.

> We celebrate and welcome different viewpoints and commit to making our disagreements heard in the meeting not in the halls. We will work hard to analyze and understand perspectives that conflict with ours and will remain open to altering our positions. We will fight gracefully.

Skill Set 4: Sustaining Transparency

Making Practice Public Unlike communities that protect the right to do whatever one wants within the confines of the classroom, Accountable Communities and sometimes Collaborative Communities have overcome the norm of keeping one's practice private. Because they understand that the best that any one member knows and is able to do should be available to all, they are willing to expose their practice and their results to scrutiny of colleagues. More important, they have found ways of doing so even within the narrow confines of the typical school structure. They make appointments to observe one another; they drop in on one another; they pool and discuss tapes, invite expert colleagues to demonstrate, swap students for a particular unit, or engage in collegial consults. They put student products and artifacts of their practice on the table for public consideration. Nested in a trusting environment, members of the highest performing groups feel obligated to give honest, data-based feedback to their colleagues even when it might be perceived as negative. As Lencioni notes, "if team members are not making each other uncomfortable at times, if they are never pushing one another outside their emotional comfort zone, then it is extremely likely that they're not making the best decisions for the organization" (2005 38).

Control

Conviction is the shorthand for the beliefs that sustain high-performing groups, and Competence stands for the skills groups need in order to solve student learning (or adult performance) problems. The third "C," Control, focuses on the surrounding conditions that can support or hamper a professional community's work.

Nuts and Bolts

Time is a hobgoblin that haunts all skillful leaders and all high-performing groups. People who are motivated by their convictions and encouraged by the sense of participating on a team where everyone pulls his or her weight, will generally donate large amounts of time—perhaps more than they can always afford. But time to think and work must also be pried loose within the "duty day." At the school level, the quantity of time a skillful leader can liberate through creative scheduling and coverage is certainly important, but the quality of time use is equally so. Because Toxic and Laissez-Faire Communities decry time set aside specifically for collaboration as counter to their own beliefs and priorities, they consume whatever is available and are rarely satisfied with either the allocation or the aftermath. Congenial Communities consume large amounts of time on friendliness and good feeling; people have a sense that they have donated their efforts because they have participated in social activities that take place at school and often become frustrated when more is required. High-performing communities, in contrast, manage to balance task and relationship; they try to use every available chunk of time together productively. Skills such as those listed under Competence above help them to do so.

High-performing communities find and use other snippets of time and other ways of communicating beyond those officially set aside by someone in authority. They grab 5 to 10 minutes with one another to talk through an idea, fill someone in on how a strategy went, pass along a good tidbit, or discuss a struggling student. They email files and stick their heads in one another's classes not to check on social obligations but to follow up on goals or plans. They make phone appointments, grab coffee together, or plan over lunch. Finally, how leaders use time, honor agendas and deadlines, and cede control over time allocation when appropriate send important signals to communities about what is expected of them and what they are capable of doing.

Space often helps or hinders time-grabbing, idea sharing, or making practice public, yet it is one of those commodities doled out for the convenience and comfort of influential adults rather than for its strategic value in advancing the goals of the school or improving the quality of instruction. Although breaking up a toxic duo or a highly social corner of the building by reassigning space may generate short-term pain, long-term gains can be surprising. Griping with your next-door neighbor is easy. Griping with someone on the other side of the building or three floors up takes planning and effort. However, the more important concern with space allocation is

---

FIGURE 3.6 Control.

Control: Adequate structures, processes, and resources to support groups charged with improving student achievement and carrying out the mission of the school.

- Nuts and bolts (time, space, technology, and materials)
- Focus of efforts
- Influence or authority
- Incentives, rewards, sanctions
- Freedom from distraction (inappropriate interference, micromanagement, competing urgencies)
- Alignment of key systems that impact the work (e.g., supervision and evaluation, professional development, or student assignment and scheduling)

---

ease of communication for those who are trying to work together on students' behalf. It is hard to be an active member of an Accountable Community when your colleagues are miles away, there is no common meeting space, or when you are separated and surrounded by naysayers. Making it easy for adults to work together means eliminating physical barriers whenever possible.

Skillful leaders have increasingly come to recognize *technology* as a tool to support effective collaboration. Although the benefits of email, scanners, file sharing, and the like seem obvious, not all districts or school leaders make the investments needed to link community members efficiently. Easy access to data online, the creation of ways to network and share questions and findings, plus such resources as printers, copiers, laptops, and whiteboards or easels for public note-taking send signals that leaders believe in the value of the group's work.

Focus of Efforts

Burnout is a danger of collaborative work. Skillful leaders understand that not all problems are best solved, and not all work is best done, collaboratively. Collaboration can generate energy if it is focused on issues of immediate importance to the group's students and on issues for which no one person in the group has a ready answer or highly successful approach. However, sometimes teams think that all aspects of their individual practices must be negotiated and uniform for collaboration to be successful. Continual negotiation on technical challenges for which one or more members of the group already have a repertoire and/or a relentless press toward uniformity can drain energy. Recognizing that not all instructional decisions are equally compelling or urgent, skillful leaders help groups to select the focuses that will add to their shared understanding and capacity and to let go of the need to work through every detail of their year.

Influence or Authority

Low-functioning or emerging groups often feel that they are victims of circumstance and have little opportunity to influence organizational choices. Even when members perceive opportunities to improve a small part of joint practice, they may claim that change beyond their own classroom is neither their responsibility nor something they can affect. If past actions and experiences have taught them that someone else, often far removed from the arena in which they work, will undo 10 months' efforts with a pen stroke, such claims are understandable. Skillful leaders recognize the importance of establishing and clearly communicating explicit guidelines about:

- What decisions are within a group's purview to make independently
- What changes they may implement without being countermanded
- How they can raise concerns and get rapid answers to questions
- What processes they need to follow if a proposed improvement is one that must be negotiated

Easy, regular access to the decision makers who have the authority to affect what a group does is also an important aspect of control. When leaders have open office doors, share key information about their thinking, make sure groups know what is affecting other parts of the organization, or routinely update data that may be useful to the team, they send the message that the professional community is respected, included, and treated as colleagues in a problem-solving endeavor.

Incentives, Rewards, and Sanctions

Leaders often focus on the issue of monetary incentives and rewards under the assumption that their availability is an essential precondition for individuals to participate in collaborative work. In doing so, they may accidentally feed into one of the many excuses that Toxic and Laissez-Faire Communities offer up to explain their resistance, namely that collective problem-solving is an add-on and extra burden rather than an integral part of professional life. Our experience suggests that benefits such as money, graduate or continuing education credits, or comp time only serve to reinforce mediocrity when they are:

- Substituted for important goals as the incentive for participation
- Viewed or treated as entitlements
- Distributed with no regard for actual performance or the quality of participation and investment
- Presented as equivalent compensation for time spent

Incentives and rewards become valuable only if they signal respect and appreciation for genuine investments and are understood to have been earned through effective effort. When they talk about meaningful rewards, high-performing teachers and principals often cite influential small gestures or quid pro quo acknowledgments of a group's contributions, such as an invitation to or travel funds for a conference, a journal subscription or an account to buy books that will illuminate a problem, a much-desired piece of equipment located closer to the group's work space, coverage to observe at another school, repairs or technology trouble-shooting quickly and graciously accomplished, an invitation to participate in a focus group or offer one's opinions to an outside evaluator. First, these actions are likely to have a more immediate impact on one's sense of being respected and supported as a professional or as a professional group than a small stipend parceled out from paycheck to paycheck. Second, they can be directly tied to identifiable performance and results, to the donation of extra time and effort. Unlike stipends or step increases, they can be treated as one-time events. Differentiated and matched incentives run less of a risk of becoming entitlements; they are not expected to repeat year to year without regard to the quality of the year's input or output.

Control involves dealing with consequences and sanctions for non-performance as well as with rewards. The environment in which groups do their work should not signal that any superficial compliance or activity for activity's sake may be considered effective teamwork. Many districts experiment with a range of rewards but fail to consider what will constitute evidence that the reward has been earned. Although contracts may permit a district to mandate professional development in response to nonperformance or to withhold credits, stipends, or step increases, the criteria under which such sanctions might be used are often ill defined. Thus they are rarely implemented even for well-documented individual cases. For some players, their absence signals that business as usual is just fine with everyone.

Freedom from Inappropriate Interferences

Part of Control is the ability to be tenacious and to come at a problem repeatedly over time. Sustaining such a stance and focus requires Conviction and Competence, certainly. However, even the most accountable groups can find their efforts and will undermined if they are subject to a barrage of unnecessary interference. For example, meetings of teams and formally established professional communities are like nectar to worker bees from a variety of departments, programs, and special interests in a school system. The latter, understandably, see officially scheduled meeting times as opportunities to get their messages out and to recruit attention and participation. Sometimes these distractions are a direct result of inescapable mandates from Central Office, the head of school, or the board of trustees. More often, however, distractions and competing urgencies occur because leadership has not established a thoughtful process for determining what agenda items may be brought to the group. Protecting school or team time is a critical competency for skillful leaders (see Chapter 2 "Confronting Blocks to Organizational Learning"). Items need to come to team agendas because they are genuinely urgent and important for solving current or long-term student learning problems, not because they are urgent on someone else's to-do list. Leaders' conduct should never signal that they think a group engaged in analyzing student work, doing error analysis, or determining how to help a group of at-risk learners has nothing planned or nothing better to do than to have its agenda filled with outside interruptions from people who have begged a favor from the boss.

Protecting time when there is so little of it is one struggle for skillful leaders and high-functioning groups. Sustaining the delicate balance between paying attention to and monitoring a team's efforts and performance and micromanaging it becomes another challenge, particularly when the organization is trying to shift from a centralized notion of leadership to one that distributes responsibility and influence across a wider spectrum of the faculty. Establishing early expectations for attendance, norms, reporting, problem-solving processes, rotating leadership, and facilitation can all help a concerned administrator turn over day-to-day responsibility to a professional community. However, both informal and formal groups quickly become disillusioned if they think they are being manipulated in order to put a wash of legitimacy on some pet project of administration. If the right answer, the right agenda items, and the right behavior are already selected and clear to the boss, then communities may end up simply trying to comply with a thinly disguised demand rather than identifying ways to best help their students learn.

Alignment of Key Systems

Professional Development One of the hallmarks of high-functioning communities—and particularly of accountable ones—is their commitment to getting smarter and their ability to face up to what they do not yet know and cannot yet do. Groups that are trying to get smarter at what they do need the ability to influence both the content of professional development and its timeliness. To develop their Competence, they cannot "wait until next year's committee sets the agenda" or next year's grant comes in for help on needs that range from content understanding, to the design of an interim assessment, or their own ability to engage in a difficult conversation with a parent. For purposes of thinking about Control, a group does not necessarily need a whole pre-planned program of training. Laying out a year of learning how to function effectively might be the best match for a Toxic or Congenial Community that must acquire skills that are foreign to its culture. For Laissez-Faire Communities, the ability to self-assess and select priorities from a list of required content or to draw upon colleagues' expertise may be more effective.

In addition to its inflexibility, mediocre professional development is distinguished by its fragmented, single-shot, one-size-fits-all approach. Often conceived and designed in a hurry, at a distance from practitioners, and with an eye to filling up open space on the calendar, it diminishes both a leader's and a group's control over the essential conditions needed to support progressive problem solving. Aligned professional development, on the other hand, is differentiated by grade, group, or content and targeted. Its content and delivery have been carefully matched to the identified and emerging needs of groups by using:

- Data about student achievement and targets for results
- The community's own self-assessment data from prior efforts
- Focused feedback on performance provided by administrators, coaches, or other designated "critical friends"

Finally, aligned professional development sends clear signals about the school or system's goals and about what the organization most values. It does not pull communities away from their explicit focus on improving the core of teaching and learning.

Supervision and Evaluation   Rather than seeing collaboration and shared accountability as an essential aspect of their work as professionals, members of low-functioning communities often describe it as an "add-on" or imposition, a fad to be ignored, or, in the worst scenarios, the whim of an imperious administrator who is encroaching on traditional labor rights. All of these responses may suggest that the requirements of the supervision and evaluation system are out of alignment with the organization's need for adults to pool mental energy in service of student learning. Thus groups do not have the conditions they need in order to function effectively. A more likely explanation for such a response, however, is that supervisors and evaluators have consistently failed to acknowledge high-level collaboration and problem solving or demand improvement of same from an individual or group of individuals functioning at a mediocre level. Thus members of Toxic Communities will have received commendable ratings on the standards for professional collaboration merely because they showed up at meetings the requisite number of times. Or collaboration will have been confused with cooperation; individuals who got their grades in on time or were always present and amiable at back to school nights will have been rated as meeting their responsibilities for working with colleagues effectively.

We see an increasing number of supervision and evaluation systems that contain provisions for years devoted to professional growth and/or collaboration in lieu of the kinds of formal observations and administrator feedback that characterize traditional clinical supervision. However, we also see few attempts to make the alignment between the expectations implicit in these system provisions and the work of professional communities clear and explicit. Instead, we see the perpetuation of an arbitrary misalignment: a division between work that is to be subject to evaluation and work that is real, i.e., focused on taking risks and experimenting with new strategies that will help reach struggling students. The misalignment is evident as teachers madly scramble to do projects that allow them to check off a professional growth requirement but drain time and attention they can bring to the work of their teams. The misalignment is also clear when supervisors repeat the cherished misconception they are not allowed to use information about the teachers' thinking, problem-solving skills, ability to help a group make progress, willingness to take responsibility, or conviction about students' ability to learn that has been acquired while attending a meeting or observing a group at work. In either case, the organization wastes a valuable opportunity to get smarter by narrowing or limiting channels of communication and information sharing.

Summary

As our understanding of the potential power of adult collaboration increases, it becomes clear that high-functioning professional communities are an ideal rather than a reality in many schools. In this chapter, we consider a continuum of community function and adult learning that ranges from toxic or actively blocking to accountable or highly likely to produce significant improvements in student achievement over a sustained period. We use the 3 C's of Conviction, Competence, and Control to distinguish the capacities of our ideal, Accountable Communities, and to create an image of excellence against which current efforts in schools can be measured. The continuum and the capacities of Accountable Communities are intended to be frameworks that help leaders to:

- Analyze and describe the performance of professional communities within their own schools or district
- Diagnose the ways in which ineffective groups undermine both adult and student learning
- Identify where they need to help groups build Conviction, Competence, and Control

Here our goal is the creation of a common language and set of concepts. In subsequent chapters we will consider specific strategies for confronting and changing groups that have not yet reached their full collaborative potential.

4 Community Building 101: Setting the Stage

Most groups do not evolve naturally into the idealized Collaborative and Accountable Communities described in Chapter 3. Too many competing pressures and too much old history get in the way. Leaders who want to help an organization get smarter by having people pool their mental effort have two key responsibilities. First, they must help individuals and teams expand their Conviction, Competence, and Control. These are the capacities that support *progressive interactions*, those that move the organization forward, and *progressive problem solving*, continuous re-examination of performance to identify next steps and challenges. Creating the appropriate conditions to nurture community development is the subject of this chapter. The second important responsibility, confronting low-performing communities, is the focus of Chapter 5.

Building Conviction

The task of tapping into hidden reservoirs of hope, giving discouraged troops courage, or trying to instill conviction where none seems to exist is one of the most critical but daunting challenges a leader can face. It is critical because conviction motivates people to put aside petty concerns and to pursue important goals tenaciously. It is daunting because the work begins with an examination of self and sometimes a willing suspension of one's personal doubts and fears. "What convinces is conviction," Lyndon Johnson noted. "Believe in the argument you're advancing. If you don't, you're as good as dead. The other person will sense that something isn't there, and no chain of reasoning, no matter how logical or elegant or brilliant, will win your case for you." Our experience in schools, unscientific but anchored in a collective century of work, suggests that faculties may not always agree with a leader's convictions. However, they will most often respect individuals who are clear, consistent, and passionate about what they stand for and why. The respect will lead them to try actions in which they do not yet believe.

Setting the stage for community development, then, begins with a self-assessment. It requires us to:

- Explore what Senge calls our own mental models, the tacit, often unrecognized and untested assumptions that we carry around and use to explain events (7)
- Inquire about and reflect on the messages that people are getting from our deeds as well as our words

This act of taking stock is necessary for several reasons. Many educators have been shaped by what Gordon Donaldson describes as "the planetary culture" and "individualistic ethos" of American schools (26-30). If we began our careers ten or more years ago, our experiences—and thus our mental models—may not have featured powerful and accountable collaboration that improved our teaching. Most likely we were the lonely rulers of our small classroom kingdoms; we faced only sporadic visits from outsiders whose prognostications resulted in little change in what we chose to do. Now we need to convince others that they must be accountable to and honor the decisions of a team of people, even when those decisions represent significant departures from preferred modes of operation and when those decisions guarantee extra work.

Educators also tend to prefer harmony over disagreement, affirmation over challenge, and "right answers" over ambiguity. Truly Accountable Communities, however, seek out and attack vexing problems for which they have no obvious solution. Suddenly teachers trying to collaborate effectively and leaders who think they want to tap into the power of collaboration have to increase their tolerance for temporary pain and their willingness to endure messiness in service of new learning. In the early stages of joint work, the gain for students may not be readily apparent, but the increased investments of time and the loss of autonomy will be. Leaders must recognize and be ready to do battle with their own tendencies to back off immediately in the face of assertions that "this isn't working, and I told you it wouldn't."

Finally, taking careful stock of our own beliefs and actions is necessary because district and school leadership often fall prey to "Do as I say, not as I do" syndrome. Everyone in school is in a hurry, under pressure, and attempting to respond to multiple demands. Leaders have to implement mandates from boards, the state, or the federal government that may not be well known or understood by faculty. People in power may be pushing for certain approaches or programs. Thus administrators tend to move quickly, fire off memos and emails, and take shortcuts that cut others out of deliberations. Those actions leave staff wondering how decisions really get made and why anyone ever asked them to weigh in. When we tell teachers and specialists to work together to solve important problems but then inform them of what their solutions must be, we undermine both their conviction and our own credibility.

To help in assessing and building conviction, let's return to the categories of convictions we presented in Chapter 3 and consider two different mental models leaders might hold about them. We'll call one model *debilitating beliefs*[1]; they are the mindsets and opinions that sap energy and undermine adult and organizational learning. The contrasting model will be *driving beliefs*, that is the attitudes and assumptions that work to support learning and propel a group's development in positive directions. In Table 4.1 we summarize the categories and suggest what indicators of each might sound like.

TABLE 4.1 Indicators of Debilitating and Driving Beliefs

Conviction Category	Overheard Indicators of Debilitating Beliefs	Overheard Indicators of Driving Beliefs
Ability to Learn	It's a function of IQ and out of our control. "Whether a group can collaborate effectively is all about personality and smarts. Some teams perform well just like individuals do; some don't have it. That's to be expected. The best you can do is try to contain the damage and work around the ones who can't get it together."	Hard work and strategies help you get smarter. "That team can improve. They're just stuck in some old crummy patterns. Have we been clear about what we expect—and that we know they can take this [named performance] on? Let's figure out what they need and get them some help. Should we give them an off-site retreat to get started?"
Development of Expertise	Some have expertise; some don't. "If we can get one or two star players, you know, the creative ones, we can feed them stuff, and they can carry the team. You've got to have followers, so spread the lightweights out to minimize their impact and figure they'll just go along."	Expertise is a habit of finding and solving problems that can be taught. "Everyone has something to contribute here. We've all got to push our thinking to come up with some completely different approaches to this problem because the way we've been carrying on isn't helping a whole lot of kids."
Need for Autonomy versus Collective Commitment	The part takes precedence over the whole. "I tell my people that what they do in their classroom is their own business; they're the experts. No team really has the right or knowledge to tell someone else how to conduct his business."	The whole is greater than the sum of its parts. "Folks, you can discuss and debate and wrestle around with this problem until you define what will be the best for students. But once you all make the decisions as a team, everyone has to uphold them with 100% effort. Where this initiative is concerned, there is no 'I' in team."

[1]See Platt et al. *The Skillful Leader: Confronting Mediocre Teaching* (2000) Chapter 2.

TABLE 4.1 (continued)

Conviction Category	Overheard Indicators of Debilitating Beliefs	Overheard Indicators of Driving Beliefs
Ownership and Responsibility for Results	It's not our problem because it's not our fault. "How can you blame grade___? Look what they got sent. Central Office has got to start forcing ____ to cover the curriculum the way they're supposed to."	It's our job; no excuses. "Hey, whatever we got here is now ours. We own these kids till they leave us, and we're going to do whatever it takes to help them make progress."
Urgency and Hope	Why rush? Nothing is going to change. "Change takes time. Rome wasn't built in a day. These are good people and I have to bring them along slowly, let them pilot a little bit and see how it goes. I want them to be comfortable with what the district wants. We're fighting a losing battle here."	Lives need turning around and time is running out. "Ladies and Gentlemen, these kids are losing out. They don't have much time, so neither do we. We're going to have to go with some short-term pain to get long-term gain. This year is our marathon, but we're going to make it."

Checking on Debilitating Beliefs

As we noted in *The Skillful Leader: Confronting Mediocre Teaching*, debilitating beliefs are deeply rooted assumptions and shared myths that shape the way members of an organization tackle their work. Typically we do not think of the statements we make about perceived "facts of life" or "the way it is around here" as debilitating beliefs. Few leaders would actively go about collecting and spouting a set of statements meant to undermine learning. By their very nature, debilitating beliefs are usually hidden and unexamined. We recognize them only when we put certain of our statements under the microscope to examine their underlying assumptions and when we imagine the logical consequences of thinking or acting in certain ways. Consider how the following example of selected debilitating beliefs can drain conviction from a professional community.

EXAMPLE Debilitating Beliefs

1. **Adults can be sorted into low groups and slow groups just like kids; it's an inevitable fact of life.**

   Sounds like: "The social studies department is a disaster and always has been."

   Looks like: The elementary principals have been bypassing the reading teachers and using their grant-funded coaches to conduct literacy training for the last three years.

   Drains conviction because: Leaders who decide that some communities of adults simply do not have the innate ability to learn what they need to in order to collaborate well for students give up on those adults. The resulting pockets of stagnation create inequities for students who must depend upon the low-performing adult groups and for other adults who have to carry the increased load. With part of the organization malfunctioning, investments of salary and time yield fewer results; hardworking and thoughtful members at different levels then find their own confidence in future success undermined.

2. **Adults ought to be able to do what you tell them to do the first time you tell them; they shouldn't have to be helped or given a second chance.**

   Sounds like: "I empowered them and they blew it. I told them they needed to get together in their teams, look at student work, and figure out how to get our scores up. It's been a wasted year. I'm taking the release days back."

   Looks like: Every member of a high school faculty is assigned to a small learning community that is to meet once a week and "talk about data." The communities are left to their own devices after the initial meeting with the principal. In May they report that using their prep time in that way was "a waste of valuable time," and the principal scraps the experiment.

   Drains conviction because: Rather than ascribing the poor collaboration to lack of clear criteria for success, training, practice, and feedback, or monitoring and adjustment of time and structures, all participants are left with the notion that they are inadequate and that collaboration is an ineffective approach to improvement. The unsuccessful experience, if not correctly interpreted and corrected, can leave a reservoir of resentment and self-doubt that erodes willingness to engage in joint work the next time it is requested.

3. **Some adults know more than other adults; they should not be asked to waste precious time helping struggling colleagues solve their instructional problems.**

   Sounds like: "I know she's difficult, but she's brilliant. She's got a point when she says she knows this stuff already. The proof is in her classroom. To keep everyone happy, I'm going to let her go to the assessment conference and work on an independent project."

   Looks like: Three members of the administrative council have been excused from attending the last three data analysis sessions because they either "did that already in their departments and have other pressing issues" or because they feel very strongly that they have nothing to learn from looking at some other subject area's test scores.

   Drains conviction because: Instead of conveying the message that everyone's effort and knowledge must be pooled to help struggling students and that the welfare of those students is everyone's responsibility, this approach tells people that collaboration is for the benefit of adults. It sets up a double standard: those who feel like it or have nothing better to do with their time should attend; people who need remedial help should attend; the rest of us are better than that and our time is more valuable. Ultimately this approach undermines the notion that one has to sacrifice some degree of individual autonomy in order to work collectively for improvements in student learning.

4. **People are going to do what they want when they close their doors. The fact that the team decided something isn't going to change behavior any more effectively or any faster.**

    Sounds like: "So we know you have your own way of doing things and it's hard to change course in midstream but hopefully you'll find something here that you can fool around with. No pressure. We can't turn this around overnight, but it does sound like there were some good suggestions today. We can take this slowly and see how it goes."

    Looks like: The 7th grade team decides that all academic classes will begin with a 7-minute focused writing called "explain yourself" at least three times per week in order to help boost students' performance on the constructed response items in the upcoming state assessments. Leo, the basketball coach, tries it once but then stops because he needs to return calls at the beginning of the period and usually lets the kids talk and "decompress for 5 minutes or so" while he is doing that. When the team complains to the vice principal, they are told that "Rome wasn't built in a day" and "Leo will get it figured out in a way that works for him eventually."

    Drains conviction because: The message here is that students' needs and the potential for improved student learning are not urgent enough motivators to cause dedicated professionals to abandon their usual routines and practices. The positive presupposition—that excellent teachers will seek to use the best possible thinking available and will honor commitments they have made—is missing entirely. Rather than signaling high positive expectations and hope for a changed future, these actions suggest resignation and business as usual.

Acting on Driving Beliefs

If leaders are going to successfully raise student performance, they must believe that they can structure a work setting and culture that allows people to show themselves at their very best and to grow in areas where they are currently weak. Driving beliefs undergird leader actions that help people work together effectively; they include:

- We can all—administrators, teachers, students, and organizations— get smarter.

- If we work together judiciously, effectively, and with hope for a changed future, we can solve some of the student learning problems we currently face.
- Each of us is responsible for contributing to group knowledge and understanding and for making our voices and opinions heard.

LEADER ALERT

Chemistry Is Not the Answer to the Question Beware of attributing a group's effective or ineffective performance to personalities, chemistry, or the innate intelligence of some of the members. Chemistry explains strong relationships; however, it doesn't shed much light on ability to use data to identify a problem or willingness to be responsible for results. Those capabilities may be more a function of members' prior knowledge, experience, or training than anything else. If leaders believe there is a bell curve for innate ability to collaborate, that some groups are just naturally great and some are not, they will make decisions that inadvertently reduce group conviction and encourage dysfunctional group behavior.

All Levels of the Organization Can Learn

This driving belief assumes that the skills and habits of mind for effective collaboration can be taught, learned, and monitored. Both administrative and teacher leaders can get better at facilitating investigations, using data, building on colleagues' ideas, or asking hard questions. Teachers and leaders at all levels of the organization can improve their ability to reach students and remove barriers to learning. Organizations can get smarter and more strategic about the ways in which they share knowledge from one level to another, support teachers, tap into their expertise, and reward and protect their ability to solve learning problems.

Collaboration Is Important

A conviction that collaborative work can solve student learning problems includes several component beliefs: (1) that the whole is greater than the sum of its parts, (2) that good teachers know a great deal about how to help students and should be listened to closely, and (3) that there is a pool of professional knowledge drawn from both research and daily practice that we can tap into.

Every Individual Is Responsible

Pooling intelligence, collaborating to solve student learning problems, and implementing improvements that result from effective collaboration are not optional activities. To be considered an excellent teacher, one must be able to be part of a high-functioning team or collaborative initiative when that is the most appropriate way to deal with adaptive challenges.

Some Values Are Non-Negotiable

Jon Saphier identifies four levels of values-communication that can help a leader determine how to present and pursue particular convictions (personal communication 2007). Note that thinking in this way also helps a visionary leader prevent the imperative overload that occurs when every potential conviction carries equal weight with every other in discourse or directions.

> Level 1 **Non-negotiable** are those values or priorities that are not up for debate—clarification, but not debate.
>
> Level 2 **"Stand for"** is something you advocate for but would not force on anyone.
>
> Level 3 **"Invite"** is something that you are interested in promoting as a thought to study or investigate. You may not have enough data to have a "stand for" position.
>
> Level 4 **"Support"** category refers to things that you have not initiated but would support.

Recognizing the presence of debilitating beliefs and the ways in which we all interfere with our own best intentions helps leaders build conviction. Examine the following sample of strategies to determine which ones you are either doing already or could do more purposefully as you work to support the growth of professional communities within your schools and districts.

STRATEGIES TO BUILD CONVICTION

- **Communicate your beliefs, values and "non-negotiables."** Make your convictions clear and explicit. Share your core values about standards, expectations, motivation, and persistence. Repeatedly refer to what you believe about student capacity to learn, the power of teaching to transform student lives, and the importance of collaboration, not in ways that reproach people but in ways that tell others what your personal vision of a better future has to encompass.

- **Walk the talk.** As obvious and stereotyped as this bit of advice seems, the contrast between leader words and leader actions remains one of teachers' strongest complaints. Critically examine the recurring situations or events that allow community members to deduce what you most value: faculty meetings, morning greetings, hall exchanges, supervisory conferences, problem solving around student behavior, and event planning. Determine what messages about beliefs and values these interactions are sending. Is it really "We pool our thinking and solve problems together?" Or is it "I talk, you listen." Ask for feedback to make sure that your actions are consistent with your words.

- **Listen carefully to all points of view and do not shut down debate too early or too often.** The sense of urgency and the drive to reduce messiness can cause well-intentioned leaders to dismiss important information or criticism that is essential to identifying the right problem to solve. See researcher Tom Levine's Leader Alert.

- **Help teachers choose a problem/focus for improvement and community action that is important to student success and shared by many different disciplines.** Make sure early collaborative efforts aren't around technical issues that are unlikely to make a dent in student performance problems that teachers worry about. Focusing on writing, reading non-fiction texts, representing and analyzing data in science, math, and social studies, for example, can help foster a sense of shared purpose and a sense that the faculty is investing collective effort in something significant that is a persistent barrier to student success.

- **Develop goal-oriented "chants and refrains."** In part, leaders build conviction through constant repetition of key phrases or metaphors that capture the moral or visionary essence of what the school is attempting to do. These chants cannot be meaningless rhetoric. They should summarize or signal actions a team or the entire school community has committed to taking, e.g., "No going backward; no excuses" or "We take care of ourselves. We take care of each other. We take care of this place." or "We look for gaps so we can close them or bridge them." Not all such chants need to come from formal leadership. Often influential informal teacher leaders have developed powerful refrains they live out in action with their students. We think, for example, of the second grade teacher who told her class "Be strict with yourselves; you're teaching yourselves lessons that have to last the rest of your life." The key is listening for, repeating, and thus honoring powerful classroom-based chants so that they can become meaningful for a larger community.

- **Organize problem solving to identify mid-point benchmarks and indicators of progress; organize data gathering to capture incremental growth toward goals.** As Schmoker and others have suggested, teachers need the encouragement provided by tangible evidence that their efforts are making a difference (2001). Schools often build agreements around actions they will take to implement programs and forget to identify how they will assess those actions. By focusing on outcomes and how to collect evidence of progress toward those outcomes instead of the more typical emphasis on activities, leaders can help communities find the incremental gains that will motivate and sustain them.

- **Ask groups to identify and change an accepted but ill-considered practice that is getting in the way of student learning in the school.** Problem solving includes the challenge of problem identification.

Accountable Communities need to ask themselves hard questions such as "What are the standard operating procedures and cherished practices that are no longer working to help students learn?" They must test their beliefs by facing the anxiety or potential conflict that is likely to arise when something long held to be a truth is called into question: for example, giving zeroes for missed homework and averaging them into a student's grade, refusing to allow students to earn a higher grade from a test re-take or project rewrite because that grade wasn't earned on the first try, or reserving summer school classrooms only for those who have failed.

- **Establish common research-based instructional or assessment strategies.** The consulting group Focus on Results recommends adding common "evidence based teaching practices" to support a school-wide instructional focus (Nelson et al. 48).[2] For example, Balboa High School, San Francisco, CA adopted the common practices below to support its "Writing Across the Curriculum" initiative, and Daniel Webster Elementary School in San Francisco adopted and posted agreements about assessment practices.

- **Communicate criteria and models for successful teams.** Building conviction often involves helping others create a concrete image of a successful future in which the changes they seek are working well. Provide either newly minted or long-standing groups with information, criteria, and models for what high-functioning teams do and how they behave. Descriptions of community capacity from Chapter 3, Saphier's criteria for high-functioning teams in *John Adam's Promise*, or Lencioni's functions and dysfunctions of teams can serve as useful starting points for reflection and self-assessment. Other strategies for raising awareness and clarifying what good performance looks and sounds like include:

    Presenting video examples of high-functioning teams and teams that are struggling

    Inviting team leaders to visit meetings of exemplary groups in operation throughout the system or in another location

    Posting and regularly checking on group norms at each meeting

---

EXAMPLE Balboa Small Learning Community Initiatives

BBC (Blackboard Configuration) must be used school-wide daily to guide instructional delivery and clarify for students the part of the content standards to be mastered that day. All elements must be clearly visible, complete, and current for every subject.

Writing strategies and rubrics developed by the English Department will be used school-wide.

---

[2]See also www.focusonresults.net, Saphier (2008) and Marzano (2001) for information about research-based teaching practices.

Vocabulary will be improved school-wide by learning the connection between roots and prefixes and content-specific terminology.

Organizational skills will be built by teaching and using Cornell note strategies school-wide.[3]

EXAMPLE Assessment Agreements Daniel Webster Elementary School, San Francisco

Monthly writing samples 1st Wed. of month. Prompts to be decided by grade level.

CELL/EXLL assessments three times a year.

Monitoring tests after every HM theme 2nd through 5th grades.

Notes on two children daily, running records, observations, etc.

District Harcourt Brace assessments after each unit. Problem-solving assessments need to be made.

Use fluency rubric to directly teach fluency 2nd through 5th grades.

Students complete five writing projects to be shared at Author Fair in the spring.

LEADER ALERT

Are you open to changing practice, receiving influence, and taking teacher concerns seriously?　　　　　**by Tom Levine**

You want teachers to be open to changing practice, receiving influence, and taking your concerns seriously. Are you similarly open to changing practice, receiving influence, and taking their concerns seriously? As you try to shift the way teachers work together, you may hear—or overhear—critical comments about you, your work, or the reforms you support. Teachers don't have practice providing analytical feedback to fellow adults and may react with a bitter tone honed through work in a non-collaborative if not a Toxic Community. When you meet with teachers to promote your agenda, it is likely that you will be the "elephant in the room," silencing open reaction to "your ideas" for school reform. With low-performing communities, you will have to help teachers talk directly about your actions or the larger work you are supporting.

[3]For a download model of Cornell notes see www.dartmouth.edu/~acskills/docs/cornell_note_taking.doc

When they do speak, teachers may express strong emotions that make it difficult to hear the underlying message. You may need to acknowledge these emotions and give them space before confronting underlying issues. Your first reaction to teachers' feedback and criticism will send a message about whether such feedback can be given openly, or must remain subterranean. Sometimes, beneath the griping, pain, or exhaustion, there will be important information for you as a leader that goes beyond the emotional state of the teachers. If you hear reactions or ideas that are new or that you don't totally understand, try to check your own instinct to defend yourself, and ask more questions to explore the issue. You can defend yourself or respond more thoughtfully later, but hearing more may let you grasp pressing issues and determine how much merit there is in the concerns.

The point is not simply to agree or yield to teachers when you hear their concerns, but to seek their perspective, to understand what they're seeing and experiencing, and to hear what could be valuable in their feedback while simultaneously getting them to hear you. Expect that you'll need to grow in ways you can't foresee, just as you want teachers to grow. Your example could do more than your words to help teachers become open to change and to work in ways that are collaborative and accountable.

Building Group Competence

Building Conviction about the power of effective collaboration often depends on helping people behave their way into new beliefs. Seeing positive results for students convinces skeptics. To get those results from collaboration (as opposed to the sense that hours have been wasted on talk and wheel-spinning), teachers and administrators working in concert need to be skilled and knowledgeable. That capacity we call **Competence** (see also Chapter 3 definition). Fortunately, it is the one a skillful leader can influence significantly.

Start by Building Trust

Knowing how to establish and protect trust is at the heart of building group competence. Lencioni defines trust as "the confidence among team members that their peers' intentions are good and that there is no reason to be protective or careful around the group" (2002 195). He noted that lack of trust is a major reason teams malfunction, because it limits members' willingness to be vulnerable and open to opportunities for growth. A team member lacking trust will not want to give or receive feedback.

The vulnerability that community members feel and show can be about interpersonal shortcomings such as difficulty building good relationships with students or parents. It can be about skill deficiencies such as difficulty using technology or about a complex instructional problem such as how to help students with reading difficulties use primary sources in social studies. One key indicator of trust is public acknowledgement of a need to learn more and public willingness to seek and use assistance. Leaders must model that quality in their talk and in their actions. Their openness to other ideas and influence frees staff to sort through cherished activities for those that must be changed and helps build ownership for implementing decisions. If they do not work to build trust, leaders may find themselves stymied by teams who comply superficially on matters that do not make a significant impact on their practice but are unwilling or unable to make any substantive changes. Small investments in explicit trust-building strategies pay off. There are times when groups should participate in shared experiences that allow them to practice taking risks and being open to feedback. The best context for trust building would be an "off-campus," non-academic retreat led by an outside facilitator, but leaders can certainly plan some more modest in-house icebreakers and team builders at key points during the year.[4]

Of course trust, by itself, does not guarantee that a group will develop the competence it needs. Groups who trust one another can still engage in unpromising practices that undermine their learning and effectiveness. For example, members may:

- Value getting along over facing difficult facts and questions and fall easily into group conformity and complacency
- Approach every problem by drawing only on existing group knowledge without seeking research and outside knowledge to test their ideas
- Waste valuable time in a constant recycling of the same problems without arriving at any commitment to action because they do not use problem-solving protocols
- Fail to anchor their work in data, standards, and clearly established norms, thereby spending time on the wrong issues or questions

To counter the effects of these and other unpromising practices, we need practical strategies for building competence.

STRATEGIES TO BUILD COMPETENCE

- **Make sure groups specify and adopt norms describing *how* they will work together and the mechanisms to monitor the adherence to those**

[4]For activity and retreat ideas, see the Project Adventure web site: www.pa.org

norms (in Chapter 3, see "Skill Set 3: Anchoring the Work"). Unexamined norms can damage trust and hinder productivity. Toxic and Laissez-Faire Communities, for example, may adhere to a norm that allows any member to use sarcasm and complaint in response to another member's observations. When they are subtly punished for offering an opinion, newcomers in Toxic Communities may quickly recognize that they are expected to be quiet, self-effacing, or deferential to veteran colleagues for the first several years they are in a group. Requiring all groups to go through the process of stating what they do want to have happen as they work together, the way they want colleagues to behave, and what they do not want usually uncovers behaviors that have been getting in the way of learning. For examples of norms and ideas for working with groups see "Norm Handbook" www.ready-about.com

- **Help groups examine and discuss the characteristics of effective teamwork and then participate in self-assessment and goal-setting activities using those characteristics.** Tapping into the pool of research on how high-functioning teams work can provide groups with a common language and concept system to use in judging their own progress. It can take away confusion about what a school or district expects of an officially constituted group. Finally, it can validate the kinds of informal arrangements that colleagues have made and give them new life. Once a common set of criteria for good teamwork have been explored, groups can then assess their own functioning, give themselves a grade, and set goals for improvement that also incorporate student learning.

- **Increase group proficiency in "taking on the tough stuff."** Consultants, such as Patrick Lencioni (2002), who specialize in team-building recommend that groups complete and examine some kind of personality type or problem-solving inventory that helps individual members to gain insight into their own and others' default responses to conflict, ambiguity, etc. These typologies give participants language and a frame of reference to use in place of the assumption that someone is reacting negatively out of personal animosity or spite.

To demonstrate your own confidence in the value of healthy debate for surfacing important ideas, plan for and use processing structures that help to bring out contradictory information and opinion during meetings. These might include T-chart activators that ask people to respond to what they are pleased about or struggling with or to evaluate the pro's and con's of an argument and brainstorm without judgment. Another processing structure asks individuals to go to a particular corner of the room to signal their opinion. Make a conscious and consistent effort to include all voices in a discussion and to value those who offer ideas that are contradictory to current group thought. If you sense that important conflicting opinions are being suppressed and that this will later harm the group's efficacy, use short on-the-spot response strategies to get data about how people are feeling and what they are thinking.

Last, but not least, know yourself. Skillful leaders are patient with productive debate. Experience has convinced them that the ultimate product of that debate will be stronger and more useful than it would have been had they allowed the group to jump to an immediate solution to a problem. Is your default mode speed and efficiency and your favorite line "let's move along?" Do you tend to be irritated by anyone who wants to consider an alternate viewpoint once a seemingly straightforward solution is at hand? If any of these descriptors fit, get outside help to determine whether you are regularly shutting people down. Groups cannot practice getting more capable and responsible at handling generative conflict about important ideas if their leaders regularly signal that there is no time to talk.

- **Involve teams of teachers in determining important student learning problems and the processes to address them.** Leaders in a hurry tend to want to jump into action: pick programs, adopt textbooks, get training, and get moving. The urge is understandable, particularly in schools where achievement problems are severe and the staff has been floundering. Jumping in and solving problems oneself can become a habit, however. Groups cannot develop competence in problem-identification if they never have opportunities to analyze data and find the problems. Tom Levine (2006) cautions leaders to allow buy-in time and plan experiences that help teachers understand and own proposed changes. School leaders must negotiate a delicate balance: they must allow teachers to share control of the process for identifying pressing student needs and at the same time prevent suppression of difficult information or proposals that cause discomforting moves away from business as usual.

  In one school where the principal usually made the problem-process decisions, teacher buy-in and participation seemed to be limited. The principal, who was in her first year leading a school, acknowledged that she "didn't necessarily allow people the buy-in or allow people the space to create it [the program] so that it worked for them." This principal's active participation and norm-setting did, however, break toxic patterns of talk and blame, and pushed teachers to focus on aspects of teaching they might not have raised on their own. Teacher groups can create an unspoken consensus about what issues are acceptable to discuss and what should be kept out of group conversation (Little 2002, 2003). In year two, this principal negotiated both the topics and activities for collaborative work without relinquishing her right to influence group work. "Teachers' participation improved considerably, and the principal was aware of the more developed sense of ownership" (Personal correspondence October, 2006).

- **Learn how to use a variety of processing structures to help communities focus on important student learning needs.** Burnout, disillusionment, or the reinforcement of negative beliefs can be the unwanted consequences of unfocused, time-consuming group work that yields little in the way of results for students. Training to use a variety of structuring models can help groups with little prior experience in collaboration move beyond the "blame game" to determine where they can take action (see Case 4.1). The options below, listed here for reference but detailed in Chapter 7, all provide carefully delineated ways to facilitate collaboration:

1. **Protocols** are structures that help groups to focus and monitor the flow of conversation about a particular question or issue.

2. **Peer Observation** models can provide structures to facilitate shared understandings about practices and their impact on students.

3. **Lesson Study** is a special collaborative structure developed in Japan that pays intense attention to lesson planning as a way to improve student learning.

4. **Error Analysis** focuses the group's attention on barriers to learning and designing alternate ways to re-teach a concept that students are struggling to learn.

5. **Study Groups** allow clusters of teachers with different training and experience to examine research, acquire common background knowledge about an issue or approach, process joint observations, or share findings from their experiments with improving instruction.[5]

Menus of structured models are useful because they allow a leader to match the approach to the circumstance. They should never be regarded as a checklist of best practices each school has to do in order to be modern or progressive. The activities need to be carefully aligned to an objective and to the people who are going to carry them out. Lesson Study, for example, requires high levels of trust and the ability to be analytical and patient with repetitive refinements. Finally, there are two other dangers to keep in mind as you use structured models to build community competence. First, if members have not been involved in selecting the tool to focus their work, they may have little ownership in its success. Second, there is always a danger that the process becomes so appealing and comfortable that doing it becomes the goal rather than using it to focus work and solve student learning problems.

EXAMPLE Self-improvement Goals Set by Teams

Commitment to Using Standards Through our self-assessment, we determined that last semester we spent too much time talking about individual students' problems and did not really look at how our students were performing in relation to the new learning standards. We will identify the most important learning standards to serve as our

---

[5]Murphy and Lick suggest the following guiding question for study groups: "What do our students need us to do so that they can most effectively learn what they need to know?"

focus for the remainder of the year and examine what we need to improve to get more students to meet those standards.

Sustaining Transparency In our self-assessment we found that we have not created enough opportunity to meet the school goal of publicizing our practice. In the next three weeks we will agree to observe in a colleague's class for 30 minutes and report back at the next meeting on what we observed.

Dealing with Conflict In our self-assessment we found that we avoid disagreements and do not discuss negative data. We need to get better at handling conflict and facing difficult facts. We will ask for district support for a session on managing conflict and practice the strategies. We will assess how we did on this norm after each meeting.

CASE 4.1 **Structuring Collaboration for Student-Oriented, Progressive Interaction   by Tom Levine**

Every Monday morning, one 9th-grade team of teachers exchanged and analyzed information about individual students. There were no structures or prompts beyond sheets teachers filled out to provide peers with information about student performance. Without any intervening structure, these teachers had conversations that did not reveal any sense of their own agency or potential to affect the outcomes they discussed. Conversations about struggling students were often framed in terms of what students needed to do, what problem they had, or how family or friends contributed to a problem. ("I'm really concerned about Josie. What worries me is that her mom enables her, and doesn't think about Josie's responsibility.") If teachers don't push beyond this kind of description of external variables to consider how they can make a difference, such collaboration produces adult-oriented, regressive interaction.

These same teachers then received training to engage in tightly structured collaboration. On Tuesdays and some Wednesdays, they used formal processes such as the critical friend protocol: One teacher spent 8 minutes describe a teaching dilemma in detail, others asked clarifying questions, then everyone but the presenter offered suggestions or reframed the problem (see Chapter 7 and MacDonald, Mohr, Dichter and MacDonald for more on protocols). The group debriefed their use of the protocol each time they used it, and an outside coach guided the process. On other occasions, the principal or school coach identified areas of concern, and created prompts requiring teachers to share and explore their own work. During the more structured collaboration, this same group of teachers shared their own teaching practices much more frequently. Such discussions let teachers focus on what they actually do and could do, thus bringing their own sense of personal efficacy into focus, and creating opportunities for reflection and mutual learning. For communities that are not used to collaboration, or who are used to attributing student learning to factors beyond their control, formal structures can provide scaffolding to help teachers and administrators to engage in more student-oriented, progressive interaction. On the other hand, if teachers do not understand the nature and rationale for adding structure and have no input in selecting and adapting the structure, making collaboration more structured may alienate teachers or produce surface compliance. Teachers are more likely to master new structures and use them for generative work if they receive training, receive feedback from a coach, reflect explicitly on their work together, and decide how to adapt activities to be more appropriate for their ultimate aims.

Create and Support a Data Team[6]

Love (2002, 2007), Reeves (www.makingstandardswork.com), and others have raised the bar for collaborative work by developing tools and training options to help schools build data teams. A data team is a group of four to eight teachers and administrators who work together to use data to improve student learning at the school level. Data teams can be newly constituted groups or subgroups of an existing Instructional Leadership Team, School Improvement Team, or steering group. As their name implies, they carry out a range of data functions that include:

- Collecting and analyzing a variety of types of school data
- Developing or adapting common assessment instruments
- Using data to surface and monitor equity issues
- Using processes, tools and protocols to identify student-learning problems, verify causes, and generate solutions
- Consulting research to investigate problems, causes, and best practice
- Developing data-supported action plans
- Overseeing the implementation of the plan (school-wide or by vertical team) and/or implementing instructional improvement in their own classrooms (grade, course, or subject teams)
- Sharing successes and challenges from their own classrooms and/or at the school level

At their best, data teams become models for the progressive interaction that we call an Accountable Community.

TIPS ON CREATING DATA TEAMS

✔ **Consider converting existing teams into data teams.** There may be a group already in place that you can tap to take on the challenge.

[6]Thanks to Nancy Love for her generosity in sharing the information in this section, much of which is extracted from Nancy Love, Katherine E. Stiles, Susan Mundry, and Kath DiRanna, *A Data Coach's Guide to Closing Achievement Gaps: Unleashing the Power of Collaborative Inquiry*. Thousand Oaks, CA: Corwin Press, in press.

Teachers and leaders are drowning in meetings and may groan when a new committee is established (York-Barr 2006).

✔ **Set a purpose for your data team and use that as a criterion for membership.** For example, if the purpose is to improve a particular subject area such as language arts or mathematics, your team should include teachers and other staff who have responsibilities in this area, such as members of the district's curriculum committee and staff who have been involved in related initiatives (e.g., textbook selection and professional development planning in these subjects). If the purpose is to look across all subject areas, you will want to balance the representation to include members from across the different curriculum areas.

✔ **Be inclusive in membership.** Seek out racial and ethnic diversity and inclusion of specialists such as teachers of English Language Learners or of students with exceptional needs.

✔ **Actively seek people who are opinion leaders, reflect different perspectives, and can be ambassadors to others for the project.** Relying on the "usual suspects" who volunteer for everything can sometimes result in a team of people with too many competing demands on their time who are not representative of the diversity in your school or district. Membership may be voluntary, but seek out teacher leaders who might not be involved on other school initiatives (see Chapter 6).

✔ **Consider tapping individuals who are skeptical of the process.** These individuals can be particularly helpful in identifying roadblocks and concerns that others may be thinking, but are not comfortable voicing.

Giving Groups Control

Control has to do with the circumstances in which professional communities do their work. When we raise questions about control, we are not merely asking about the ability to be in charge of something. We want to know whether groups have adequate structures, processes, and resources to tackle important learning problems and make significant improvements for students.

"We need more money" is almost always the answer to any inquiry about whether professional communities have adequate resources. As we begin this section, we need to acknowledge the power and potential impact of appropriate funding. Student learning can benefit from many supports that cost money ranging from longer school days, enrichment summer programs, or weekend extra help, to better science equipment and up-to-date technology. Teachers who are trying to design assessments, improve curriculum, and learn new practices need paid professional development and meeting time just as their counterparts in businesses do. Consider, however, the word *potential*. Control is only one of three key capacities that professional communities need. In the hands of a group with little conviction or competence, lavish funding is likely to go to waste.

Beyond a lack of financial resources, a number of unpromising institutional practices undermine a group's control. Unlike the problem of getting funding, these are practices a skillful leader can change relatively quickly. For example,

- Time, space, technology, and training are not in place to support collaborative interaction.
- Effort is diluted by inefficient use of meetings.
- There are few incentives and rewards for good work.
- Leaders ask teams to respond to "whiplash" demands that constantly shift effort away from important goals.
- Evaluation and professional development systems either do not accommodate or actually hinder collaborative efforts.

Many of the following practical approaches to setting the stage for collaboration may be familiar ones. If so, then you are well on your way to eliminating institutional practices that hamper a group's ability to work efficiently and effectively. We offer the basics primarily because we see their absence so often in schools with malfunctioning professional communities. We see and hear the negative responses and growing cynicism that result when seemingly simple actions like the thoughtful arrangement of space or planning ahead for technology are blatantly ignored.

Create Common Planning Time

All professional community advocates from Dufour to Schmoker, Saphier and Reeves indicate that allocating regular time during the school day is a necessary if not a sufficient condition for collaboration. Reporting on New American Schools' efforts to scale up improvement, Bodily et al. noted that the incorporation of time for committee work or common planning was a constant and essential characteristic of all the designs member schools used (109). So how do skillful leaders find such time? Some build schedules that contain double planning periods two or three times a week for teachers who have the same course assignments. Some try to combine a planning period with other paid non-instructional time. A few fortunate districts build schedules that contain different lengths of school days: students have four long days and one day a week that ends early so that teachers can plan. Some schools are able to release teachers from all administrative duties or to arrange for skilled substitutes or specialists to cover team planning time. Whatever the model, the critical concept is weekly time that enables continuity and efficiency, not three release days three months apart.

Organize Space for Collaboration

Providing space compatible with productive adult interaction requires some planning. Sitting on one foot chairs in a 1st-grade classroom or at the posterior-challenging fold-up lunch tables in the cafetorium does not encourage collaborative discussion. Furthermore, perpetually forcing people to accept discomfort sends a message that the leader does not think the activities being undertaken by the group are worthwhile. Not all schools can provide a dedicated adult learning space as does the Edison Middle School in Boston, but attention to the following basic criteria can help leaders make the most of what they have available:

- Find or partition off a space that is large enough for people to move around and divide into task teams but intimate enough for all members to be able to hear one another easily.

- Provide face-to-face seating at easily accessible tables and chairs with back support.

- Use circles, horseshoes, and open rectangles rather than auditorium-style seating to maximize eye contact.

- Have a mechanism for public recording of ideas and decisions (flip chart, markers and tape, smart board, or computer and projector) readily available.

- Make sure norms are posted and readable.

- Set up a work counter or cart or provide table baskets that contain basic supplies people need in order to get tasks done: staplers, punches, paper, clips and post-it notes, and highlighters.

In the absence of decent conference or staff rooms, multi-purpose specialist space, stages, corners of cafeterias, vestibules, or libraries can all be pressed into service for short meetings. However, the most skillful leaders we know work hard to beg or borrow off-campus meeting spaces specifically designed to give adults a comfortable work environment whenever meetings extend beyond 2 or 3 hours.

Provide Supportive Technology and Materials

Technological advances make idea and document sharing so much easier than in the past and can encourage such collaboration-friendly acts as posting results on a jointly developed assessment, emailing the latest re-teaching strategy, or forwarding an article to all members of the team. When team members are locked out of computer labs, denied access to buildings after hours, forbidden to use copiers, forced to walk two flights to find a working printer, we would say they do not have even minimal control over the conditions they need to do their work. Accessible copy machines, Internet access to professional journals, laptops for teacher use, dedicated bulletin boards, projectors, and smart boards all signal to professional communities that communication is important and that they will be supported in their efforts.

Make Every Meeting Worthwhile

Ask a broad sample of teachers what they think of formally organized meetings. You will find that most consider them time wasters. In schools that have not organized themselves to support powerful collaboration, meetings often reinforce negative interactions and bad behavior. Just say "faculty meeting" or even "department meeting" and watch for yawning or rolling of eyes. One reason for this response is leadership's failure to see the meeting as an important investment of resources and to plan for it well in advance. Another is administration's tendency to use meetings as substitutes for other kinds of communication tools. Thus meetings become a variation of the same lectures teachers are giving to students. Attendees sit passively and listen to a string of reports and information items or reviews of technical procedures. Little mental effort is required, and no insights are pooled in service of student learning.

Skillful leaders craft meetings as carefully as skillful teachers craft lessons. Their agendas reflect a commitment to invest the professional community's time and effort wisely. First they clearly differentiate the focus of and desired outcomes for the meeting or of specific parts of the meeting. For example, time might be designated for student intervention, data analysis, feedback and data gathering, design, or decision-making. The amount of time to be spent and the specific structures used to focus that time will all be carefully matched to the desired outcome. Good meeting agendas that convey a sense of a thoughtful underlying structure include:

- Overall purpose of meeting
- Items listed as topics or questions
- Time alotted for each item
- Item classification such as information, feedback and data gathering, goal setting, problem solving, and decision making
- Roles and individuals assigned to fill them: facilitator, timer, recorder, process observer
- Goal for each agenda item
- Summary (implement the "last 5 minutes guarantee")

Finally, skillful leaders communicate the results of a meeting and perhaps the alerts for what will come next. They may post and revisit important agreements from the last session or look at minutes of discussion. They may plan an opening experience that helps people get actively engaged in the topic at hand, remember where they were in a process, and recall their thinking. The message is always that the community's work is important, all members' contributions have been recorded, and everyone's brain is needed for the next step.

Identify and Celebrate Small Gains

Part of giving groups a sense of control is helping them to track the progress they are making so that the long-term goal does not become something that seems unrealistic and unattainable. As Schmoker notes, "Research and common sense point hard to the supreme importance of continuously recognizing and celebrating specific, short-term accomplishment that bring us closer to goals" (2006 146). Using the work of data teams or creating and tracking benchmark assessments can provide the necessary structure to take away the sense of helplessness in the face of enormous aspiration that sometimes affects groups.

Protect Groups from Unnecessary Distractions

Although it sometimes places them at odds with colleagues at the district level and parents or community members with agendas, skillful leaders run interference for their teams and work groups. Every request for time at a meeting, each item inserted on the agenda of a work session, or the use of a team planning period is scrutinized for its contribution to the goals of the professional community and for the likelihood that it will help that community improve student learning. Some leadership teams work with grade levels and departments to craft a school policy that guides responses to requests for time on a team agenda so that there will be consistency throughout the school.

Rigorously Monitor the Focus of Efforts in Common Planning Time

Unmonitored teams will often avoid getting to instructional deliberation by wasting valuable time with nuts and bolts business and housekeeping. Even higher operating collaborative teams may spend too much time discussing individual students. Teams need explicit criteria for their meetings and a way to assess how well they are doing. Provide an orientation that presents different ways to structure time so that instructional issues almost always come first or always occupy the greatest amount of time in an agenda. Model different activity structures that help people get to the point or collect data quickly and efficiently. Collect and scrutinize agendas or visit teams from time to time to see how well they are doing at keeping their focus on instructional challenges and instructional improvement.

Make Connections and Alignments Conscious and Explicit

People begin to feel overwhelmed and as if they have little control over outcomes when everything on their "must do" list is a separate item not aligned or connected to any other item (in Chapter 2 see "Organizational ADD"). Without alignment, every change in practice becomes a burdensome add on or feels like a new initiative that will compete with an old one. Several aspects of alignment help community members see their work as interconnected and meaningfully directed toward clear outcomes. One is the idea of parallel work: professional learning communities should be doing the same kind of work at all levels of the school district, including the classroom. That means all working teams, from Central Office to 1st grade, and all classroom teachers would be using standards and data, problem-solving processes, feedback, clear expectations, and norms and assessments that help them know when they need to modify what they are doing to improve it. A second aspect of alignment is a shared consistent focus on student learning. If an activity is not clearly and convincingly connected to our current learning goals for students, it is out of alignment and does not belong on the current agenda.

Finally, two other resources discussed in detail in Chapter 3 are worth mentioning again under the heading of giving groups control. First, timely professional development appropriately matched to the instructional improvements teachers are trying to make and to the learning goals of professional communities is an essential condition for success. When professional development is scattershot and disconnected from community priorities, it slows progress at best. At worst, it drains energy and conviction and pulls effort off onto unimportant activities that may subsequently undermine learning. Second, supervision and evaluation that give teachers feedback on the products and processes of their collaboration as well as on their individual efforts in the classroom validate that joint effort. Supervision and evaluation systems that "disallow" all evidence of a teacher's accomplishments in collaboration with others or disregard teachers' contributions to an Accountable Community send the message that collaboration is not necessary or important.

Summary

This is the first of three chapters that consider strategies to help adults work together in service of student learning. In this chapter we considered how to create the basic conditions needed to support the three capacities associated with high-performing groups: competence, conviction, and control. Creating the conditions for effective teamwork is the starting point to building a professional community that boosts student learning. Chapter 5 presents cases and strategies for leaders to confront low-functioning communities (malfunctioning groups). Chapter 6 provides tools help move Collaborative Communities to Accountable Communities.

5 Challenging and Changing Malfunctioning Groups

I f effective adult collaboration magnifies children's opportunities to learn and enables overall improvement on a far greater scale than one teacher acting alone can achieve, then establishing the essential conditions for that collaboration is a critical part of a skillful leader's work. In the real world, however, leaders bent on transforming their institutions rarely get the time or opportunity to design the perfect backdrop for action-in-common before the players appear. Unless they are taking over and clearing out a failing school, opening a new building, or regrouping after school closures or redistricting have radically changed faculty make-up, they are likely to inherit at least some existing communities who do not yet function the way they need to in order to help all of their students learn. They are likely to face groups whose interactions are regressive, i.e., they push organizational problem solving backward, and they push people apart. Anyone attempting to improve school performance usually faces a drama that is underway and characters that have already adopted roles. The challenge becomes how to redirect action that is going nowhere or accomplishing little.

In *The Skillful Leader: Confronting Mediocre Teaching* (2000), we focused on strategies for describing and intervening in *individual* cases of mediocre performance so that every child could be guaranteed an expert instructor. We still believe in confronting mediocre instruction through supervision and evaluation when the case warrants, and Chapter 9 focuses on dealing with individuals who undermine group efforts. However, watching hard-working colleagues' efforts over the last five years, we have also come to appreciate the stalling power of a negative culture and nonperforming groups. When the education of hundreds of students is at stake, intervening with individuals through the cumbersome stages of formal evaluation is insufficient. To improve core practices in many classrooms as quickly as possible, skillful leaders must do something beyond setting the stage. They need to confront and change groups that are malfunctioning.

Educators are optimistic people in general: we assume that good people will rise to the challenges in front of them, work hard, and uphold the efforts of their team, department, or school—in short, carry their load with skill and good will. But what happens when: 8 Gold decides it doesn't want to reach out to failing students, when only the English department at Mid-Balkans keeps its promise to do "whatever it takes," or when feuds between principals and Central Office staff divert important resources away from students who need them? What happens when a group starts well and then stalls in splendid complacency? The literature on professional learning communities presents many ideas for developing healthy school communities but only limited intervention strategies for dealing with those that are not meeting expectations (Dufour 1998, 2004).

In this chapter, we consider a series of short case examples of groups whose current performance is either undermining organizational improvement or moving the institution backwards. These are stories of work in progress; some are drawn almost entirely from one location, and others combine several similar examples. They are intended to capture the messy, taxing challenges leaders face as they attempt to transform regressive or nonproductive interactions into progressive ones. Because such work is relatively new, we offer the cases primarily as prompts for reflection and discussion rather than as exemplars for action. Real-world situations rarely match prototypes in every detail. However, for purposes of discussion, we have sorted the examples that follow according to their predominant resemblance to the three specific kinds of malfunctioning communities that we discussed in Chapter 3.

Group I: The Toxic Communities
Hazardous High
Expect Little Elementary
Misery Magnet

Group II: The Laissez-Faire Communities
Freewheeling High
Grade 8 at Miraculous Middle School
Autonomous Unified School District

Group III: The Congenial Communities
Muddy River's Math Department
Edgeland Elementary

We'll consider what challenges each case poses and identify potential ineffective responses versus skillful responses.

Finally, legal notes intended to help readers working in districts subject to collective bargaining appear where they are appropriate throughout the cases. The notes have an overall theme: to make decisions and take actions that will improve student learning, skillful leaders must know their school or district contract thoroughly, be clear about the roles and responsibilities of unions, and have a sense of ownership and responsibility for the process and outcomes of the collective bargaining.

Facing Toxic Groups

Some leaders face entire schools they would describe as toxic; others find themselves doing battle with a part of a school—a grade level team, a department, a group of old allies or new prima donnas—whose anger and seeming resistance can be confounding and exhausting. Understanding the forces behind the behavior becomes essential. As we noted in Chapter 3, toxicity may be fueled by any number of factors ranging from a history of gross district neglect, broken promises, untrustworthy leadership, or bitter union-management battles to the unchecked dominance of a few ringleaders skilled in negativity. It can also be generated by dangerous institutional conditions. Although the reasons for toxic behavior may differ, the public profiles of different malfunctioning groups are likely to be quite similar. Because Toxic Communities are focused on protecting members and others from perceived threats, anticipated disappointments, and "unfair" demands, they most often present a hostile or resistant stance to outsiders. Establishing or re-establishing trusting relationships through integrity, consistency, and clear, frequent communication about important ideas and shared goals is essential. Members of toxic groups often perceive that have been used and bruised; they will not "roll over and play nice" just because another potentially ineffective leader asks them to do so.

Exchanges in toxic groups have been sometimes been called "NBC talk" (nagging, bitching, and complaining) or BMW (bitching, moaning, and whining) (Kegan and Lahey 18). To stay centered, skillful leaders need to recognize that cynicism and sarcastic humor may be habitual responses to mask fear or pain rather than part of a calculated strategy of personal attacks. Being open to the former interpretation allows the leader to acknowledge the discouraging effects of past negative history while at the same time checking on a speaker's actual intent re the present request. When dealing with toxic behavior, skillful leaders need patience, significant self-discipline, and self-awareness in order to resist being diverted into heated exchanges, retaliation, or futile attempts to gain a naysayer's approval through concessions. They expect the turnaround process to be both slow and pockmarked with minor setbacks, and they report that they work hard to keep a brave positive face in public even when they feel discouraged in private. Consistently, those who have successfully worked with toxic groups talk about changing the focus of the discussion from adult rights, accusations and recriminations, or exhortations to a relentless, respectful focus on "pooling what we know in order to help those students who most need our expertise." When these leaders confront toxic behavior, they do not do so by attacking individuals or by labeling and punishing the group. Instead they name the consequences to students that result from the unproductive interactions: the lost opportunities to share knowledge with colleagues, the broken relationships with parents, the resulting alienation from other parts of the organization that might help. Skillful leaders make those consequences evident and at the center of all discussions in a calm and compelling way; then they state that the behavior producing such consequences must change.

In addition to getting help on defining the problem, leaders need an outside support system that helps them stay centered after daily immersion in acid and innuendo. Hostility, disapproval, and negativity are catching. Support systems provide a counterbalance to our tendency to tell ugly stories about the people who are frustrating our efforts to change. Once a leader has fallen into the trap of characterizing most of the members of his or her department, school, or district as villains, it is hard to come to work and interact productively.

Finally, leaders need data that will pinpoint a student product or performance that needs attention and that is likely to improve significantly if instruction improves. Leaders also need good process skills for getting the effort underway. Toxic Communities often have little real experience of effective collaboration or of making a difference in learning; they need immersion in a productive, objective process that shows doubters what an alternate kind of interaction might be like. Without something positive to work on, such communities will fall back on old patterns of behavior. They cannot be left alone to undertake work without skilled facilitation and a relentless, positive assurance that they do not have to do business the same way they have always done it.

We begin with a case of a failing urban school—one of the most difficult places to enact change. Schools that feel unsafe are frequently failing schools, and the larger school community often presents itself as toxic. Once leaders have tackled the conditions most immediately responsible for undermining learning in dangerous schools, they face new barriers and new difficulties. Consider the following work in progress:

CASE 5.1 **Hazardous High School**

Ms. Devins is a high school principal in a medium-sized urban district. She entered a school with 30 percent annual turnover in staff, high dropout rates, and gangs with guns who operated within the school. Teachers had essentially given up; virtually no instruction was taking place. An assistant principal handled all the discipline, even for minor issues that other faculties might have dealt with themselves. "Kids were sent to the assistant principal for things like sleeping in class," Ms. Devins reports. In her first year, therefore, she focused on making the school safe and on creating a climate where students could have more intimate contacts with adults and where teachers would assume responsibilities for minor infractions. She created what she called "clear corridors." With the number of major disruptions significantly reduced, the school became safer, and both faculty and students felt more secure. She also formed small learning communities (SLC) that gave teachers a structure for working together and pooling their knowledge.

In year one, administrators and teachers made considerable progress toward the goal of a safe school. SLC's were successful in creating a first line of discipline and better relationships with students. Guns and gangs were a phenomenon of the past. Ms. Devins also attempted to impact instruction by returning the schedule to 45-minute classes in place of the 90-minute blocks she had inherited. Teachers, she noted, were not skilled in planning for long blocks and seemed to have difficulty using the time productively, as evidenced by the common direction to "Take the last 15 minutes and begin your homework." Even with the schedule change, however, students still slept in class and were either disengaged or constantly engaged in low-level disruption rather than in learning. Reflecting on year 1, Ms. Devins said, "After that first year, I was so sure that we would move up [the student performance] but it just was not happening in the classrooms.... Just because we had cleared out the halls and created SLC's did not mean there was much time on task in the classrooms." Although chaos had been eliminated, students were still off task, instruction had not changed, and neither had achievement results.

In year 2 Principal Devins made some changes in the school administration to build a competent team that could share the vision and leadership work. To tighten classroom discipline in year 2, she established an escalated discipline policy clearly specifying what infractions were the teacher's responsibility, how the SLC could support individual teachers, which problems were really counseling issues, and which problems should be dealt with by the assistant principal. Finally, she established common planning time, which was used mainly for discipline support. The procedures worked well, and classrooms became more focused and under control. But instruction and achievement still did not improve. Unlike some of the veteran teachers who equated real changes in climate and order with school improvement, Ms. Devins was not happy. She began to realize that order might be a necessary prerequisite to turning a school around, but it did not ensure improved instruction.

Even during her first year, Ms. Devins had confronted poor performers; she worked to counsel them to move on and tried to replace them with more enthusiastic teachers. Forty percent of her faculty turned over in the first two years. Year 3 was the year to begin to move on instruction, "Year 2 we had a literacy support class; it did not really impact the gap. So we volunteered as a pilot for implementing the Reach program (in year 3); a teacher coach was given a period for coaching. The next year we had a coach in four disciplines to work with teachers on teaching reading and writing across the curriculum—which remains a priority five years later!"

Ms. Devins anchored this work in school-wide agreements. One of the priorities was to adopt Lorraine Monroe's "Bulletin Board Configuration (BBC)" a format for communicating objectives and agendas. However, here she ran into another block to instructional improvement: "We established Lorraine Monroe's Bulletin Board Configuration (BBC), but we did not follow up, and teachers did not follow the agreements. So we instituted BBC checks with three administrators rotating through every classroom. We gave feedback to the entire staff. They complained, but they did it."

Ms. Devins also began to use data to report results and to make the natural consequences of teachers' inaction clearer. After manipulating data by hand for a few years, she noted "I attended PD–Data Works; it helped me to be an instructional leader by providing strategies for monitoring reform." When teachers claimed that students knew how to read, she confronted them with the "brutal" data that 60 percent of the students had not passed the state reading test. Slowly they became convinced of the problem. Ms. Devins was driven by a sense of urgency that gradually infected others: "I was at war with underachievement and anyone who did not see the sense of urgency. There were written policies placed in the Principal's Expectations and in evaluations that reflected the teacher's willingness to adhere to policies. I had a critical mass of staff who agreed with the data and did not blame the students; so we moved forward and devoured those who showed movies, had parties, and gave students days off."

Challenges for Leaders

Unsafe schools present the leader with no choice about starting points; before communities can focus on instruction, leaders must attend to what Maslow might call second level needs, real or perceived security and safety concerns that interfere with teachers' ability to think about their practice or the goals of the school (1987). Leaders who enter dangerous schools must start reform by making the environment safe for teaching and learning. This includes building effective discipline systems while simultaneously establishing more intimate staff-student connections, often through structures such as small learning communities, special interest groups, or advisory programs. Building these human connections, especially between students and teachers, forms the trust so important to establishing a healthy learning environment. Although structures and strategies that lead to safer, more secure schools may provide a foundation for improved instruction, they do not automatically translate into better teaching and learning. As we see in this case, instruction remained largely untouched despite structural changes—changing the bell schedule, setting up small learning communities, or establishing common meeting times. The mission of improving the quality of teaching required two additional leadership interventions. From the beginning, the principal worked to counsel out the worst performers and also began a directed focus on school-wide agreements that would raise the quality of instruction.

Ineffective Leader Responses

- **Assume that improving safety and discipline will improve instruction.** Establishing sound discipline policies may lead to a more organized environment but does not create high-quality, standards-based instruction.

- **Rely on the activity of restructuring faculty and students into smaller groups to fix instructional deficiencies.** Implementing small learning communities (SLC) definitely sets up a support system and creates more intimate student-teacher interactions. However, without a skillful leader's intervention, common planning time agendas often default to discipline issues and other concrete, easily addressed organizational matters. Hard questions and worries about how to help students perform successfully are then left to the individual teacher or not addressed at all.

- **Subscribe to the idea that change happens incrementally and therefore requires "rest periods" and times when leaders should expect less.** Students have only a limited time in which to meet performance standards and to learn what they need to learn in order to be productive citizens. Changing student performance requires a strong sense of urgency, constant fine-tuning, and a relentless quest for the next solution to pressing problems.

- **Assume that individual teachers who are very low-performing will spontaneously improve their practice because of a new structure.** Underlying such a false assumption is the idea that teachers were low-performing because of structural problems. In most instances, low performers lack either the requisite knowledge and skills to get the job done or the will to persist when the work is hard and the rewards are uncertain. Putting poor performers into a group without providing them with focused feedback and training means that the leader runs the risk of dragging down the energy and performance of other members who must pick up a bigger share of the instructional load.

- **Assume that current staff have the skill to make the instructional changes needed and that supervisors can provide the necessary support.** Taking this tack means the leader believes that people are not getting the job done because they are willfully withholding their skills and capacities. In fact, current staff may have been under-trained for the complexity of the tasks they face and may need far more coaching than an overworked supervisor can provide through sporadic observations.

- **Assume that adopting outside programs will automatically improve instruction and close achievement gaps.** Even the best-designed programs are useless if they are not implemented or are improperly implemented by people who neither understand nor believe in them.

- **Subscribe to the idea that accepting a one-year position is a good** strategy when the goal is to "clean up" the place. Many toxic schools feed on their principals. A minimum of three years is necessary in order to build the necessary structures and hire the right people for the work. Superintendents should offer no job and principals should accept no job involving confronting toxicity with less than a three-year commitment.

- **Become an autocratic, authoritarian leader; decide to ignore the contract, get the job done, and let the grievances fall where they may.** The tough, counterpunching, drill sergeant leadership style is often an appealing match for a toxic and failing school, especially when the charge is to take back power for the administration. Even with a clear mandate from the school board and superintendent to wave a big stick, leaders make a mistake if they can think they can ignore the teacher contract or refuse to deal with union representatives.

Skillful Leader Responses

- **Solve problems of school-wide safety and discipline and provide support and training in classroom management to provide the strong base for instruction.** This principal found that school-wide discipline did not even ensure good classroom management and time on task. Major problems threatening safety were substantially reduced, but established classroom habits did not change correspondingly. In addition to establishing clear classroom discipline policies backed by the administration, the leader needs to raise issues of quality instruction.

- **Establish clear student learning goals as the focus for restructuring of schedules, space, etc.** Restructuring schedules to create common planning time is important; however, it is very easy for such time to be consumed in the discussion of low-level administrivia or student behavior problems. Consider differentiating meeting time so that student issues do not consume every agenda.

- **Communicate "I am here to stay for awhile" and stay for awhile.** Ms. Devins stayed eight years. As a way of filling openings in unpopular, toxic schools, many districts cultivate short-term, "quick fix leaders" and promise them they will be able to move on quickly. As a leader entering a failing/toxic school, consider that you will need a minimum of three years to turn it around. All of the leaders whom we have studied stayed a minimum of three years, and several stayed seven or more.

- **Build a leadership team.** Much less has been written about leader isolation than teacher isolation. With the support of Central Office, this principal brought in a powerful administrative team to help with strategic planning.

- **Adopt common, school-wide instructional agreements, but don't trust implementation to happen.** This principal found that verification and feedback was needed to establish the shared practice of posting the

BBC. Initially, as the skillful leader builds group competence, it is important not to prematurely release responsibility for implementation. Over time, the leader can turn accountability over to teams who are developing the capacity to self-monitor and to direct their own learning.

- **Decide what you need to learn to become more skillful and astute in using data.** Almost all schools that have had positive student achievement results get smart about using data. Leaders lead the way.

- **Present the data on learning.** In this case the SLC's role of focusing on discipline did not lead to better learning. The second year the principal found that "60 percent of the students were passing their classes but could not read as measured by district tests." Even though the school was safe, instruction was still weak. The principal presented test data and asked the SLC to analyze them, identify likely causes for the poor performance, and report back to the leadership team.

- **Hire expert coaches.** Because of time limitations, their role as a primary evaluator, and limited expertise, principals need to enlist experienced teachers as coaches. Although conventional thinking holds that coaches should not evaluate, they do in fact need to identify gaps between the necessary standard of performance and current reality. They also need to be able to give meaningful feedback to teachers about these gaps. They do not write teacher performance evaluation, but they do evaluate the quality of instruction.

- **Get the right teachers (Collins 2001) and get rid of the wrong teachers by creating a sense of urgency.** In this case, 30 percent of the teachers left after the first year, and 25 percent of the teachers left in year 2. Of that number, about 75 percent left because of pressure from negative evaluations and 25 percent because of counseling out. All of our turnaround leaders spoke of the tricky balance between putting pressure on individual mediocre performers through the evaluation process and developing positive, learner-focused communities. These leaders all spoke about the need to do both but to resist jumping to individual evaluation until the mid-year point.

- **Expect an initial outburst of resistance, complaining, and criticism.** Reforming schools requires asking people to change their comfort zone. Leaders who overly personalize the reactions of staff under stress tend to burn out. Keep firm, be clear, and don't take the reactions personally. Use the "free speech" mantra that people have a right to their opinions and can express them in appropriate forums.

Some schools are physically safe and orderly places with clear discipline policies and good management in the classrooms. Teachers may have reasonably good relationships with students and are committed to traditional forms of instruction that keep students busy and occupied without producing significant learning. The school community does not appear to be toxic until it is galvanized by a demand for change in response to poor performance. We see this kind of toxicity when a new principal follows a long-

LEGAL NOTE 5.1

Teacher Rights to Free Speech

School leaders can sometimes be disturbed when teachers make statements to students and parents that are critical of proposed changes and new directions the leader may be advocating. Because public schools are staffed by public employees, leaders must be knowledgeable about a public employee's free speech rights under the First Amendment to the U.S. Constitution. Although a public employee's free speech rights would protect them in some contexts, even when they are critical of their own employer's actions, their free speech rights are not absolute. For a discussion of relevant case law regarding a public employee's free speech rights, see *Garcetti et al. v. Ceballos* (May 20, 2006) at http://caselaw.lp.findlaw.com/scripts/getcase.pl?court=us&vol=000&invol=04-473

term mediocre principal who has protected poor teaching in exchange for cooperation around noninstructional matters. Here is such a case.

CASE 5.2 Expect Little Elementary School

For 18 years the male principal of Expect Little Elementary, a small school tucked away at the edge of a large city, ran a well-managed, smoothly functioning building. He described himself as a leader "in partnership" with his faculty, whom he praised lavishly and supported against all comers. He often told outsiders that his teachers were so good the "building could run itself." In fact, with full knowledge of the staff, he would nap (undisturbed) in his little office in the center of the building for 40 minutes or so after lunch each day. The school culture was a cozy if unrecognized collusion to support mediocrity. Teachers were never evaluated. Classroom instruction focused on low-level memorization and "make-work" that was justified, staff often said, by the socioeconomics of the school. As accountability measures increased, data about school performance became public, and achievement gaps between subgroups within the school and between Expect Little Elementary and other comparable schools widened, the teachers evinced little sense of discomfort or urgency. They felt that they were doing "the best they could in light of student demographics." As he retired, the principal agreed heartily.

The new principal, a young woman freshly certified, was charged with raising the achievement scores of Expect Little Elementary's students. Wanting to establish a culture for improvement in student learning and knowing that the transition would be a challenge, she decided that the community-building activities she had learned during principal training would be essential in the first year. Thus armed with strategies to help people feel motivated to change and willing to collaborate, she commenced her culture-building project. Unfortunately, her activities were unappreciated. "Compliment

Cups" intended to signal her appreciation for individuals were crushed and placed back on her desk. An effort to build a faculty study group around "Who Moved My Cheese?" was met with a united group of "nonreaders." One participant said: "We know all about change; that's how we have survived for 30 years." They even snickered at the homemade cheesecake brought by the principal to support their discussion.

Efforts to derail the leader and her agenda were led by two individuals—one a union representative who had had a good relationship with the previous principal. Whenever possible, individuals identified and pursued grievances for what might otherwise have seemed straightforward acts such as the principal's attempt to change the duty assignment of a 25-year veteran. Year 1 was very difficult; the school principal felt she was alone against a united front of toxicity. More important, students were still losing out.

After a long vacation and significant reflection, the new principal started her second year with a new plan. She focused all of her energy on quality implementation of the literacy program that the school had been required to select from a district menu. In place of faculty meetings she organized regular "Looking at Student Work" sessions. All of her informal observations and formal supervision and performance evaluations focused on implementation of the literacy program. With support from Central Office, the principal transferred two of the most negative teacher "leaders" out of the school and replaced them with new teachers who had completed literacy training as part of their preparation programs. This too became a grievance, but the transfer was sustained. The combination of these interventions began to turn the school community around. The school became less about teachers and more about students and their performance. Student achievement began to improve. In the next year there was further progress in the evolution to a Collaborative Community. Teachers were beginning to examine data independently, and scores were improving significantly. Regrettably, the old school was closed at the end of that year even as they began to use data to examine their progress and began to plan for peer visits. The road to Accountable Community ended abruptly.

Challenges for Leaders

This case describes a school that was not physically dangerous but that certainly compromised students' long-term educational development. Although its needs were less immediately obvious than those of Hazardous High, it was also a school that required serious attention. Over time, the laissez-faire principal created and nurtured, perhaps inadvertently, a change-resistant, adult-centered, community whose primary orientation was to protect itself from any demand that challenged a comfortable set of beliefs and practices. New faculty were quickly introduced to the norms of the community they were joining: (1) the deal from the leader is "You work with me on administrative requests, and I will support you in discipline and won't demand much" and (2) the deal about getting along with the rest of us is "understand the pecking order, do the basics, and don't rock the boat by raising questions or asking to do things differently." Describing the previous principal's expectations, one young teacher said, "He was a coach kind of principal. Some teachers liked him because if you were nice to him and you showed up on time, you were all set with him." Discipline data and low numbers of faculty grievances would have suggested that the school was "running smoothly," and would have given a "false positive" reading about its health.

In this case a comforting order and predictability masked low expectations for student learning. While Hazardous High's faculty could at least recognize and name the outward symptoms of its problems, this faculty had repeatedly been told—and had perhaps convinced itself—that it was doing the best job it could be expected to do given the limitations of the children it served. When the new leader arrived with a mandate to raise student performance and instructional standards, the ground rules about what was accepted, tolerated, or taken on changed. She accidentally complicated the situation further by focusing on the wrong problem, that is whether the faculty was behaving as a collaborative, student-oriented group. Enough powerful members perceived the introduction of criticism about children's performance and the challenges to "the way we do business around here" as an attack that they and others responded with a protective outbreak of toxicity. Because the school was small and the faculty hitherto used to a sort of "peace at any price" approach to issues, the negative faction was able to exert enormous peer pressure on members who might not, in other circumstances, have automatically agreed with its stance. Thus they forced colleagues into silence and further isolated the new principal. In year 2, however, this new leader found and focused on the right problem: the gap between children's actual literacy and what they needed to know and be able to do that was the consequence, in part, of the adult behavior.

Ineffective Leader Responses

- **Underestimate the effects of change.** When new leaders begin to make changes, they are asking teachers to make not just technical change but adaptive change (see Chapter 2). This principal was surprised by the response and underestimated how even the modest request to participate in a study group caused hostile behavior.

- **Focus activities and interventions on the symptom of the problem rather than on the problem itself.** While culture-building approaches like team-building, motivational speakers, study groups, or personal notes from the principal can all be part of a comprehensive turnaround strategy, they are not a substitute for initiating the hard conversations about student needs and student performance. They also allow Toxic Communities to be offended by and angry about superficial bits of a leader's practice and thus avoid facing their own worries or fears.

- **Assume that Congenial Communities are a step to better learning for students.** Our experience suggests that it is a mistake to try to influence Toxic Communities to become congenial as a first step to dealing with important achievement gaps. Congeniality does not guarantee either effective substantive collaboration or shared accountability. In this case the attempt to create a kinder culture backfired. This principal made the understandable mistake of believing that the faculty would respond to attempts to create a friendlier culture, a tough order when teachers are quite content with the status quo and equate change with increasing their workload.

- **Underestimate the power of negative leaders.** New principals often underestimate the power of one or two toxic teachers to influence negatively a largely competent, if "stuck," faculty accustomed to operating unchecked in a laissez-faire or toxic culture. Those who must work with negative colleagues day in and day out are likely to assume that the principal will go first and thus to choose pacifism over defiance in the face of a colleague's displeasure.

- **Assume that changes can be made with current staff.** Our experience is that firmly entrenched Toxic Communities are almost impossible to change without at least some small shift of personnel. This is a Control issue (see Chapter 3). Leaders need to be realistic about changing a toxic culture without changing some of the personnel. We recommend that, before accepting a position in toxic schools, leaders negotiate some personnel agreements (see Legal Note 5.1).

- **Avoid any action that might result in a grievance.** We are not proposing that all union leaders or unions are against change. But often in these situations where there is a fight to keep the status quo, serial grievances become a tool to throw the leader off course and block initiatives. An ineffective response is to avoid tough decisions because there might be a grievance.

Skillful Leader Responses

- **Refuse to be chased out.** If the leader can survive the first year, the Toxic Community will have failed in its primary goal—getting the principal to move on. This is particularly true for schools that have been successful in chasing out idealistic or impatient leaders. Many of the schools we have examined have had four to five principals in ten or fewer years. Ironically, the revolving door leadership that toxic groups create then further fuels their sense of vulnerability and need for protection. There is little they can count on except themselves; everything and everyone else will pass through and pass on.

- **Try to open channels of communication with union leaders or key teacher leaders.** When new leaders acknowledge union concerns, listen to issues, and clearly set forth their understanding of contractual

LEGAL NOTE 5.2

The Grievance Procedure

Though no administrators like to have a union filing grievances that challenge their decisions, the grievance and arbitration process that appears in most collective bargaining agreements is a mutually agreed way to dispute resolution. To be an effective leader in a unionized working environment, it is necessary to recognize the grievance procedure for what it really is, i.e., a private judicial system to resolve disputes that arise during the implementation of the contract language, often in a context that the drafters never anticipated or where the language is ambiguous and must be applied to new circumstances. Frequently, administrators who have little, if any, first-hand knowledge of the context in which the contract was negotiated are faced with interpreting the contract. Change agents, especially those who may be new to the district, should proceed cautiously and in consultation with those more experienced with the culture and the contracts. Often, prior consultation with Central Office personnel and the district's legal counsel can help leaders new to the district to avoid grievances or at least resolve them in ways that do not compromise the integrity of the goals they may be trying to achieve.

obligations and responsibilities, they signal that they are not trying to be either disrespectful or abusive of teachers. At the same time, it is important for skillful leaders to explain themselves, their goals for children, and what they are trying to accomplish in the school rather than leaving a communication void for others to fill. Establishing regular channels of informal communication can help to clear up misunderstandings and defuse the sense of being under attack which some Toxic Communities have developed whether the evidence justifies that perception or not.

- **Get the data about student performance and make examination of it regular and public.** Student performance data can highlight an important problem worthy of the whole school's consideration and one for which no one has an immediate right answer. If done respectfully and in a spirit of inquiry, worrying together about what causes a gap in performance and how to plug it can allow a principal, curriculum director, or coach to become a colleague in the problem-solving effort. The data can objectify the problem to be solved so that it does not appear to be an unfounded attack on the way things have always been done.

- **Focus on curriculum implementation.** Focusing steadily and without blame on curriculum implementation to meet important student learning needs helps a leader blunt the impact of personalities, personal agendas, and complaining. It also gives an opportunity to organize the work beyond an individual classroom and begin to establish peer work groups.

- **Create a support system.** Lonely small school principals lack an internal support network. Without an administrative team, they often depend on a counselor or lead teacher or coach or even a competent secretary for collaboration and thus run the risk of appearing to play favorites or to create in groups and out groups. In this case the principal wisely sought support from neighboring principals and, most important, from her deputy superintendent who made frequent visits to provide the overt message that Central Office expected change. Once the principal was able to hire new staff, positive teacher leaders emerged who could be part of an informal leadership team.

- **Do not let grievances distract your focus.** Leaders often pride themselves on being able to communicate openly, build good relationships, and get along with others. Grievances become a personal affront eliciting either discouragement or an angry reaction. Do not react personally to grievances. If the grievance is a reasonable one or if it highlights confusion or misconceptions, be open to negotiation. If the grievance is unreasonable or simply signals that the leader is doing his or her job as it was meant to be done, pass it to the next level and sleep well.

- **If possible, invite the most negative leader(s) to transfer or (in a worst-case scenario) carry out an involuntary transfer to change the dynamics.** In small districts or those with rigid contract restrictions, such a strategy may not be possible. However, in large districts where personnel move from school to school fairly often, the firm request that an individual find a better match for his or her preferred leadership style or environment can be part of a leader's repertoire with two caveats: (1) the individuals to be transferred must be competent and able to help students learn and (2) the transferring principal must respond honestly to the receiving principal's questions re the cause. Especially in a small school, exchanging two teachers can make a large impact on the quality of the community. Breaking up an unhealthy combination of people and/or taking away a self-appointed spokesperson can release reasonable teachers from the overwhelming social and emotional pressures, the need for protection, and the fear of emotional violence that day-to-day life in Toxic Communities engenders. Leaders taking on tough schools should be very clear about contract provisions regarding movement of personnel and should negotiate an entry agreement around replacing a certain number of staff if they find they need to do so.

In order to develop more teacher-student connections, increase flexibility and responsiveness, and develop shared accountability, districts have been moving to break up large, poor-performing high schools. They have either replaced them with small magnet schools or have restructured the faculty and students into small learning communities (SLC's). Supported by powerful players in the school reform arena like the Gates Foundation, the small schools movement has had mixed results thus far. Preliminary findings point to some unsubstantiated or misplaced assumptions about adult autonomy and about the connection between restructuring and changes in instruction. Consider this cautionary tale:

LEGAL NOTE 5.3

Changing Personnel Assignments

Changing personnel assignments often implicates both legal and contractual considerations. Procedures, bidding clauses, job descriptions, seniority clauses, language that governs transfers, certification or licensing requirements, leave of absence clauses, and tenure laws that require personnel changes can all be implicated in decisions intended to improve the quality of education for all students.

Caution! Well-intentioned suggestions can set off a whole series of unintended consequences that can undercut the effectiveness of change agents before they even show up for the first day of work. If your state law, local collective bargaining agreement, or even just your school board policy contains transfer language, bidding procedures, and/or seniority rights (not to mention procedures that delineate if and how personnel can be removed or involuntarily transferred), it is highly unlikely that new leaders taking on "tough schools" will be able to negotiate entry agreements that run up against any of the entitlements created by the aforementioned legal constraints.

CASE 5.3 **Misery Magnet School**

In a move similar to those going on in other parts of the country, District X (a medium-sized urban district with approximately 59,000 students) restructured its most toxic and ineffective high school into four smaller magnet schools housed within the same building. Faculty members were allowed to indicate the school they wished to join but were supposed to obtain the approval of the incoming principal. Wanting change and leadership not corrupted by the existing culture, the district selected principals from a combined pool of experienced and newly certified leaders who had worked in other parts of the city. Thus the incoming administrators knew little about the staff they were inheriting. Most, like Dr. K, Misery's new head, chose to assume that staff had good intentions and to start off on a positive note by accepting all applicants.

In the first year of Misery Magnet's existence, toxicity actually increased. District leaders had insufficient data about the real problem that needed to be addressed (instruction), wanted a quick fix to a long-standing achievement gap, and were understandably concerned about the students whose education was being compromised in the larger school. Thus they were willing to shortcut the process of staff "buy in." Once class sizes decreased and teachers had greater autonomy, reformers reasoned, faculty would be able to work together to solve student learning problems. Meanwhile, each new small school leader was given a mandate: do what you need to do to motivate staff, clean up the negativity, and get the schools on track to raise student achievement.

Attempting to adhere to that mandate, Dr. K ran into problems almost immediately. In the original big high school, faculty had enjoyed a great deal of autonomy. They were accustomed to a laissez-faire environment in which they paid only lip service to district standards and curriculum. Behind the closed doors of their classrooms, they routinely acted on their own limiting beliefs about what their students might be capable of doing by providing a steady diet of low-level make-work. Teacher supervision and evaluation was perfunctory to nonexistent; poor student performance was always the students' or their families' fault. More savvy young people removed themselves from ineffective classrooms; those who did not do so either suffered in silent compliance or dropped out. In the large school, moreover, colleagues saw no need to collaborate; everyone understood what the problems were and the code of the school was "you mind your own business and take care of your own messes; I'll take care of mine." Autonomy as Dr. K and school reformers imagined it in the restructured schools, however, meant that teachers would have the freedom to think together about what needed to change and to make decisions about programs and practices most likely to help their particular student population meet achievement target. Autonomy did not mean "I get to do what I want to do when and how I want to do it without any questions from either my colleagues or the so-called principal." Immediately, Dr. K's presence in classrooms and her pointed questioning in meetings began to be challenged by union representatives.

In Misery's first year, as intended, students did indeed have more personal interactions with faculty and far fewer options for escaping from poor quality teaching. "Smallness" shed daily light on individuals whose exchanges with students were toxic; it also brought into sharp relief the performance of certain individuals who did not understand the content sufficiently, who were not aware of new performance standards, or whose repertoire of teaching strategies seemed limited to drill and kill. With protective covering removed and no place to hide, several senior faculty members began acting out in planning meetings, sending large numbers of students to the office for minor infractions, and pursuing a series of grievances that focused on Dr. K's "lack of respect" and "personal vendetta against veteran teachers." They also indulged in loud and intensely negative public confrontations with the new principal that wore down both her energy and that of their colleagues. She responded by clamping down: increasing supervision, monitoring all planning meetings, and requiring that teachers submit lesson plans, post standards on the board, and offer alternative assessments to struggling students. Horrified by what she saw in several classrooms, she decided she needed to take on the worst of the poor performers and her Central Office supervisors agreed. "In the fall of my first year, I wrote with the help of Central Office, a detailed evaluation of an awful teacher. It was 38 pages, quite specific, and set out a clear mandate for change and with that the whole building blew up."

Because the community was small and a closed society, the impact of Dr. K's decision was magnified. It fueled rumors that she was there to "fire everyone" and diverted most faculty members' attention and effort, at least temporarily, from helping students to protecting their rights. Hours spent on rebuttals to supervisory feedback were hours not spent on lesson plans, giving students feedback, designing projects, or creating benchmark assessments.

Dr. K changed her strategy in year 2. Although Central Office withdrew its support for "evaluating the incompetent teacher out," a number of faculty members reported that they felt threatened and "ran to the other schools, which gave me some openings so I was able to hire. The people who stayed were serious about teaching and wanted to make a difference." Instead of her previous emphasis on trying to use evaluation to move instruction, Dr. K focused on meeting with teachers to examine student performance data and design strategies to help struggling learners.

Challenges for Leaders

Leaders who are charged with turning around low-performing schools or units must balance effort spent on developing powerful learning communities with effort spent on confronting individual cases of mediocrity or incompetence. The question, we think, is not whether one should stand up and speak up about poor performance but rather when that accountability conversation should take place and in what ways. Consider the modus operandi of the two Toxic Communities we have discussed: to mind one's own business, stick to one's own shop, and follow one's own rules. Neither the faculty of Expect Little Elementary School nor that of Misery Magnet had had any experience with collegiality and collaboration. They might have shared materials and worksheets. They might have talked about "a great activity the kids like." They were unlikely, however, to have ever seen one another teach, to have looked at one another's tests and projects, or even to have compared and analyzed completed student work. In such communities, colleagues may guess—by piecing together student complaints, observed interactions in halls and cafeterias, and behavior in meetings—that someone else's practice is perhaps less stringent, varied, or empathetic than their own. The code of silence in all three types of regressive communities means that no questions will be asked and no comments will be made. When teaching is private and not subject to questioning or reflection, as it is in Toxic Communities, no one really knows what anyone else does, how it works for students, or what results anyone gets. Thus there is no basis for making an informed judgment about whether learning is taking place and learners are being well served. Because there are no shared agreements about practice to provide grounding for thinking about why an administrator might be asking someone to improve, fear fills the void. "If she can go after him," teachers in such communities often say, "then what's to prevent her from going after me?"

Ineffective Leader Responses

- Assume that people who have never worked together effectively before will immediately know what to do when they are put in a group, be willing to be open and vulnerable about their practice, and be able to trust one another and the leader without any further effort on the leader's part. Restructuring creates its own kinds of stresses and insecurities. Even when faculty has participated fully in the design and decision-making about change, restructuring is likely to upset familiar patterns and relationships, disrupt routines and make people feel that they have lost their old identity without necessarily acquiring a new one. Short-circuiting the process of building relationships, exploring ideas together in groups, or establishing norms of action often results in what teachers call "communication problems," i.e., "I don't know who you are, what you want from me, how you want me to do it, or what secret agenda you and others have.

- Assume that changing the size of the potential professional community will automatically lead to better teaching. Creating smaller groups of teachers who have hitherto been unsuccessful in raising student achievement or addressing pressing problems that impact learning may help to give members a sense of connection and support. It may boost morale and re-engage attention. However, without carefully designed training, facilitation to look at performance data, or coaching to change day-to-day instruction, the small group is more likely to assume support means ignoring or reinforcing existing ineffective stances rather than giving one another the courage to look critically at practice. In this case, the principal's attention was so diverted by the cases of genuine incompetence that she did not actively work to help other groups develop an alternate sense of what might happen in the classroom. Without an alternative vision to consider, small groups correctly assumed that their "targeted" colleagues' instruction was similar to what everyone had always done without any problem or repercussion. And they incorrectly assumed that the principal's efforts to specify what needed to change through elaborate evaluation documents meant she was being unfair.

- **Invest large amounts of start-up time and effort on evaluating and trying to reform one or two poor performers.** Leaders trying to change instruction need to consider how to spend effort in the first year. This principal had the dual pressure of her own supervisor's charge to "clean up" the non-teaching going on and her own moral outrage at what she believed her students were missing. Her response was understandable. However, the time and effort required to developing and try to follow up on a 38-page analysis of one teacher's shortcomings and to respond to the grievances, meetings, hearings, and steady drumbeat of negativity that resulted was time and effort that did not get spent on improving instruction in any other classrooms in the school.

Skillful Leader Responses

- **Build bridges before lighting fires (Lencioni 2002).** Leaders who are new to schools and faculties are often charged with fixing some long-standing, festering problem. They describe feeling under the gun to take action and recognize that they will not have their own supervisor's support and patient understanding for long if they do not make overt gestures that signal that business as usual is over. Relationship building, which assumes a long-term view of change, can feel like a waste of time or a misplaced priority in such an environment. However, if the leader has no prior positive relationships to draw upon and takes no steps to create new ones based on shared values and common concerns for students, every one of his or her actions is subject to misunderstanding and misrepresentation. Moreover, in the absence of relationships that allow people to quietly check out rumors and fear-filled perceptions, the loudest voices are likely to sway opinion. As Dr. K noted, "I learned that you've got to do some building before you do some taking down...it became hysteria, fear, hostility, and I could not get anywhere (in the first year) because of that one evaluation."

- **Acknowledge the strengths and weaknesses of year 1's strategy and come back (as promised) for year 2.** In addition to communicating belief and a commitment to the long haul with faculty, effective leaders lay out their change strategy, identify short- and long-term indicators of success, and regularly assess progress with their own supervisors. In this case, as in previous ones, a small but powerful set of faculty members hoped that providing a stream of complaint to the central administration and going around the new principal to stir up fear and insecurity would eventually result in either transfer or resignation of the principal. Dr. K, however, had warned her own deputy superintendents of her approach and the anticipated response. When she did not receive support for dismissing the worst performer, Dr. K shifted tactics and sought to bring change about in other ways.

- **Initially, collect data about, and focus attention on, patterns of instruction.** Leaders charged with improvement need to define the problem they are trying to solve. Thus they need data about patterns across many classrooms first before they begin to work on individual cases. Spending a few months observing what the building or unit is currently accepting as good teaching and capturing the range of demonstrated expertise present in the faculty can help a new instructional leader determine what the majority of the professional community knows and is able to do —and what it does not yet understand. That information can be reported back to teams or grade level groups and be used in conjunction with student performance data to determine where professional development is needed. Reporting on "worrisome patterns" and "areas of learning for all of us" allows a leader new to a building to signal where expectations are changing without getting into confrontations with non-performers right away. Moreover, the mere act of being highly visible learning about classroom life before raising issues can help build a leader's credibility.

- **Raise the expectations and demands for all, not just for underperforming teachers.** From the start, skillful leaders communicate the belief that supervisory feedback, like data analysis and problem-solving with peers, can help members of a professional community identify areas where they can improve practice to help students learn. Thus they make supervision and evaluation a regular occurrence, an "ongoing conversation about standards" rather than a one-time, high-stakes exam. Everyone in a restructured school learns to expect scrutiny and to answer hard questions about decisions and actions— not just the targeted underperformers.

- **Recruit and hire teachers who can demonstrate that they have a track record of self-assessment and self-correction.** The obligation to take stock of instruction, determine whether it is working to help students meet standards, and make adjustments as needed should not belong to administrators alone. Skillful leaders work hard to make the standards and criteria for performance evaluation transparent and to encourage teachers to do their own critical assessments. They do not choose new hires who are complacent or sure they have all the right answers. In Dr. K's case, whatever critical faculties many of her inherited faculty members had possessed had been blunted from years of disuse and union protectionism; they had been conditioned to assume that whatever they chose to do was fine unless someone told them otherwise and only if that someone could make the charge stick.

Transforming Laissez–Faire Communities

Both Toxic and Laissez-Faire Communities exhibit a pattern of low or unequal expectations for student learning and place the blame for student performance problems outside the school. The interactions of both types of communities are unhealthy and unproductive. However, Toxic and Laissez-Faire Communities have developed for different reasons and require different starting points for intervention. Members of Toxic Communities know that they are unhappy; they have complaints. If there is a long enough history of battles and bruises or gains and losses to draw upon, many members may even recognize that they present a problem for school leadership even though they do not accept responsibility for their behavior. A leader's initial strategies, then, can include acknowledging the presence of a problem and the need for change. Faculty who have operated successfully in Laissez-Faire communities, however, are less likely to consider themselves unhappy and far more likely to have been rewarded for, or encouraged to pursue, the behavior that skillful leadership is now trying to label a problem. That is, they have always been expected to take initiative and responsibility to get what they need to survive regardless of the impact on others. They have been rewarded for complying with low-level administrative requests by being left alone. They have learned the survival techniques of making small-scale technical changes when they can't be avoided, and they have internalized a belief that one's classroom is one's kingdom.

Communities that most closely resemble the Laissez-Faire profile frequently develop in response to voids: the absence of clear, coherent program standards and expectations, a decentralized decision-making structure not counterbalanced by commitments to shared goals, lack of instructional vision or expertise at top leadership levels, hidden or highly politicized criteria for the distribution of resources and rewards, or the absence of any structural supports for collaboration. Left to fend for themselves, individuals and small cliques adopt turtle-like survival mechanisms. They mind their own business, do their own deals to get what they need, and pull their heads into their shells in the face of controversy.

At best, communities that fit the Laissez-Faire profile expect their administrators to pay attention to and provide protection for individual faculty members' autonomy. At worst, they may expect leaders to tolerate and support eccentric interpretations and personal performance rules. Confronting a Laissez-Faire Community means changing the characteristics of the teacher-administrator relationship from collusion in overlooking low performance and low expectations to professional collaboration in service of high demand and high achievement. Doing so requires seeking out and making sense of the underlying forces supporting that collusion:

- Has the previous administration operated through fear and intimidation?

- Have others "managed," or do others continue to manage, the school or department through hidden deals and trade-offs?

- Is there a recognized (but not discussed) "old boy" or "old girl" network that dispenses favors and punishments using criteria known only to insiders? Are people in power such as veteran assistant principals or K-12 directors active members of such groups?

- Is parochialism or limited experience a problem? Have well-meaning specialists, chairs, directors, and teacher leaders been left to create order without any exposure to other viewpoints, to data they need to make intelligent decisions, or to professional training and feedback that might help them shape their leadership practice?

- Are there unhealthy patterns of communication that allow individuals to bypass traditional decision-making processes or to get decisions reversed at another level of the organization?

In most of the laissez-faire schools we have observed, more than one of the variables above are present. Some contributing factors such as the use of fear and intimidation surface quickly when leadership changes and are more easily addressed than others. Both those who have taken on leadership roles after being members of the community and those who are outsiders to a culture need to step back and take a long, skeptical look at standard operating procedures within a school where there is little effective collaboration. Those largely hidden daily practices may subtly but steadily undermine community development.

Finally, confronting Laissez-Faire Communities often means asking people to give up traditional perks and privileges, to work harder, or in many cases to work differently. As one leader recently noted, it means running the risk of making people miserable who have not been miserable before. Skillful leaders understand that they must carefully, consistently "walk their own talk"; they cannot tout collaboration while eliminating meeting time or using it up on trivia and haranguing, urge teachers to share while withholding important information, or behave in ways that favor a selected few "cooperative" individuals at the expense of others.

CASE 5.4   **Freewheeling High School**

Freewheeling High School is a mid-sized urban school that serves students from a wide variety of socioeconomic backgrounds. It has a reputation as a smooth-running, safe, pleasant place to work and as a place where students can do reasonably well if they are able to make it into the top groups. Until the advent of high-stakes testing and the federal requirement that subgroups within the school be able to make AYP, Freewheeling attracted little public or Central Office attention.

Beginning with the district's wholesale adoption of "school-based management" almost 20 years ago, Freewheeling has been led by a succession of principals with weak instructional but strong management skills. Each relied heavily on department chairs to make instructional decisions for the school. The most recent principal, who came up through the system, also believed in and strengthened decentralized decision making. He often touted his ability to "honor and work around the distinct cultures" of the academic departments and to let them take the lead in determining what was best for their programs.

Not surprisingly, the school is a collection of "mini kingdoms." Most of the department communities represent variations of the laissez-faire profile and are peopled by a mix of royalty, entrepreneurs, masterful teachers, and designated drones, each following just as much of the suggested curriculum and instructional approaches as s/he sees fit. Department chairs participate in monthly School Leadership Team meetings but view their role solely as protectors of and advocates for their particular subgroup. The chairs are also responsible for most of the hiring process and usually get the final say in selection of candidates. In turn, induction of new teachers is entirely a departmental and not a school responsibility. As a result, most new teachers adopt the prevailing mores of their departments and rarely encounter colleagues who think or behave differently. Newcomers expect to pay their dues by enduring a certain number of years with students who "don't want to learn"; many say they expect to have to wait years for "the seniority rights" or a retirement that will allow them to teach the honors level classes. Finally, tenure is largely determined by the recommendation of the department chair.

The transition to a standards-based curriculum has not been a smooth one. Some might question whether there has been a transition at all. Departments generally view external standards as interfering with their individual interpretation of the curriculum and their academic freedom. They see data as a top-down way of creating an "NCLB lockstep curriculum" and usually wait until someone from central administration appears in a meeting before they expend any energy analyzing results. Professional development is a buffet approach with individual teachers taking courses or programs they find interesting. In-service days always feature lots of time for teachers to be in their classrooms.

Union identification remains strong at Freewheeling. The school is still largely served by a veteran staff who readily recount war stories about a strike that occurred 15 years ago. Thus elements of toxicity exist close to the surface. Much of the union negotiation team comes from the high school, and it bargains unabashedly for veteran teacher benefits and contract provisions. In seeking comparable benefits and wages to neighboring suburban communities, the union's constant argument is that teachers deserve raises because of the high numbers of ESL and disadvantaged students served by the school

Roughly 40 percent of Freewheeling's students qualify for free and reduced lunch. Teachers hold only a tiny group of high-performing students, usually those who entered Freewheeling with previously honed skills and well-developed work habits, to high standards. In 80 percent of Freewheeling's classrooms, students face a classic teacher-centered pedagogy of lecture and note-taking, worksheets, and questions at the end of the chapter. In the remaining 20 percent, quietly determined teachers make an effort to connect instruction to students' background or learning styles, but the positive results they get are never examined or shared among faculty. Thus their methods do not catch on.

When the topic of the school's poor achievement scores comes up in meetings, teachers routinely blame students, homes, and resources. Rarely does anyone publicly question his or her own practice or ask for help in thinking through a challenging problem and developing common action. Instead, teachers defend the status quo. Conversations revolve around teacher rights and benefits not around students. It is clear that the norms support individual action, not collective action. As a result there is great variation in the quality of the teaching and the outcomes for students. It is a "pass through the lottery school" where students get the luck of the draw—some good teachers, some poor, and most mediocre.

Challenges for Leaders

Groups and cultures that are toxic usually reveal themselves to outsiders fairly quickly. However, schools or smaller units like departments, grade-level teams, or job-alike clusters that fit the laissez-faire profile do not necessarily look problematic at first glance. Often described as efficient, smooth-running, or even "self-starters who need little direction," a Laissez-Faire Community can contain large numbers of teachers who are doing a "decent" or even superior job in their classrooms. Members of Laissez-Faire Communities may behave like private contractors; however, they are not necessarily terrible classroom teachers, and they are usually not poisonous.

Ironically, the academic freedom and autonomy that some highly successful members of laissez-faire faculties cherish protects them from the scorn of less capable, energetic, or committed colleagues. Because practice is private and there is no communal examination of how effectively individual choices work to help students achieve, high-performing teachers can raise standards, introduce more challenging curriculum, offer extra help—all without having to fight the political battles of department politics or suffer the barbs of jealous colleagues. In our work with schools, we often ask teachers if we may share their insights and innovations with others. When we hear, "Yes, but don't put my name on it" or "Yes, but don't say it came from me," we suspect the individual's so-called professional community is not functioning as it should.

The challenge for leaders then is to generate conviction and competence within everyone in a Laissez-Faire Community without alienating teachers who have already excelled and toppling the group into toxicity. Because the sudden spontaneous outbreak of collaboration in the absence of strong leadership is unlikely, leaders need to provide training and actively model, inspire, and reward the new behavior they are looking for. Leaders must also exercise strong, proactive, but not punitive, monitoring of the decision-making processes of existing groups and their ability to take action in service of students.

Ineffective Leader Responses

- **Keep hands off department affairs; declare the departments to be teams; trust them to focus on the right things.** This case illustrates the most common ineffective response to Laissez-Faire Communities: noninvolvement and lack of vision dressed up as "noninterference with the work of dedicated professionals."

- **Create a leadership team that gives all departments "representation and influence for their constituencies" in order to manage the politics of the school and try to create buy-in.** Such an approach merely emphasizes the notion that subgroups have a right and responsibility to pursue their own concerns regardless of the impact on students.

- **Delegate work with sub-group leaders or influential teachers to old-timers who have been in the building a long time and "know how to motivate people and get things done."** New leaders are sometimes told not to "mess with a good thing" or instructed to take their cues from folks who have been managing a school community for a long time. While that advice can sometimes be appropriate, sitting in one's office while the vice principal, athletic director, union president, or most influential department head runs a meeting "per usual" is a risky choice. It can be tantamount to saying that under the surface nothing has changed and that deal making will go on regardless of any pronouncements to the contrary.

- **Assume that all members of an officially designated group have a shared set of curriculum standards, goals, agreements about practice, or view of what students need in order to be successful.** Laissez-Faire Communities often develop procedural understandings that make classroom and school management easier. They will report such understandings to a new leader as evidence of how efficiently they work together. However, such procedural agreements rarely affect what or how students learn.

- **Reorganize rapidly to eliminate previously ineffective structures and introduce a number of new activities requiring collaboration.** Leaders who jump to making previously isolated individuals engage in activities that require them to "give in" to others and/or to let go of cherished practices run the risk of precipitating the community into a toxic type of response. Without a clear understanding of the problem they are trying to solve and some concrete evidence of the success to be gained by "giving a little," individuals who have previously believed themselves to be successful may experience an overwhelming sense of exhaustion, disorientation, or loss.

- **Take away all opportunities for autonomous decision-making; standardize forms, policies, and practices; and require all changes to be approved by school administration.** This approach assumes that one solution fits all circumstances and that the best cure for occasionally unproductive resourcefulness is to kill it. Rather than focusing Laissez-Faire Communities on the degree to which they have become their own worst enemies, this approach is likely to galvanize the group into a mutually agreed-upon dislike of leadership and its policies and runs the risk of pitching members into protective toxicity.

Skillful Leader Responses

- **Bring the problem to light frequently, openly, ruefully, and with hope that it will change. Establish a new vision in which students benefit from the pooled knowledge of a skilled faculty.** In public and private talks, highlight student needs for and faculty benefits of focused, effective collaboration and contrast those benefits with the way in which the community presently squanders its potential. Start with a widely acknowledged learning or performance problem and convey a graphic picture of what students might accomplish if all adults targeted their knowledge and skill toward solving that problem.

- **Spend significant personal time and effort on leadership skill development and on building department heads as a team accountable to the school as a whole.** (See page 149 "Creating Model Teams.") Perhaps the most important work the leader of a large school can undertake is to build the capacity of the leaders of sub-groups within the school and to model the kinds of processes and interactions that should characterize all productive communities. That means that, at least initially, leaders must be directly and consistently involved in collaborating with faculty around important student learning issues—not in issuing orders and making pronouncements about what others should do. Individuals who have never had experience with effective, school-wide collaboration need safe, repeated, and gradually more challenging opportunities to work together on important common problems and to achieve success.

- **Establish clear, problem-solving structures and facilitate making problem solving a central part of all groups' meeting agendas.** Underlying this strategy is a key definition of a "problem" as an identified gap between actual and desired student performance—not an accusation or a label to be dodged (e.g., not a "problem child" or a "problem group"). Thus a group can be considering how to help students deal with large volumes of content area reading, how to help students form and test hypotheses, or what kinds of homework would best help ELL students acquire the math vocabulary they need in order to enroll in higher level courses.

- **Use student performance data to connect departments with related concerns and to surface places where cross-curriculum initiatives would make a difference to learning.** Like the previous strategy, this approach focuses people on the challenges they have in common and on the ways in which everyone might benefit if a gap could be closed. The collaboration across curricular areas needs to be done not for the sake of collaboration alone but rather because pooling the understanding of two groups is likely to help eliminate some of the existing barriers to learning.

- **Build competence through explicit training, practice, and feedback.** Providing common training experiences for a leadership team, a task force drawn from across the building, a department, or a voluntary study group can help reduce the prevailing sense of isolation and disconnection, particularly if that training is designed to help groups achieve something that they care about. Focus on one or two attributes of Collaborative/Accountable Communities, for example having faculty create, apply, and analyze the results of a set of benchmark assessments and structure task and time around practicing tasks connected to those attributes. Monitor efforts and provide—or better yet assign the task of providing—feedback that lets the group know how it is functioning.

- **Monitor Time.** Ideally you may already have meeting time. This is imperative. All success stories cited by Schmoker (2001) have been based on common meeting time. Although it does not guarantee effective collaboration, collaboration is unlikely to occur without significant time being set aside for that purpose. Leaders seeking to transform Laissez-Faire Communities also need to model how time should be used and to expect and perhaps lead groups in establishing norms and agreements about focused and effective participation. They also need to scrutinize data that show how the time is actually spent, to provide feedback, and to coach groups to modify their practices if they are struggling.

- **Help teams develop short-term (2- to 6-week) instructional goals based on data.** Work with available standardized test data and teacher-designed materials to help individuals who teach the same course, grade level teams, or departments to identify specific skills and performances that students need to improve (e.g., factoring, com-

LEGAL NOTE 5.4

Finding Time for Team Meetings

Finding time for group and team meetings within the parameters of the current teacher workday often presents an enormous challenge for school leaders. In most cases, as a result of contract language or past practice, teacher preparation time may not be available for the administration to tap for group meeting time. Consequently, it will usually require negotiations with the union unless the district has substantial resources to provide the coverage necessary to release groups of teachers. Finding these resources is challenging as built-in costs such as step and lane changes on salary schedules, double-digit increases in health insurance cost, and negotiated salary increases are consuming more than the available new money from increased tax revenues and state aid. Nonetheless, if a school district is serious about the need for common planning time, it will have to find a way to implement it.

posing effective essay responses to open-ended questions, using science formulas, etc). Help them to identify a concrete level of performance they want all students to reach at the end of a targeted 2- to 6-week intervention and the ways in which they will check that performance before and after their instruction. Help groups plan for quick, formative assessments and for re-teaching if some students are struggling. Stick with a team through at least one full round of instructional goal setting in order to identify where they need further support and training. Encourage all members of an administrative or instructional leadership team to attach themselves to and participate in at least one round of instructional goal setting per semester and discuss findings in Instructional Leadership Team meetings.

CASE 5.5   **Grade Eight at Miraculous Middle**

Thanks to the extraordinary work of teacher leaders and teacher teams, strong Central Office support, and a dedicated group of administrators, Miraculous Middle has almost completely transformed itself. Once a school on warning that lost 20 percent of its enrollment to competing private and charter schools each year, Miraculous Middle can now point to dramatic gains in 6th and 7th grade student achievement across all subject areas. In contrast, the drop off in 8th grade student achievement has become more obvious and acute. The three administrators and most of the members of the Instructional Leadership Team think the primary difference is the performance and capability of teams at the different grades. The 6th and 7th grade teams collaborate effectively; whenever any one member determines that a practice helps struggling students, colleagues adopt that approach. However, 8th grade teachers have never been able to agree on the necessity to help low-performing students or strategies for doing so. Members are unwilling to move beyond their narrow comfort zone in order to experiment with methods that colleagues have used successfully. As a result, the quality of instruction varies widely from classroom to classroom.

Three retirements finally allowed the principal to bring some new faces into 8th grade. To keep them from being infected by the predominant culture, the principal and his two assistants jointly decided to put all three newcomers into 8 Platinum this year and give them support. The beginners are struggling to figure out the curriculum pacing and handle the disproportional share of special needs students, but at least they're getting along well with one another.

The other two so-called teams, 8 Silver and 8 Gold, are really loose collections of genuinely excellent teachers, one or two marginal performers, and several difficult-to-work-with people who have, over time, intimidated others into giving them the working conditions and student loads that make their teaching life easy and predictable. No one really knows how anyone else's students do. The 8th grade experts cherish their autonomy and have thus adopted a live-and-let-live approach to colleagues. In fact, the 8 Silver and 8 Gold teams come together only to oppose administrators' requests. Recently they were asked to collaborate and come up with restructured schedules; their new configurations had to provide built-in opportunities for re-teaching any concept that 30 percent of their students had not mastered. That request provoked a scathing open letter to parents and the community authored by two of the self-appointed "deans" of the 8 Gold team. The letter claimed to represent many other faculty members and warned readers that the quality of their children's education was being sacrificed to meet the needs of a few "limited ability" students. Two of the most effective 8th grade teachers already provide such time. Privately they disagree with colleagues, but neither was willing to speak up in a public meeting.

Challenges for Leaders

One popular response to the problem of malfunctioning sub-groups in elementary and middle school is to break them up and disperse their members to other groups. Another is to "salt" a group with new faces and/or strong teacher leaders who know how to get the job done in the hope of changing the predominant tone and stimulating new thinking. While both approaches offer hope of a short-term solution, neither addresses the long-term problem: holding non-performing teams accountable for their own behavior and for student learning. Moreover, both typical approaches run the risk of appearing to "punish" those teachers who have helped to create successful, high-functioning teams either by upsetting the productive working relationships and competencies they have created or by putting them into situations where they are likely to feel or become isolated and uncomfortable.

Ineffective Leader Responses

- Carry out a major shift in personnel; break up the two veteran 8th grade teams who are not getting the job done and disperse them among other grades and teams. Assign teachers who know how to get results to 8th grade. This approach is as likely, or perhaps more likely, to hurt overall achievement as it is to solve the grade 8 problem. First, even if teachers know how to get results with a particular grade level and program, it may take them some time to recalibrate their practice to deal with older or younger students and new material, and now every grade will be dealing with disruption. Second, previously high-functioning groups may find themselves diverting significant energy and attention to dealing with an angry colleague who has been involuntarily transferred. Unless there is compelling evidence that people would behave differently if they did not feel themselves under the thumb or influence of another colleague, this strategy simply serves to punish those who are working together well.

- Make a minor but strategic shift in personnel. Transfer highly capable teacher leaders from 6th and 7th grade to 8th grade in order to salt the non-performing groups with people who know how to get the job done for students. Some principals actively recruit and persuade skilled personnel to change grade levels in order to solve achievement problems and provide leadership where there are voids. Because it presumes that others will follow the lead of the newcomer as opposed to isolating him/her, this approach is also risky. It may merely exacerbate the "each man is an island" quality of such groups by forcing the newcomer to retreat into protective solitude to be able to save energy for students.

- Bring the full force of the evaluation tool to bear on the two "ringleaders" and "send them a message." Write them up for lack of variety in instruction, failure to differentiate instruction, and whatever else surfaces through observation. For good measure, compare their practices to those of the collaborating newcomers. Unless clear and compelling data suggest that students in the ringleaders' classes consistently under-perform students elsewhere or that over time one can demonstrate that clearly defined sub-group students of these teachers lose ground, this approach simply drains resources without solving the achievement problem. It may cause short-term changes in some classes, or it may simply galvanize other colleagues to rally around the "injured parties" and to make sure they never have questions or appear vulnerable. Rather than supporting a habit of non-defensive self-examination of practice and productive problem-solving, focusing first on catching people doing something wrong in class usually undermines trust.

- Address the unprofessional behavior and potential insubordination—of the open letter to parents, but otherwise decide there are some battles not worth fighting and ignore the behavior of the two 8th grade teams until someone retires. Deciding that this is a battle not worth fighting is tantamount to telling all the other teams that there are different or unclear standards and expectations and that the hard work that they have done does not matter. In essence it says that if you act out, you can get away with it.

Skillful Leader Responses

- Make sure that there are no secrets or hidden agendas about what constitutes effective professional performance on a team or committee. Work with other administrators and union personnel both inside your school and in the school district to develop a clear jargon-free description and/or set of criteria that capture what outcomes a team is expected to accomplish and what standards of effective team performance it is expected to meet in service of student learning. Communicate the standards and criteria (without blame or accusation) to all teams with the public statement that the school district/school supports and expects professional collaboration and has no secrets about what the standards for that collaboration are.

- **As an administrative group or instructional leadership team for the building, take time to identify, clarify and communicate the "non-negotiables" re team and individual behavior.** Especially in schools that have experienced significant administrative turnover, principals, vice principals, coaches, curriculum specialists, and guidance directors may all be communicating different messages about what is important and what they will tolerate. If one particular administrator does not believe in the value of collaboration and has overlooked certain behavior for years, it is not surprising to find resistance when the rules change.

- **Collect diagnostic data about the malfunctioning team or group.** Observe how the malfunctioning group uses assigned meeting time, how it exchanges information and works or does not work to help a wide range of students, how it identifies learning problems, and who takes (or does not take) responsibility for those problems. If necessary, take notes on participation and on specific quotes that reveal the group's beliefs about learning and competence in pooling information and know-how.

- **Use the diagnostic data and standards to identify and name the gaps between present and desired performance.** Figure out what students are (or may be) losing when adults do not work together in an Accountable Community. Meet with the team and name the gap that you see and the data that lead to that analysis. Ask each member to reflect privately, in writing, and perhaps anonymously, about what might be causing those gaps. Ask what support, training, or other kinds of help s/he might need and the group might need to change the nature of the interactions.

- **Help the non-functioning team use the standards and feedback to identify a change goal for itself, set out the ways in which it will monitor its own performance, and identify a target date for providing its agreed-upon evidence of improvement.** Groups full of people who think of themselves as better than or different than others, as is the case in these 8th grade teams, often respond well to being given the responsibility and independence to participate in designing their own charge. The administrator who has identified the problem makes the development of the charge non-negotiable. However, s/he also indicates his belief that the group members are skilled enough and professional enough to identify a worthwhile target. If members cannot do so with some facilitation from the building or team leader, then the charge can always be set for the group.

- **Provide targeted professional development and coaching to help the group move from isolated to collaborative problem-solving.** Report back on the group's own self-reported needs. Be explicit about how you have combined that information plus your own data analysis to identify what professional development would be most useful or relevant. Unless the group is so dysfunctional that it needs to focus on very basic understandings one step at a time, link the professional development to solving a real student issue rather than having it delivered as an abstract experience (e.g., a seminar on effective conflict management).

- **Signal that: "This work is important. You can do it well. I will help you—I won't give up on you" through deeds as well as words.** Stay actively involved with and provide feedback to a team that needs to transform itself for anywhere from six months to a year so that individuals are very clear that this is not a passing fad or something that can be ignored once they have complied with a set of superficial training activities.

CASE 5.6 **Autonomous Unified School District**

Autonomous Unified was created 12 years ago when five, small, rural towns yielded to overwhelming economic pressure, declining enrollments, and state demands. They reluctantly banded together in a regional school district after a protracted and controversial process that exposed but never reconciled deep-seated stereotypes and mistrust between towns. To get the deal done, negotiators made a number of concessions. Each community retained its own elementary school and principal; each also was allowed a four-member school board that would be eliminated after ten years. Despite protests from both faculty and parents, Kingsford's Junior/Senior High School became a regional middle school. Jewel, whose schools were already in a campus arrangement that could be adapted, kept its high school and absorbed students from all the other towns. To realize cost savings from the regionalization, the total number of certified staff had to be reduced by 30 percent; that task was accomplished through what teachers perceived to be wheeling and dealing between principals, some of whom were more politically connected and astute at the process than others. Jewel's high school principal, for example, managed to keep not only his own job but also most of his faculty, a result that earned him their unquestioning loyalty.

For the first ten years, three different superintendents attempted to manage the politics and conflicts of Autonomous Unified RSD through decentralization. All allowed principals the freedom to choose programs, hire and fire staff, and allocate budgets once the bottom line had been set. Principals were also free to design their own responses (or not) to evidence of growing gaps between the preparation and performance of students from different feeder schools within the district.

Several superintendents tried to hold, and then abandoned, monthly regional principals meetings; the tensions were too great between high school and middle school. As elementary principalships turned over, all three of the superintendents put a priority on attracting fresh leadership from beyond the district's boundaries. New hires found the role lonely and sought one another's support. Thus the "outsiders" created small alliances and subgroups that worked together effectively and gradually began to standardize practice across some of the member schools. Central Office staff spent hours attempting to work with each separate school, provide targeted professional development at each site, and negotiate curriculum changes that would be accepted and hold across the district. Not surprisingly, turnover of both district and local leadership was high.

By the time that Dr. B was hired as Autonomous Unified's fourth superintendent, its middle school was on a state warning list and its principal and faculty appeared paralyzed by despair. A growing number of parents were expressing their disapproval of the high school and were threatening to enroll their children in a newly created charter school. Two of the district's most creative and successful elementary principals were threatening to leave if collegiality and collaboration did not improve.

Challenges for Leaders

In cases such as this, district leaders face the challenge of building common ground and common practice in places that have routinely valued difference. The tradition of rural independence supports a public perception that each town ought to have autonomous control over its schools. School buildings may be central gathering points that are heavily used for community events. Attendance at school functions may be one of the ways in which the community comes together and affirms its identity as a place with a special spirit or history. If school administrators spend their entire lives in a town, they are likely to develop extensive networks of like-minded community members who provide a solid base of support for protecting a school from any kind of outside interference, even if that interference is from district leadership. Finally, routines, myths, and tacit treaties that evolve over the years provide much-valued continuity and stability; actions that threaten the status quo are likely to be suspect unless the need for change is both clear and widely acknowledged. District leadership must be able to balance the pull of independence and history against the obligation to ensure an equitable education for all students no matter where they live.

Ineffective Leader Responses

- **Continue to negotiate changes with each school individually.** This approach does not impact overall student performance nor help to build capacity for continued growth. It inevitably produces special deals and compromises that exacerbate competition and ill will between schools and dilute the district's ability to uphold standards for teaching and learning. At best it is a way to manage schools but not improve schools. It drains the time and energy of Central Office staff, makes it unlikely that anyone will be able to pay adequate attention to learning issues, and encourages schools to hunker down and wait for initiatives to pass.

- **Set up a system of financial rewards and benefits for those schools who meet performance goals and identify financial consequences for those who do not.** Conventional wisdom holds that such systems will motivate schools to compete with one another. In reality, however, resources are often so scarce that rewarding one school means denying needed services to another whose students are likely to be struggling already. These divide and conquer approaches can set up unhealthy rivalries, secretive behavior, and continued noncollaboration. They can result in the creation and perpetuation of "fiefdoms" led by virtual robber barons who are particularly skilled at political maneuvering.

- **Remove all local influence on curriculum, instruction, and personnel and replace them with a set of district mandates about the programs and practices teachers must implement.** Exhausted Central Office staff who have routinely tried to divide themselves into pieces in order to be responsive to schools report that they entertain fantasies about just ordering people to do something—or else. Those leaders who take such an approach are often driven by a strong sense of urgency and dismay at the chaos that they find. Mandates have a place in a leader's repertoire, but they are rarely effective unless considerable effort has been expended to build a sense of ownership and responsibility among the people who must carry them out. Mandates set forth without consultation and adequate debate usually cause endless complaints, elaborate attempts to circumvent requirements, or superficial responses intended to divert attention from real change.

- **Limit meeting times and meeting obligations so that administrators do not feel they are being pulled away from their buildings and from more important matters.** Subscribing either in word or deed to the idea that a district level agenda for shared action is far less important than an individual one is a recipe for continued dysfunction.

- **Avoid open discussions of polarizing issues when building leaders are together.** Facing potentially divisive questions, many leaders opt to keep the tough discussions private and focus on the positives when people are together: e.g., building an administrator group that has a good time together and gets along well, raising morale, and celebrating life events. All these activities have value. However, if communities never learn to deal with conflict openly and productively, all discussions go underground and more energy is spent on denying problems than on solving them.

Skillful Leader Responses

- Use the external pressures for accountability (NCLB) as levers to move local boards and community groups toward identifying shared challenges and engaging in collaborative problem solving. If accountability measures identify clear performance problems faced by the majority of schools in the district, choose one as the first step to building common ground. Focus on curriculum articulation and common staff development programs that will help faculties that are feeding students into the larger regional schools.

- **Set and pursue district goals for effective collaborative problem solving.** Communicate the reason for taking the goal and the data that show such a goal is necessary to all parties who will be involved. Develop a professional development plan that will help the administrative team acquire the skills it needs to function well as an Accountable Community. Identify clear criteria for success and devote regular meeting time to self-assessment on those criteria.

- **Carve out and protect time for leaders to be away from their personal turf while they are learning to be a team.** Create semiannual overnight leadership retreats that include team and professional development, planning, and problem solving. Bring board and community leaders, administrators, and teacher leaders together in neutral settings to identify the hopes and aspirations they share and the achievement goals they want to set.

- **Use technology to overcome the disadvantages of large distances between schools and to increase information exchanges and collaboration.** Teleconferencing, distance learning, bulletin boards, software that allows several users to work on a document simultaneously can all help reduce the distrust and sense of isolation that result when individuals rarely have contact with one another and thus have no way to judge the value of pooling mental effort.

- **Create a teacher leader/facilitator institute and task force to increase the pool of skilled collaborators.** Districts can partner with a university or professional development provider or create their own program that trains, certifies, and perhaps rewards teachers for competence in facilitating collaborative problem solving. If admission to the institute is competitive, its activities are stimulating, and its work respected, the district can accomplish a number of goals simultaneously. It can augment the capacity of small schools to run multiple work groups. It can offset the limitations of a particular building administrator who is struggling to learn new skills, and it can build a pool of potential new administrators that already know how to support collaboration.

- **Establish required monthly district meetings with plenty of celebration and serious deliberation.** Rotate the meeting sites and have the principal host a walk and school tour prior to the business meeting. Make sure the food is high quality and worth the visit. Have a problem case of the month.

- **Invest time and effort in implementing a common supervisory model focused on shared standards for teacher performance.** Provide training for supervisors and evaluators and sustained oversight by the superintendent to ensure it is being done consistently and well.

Motivating Congenial Communities

Communities whose patterns of interaction and information exchange can generally be categorized as toxic or laissez faire are usually easier to spot than those whose malfunction is excessive concern with congeniality. On the surface, congenial groups look better evolved and more likely to be able to do the hard work of improving student learning. Interactions are pleasant and positive; administrators and teachers usually get along well and speak positively about one another. Just as personal relationships establish a foundation for student learning in a classroom, so forming congenial relationships can be starting point, albeit a limited one, for adult community building. Teachers who interact with each other on a number of different dimensions can develop the high levels of interpersonal trust and some of the effective patterns of communication essential for effective team function. Communities that establish congeniality as a goal in and of itself, however, tend to let that value stifle their own growth and development in response to challenge.

Members of Congenial Communities connect to each other around outside interests, celebrations, and personal successes or difficulties. They embrace newcomers who are willing to be social, open, and at least superficially engaged in others' lives, and they are uncomfortable with individuals perceived to be "distant" or "loners." Groups may gather before, after, or outside of school; subgroups may play sports together or organize outings. Members extend and receive support and sympathy during times of family crises; one another's stories are known and factored into any calculation of a response to change. Thus leaders new to a Congenial Community often find themselves listening to a litany of outside issues and circumstances offered up by concerned colleagues to explain why a team member cannot be expected to perform certain tasks, meet certain requirements, or work with certain students. Those who have moved into leadership roles are expected to factor in all the history they know and to be bound by it when making decisions.

The danger for communities that closely resemble the congenial profile is that preserving relationships, strong morale, or "happy family feelings" is consistently valued more than attending to students and their performance problems. Leaders who focus on building or sustaining Congenial Communities are preoccupied with making teachers happy. Happiness is assumed to derive from presents, prizes, acknowledgments of personal needs, praise and rewards, or low stress and low demand for improvement. Teachers are not expected to be deeply satisfied by their ability to take on and master a difficult educational challenge. We often hear administrators saying "My teachers know I put them first; I'm there to get them whatever they need" or "This school is like one big happy family; we take care of each other." Such care and concern for adults is admirable and can help maintain the long-range health and productivity of a professional community. However, it cannot be allowed to stifle debate, restrain consideration of alternative approaches that might help children who are not currently learning, or justify mediocre instruction.

Garmston and Wellman label groups that want to protect congenial relationships at all cost as "pseudocommunities—the stage of extensive politeness. Being comfortable is the goal. Members of pseudocommunities ignore or make light of problems, withholding their true feelings. They ignore individual differences and avoid people that make them uncomfortable"(268). Information is exchanged in guarded, oblique or tentative ways that usually fail to make the group more productive or open-minded. Members do not question one another's assertions or ask for data to support proposed courses of action and tend to ignore or reduce problems to simplistic solutions. Congenial teams are very protective of their members. They will shield weaker members with excuses such as "Her plate is too full" to justify mediocre performance. Congenial teams also work hard to keep their sunny, cooperative reputation intact. Inquiring administrators may find it difficult to get an honest assessment of what is really happening. Senge calls these mediocre teams "smooth surface teams" where "members believe they must suppress their conflicting views in order to maintain the team" (1990 249).

Skillful leaders who face or inherit Congenial Communities need to figure out how to help such groups stretch beyond their narrow zone of comfort and tackle hard challenges without tipping them into either toxicity or self-protective isolation. As is the case with both Toxic and Laissez-Faire Communities, collecting and using good data about how well students are performing and what they next need to learn can help Congenial Communities get a sense that they are rallying around shared problems and shared goals. Leaders also need to introduce, model, and consistently use safe, transparent processes for surfacing and honoring multiple points of view and for managing conflict. Finally, Congenial Communities can benefit from shared professional development that allows them to read about, think and talk about, or experience the ways in which "productive tension" or learning and communication style differences can enhance what they already know and are capable of doing. Unlike toxic or laissez-faire groups that can become threatened and grumpy in the face of self-assessments that expose their dysfunctions, Congenial Communities are often interested in tools that let them identify their own limitations. The underlying presumption of trust and good will can serve as a foundation for discussion and for considering new courses of action, particularly if the group believes it is operating from a position of strength.

CASE 5.7 **The Leaderless Group**

Muddy River Jr. High was improving. As he led the faculty in converting what had been a traditional, adult-oriented environment to a school clearly focused on the needs of early adolescents, Principal Harry Readmore could see the changes in achievement. Strong collaboration between the social studies, science, and English departments had contributed to significant improvements in reading and writing performance. The school was still struggling to meet AYP in reading for special education students, but his three high-functioning departments were energized by the challenge and were implementing assessment and re-teaching practices that he knew would pay off.

Four years into his Harry's tenure, however, Muddy River's mathematics achievement had stalled in a headline-grabbing two years of failure to make progress. Results for all subgroups were poor; even students with high grades scored at the basic or below basic level in geometry and problem-solving skills. Harry was embarrassed and worried. The math department stood out in his mind as one of the best-adjusted, happiest, and most supportive adult groups at Muddy River. Nicknamed the "Friendly Team" after their leader, Sally Friendly, members of the math department prided themselves on always being "there for each other" and "there for our kids." They were personal as well as professional friends and socialized every Friday at a nearby watering hole for an end of the week "unwinder." Harry could count on the Friendly Team to show school spirit. They always provided volunteers for the staff golf tournament, the annual holiday shopping trip, and the student-faculty basketball game. He had noted, however, that math department seemed more focused on their relationships with each other than on tackling increasingly pressing achievement problems.

A quick look at the individual group members made the challenge clearer. Most department members were, Harry thought, competent; to a person they "loved kids." Mr. Y seemed to earn students' and counselors' greatest respect. He ran a traditional, teacher-centered classroom but worked hard to make his instruction engaging and clear and was always ready to help students who showed some effort.

Besides Sally, there were three other females, all in their late 30s and 40s, in the department. Ms. W was a self-professed "townie" who had left the local bank in order to have better work hours and a better retirement system. With a keen sense of humor, she was popular with both the students and her colleagues. She had, however, uneven standards and expectations, demanding much from the good students and little from those who struggled. Harry thought Ms. W exhibited signs of "arsenic sympathy." She often told stories of how she "cut kids from the flats a little slack" and could be counted upon to explain that poor student progress resulted from a lack of support at home. Mrs. K was in the process of acquiring a certificate to be a nutrition and stress management counselor at a local fitness center. She was more interested in 3 R's (Rescue Rather than Rigor) and often said "I really think we have to be careful not to stress these kids out and ruin their self-esteem. They are facing so much at home. We have to be realistic." Mrs. P had been transferred from the high school because of her questionable math knowledge but engaging personality just as Harry took over as principal. When she made the switch, the assistant superintendent told him "Mrs. P will be a better match for what you want to accomplish—not much math but much warmth."

One amiable, but low-performing, veteran teacher rounded out the Friendly Team. Fondly referred to as "Numbers," Mr. Arnold Beenaround entertained much and taught little. He got his nickname from the games he played and his eccentricities around math. He always carried $.39 in his pocket with 4 shiny pennies. He told endless stories always with little math facts. The students learned the number of students in his high school graduating class (37); how many students had gone to college (3 including him); how many pets he had (5 including a boa constrictor) all named in sequence for a number in a different language. He also was greatly respected because he could hand draw a perfect circle. He was celebrated for his quirkiness and any perceived shortcomings were waved off with unwarranted, humorous forgiveness. "Old Numbers may be a bit past prime, but he is an institution."

Department Head Sally Friendly had come up through the system, taught 6th grade for 13 years and then was promoted for her nonacademic contributions to the school. (For a review of her teaching career, see *The Skillful Leader: Confronting Mediocre Teaching*.) Known by administrators for her pleasant disposition but mediocre teaching, it made little sense to promote her to department head. However, no one else wanted the job. One interested younger teacher, since departed, who was universally recognized as having more leadership potential, deferred because of Sally's seniority. Saying "She deserves it. She has put in her time and has earned the opportunity to bump up her salary for those last years before retirement. Sally will serve us well," he graciously stepped aside during the perfunctory interview.

Sally did not, however, serve kids well. She did little supervision of her colleagues during her two periods of release time, and she wrote soft evaluations. Her summaries weighted climate, not learning. A sample included: "Students experience a comfortable climate" and "Mrs. P develops a positive learning environment" or "Mr. Beenaround should be congratulated for being an active member of our professional community." Recommendations, if present, did not focus on performance gaps but emphasized (even for low performers) conditional syntax. "Arnold, you might consider spending a little less time on games" and vague ideas such as "Continue to work on engaging all students." Sally never scheduled any follow-up.

Although she was a mediocre supervisor, she was not a terrible organizational leader. During her tenure, the math team completed all paperwork on time and cooperated with the administration cheerfully on scheduling issues and administrative requests. Under Sally's "leadership," weekly meetings consisted of extensive personal check-ins around snacks, demos by "Numbers," and agendas focused on planning the Math Fair Collaborative Project. Some meeting time was allocated to sharing strategies to deal with discipline problems, and four times a year they would have a "Share-In" where people would swap "grabbers" to motivate students.

This congenial team treated students well and had some consistency of demand. One high-performing student reflecting back on her math experience in middle school said:

> *The Math department was very demanding. Its just they demanded the wrong things—like where your name was on the paper and having homework every night—not on what we were to learn. Everything seemed right or wrong with no real explanation. Good thing I know math and my father is an engineer; many kids were lost but got pretty good grades if they completed everything."*

Even though the results were poor, the leader defended her department at the Instructional Leadership Team as "doing the best they could in light of the elementary school preparation and the nature of the kids."

Challenges for Leaders

Muddy River has a weak subunit in an improving school. What makes it more challenging is that the group is pleasant to deal with and cooperates with organizational imperatives outside the core of instruction and learning. Because Congenial Communities create supportive (albeit low-expectation) climates for students, most leaders think they would rather deal with them than toxic ones. As a flavor, sugar beats acid any day. Congeniality serves strong needs for affiliation, i.e., to be socially connected, supported, and accepted. The resistance to change that Congenial Communities exhibit is more subtle, has less edge and less overt push back. However, Congenial Communities can be just as hard to change as Laissez-Faire Communities and are prone to turning toxic under pressure to deal with topics that expose less congenial undercurrents.

Secondly, this case also highlights the "leaderless group" challenge. The behaviors of congenial group members may be perfect reflections of the priorities and competencies of their leader. Individuals who have been promoted by default or seniority rather than competence and who have themselves known only flabby feedback and inflated praise may lead the way they were led. They model their supervision on their experience; thus they too inflate evaluations, and rarely check anything but the highest performance rating. Even in the case of low performance, recommendations rarely pinpoint teaching and learning gaps. Whether they are formal evaluators or not, these "leaders" ask no penetrating questions, expose no "brutal facts," and simplify problems so that no boats get rocked. Positive and supportive to a fault, they will find a reason to excuse even horrible teaching. On the school leadership team, these congenial leaders believe their role and value lies in their ability to protect their group; thus they often choose to advocate strongly (or explain or excuse) "their" teachers. Although they like students, they are not student advocates, and student learning problems take a back seat to teacher comfort.

Ineffective Leader Responses

Leaders incorrectly assume that:

- **Pleasant compliance with organizational demands will lead naturally to team development "over time."** Congenial groups are meeting teachers' need for adult affiliation; they neither look like nor feel like classic "dysfunctional" groups to members who have thrived on the comfortable interactions for years. Thus, unless there is a crisis or someone "calls the question" and asks the group to deal with ineffective instruction, there is little reason for the behavior to change on its own.

- **When confronted with data that signal gaps in student learning, a congenial team will become motivated to examine practice.** Leading with a data focus is not necessarily the first step in changing congenial to collaborative. Unlike Laissez-faire and Toxic Communities where the right entry might be to lead with facts and program implementation, Congenial Communities are motivated by relationships and connection with people, not facts.

- **Selecting a protocol to structure team collaboration is a good starting point.** All protocols can be undermined by assumptions about what is "nice" or "not nice" or "unkind" behavior; thus the implementation of the protocol is critical. The authors have witnessed many compliance level "Looking at Data" sessions where conversations avoid connecting gaps in learning with gaps in instruction and participants slip easily into a collective student-blaming symphony (see Chapter 4 on "Community Building 101: Setting the Stage").

- **Promoting an internal candidate for department (or other unit) leadership will bring the right skill and knowledge to move to more progressive community interactions.** This is tricky business. There may be a limited number of available teachers to draw from and a natural proclivity to reward senior members. Often, however, administrators miss the opportunity to bring in a new individual with no history who can influence a culture change. Because there are so many treaties, agreements, and expectations of unswerving support operating, teachers who have been active members of Congenial Communities may find efforts to alter the group's orientation and behavior very difficult.

- **Congenial interactions are a necessary step to becoming collaborative.** The strength of Congenial Communities is the trust that the members have for each other; but when communities are stuck on preserving congeniality, trust can be used to protect members' narrow focus of conversations and avoid unpleasant facts (see also Case 5.2). High-performing communities too have developed trust. In these cases trust is used to support learning, risk taking, and public exposure in order to tackle complex teaching and learning problems.

Skillful Leader Responses

Many of the effective leader responses cited in previous cases apply to congenial cases as well. Here we will focus on responses unique to the Congenial Community profile.

- **Lead with relationships not data and build on the willingness and readiness of Congenial Communities to cooperate with authority.** Congenial Communities may not spend much time focusing on student results, but they do care about students. Acknowledge the good intentions and good work on behalf of students. Appeal to this strength. Remember these groups are not driven by the norms of autonomy so present in laissez-faire groups. Connections and a desire to cooperate are paramount to congenial groups. Unlike toxic and laissez-faire groups, they also respond to authority. Drago-Severson calls one of the ways in which adults make meaning a "socializing way of knowing." She notes that individuals who use this style are often dependent on external authority. Acceptance and affiliation are high priorities and criticism and conflict are threats (26). The skillful leader capitalizes on these characteristics to reframe how time and effort is spent.

- **Identify and acknowledge the role of external forces about which teachers have little control but reframe challenges in terms of what is under their control.** Explicitly acknowledge the frustrations and limitations of testing, the potential impact of poor past instruction, and the challenging backgrounds that account for some of the performance gaps. Accepting and listening to feelings of frustration is especially important to congenial groups. Lead them to name and consider factors they can control, e.g., the content they teach and how they teach it, the ways in which they use data to inform their instruction, the standards of performance they set, and the high- or low-expectation messages they send students.

- **Help congenial groups be more accepting of productive conflict.** Congenial groups benefit from processing structures that set up "safe" dichotomies or comparisons, that surface multiple ways to understand an issue, or that value evaluation and weighted rankings. Such structures allow the group to expose existing ranges of opinion and understanding in ways that do not threaten their basic respect for one another. Leaders or facilitators may have to explicitly communicate criteria for "healthy debate" and to refuse to let the group make decisions if such debate has not occurred.

- **Acknowledge your role and responsibility for the existing gaps in performance before inviting a team own a piece of the problem.** While such a strategy helps to establish a leader's credibility with any community, congenial groups especially need to feel that the press to improve is a shared enterprise and not an accusation.

- **Get the right leader. Assess whether leadership capability exists within the team, and, if necessary, assume leadership of the team.** Select a teacher leader who has been part of a Collaborative Community and/or who understands limits to congeniality. There are times when a principal or an assistant principal should temporarily take over organizing and leading meetings. An experienced high school principal highlights the challenge:

> *If there is no high-quality leader available, then it is better to re-advertise and continue the search with the team being members of the search team, along with a parent or two and a student with the principal modeling the process and establishing the expectations—for as long as it takes to fill the position with a leader. It is was painful not to have someone in place, but it communicated clearly the importance of the right match and not accepting mediocre leadership.*

- **Escalate your visits and feedback to poorly performing teachers, but reassure others that you are not "after everyone."** Congenial folks can turn paranoid very quickly. After earning trust of the group, you cannot ignore poor individual performance. This is a balancing act. You want to build the capacity of the team to set standards for their colleagues, but if kids are losing out in the meantime, leaders cannot ignore that.

- **Create a sense of urgency by putting the data on the table. Persuade the group that there is some risk to change but a higher risk to not changing through a process of "unfreezing."** Robert Evans in *The Human Side of School Change: Reform, Resistance, and the Real-Life Problems of Innovation* gives us some pertinent thoughts.

> Unfreezing is a matter of lessening one kind of anxiety, the fear of trying, but first of mobilizing another kind of anxiety, the fear of *not* trying. Unless something increases the cost of preserving the status quo, the conservative impulse and the cumulative impact of culture and past learning are too strong to prevent innovation...the change agent must make clear his caring and support, his commitment to working with people to take the difficult steps toward new learning. He must convey two essential, contrasting messages. The first is "This is very serious, the risks of inaction are very real and we must change." The second is "I value you as people, and I will help you get where we need to go."

This counsel about "unfreezing" certainly holds for Toxic and Laissez-Faire Communities, but is absolutely imperative for congenial groups because of the apparent satisfaction with a pleasant status quo.

- **Share the attributes of congenial and collaborative teams and invite them to assess where they are.** This might be part of a school-wide self-assessment.

CASE 5.8 **Edgeland Elementary School**

Edgeland Elementary sits on a lovely plot of land in a once-solid family neighborhood whose population has changed dramatically over the last six years. Its principal, Marvin R, grew up in the town and knows "everyone who's anyone" in both local politics and the school department. Marvin says Edgeland is a "big, loving extended family; once you're part of it you don't need anyone else." Many of his staff are sons and daughters of old (or new) friends; his assistant principal is a former student, his cousin is the guidance counselor, and his aunt runs Food Services. Staff work at Edgeland for years or for their whole careers; thus everyone knows everyone else's personal business, and, until recently, everyone knew the students' families and stories.

Because of his connections, Marvin can pick up the phone, call in a favor, and get almost anything done. Over 20 years he has "smoothed the path between town and gown" for at least a half dozen new Central Office administrators and two superintendents. Most have taken his advice and help. In return, all he asks is to be "respected enough to be left alone to manage my building as I see fit." Newly appointed principals, particularly if they have been hired from within the district, tend to see Marvin as an informal mentor. He puts himself out to welcome them, tell them the inside scoop and the way things run, give them advice on managing their buildings, and introduce them around to the various board and department heads in town. In return they support his positions with the "know-nothings and eggheads" who have, Marvin feels, taken over the Central Office.

Marvin's response to requests for change or new initiatives sets the tone for his faculty and for the people he brings along and recommends for positions throughout the district. He tends to support the status quo; he believes there is "no reason to mess with a good thing," and he believes that the succession of "outsiders" who have held Central Office responsibility for curriculum cannot possibly appreciate what he has built. Staff learn, and teach newcomers, that it is best not to "make waves"; rarely does anyone bring up difficult topics either in school meetings or at the district level.

Edgeland's achievement scores teetered at, or just below, state average for a number of years. Even when other elementary schools in the district began to address their student performance issues and to show improvements in their outcomes, Marvin was neither worried nor particularly interested in others' experiences or insights. At the superintendents' monthly administrative roundtables, he always "shared" a fistful of positive newspaper articles, letters from politicians, and pictures of happy children for which he inevitably received congratulations. Although there was never time to talk about learning issues at this roundtable, if someone did bring up a question at a break, Marvin often urged them not to disrupt the tone of the meeting with "negative stuff."

Then two years ago, student performance in both literacy and mathematics went down precipitously; the school has been unable to make AYP since then. In response Marvin has initiated a whirlwind of requests and activities: he demanded the Central Office find funds for new books and programs; he wanted extra special education staff, more testing of individual students, more outside placements and some big-name speakers to motivate his staff. He announced that his problem was not like anyone else's and that he was too busy to come to district meetings that were all theory and had nothing to do with his problem. Lately he's always late to required events; he skips important program and curriculum meetings without apology or excuse. Other members of the administrative team are irritated and beginning to imitate him in self-defense (they say).

Challenges for Leaders

This case presents two layers of community malfunction: one at the school and one at the district level. At first glance, mobilizing the different subgroups within Edgeland, as well as the entire staff, to move beyond their perceived comfort zone and take actions to improve student achievement may seem to be Marvin's problem. He has either consciously or unconsciously valued surface agreement and cheerfulness over the kind of intense, professional reflection and debate that might allow his teachers to jointly diagnose what students need. Ultimately, attention has to go to the actions that will help Edgeland's grade level groups and specialists uncover their concerns and capabilities and evolve into Accountable Communities. However, we think real change is unlikely unless the inadequacies of Marvin's own supervisors and professional community, the so-called administrative team for the district, are addressed.

District leadership has allowed (and perhaps even protected) persistent patterns of mediocre learning and teaching at Edgeland. In the interests of honoring and tapping into Marvin's political expertise, maintaining congeniality among principals, helping Marvin save face, and thus ensuring his cooperation with management dictates, Central Office leaders have avoided confronting the gap between what Edgeland's students need to learn and what they actually master. In essence, district leadership has signaled its approval of Edgeland's outcomes. Although the data revealing patterns of decline and deficit has been available for years, no one at the district level has had the conviction (or perhaps competence) to challenge Marvin's explanations for that poor performance or to help him analyze what is happening in his building. Moreover, a succession of superintendents and assistant superintendents have failed to structure processes, provide training, pose problems, or facilitate information sharing in ways that would build a genuine administrative team. Principals have not been invited or expected to raise questions, show vulnerability or support, and advise one another in tackling difficult student learning problems. In fact, any controversy or potentially testy exchange is usually anticipated and suppressed so that monthly leadership meetings are largely devoted to administrivia, "sharing," and "updating," i.e., the ceremonial reporting of arrangements and agreements that have already been made.

Lacking supervisory feedback, experience as part of an Accountable Community at the district level, or an evaluation that might have convinced him to stretch his repertoire, Marvin has not surprisingly assumed that his choices for Edgeland are effective and admirable ones. No one has complained about his behavior or confronted him about his thinking. He is managing his building efficiently; as far as he knows or is able to admit, his teachers, students and parents are happy. When the crisis hits, Marvin is stuck without clear models of what to do next. He only knows how to relate to his administrative group as "the dean" or "the master politician." He has never participated in the kinds of collaborative exercises that his bosses might now expect him to structure for his teachers; therefore, he doesn't even know what such data-based, problem-solving sessions might look like or sound like or produce. He has not observed how others in the town that he loves have helped similar populations of students to make progress; thus he has little to challenge his negative beliefs and build his conviction that his school, too, can make a difference.

Finally, Marvin's behavior threatens to throw the administrative group profile backward along the continuum from congenial to laissez-faire at just the point when all parties need a different, more powerful way to pool their mental energy and experience in service of student learning.

Ineffective Leader Responses

- Recognize that the principal's behavior is the result of stress, cut him some slack, and avoid making an issue of the lateness and administrative team attendance problems while he is under so much pressure. Such a stance is dangerous because (1) it sends a message that the unprofessional behavior is okay for some individuals; (2) it signals that meetings are unimportant or optional; (3) it suggests that those who do make every effort to be present and participating despite other issues in their lives are foolish; (4) it allows an individual who may be feeling anywhere from ill at ease to desperate to dig himself or herself into a deeper lonely hole instead of using a collegial group for ideas and support.

- Agree that the problem in one school has nothing to do with or little instructional value for other schools and should not be allowed to disrupt planned reports, updates, and other managerial items on monthly agendas. Taking a narrow view of either potential topics for district-wide leadership work or for district-wide administrative meetings squanders precious opportunities to train administrators on the processes, skills, strategies, and structures they need to be able to use with their own schools. Moreover, it assumes that each school is an island in competition with others for success and resources rather than part of a linked chain of people engaged in making certain all students in the district succeed.

- **Allow the principal to define the problem he needs to solve independently and to dictate the course of action to be taken without any interaction with colleagues.** When a principal has had years of freedom to dictate a course of action without producing results or solving persistent problems, then there is little reason to assume that further isolation or a laissez-faire approach will be the most appropriate way to get help for the school.

- **Assume that other members of the administrative group are too busy or too burdened or too ignorant of case specifics to be expected to participate in collaborative problem-solving about colleagues' challenges.** This kind of assumption, which leads to Laissez-Faire Communities, arises when those who are responsible for structuring the collaborative processes do not have the competence they need— or the conviction that professional groups are capable of learning from doing such work. It may also represent a failure of vision at the district level: that is, Central Office sees each school as an island and cannot, or does not choose to, identify common goals (e.g., raise standards and expectations for children of color, address poorly written responses to open-ended test questions, and deal with difficulties in content area reading) that transcend particular boundaries and are worth working on at all levels of a district.

- **Continue to tackle all controversial questions outside of regular administrative team meetings in order to maintain comfort and a sense of congeniality and support when the group is together.** When groups never see anyone wrestling with difficult problems, challenging assumptions honestly and respectfully, or confronting nonproductive outbursts or resistance with safety, they get a sense that dissent or questioning are to be suppressed or dealt with secretly so as not to "infect morale." Honest discussions lead people to say that the time has been well spent in hammering out new understandings; listening to reports of sanitized problem solving usually causes participants to assume that all outcomes are rigged and their input has little value, even if that is not the case.

- **Assume that the school faculty are in complete agreement with the principal's approach because there have been no complaints.** Communities that have treasured congeniality have developed a number of ways to deal with things that make them uncomfortable ranging from "say no evil" to "send subtle hints" and hope someone will astutely and willingly fix the problem. Thus they have little experience or impetus to surface "dirty laundry" and usually only do so when the circumstances get dire enough that an outsider asks probing questions.

- **Agree with the principal that everyone is working as hard as s/he can and that morale will be destroyed if existing practices are challenged or changes are introduced.** School or district leaders who have confused congeniality for collegiality often assume that one cannot discuss hard topics without breaking relationships. Such an assumption reveals their lack of models and inability to identify the skills and/or experiences they can draw upon. District leaders who place a premium on maintaining good relationships with all players but never explicitly explain how one goes about doing so without compromising standards for teaching and learning may send the wrong messages to school leaders.

Skillful Leader Responses

- **Focus administrative meetings on learning and teaching.** Devote substantive time on each agenda to a collegial analysis of a school-based student learning/performance problem. Make each building administrative team responsible for sharing the data they have gathered thus far and for recording the questions and suggestions of others. Push participants to question assumptions and ask for further data. Rotate presenters and save time for updates and quick consultations at subsequent sessions.

- **Use prompts and processing structures that allow administrators to identify common goals and common aspects of challenges; push back against statements that suggest individuals have nothing to learn from one another.** Superintendents, assistant superintendents and coordinators may find themselves trying to lead a "team" of administrators who have previously been managed through intimidation or through divide and conquer approaches that pit one leader against another. Those who have survived in such an environment in the past may be used to putting one another down, dismissing one another's perceptions, or masking any revelations of uncertainty or confusion. The new leader or facilitator's job is to privately (and publicly if need be) challenge such stances and to avoid planning activities that initially call up old bad habits.

- **Identify and change Central Office behaviors that are supporting the Laissez-Faire Community behaviors.** Openly discuss and come to some agreements re the tension between building autonomy and system needs. Find ways to check in on building leaders' perceptions and understandings and to clarify where and how ground rules have changed.

- **Make standards and expectations clear.** Check to determine whether past or present leadership behaviors are undermining or sending confusing messages about these expectations. Calmly clarify and restate expectations for behavior within the administrative team and in response to problems at the building level. Point out the gap between those expectations and Marvin's (or others') current behaviors.

- **Name the gap between present and desired community capacity at the school level for Marvin.** Surface data about the dampening effects of excessive attention to congeniality through observations of meetings, teacher to teacher and administrator to teacher interactions. Establish mutual purpose, i.e., that Marvin is able to maintain and honor those strong relationships while still asking his teachers to acquire new skills and competencies or to deal with some unaddressed discrepancies in expectations for students.

- **Get involved in modeling processes for goal setting and problem solving and in helping to name the gap between current and desired outcomes at the building level.** Assume Marvin does not know what to do and is most likely trying to force fit his current problems to a repertoire of outdated or ineffective solutions. Partner with him to co-plan and co-lead some problem-identification sessions or to introduce training at his school, or ask him to work with another colleague who has successfully taken such an approach. Put the goal in writing and evaluate it.

- **Resist scattershot approaches and demands that every deficit be addressed at once.** Help Marvin figure out where he could get the greatest amount of improvement the most quickly and help him to set and pursue short-term instructional goals with his teachers. Jointly identify what formative measures he can use to assess progress and meet regularly to look at what those measures are revealing.

Summary

Malfunctioning professional communities are groups whose interactions are what Perkins calls regressive. Their performance neither helps schools and school districts solve student learning problems nor increases organizational learning and capacity. In this chapter we consider three prototypes of malfunctioning professional groups: Toxic, Laissez-Faire, and Congenial Communities. Although they produce the same stalling effects, the reasons for their low performance and the strategies leaders must use to change that performance differ.

It is discouraging and frustrating to be part of a group that cannot function well. It is disheartening for a leader to recognize the gap between what a professional team might accomplish and what it is currently doing. The eight, short case studies that illustrate malfunctioning communities and the challenges they present for leaders are all composites drawn from the stories and experiences of real school districts. Each case is meant to be a work in progress rather than an exemplar of the best way to improve a low-performing group. We hope the ineffective and effective strategies that accompany each case will help skillful leaders:

- Reflect on the reasons for the behavior of low-performing groups in their own settings
- Evaluate alternative approaches to dealing with low-performing groups
- Anticipate missteps and avoid common practices that look promising but make the problem worse

Finally, we hope that describing noncollaborative situations and individuals will make teacher leaders, teachers, and building administrators feel less alone in their struggle to bring powerful collaboration to their own settings. Use the cases as a starting point for sharing your own insights and pooling your own intelligence in service of student learning.

The following chapter takes on a different kind of challenge. What happens when leaders face groups whose interactions are positive and productive but who have not yet evolved into fully Accountable Communities?

6 Moving Communities from Collaborative to Accountable

With skillful interventions from committed leaders, many malfunctioning groups can change over time. Adults can begin to engage in the kind of collaboration that is most likely to benefit student learning. Leaders can help teams build skill and conviction through action, analysis, reflection, and revision. In the real world of schools, however, improvement in adult interaction and problem solving may be uneven and vulnerable to disruption.

Under the relentless time demands of modern schooling, settling for "good enough" and backsliding to familiar survival patterns of interaction are ever-present dangers. Once immediate (and sometimes superficial) reforms have been carried out and some degree of success achieved, groups can easily settle into complacency. A school, team, or department's evolution from a Collaborative to a self-sustaining, Accountable Community is neither automatic nor inevitable.

Skillful leaders first face the challenge of helping teams and whole schools turn around and develop levels of collaboration that help children achieve. Then they face a second challenge of continuing their development to help them to reach accountable levels of interaction and performance. To achieve widespread improvement, we cannot simply remove conditions that undermine learning; we also need to create conditions that enable groups to challenge themselves, challenge the organization, and ultimately tear down barriers that have held some children back. This chapter is about continuing growth, getting beyond early improvement plateaus, and distributing competence. In it we suggest some of the strategies district and school leaders can use to:

- Maintain the steady press for excellence
- Reward, feed, and stretch the highest performing professional communities
- Create a self-renewing pool of teacher leadership that can sustain improvement over time

FIGURE 6.1   Strategies for pushing from Collaborative to Accountable Communities.

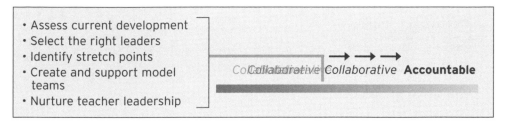

Figure 6.1 shows five broad categories of strategic effort that go into the press for excellence: assessing community development, selecting school leaders, creating model teams, identifying places to extend group competence (hereafter called stretch points), and selecting and nurturing teacher leadership—otherwise known as building a deep bench. Keep in mind that these categories are not meant to be a linear progression of steps or a hierarchy. We expect that each school or district may require a different starting point and a different mix of strategies. To put the strategies in a context, we'll consider how they apply to the case of Collegial Elementary.

Assessing Community Development

Using the community continuum shown in Figure 6.2, how would we characterize the district's highest functioning schools? How would we characterize a school's most effective communities? As we noted earlier, our experience suggests that the majority of so called teams or professional communities are really just loose associations of individuals who have the same job title or job assignment but most often function independently. Such purported communities cooperate on certain matters only as it suits their self-interest. They may or may not treat each other with respect. Some even collaborate on plans, materials, assessments, grouping, or scheduling. Only a few manage to challenge one another's thinking and practice to produce consistently higher quality instruction and learning in all of the classrooms of their members. Authentic Collaborative Communities are unusual; those that come close to our Accountable prototype are rare. Quickly contrasting these two types of professional communities will help us get a sense of the challenge skillful leaders face. (See also Chapter 3 "Professional Communities and Mediocre Learning.")

FIGURE 6.2   Communities that sustain learning.

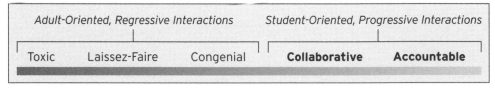

LEADER ALERT

Congeniality Does Not Guarantee Accountability   Leaders must first avoid complacency by assuming that smoothly operating congenial groups are functioning as genuinely collaborative professional communities. Second, leaders need to avoid the temptation to ignore teams that are functioning at the collaborative but not yet accountable level. This is equivalent to ignoring high-performing teachers who could improve even further.

The Collaborative Community

Whether the community is an entire school, a short-term task force, a middle school team, a high school department, a department subset such as all the teachers responsible for the 10th grade English program, or an elementary grade level group, Collaborative Communities generally focus their work on students. Together these communities exert effort and reinvest mental energy in their teaching. They have moved beyond simple compliance with administrative mandates; they use meetings productively to develop common units and assessments; they seek compromises and common ground around resources and directions; and they address problems with student learning. Individuals derive personal satisfaction as well as demonstrable student gains from the instructional improvements that their community helps them to bring about.

When they are at their best, Collaborative Communities can engage in substantive planning to help large numbers of students learn because they share common objectives and make a commitment to pursue those objectives. Groups that we are calling collaborative, however, may not yet have developed a finely tuned gauge that compels constant inquiry into what they can improve and enables them to monitor and adjust their own work *without outside prodding* or *facilitation*. This self-monitoring includes the difficult and rare behavior of confronting one another on instructional decision making that does not benefit students or certain subsets of students. On our proposed continuum (see Chapter 3), communities that most closely fit the collaborative designation are not yet functioning at a level where they can ensure that *all* students will have consistently higher level instruction.

In addition, these Collaborative Communities may not have the capacity to sustain themselves in the face of stability-threatening changes such as the loss of a key teacher leader or a key school leader who has guided, cheered, and protected them. They are more vulnerable to the inevitable forces that make working in groups difficult even in the best of circumstances: time constraints, difficulties in home and personal life that spill over into school work, minor personality conflicts that escalate when people are ill or tired, communication mix-ups, or resource shortages.

The Accountable Community

Members of Accountable Communities consistently value student learning and achievement over adult needs and preferences and over maintaining harmony. They take direct responsibility for their own actions to help students make progress and for "calling" team members on any behaviors and stances that are not helpful to students or to the functioning of the group. Accountable Communities impact the consistency and quality of member instruction more than teams functioning at other levels. Labeling a community as *accountable* means it has moved beyond merely working together well in service of students in general. Accountable Communities live a "no quarter, no excuses" existence where every choice a teacher makes is open to examination and revision when there are students who have not yet learned what they need to learn. Problem solving relies upon both the knowledge of the group and carefully gathered external expertise. Learning gaps (concepts not yet understood and skills not yet mastered) for both adults and students are addressed relentlessly.

Because of the emphasis on problem solving and the constant fine-tuning that goes on in Accountable Communities, the impact of their teaching on student learning is less random. Accountable Communities have reached a level of development that allows them to overcome the norms of autonomy and isolation that prevail in the teaching profession. Members routinely honor commitments to make improvements that their collaborative data analysis has identified as important. Although they have not entirely given up their autonomy, they accept and are proud of their ability to manage the tension between individualism and cooperation that is inevitable when adaptive changes are taking place. Bonded by this glue of common goals, common agreements, common assessment, and common students, these communities are responsible. They do not depend on external authorities to police them; they are able to connect their classroom work to larger organizational goals.

Just as Collaborative Communities do, Accountable Communities spend time tracking individual student performance and designing individual interventions. However, they also spend considerable time examining data to identify patterns of problems and needs for overall instructional improvement. They try to leverage their efforts to reach as many students as possible by looking for gaps in student achievement, setting short-term targets, and finding ways to re-teach concepts or stretch students' thinking. Regular, varied formative assessment is an essential part of all members' work; the results are public and are routinely critiqued. As a result, individuals are expected to give up cherished notions and activities, rethink assumptions, and push beyond personal fears and discomforts.

Having a theoretical frame for Collaborative versus Accountable Communities does not necessarily help us understand what might impel a leader to make changes once real collaboration is underway. Let's consider the case of Collegial Elementary at a turning point in its development.

CASE 6.1 **Is Collegial Elementary Stuck?**

Five years ago, Collegial Elementary was lagging behind other suburban schools with comparable populations and socioeconomic profiles. Its veteran principal had been marking time until retirement for at least the final 3 of his 20 years at Collegial. Student achievement and staff morale were low; a number of teachers described themselves as "just surviving" and as feeling as if they were running in place without genuinely improving student achievement. Wanting a strong, charismatic successor who would be able to turn the school around, Superintendent Bonnie Able chose Vance Hayes, then an idealistic, 35-year-old assistant principal from a nearby district.

Hayes went to work to invigorate Collegial and to reenergize some of the skilled but discouraged staff he found there. For three years in a row, he sent different cross-grade-level groups of teachers off to a summer conference with famous speakers who taught them about building professional learning communities. He introduced structures and processes for effective collaboration and rescheduled the building so that grade level teams had almost daily meeting time. Through skillful hiring to fill openings, he assembled a mix of veterans and newer teachers who regularly shared materials and strategies and played off one another's strengths. He formed a professional development committee, and together he and the teachers on the committee planned and contracted for training in both literacy and math. He volunteered Collegial as the meeting site for the district-wide math review team and salted the membership with his own teachers. They, in turn, became excited by and more confident about their ability to analyze data. To Vance's delight, they brought their newfound enthusiasm back to colleagues at Collegial.

By the fifth year of Vance's tenure, student results had improved dramatically in literacy across all grades and unevenly in math. Meeting agendas were planned so that focus on individual students was balanced with work on examining data. Two teams (2nd and 5th) had even started to develop and score common assessments. It seemed that when people talked about the school, they would talk mostly about the great 2nd and 5th grade teams; grade 4 had suffered from frequent staff turnover, and grade 6 had decided it needed to slow down and give its members more freedom. But Vance had to say he really had no "loser teams" as in the "bad old days." In fact Collegial had recently won a state award for improvement.

Professional communities at Collegial were looking good if somewhat uneven. However, the future is less certain. Is this a case of being stuck at collaborative? Will this school continue to improve? Or will effort and success begin to decline when standards are raised? Will more teams begin to resemble the 2nd and 5th grade ones, or will the latter two groups remain exceptional pockets of excellence in an otherwise capable school? Consider the growth-limiting indicators at Collegial Elementary.

CASE 6.1 **Collegial (continued)**

Collegial's initiatives revolved around its charismatic principal. He was at the center of almost everything. If teams had personnel concerns, they would ask Hayes, a consummate problem solver, to intervene. Instead of handling it within the team, the 3rd grade team leader asked the principal to speak to a newer teacher about putting down a veteran teacher with a sarcastic "Is that how you did it in the 70s?" Three members of the 6th grade team came to Hayes about a veteran member who continued to spend Friday afternoons on a social studies Trivial Pursuit® game despite a team agreement to reallocate limited learning time from fun activities to work more aligned with state-tested standards. The teacher kept insisting the kids needed time to unwind from the pressure of the week and prepare for the weekend; he rather rancorously told the team they could do what they wanted in their own classrooms but should not mind his business for him.

The high degree of satisfaction (laurel resting) expressed by the faculty despite the fact that Collegial had nearly missed AYP (Adequate Yearly Progress) for African-American and special education subgroups was more worrisome. If aggregate data were used to measure academic success, the school showed marked improvement. Disaggregating the results, however, showed that not all groups were making marked progress, particularly in math where performance had declined slightly in 3rd, 4th, and 6th grades. Faculty seemed to have lost their sense of urgency even though Central Office had warned Hayes that the state was likely to raise its minimum passing scores for math in the following year. As teachers tired of the intense effort and began to worry about how hard it would be to reach the groups who were not yet successful, cracks in the "ability of everyone to learn belief"—always present but rarely addressed directly—were beginning to show.

Around school, the talk was changing. For example, Principal Hayes had begun to worry aloud about having "realistic expectations." When the superintendent visited, he warned her that "we can't expect every team to be like 2nd and 5th—those are unique situations" in earshot of several 5th grade teachers. The facts pointing to poor math performance overall and subgroup performance particularly did not seem to motivate anyone at Collegial. Instead, Superintendent Abel heard excuses like "We're doing the best we can" (implied "with what we have") or "What can you expect when there is absolutely no support at home?" The 4th grade team found itself polarized between those who thought that the group needed to make some significant changes in its practice of sorting and tracking children for math at the beginning of the year and those who liked the existing model. Because they could not agree on whether all children should be able to meet the proposed benchmarks, they had stopped discussing and pooling items for a common assessment and agreed to continue testing in their own ways in their own classrooms. Meanwhile, 6th grade had forestalled its own battles by agreeing to concentrate on the average students and ignore the really low performers. Interestingly, none of these comments were heard from the 2nd and 5th grade teams; they reinvested themselves in trying to collect and analyze data about what was interfering with the learning of the lowest performing groups. In particular, Mary Modest, the 5th grade team leader was speaking out about "defeatist" attitudes among some colleagues.

Poised as it is at a sort of improvement crossroads, Collegial Elementary represents a challenge for both district and building level leaders. How can improvement be sustained after the first flush of success?

Selecting the Right Administrative Leader

What kind of building level leadership does it take to move from collegial to accountable? Consider the district level dilemma when the superintendent contemplates an improving school that has stalled or is beginning to slide backward. One explanation may be the unintended consequences of the initial fix-it strategy: hiring the strong leader who sees it as his or her role to stand in the forefront of all improvement efforts. Faced with a school that has performed poorly over several years, school boards and superintendents know they have to make dramatic changes. They believe they need—and frequently seek—powerful, take-charge, turnaround leaders. Often these chosen leaders are charismatic individuals with strong wills. Usually good communicators, they are able either to unite people around a vision of better learning for students or induce them to leave and practice elsewhere. They take responsibility for diagnosing the problems and create the structures and processes to force teacher interaction around the goals they have set. Successful turnaround leaders can get quick visible results, considerable praise, and, whether deservedly or not, the lion's share of credit for the outcomes. In the districts we have visited, however, we have noticed that turnaround leaders thrive on the challenge of change and are less likely to enjoy solving the problems of sustained implementation. Many choose to move on to another challenge in three to five years. The problem comes when they leave a school without sufficient distributed capacity to continue improvement. If faculties perceive that the will and wherewithal for change reside primarily with a principal, assistant principal, or beloved curriculum director, school productivity and the sense of urgency generated by past efforts can decline almost immediately with the departure of that individual. Student achievement dips often follow. District administrators are in a bind because good schools can turn mediocre in a hurry.

The superintendent's dilemma does not go away if the principal stays beyond the first few years of change. Both the district leaders and the principal must understand that the skill set needed to turn around a school in the first few years is not the same skill set needed to sustain constant improvement. The work gets more difficult in the face of escalating demands from shifting federal and state performance requirements, increased state scrutiny, funding limitations, demographic changes, or the vagaries of local politics. As a result, the quick success that motivates teachers in early stages of reform diminishes when progress is measured in smaller increments. Can Collegial Elementary, a good school and our prototypical Collaborative Community, face additional challenge and maintain its momentum? We think part of the answer hinges on the principal's skill in distributing leadership in order to create high-functioning, accountable teams at all grade levels—not just at the two that have managed to push their own practice forward. Vance Hayes may not be the right leader.

Let us examine the characteristics of administrative leaders, especially principals, who can build Accountable Communities. We are indebted to Jim Collins for giving us permission to apply his "Good to Great" leadership concept developed in *Good to Great: Why Some Companies Make the Leap…and Others Don't* (2001) to our construct of describing leaders who move school communities from Collaborative ("good") to Accountable ("great"). He describes the characteristics of CEO's who led their companies through the transition from "good to great" performance. He calls these architects of greatness "Level 5 leaders" and contrasts them with the "Level 4 effective leaders" of companies with "good" track records.[1] Almost all these "good" companies had leaders with large egos, many were household names (e.g., Iacocca). However, Level 5 leaders of companies that had made the transition from "good to great" were largely unknown outside their companies. These individuals were notably modest, very ambitious for their company, and ferociously focused on an "incurable need to achieve sustained results" (Collins 2001 39). Collins modified his Level 5 leader characteristics only slightly for the nonprofit world—which would certainly include schools. Level 5 leaders in those sectors, he noted, work more through "legislative power" than "executive power."

> In executive leadership, the individual leader has enough concentrated power to simply make the right decisions. In legislative leadership, on the other hand, no individual leader—not even the nominal chief executive—has enough structural power to make the important decisions by himself or herself. Legislative leadership relies more on persuasion, political currency, and shared interests to create the conditions for the right decision to happen. (Collins 2005 11)

[1] Curious readers may wonder about Collins' Levels 1 to 3. He labels Level 1 as a "highly capable individual" who makes productive contributions; Level 2 is a "contributing team member" who works toward the achievement of group objectives; Level 3 is a "competent manager" who organizes people and resources toward an objective.

We believe that leaders, especially principals, who are able to create accountable school communities closely resemble Collins's Level 5 social sector leaders. They *create the conditions for the right decisions to happen* by building capacity for ongoing development. Unlike Principal Hayes, they give up the need to be at the center of the work. We name this version of Collins's "Level 5 leaders," *Capacity-Building Leaders.* They are able to skillfully build the "3 C's"—Competence, Conviction, and Control—introduced in Chapter 3 and developed further in Chapters 4 and 5. In contrast we call Collins's "Level 4 Leaders" *Transition Leaders* because they are effective at changing interaction patterns from regressive to progressive and in harnessing energy of people to engage in important work on behalf of kids. However, their effort and success may not outlast their tenure. Consider the difference between these two types of leaders.

- **Transition Leaders provide the energy for change and motivate people through strong personalities.** Vance Hayes was such a leader and was able to turn the school around by being at the center of the action. He did not, however, evolve into one of the Capacity-Building Leaders who, like Collins's Level 5 leaders, "embody a paradoxical mix of personal humility and professional will. They are ambitious, to be sure, but ambitious first and foremost for the company, not themselves"(Collins 2001 39). The very qualities that make a school turnaround leader so appealing may be those that inhibit a school or district's evolution into a community that can monitor and sustain its own development. Members of the community never learn to do what the leader does. Ask the principal and teachers in an improving school who is most responsible for the improvement and calculate the "we:I ratio." Capacity-Building Leaders who nurture Accountable Communities will genuinely and accurately attribute most of the success to the staff. The "we's" win out. In schools that might be described as collaborative, some credit will also be passed along; however, the widespread stance is often "We would be nowhere if Mr. Savior hadn't come along." Transition Leaders may nourish leader dependency rather than self-sufficiency.

- **Transition Leaders may create conditions that result in successor failure; Capacity-Building Leaders prepare the way for the next leader to succeed.**[2] When Transition Leaders depart, the changeover is often difficult; those who stay behind have learned to depend heavily on a single individual and do not see themselves as capable of filling the void. The "big shoes to fill" label attached to the departing leader is often as much about personality as it is better learning for students. Because they see themselves, and often are, at the center of all change efforts, these leaders rarely think about or provide a transition designed to help the school, team, or organization function well in pursuit of a goal once they are no longer directing the action. When the center is removed, there is no bench full of leaders in waiting.

[2]Based on Collins' idea that "Level 5 leaders set up their successors for even greater success in the next generation whereas egocentric Level 4 leaders often set up their successors for failure" (Collins 2001 41).

Successors often experience either a backlash of regret or inexplicable resistance provoked by the anxiety that results from the radical change. In contrast, Capacity-Building Leaders rarely think of or portray themselves as indispensable. They make developing internal capacity by creating a cadre of individuals who are well prepared, well coached, and experienced at sustaining improvement efforts—a key part of their mission. These leaders tell us they define their own success by the fact that their leaving creates only a small ripple in the productive work of the organization.

- **Transition Leaders may have more expansive personalities than modest Capacity Builders and thus excel at interviews.** Transition Leaders may be better at jump starting change and may in fact be the leader of choice for the first round of school improvement. But after an initial turn around, the challenge should quickly shift to capacity building to sustain the change. The skill set required to release more responsibility to others may be incompatible with the personality of the turnaround stars. In addition, after a year or two, these turnaround specialists often get quick promotions to Central Office or to another troubled school. School boards hiring superintendents, superintendents hiring principals, and principals themselves need to anticipate the changing demands of leadership and build these into search processes.

- **Transition Leaders are comfortable operating in a traditional, hierarchical context; Capacity-Building Leaders seek genuine distribution of power.** Leaders operating from a bureaucratic notion of schools with traditional lines of authority demonstrate an unwillingness to share power. Murphy notes the implications for principals who seek to distribute authority: "principals who want to cultivate distributed patterns of leadership in their schools must learn to think about power differently and must be willing to share the playing field with a wider set of colleagues (134). We will return to the value of distributed influence and power when we consider our fourth strategy: finding and supporting good teacher leaders. In the meantime, let's examine how these implications play themselves out in the case of Collegial Elementary.

CASE 6.1 **Collegial Elementary II: Who should lead Phase 2 Improvement Efforts at Collegial?**

Superintendent Bonnie Able had clearly selected a Transition Leader for Collegial Elementary, perhaps correctly. Initially, the community was mired in discouragement and inactivity, and she needed a take-charge individual with a forceful personality. Vance Hayes made changes and got results. However, Superintendent Able had noted Vance's growing frustration and the shift in his level of commitment to his most difficult-to-reach students. She had also read the signs that some teams were beginning to fray at the edges under the pressure to scrutinize cherished practices and long-held beliefs about who could learn.

Superintendent Abel decided to have a frank supervisory meeting with Vance. She thanked him for his work and said "You know, Vance, when I hired you, you were the right person for the challenge. You have done everything the district has asked and more. You love the limelight and have a style that has worked well these last five years. People count on and look up to you; they think they cannot do without you and thus they aren't moving forward to take adequate responsibility for their own roles in helping Collegial close the achievement gap. You have many years of your career ahead of you— and I suspect other goals you would like to pursue. I don't want to see Collegial left rudderless when you decide you are ready to move on. As we think about Collegial's next five years, we need to focus on developing other leaders at Collegial, on distributing more responsibility and accountability, and on coaching people to be more independent and resourceful. It's going to require you to shift styles, share influence and authority—probably move into the background and let others shine. I want you to think about whether this is a match for you and whether this is a capacity you want to build in yourself or whether it simply isn't very appealing. Here are two other possibilities to consider: Murdock Middle, as you know from our administrative meetings, is in bad shape. And yesterday Bill R. from Centerville called me to see if I had any names of people who might help him with an elementary school that is about to be put on warning. I want you to think about what would be the best match for you."

Vance took a few days and came back with "Bonnie I think you're right. I may have moved the school as far I can. It is not as much fun with the AYP vise. It is just harder making progress, people are beginning to get on my nerves, and perhaps I am showing signs of burning out. I do need a change." So Collegial Elementary suddenly faced the challenge of new leadership. As Bonnie prepared her search process and committee, she decided to add interview questions that might help the district find the capacity-building leadership Collegial needed to move forward and help all its grade level teams become Accountable Communities.

Screening Candidates

How do we determine whether an individual thinks and behaves like a Capacity-Building Leader? An individual's track record and the stories others tell about his or her ability to mobilize people for effective collaboration are obviously important. We also recommend designing some of the interview questions used to screen and select leaders by working backward from the capacities of Accountable Communities: Conviction, Competence, and Control (see Chapter 3). For example, the following interview question checks a candidate's conviction about shared ownership of and responsibility for results.

What does the term accountability mean to you? How does it affect what you would do in a school?

Transition Leaders will talk about their own accountability for student results and the ways in which they should be held responsible for orchestrating change. They will speak about individual accountability of teachers. They might even talk about including student outcomes as part of teacher performance.

Capacity-Building Leaders will be very clear about the comprehensive meaning of accountability. They focus accountability on what Reeves (2004) calls effect variables, such as test scores, but also the cause variables such as extra help attendance, student resubmission of work after feedback, and homework completion rates. Capacity-Building Leaders will define accountability as including the importance of measures to keep track of targeted initiatives and the development of common assessments and benchmarks (Reeves 2004 50-55).

The next question probes a candidate's competence in building others' problem-solving and decision-making skills.

How do you balance the need to make quick decisions with the need to involve people in those decisions?

The Transition Leader will (perhaps appropriately) emphasize the need to take charge, especially in the early phases of improvement, to make quick structural changes to fix problems s/he has identified, and to communicate clearly his or her vision. Stories or examples of prior experience in helping schools improve may involve frequent use of the first person pronoun to identify how improvement is carried out ("I got everybody together and set some goals. In the second year, I wanted to make sure . . ."). Since interviewers often ask candidates to recount examples of how they have helped to bring about change, the use of the word I is not, by itself, an indicator of a Transition Leader. Rather it is the absence of a balance of attributions (i.e., credit given to other players and efforts of key staff members noted) that signals whether this individual puts an emphasis on developing internal capacity.

Capacity-Building Leaders' responses will include strategies for identifying key teacher allies, recognizing and developing the talents of various staff members, and creating high-functioning teams. They will talk about training leaders. They may talk about understanding that they cannot "go it alone" and the importance of developing ownership among constituents. If these individuals have had considerable prior experience in helping schools, they may modestly assign credit to the caliber of the faculty or to the district leadership in their prior location. The pronoun "we" will be prevalent.

Finally, it can be useful to query candidates' understanding of decision-making models and sources of authority for decision. Both types of leaders should be able to explain how they determine when decisions must or should be made by:

- Someone outside of their school (e.g., above them in the organizational hierarchy)
- An administrator unilaterally
- An administrator with input from staff
- An administrator and staff by consensus
- Staff with input from administrator
- Staff by consensus
- Staff by vote (Saphier et al. 1989)

We would expect Capacity-Building Leaders to be particularly astute at knowing when and how to share decision-making opportunities and responsibilities with staff and to be able to evaluate the advantages and disadvantages of doing so in particular situations.

Please discuss how and when you would develop leadership for resolving difficult student learning and performance problems within your school.

Transition Leaders may talk generally about decentralization, creating teams, and involving people in the work and should be fairly concrete about the kinds of tasks that the various communities within the school might undertake. They will be passionate about what needs to be done and about their vision for the school but may be less articulate about creating buy-in and ownership. We would expect them to be less concrete about how they would build skills or about strategies such as adopting or creating experiences in using a common problem-solving model. They may talk vaguely about "turning over the work" but will not know how to orchestrate that.

Capacity-Building Leaders are very articulate about the need to adopt processes and norms to support the development of collective problem solving. They are precise about how they will use professional development to help groups "get smarter." This includes how to give teams of teachers the skills to handle most of their own problems. (See Chapter 4 "Community 101: Setting the Stage" for more detail on structures and processes.)

The next two questions check a candidate's competence in taking on tough challenges.

How do you handle disappointing or negative information about student performance?

When Transition Leaders talk about what they think they need to do when the news about school performance is bad, they may discuss their responsibilities as cheerleaders or the importance of finding explanations and mitigating factors. Sometimes the implication is that bad news may be deemphasized. They may also convey their belief in the importance of praising staff and keeping morale up. Some offer variations on telling the faculty "the buck stops with me" or "I hold myself responsible for getting us out of this."

Capacity-Building Leaders talk about the importance of sharing bad news honestly and without blame, but they also make a point of needing the school to face and acknowledge the patterns revealed by performance data in order to find solutions.

How do you respond to staff conflicts or difficult interactions about goals, programs, instructional strategies, or student opportunities to learn?

If they consider that their job is to "clean up messes" and mobilize schools whose cultures have been rife with argument and discontent, Transition Leaders will sometimes downplay or undervalue the role of healthy conflict in solving difficult problems. Understandably, they may describe their job as "seeing that we get along well and are all on the same page." Depending on whether their entire experience has been putting out fires, some may be unable to provide an example where living through healthy debate or soliciting and paying attention to conflicting viewpoints actually resulted in a better solution to a problem than might have occurred if the conflict were suppressed.

Capacity-Building Leaders can clearly articulate the importance of sharing good and bad news without blame and the importance of controlled conflict. We would expect these leaders to be able to discuss the ways in which they make room for conflict over means and methods and the kinds of processes they puts in place to ensure respectful consideration of multiple viewpoints.

The next interview question checks competence in sustaining transparency.

We hear a great deal about the importance of the transparency of the process of school improvement. What does this mean to you?

Transition Leaders will talk about openness—the need to have clear lines of communication and open door availability. They will emphasize the need for honest, open communication. They will omit the nuances of transparency.

Capacity-Building Leaders will speak of transparency in similar ways but add their belief in making their own practice transparent and open to feed back and scrutiny. Furthermore, they will highlight the importance of sharing data—not only data that reveal successes but also the patterns of failures to date. They will acknowledge their own mistakes, model how to monitor and adjust leadership practice using feedback, and embody in their behavior a relentless drive for excellence. One of our leaders interviewed referred to the notion of transparency as making her school as much as possible like a house of glass with no secrets and total accountability.

The next two questions check on leaders' competence in establishing and honoring norms.

What are some of the specific ways in which you establish norms for teams and teacher leaders to be held accountable for their work?

Transition Leaders will likely talk about themselves and possibly how they might model accountability or communicate norms. Capacity-Building Leaders, however, will specify how they monitor the work of teams and teacher leaders, how they provide feedback to teams and teacher leaders, what specific standards they set in place for consistency in performance across teams, and which criteria they used to evaluate team and teacher leader success.

In teams you have led in the past, can you explain how norms were established and how the team enforced these norms?

Transition Leaders will be able to talk about development of procedural norms (see *Norm Handbook* www.ready-about.com) and perhaps some modest monitoring techniques. They will not articulate how they developed leadership through roles and norms that kept agendas focused on learning or through norms that developed participant leadership.

Capacity-Building Leaders will be very clear that they focus effort on developing individual teachers and on their Leadership Teams. Whether they use the term *norms* to describe getting clear about how the school does business or not, their answers will indicate that they emphasize distributing leadership responsibility. They can also articulate how they use norms to shape conversations about student learning.

The last sample interview question checks candidates' understanding of how to use key systems.

What professional development opportunities do you see as critical to sustaining school improvement?

Transition Leaders will be likely to point to pedagogical, curricular, and content training that supports targeted school improvement areas (e.g., literacy, math scores). They may also point to training in protocols that they have introduced—or might introduce—to facilitate teacher collaboration (e.g., critical friends' groups, looking at student work). The scope and purpose of such training are often limited and directly targeted to current school improvement goals rather than future capacity.

Capacity-Building Leaders will share much that the Transition Leader has articulated but will also reference capacity-building training that seeks to continue moving the school forward toward higher levels of autonomy and accountability. We would expect these leaders to talk about a combination of formal training, opportunities for stretch and practice, and informal coaching that nurtures and develops teacher leaders.

CASE 6.1 **Picking the Phase 2 Leader for Collegial**

Superintendent Abel appointed a search committee to replace Vance. Trying not to bias them too much, she oriented them to Collegial's strengths, the challenges the school faced, and the differences between Transition and Capacity-Building Leaders. Surprisingly to some outside the process, the successful candidate came from inside the school. Mary Modest was made principal. She was the leader of the celebrated 5th grade team that had exhibited many characteristics of an Accountable Community. Mary had only applied for the job at the urging of teacher members of the committee.

Superintendent Able knew that by selecting a respected internal candidate, she could minimize the morale drop associated with the

departure of a charismatic leader. She promised Mary that she expected excellent outcomes at all grade levels and that she would support
Mary as she tried to move the good school to a higher level of performance. To help Mary identify where she might begin to take
action, Dr. Able raised several points to consider in moving groups
from collaborative to accountable and asked Mary to come back in a
week to begin planning her entry.

Identifying Stretch Points

LEADER ALERT ───────────────────────────────────

Beware of Promises to Maintain a School as It Is   Selection
processes always include debating the relative benefits of inside versus outside candidates. Especially when they are replacing an
administrator with a charismatic personality, superintendents and
search committees should always scan internally for quiet but
extremely effective teacher leader candidates. Although the goal
may be to ensure a less bumpy transition, do not fall for the candidate who offers the promise of stability and, in effect, signals that
s/he has no intention of rocking the boat or making demands.
Capacity Building Leaders are not peacemakers nor are they complacent or prone to pacifying slightly anxious communities. Instead
they offer the promise of someone who can quietly and systematically push to overcome performance problems by helping others
become more effective.

What are some useful starting points for helping groups grow? Closing gaps
in student or teacher performance and pushing colleagues to seek excellence
is the business of skillful leaders. With so many demands, how do you determine where to invest energy and effort to help groups that look healthy on
the surface? In the next section, we suggest several points for determining
whether a stretch is needed and strategies to help work groups become more
focused on student learning and more efficient and effective in their interactions with one another.

Examine Attitudes toward Standards and Feedback

One of the dividing lines between Accountable and Collaborative Communities occurs when some individuals choose not to implement policies and practices or to settle for a lower level of student achievement. Members of a Collaborative Community have learned to work together quite effectively to help large numbers of students in their care reach high minimum performance standards. They employ a variety of rubrics, benchmarks, exemplars, and self-assessment tools to help their students get a clear picture of what "doing excellent work" looks and sounds like and to guide the feedback they give students. Such collaboration is usually satisfying for the participants as long as all members of the group or team abide by the agreements and offer similarly excellent instruction. Stress and confusion result when not everyone in the group is willing or able to carry out agreed-upon instructional changes. Then group members must choose between protecting the good feelings associated with effective collaboration by "looking the other way" or testing the bonds by asking colleagues to make changes. Using professional standards as a reference point can help depersonalize the request; professional standards require everyone in the school to use data to monitor learning and adjust instruction or to provide alternatives to paper and pencil measurement. The push for change is not an attack on one individual by another.

In general, we find that collaborative group members do not always see that adults must be held accountable for meeting demanding professional standards. As a result, they may not be comfortable giving feedback to peers who fail to live up to agreements. Learning how to give standards-based feedback, studying what the adult performance standards are and how one recognizes them in action, or practicing in small doses with new programs where no one is an expert can help build both conviction about the value of such a practice and competence in providing meaningful information in appropriate ways.

STRATEGIES TO HELP COMMUNITIES EVOLVE

- Model asking for feedback on accomplishment of one of your leadership goals.

- Conduct the first rounds of training on giving nonjudgmental, standards-based feedback with individuals whose roles would logically benefit from the skill, e.g., mentors, instructional specialists, people in co-teaching situations, teachers who are working with paraprofessionals in inclusion classrooms, or faculty who expect to have student teachers in a coming year.

- Ask members, either in a silent survey or perhaps an open discussion, what positive experiences and practice they have had with giving and getting specific feedback about current performance in relation to a desired target either inside or outside of school (e.g. in music lessons, in sports, in arts and crafts, in performances). Analyze the nature of the feedback, its results, and how teams might use a similar approach in their instructional efforts.

- Invite teams to brainstorm strategies for monitoring how well they hold each other accountable for individual contributions.

LEADER ALERT ─────────────────────────────────────

Using Data from Team Assessments   If teams are to engage in genuine self-assessment, leaders must establish an environment of trust and safety. With rare exceptions (see Chapter 8), data from team assessments of their own performance should not be included in performance evaluations. The information from such self-monitoring, however, can be used in a conference to further illustrate a pattern of problems the supervisor has already documented in other ways.

Assess How New Members Are Oriented and Supported

Members of a Collaborative Community will orient and support new members about procedures, programs, and key initiatives. They may not realize that they need to be explicit about the group's attributes and norms in relation to student learning so that there are no secrets about how questions will be considered and decisions made. As a result, new members may not fully internalize the sense of responsibility that causes Accountable Community members to demand improvement in their own and others' performance.

STRATEGIES TO HELP COMMUNITIES EVOLVE

- Meet with new teachers as a group to explicitly communicate what you value and how you define high-performing communities.

- Insist on and praise strong participation in each team. Make sure new faculty know they need not wait until they have paid some apocryphal dues before they begin to ask questions and contribute.

- Identify a team mentor to update new members on context and background and team expectations.

Check How Groups Spend Time

Determine whether groups are spending the majority of their time on the "right work," i.e., on work designed to maximize student learning (Marzano 2005). Because collaborative groups want to be inclusive, participatory, and able to influence the conditions under which they do their work, they run the risk of spending hours on what we might call "nuts and bolts" issues. If they spend too much of their time focused on modifying materials for one or two students; dealing with behavior, scheduling, or grouping challenges; or getting ready to meet with parents, they cannot focus on changes in their joint practice that might make what they do more effective. Over time, if everything is grist for the collaborative mill, they run the risk of burning themselves out.

Groups whose interactions either closely match or approach the Accountable Community profile have learned how to focus their efforts on looking at the data they have collected, on determining together what is getting in the way of student comprehension or skill mastery, and on deciding through debate and experimentation what they will have to add or change and what they may have to give up. It is important to note that accountable groups have to spend time on basic issues of implementation once they have decided they need to make a particular change. They may work together to find time for re-teaching concepts or to identify questions for an alternative assessment of students' skills. To determine whether time is being spent in the right way, it is important to look at the underlying reasons that each item is on the agenda and consuming attention and at the student learning goals that will be addressed by the investment of collaborative time.

STRATEGIES TO HELP COMMUNITIES EVOLVE

- Use the Leadership Teams (LT's) as a model for how to allocate time in service of student learning. Jointly determine how any item getting significant agenda time will positively affect student learning; then cut out or reduce agenda items that do not meet that criteria. (See later section in this chapter on "Building an Accountable Leadership Team.")

- Have teams submit agendas and minutes to identify patterns of time use and the team's ability to focus on student learning. Give feedback to the teams on time expenditure and invite problem solving around time reallocation.

- With the team, schedule meetings that clearly differentiate time spent on individual student discussion, time spent on management basics, and time spent on modifying instructional practice to address student performance issues.

Check if Weaker Members Are Challenged

Determine whether some groups have members who are not carrying their fair share or who are not yet able to meet the standards set by the group. Find out the ways in which all groups deal with their least capable or least motivated members. Collaborative Communities depend on the competence and good will of their members. As a result, they can be threatened or undone by the need to cover up for, confront, or compensate for a weaker member. Most Collaborative Communities rely on outside authority, generally school or district administration, to enforce norms and practices. Watch for two early warnings of dysfunction that can threaten the effectiveness of Collaborative Communities: the avoidance of accountability, defined by

Lencioni (2002) as a hesitation or unwillingness to "call peers on actions and behaviors that seem counterproductive to the good of the team" and what Lencioni terms "inattention to results." This inattention occurs when individual members put their own classes, subjects, subgroups, or personal needs ahead of team goals for student results. When they preserve the façade of working in harmony rather than challenging one another's teaching practices or when they believe that questioning one another's ineffective choices will threaten the well-being of the group, Collaborative Communities undermine their own effectiveness.

STRATEGIES TO HELP COMMUNITIES EVOLVE

- Offer professional development to build group competence in confronting the performance of a colleague in an open and honest manner (see Chapter 4 "Community Building 101").

- Consider using 360 feedback (Manatt 97).[3]

- Invite teams to self-assess their functioning in light of Lencioni's "dysfunctions." If appropriate, set goals.

Check the Kinds of Data the Community Uses

Examine the kinds of data the community regularly collects and uses to shape instruction. Old habits, such as the right to privacy and the right to shift the target midway through a unit, persist and are manifest in the early stages of a Collaborative Community's development. Team members may not know how to design simple measures for formative assessment; members may have spent years looking at end-of-year or end-of-unit data only (if they used such data to shape instruction at all) and/or collecting check-in data about how students are doing. Collaborative Communities may expend their early energies on the activities associated with instruction (e.g., designing projects, materials, and lessons) and forget that they need to select a means of assessment and to do regular data collection. As a result, teachers will not develop the kind of internal accountability for student growth that ultimately prepares them to respond productively to external measures (Elmore 2000).

---

[3]360-degree feedback refers to performance evaluation where personnel receive structured feedback from peers, supervisors, parents, students, and subordinates. In *The Skillful Leader: Confronting Mediocre Teaching* (2000), we quoted then-superintendent of the Danvers Massachusetts Public Schools, Richard Santeusanio as saying about 360-degree feedback "I think this process has helped administrators and teachers come up with better action plans, which presumably improves teaching. It is still too early to tell," In a follow-up conversation in 2006, Superintendent Lisa Dana commented on "360" as having some reliability problems—especially in peer rating. When asked about the impact on achievement, *"Can't say (re 360 feedback)... but critical friends groups have helped, especially at the Middle School."* Our recommendation is that time be spent on protocols (see Chapter 4 "Community 101") that build collaboration rather than on complicated data collection structures such as 360. That does not mean that it could not be instituted in a particular context.

STRATEGIES TO HELP COMMUNITIES EVOLVE

- Ask teams to develop formal and informal data sources that they could use to document their internally identified priorities. Structure analysis and problem-identification meetings around their data.

- Adopt protocols that demand data be collected in order to define problems. (See Chapter 4 "Community Building 101" and Chapter 8 "Data Sources.")

Check for Belief in Excellence for All

Watch for indicators of widespread belief in effort-based achievement and in excellence for all—with no excuses for student failure.[4] Communities teetering between being Collaborative and Accountable often say that they believe in the notion that students can get smarter but don't take responsibility for pushing students' performance beyond its initial poor level. Individuals in Collaborative Communities may balk at the work required by limiting options to A, B or "not yet meeting standard" as possible responses to student work. They may induce others to back off that stance. Under the stress of challenging old assumptions and breaking new ground, members of Collaborative Communities may revert to well-used external explanations (e.g., socioeconomic background, race, gender, or innate ability) for student failure.

STRATEGIES TO HELP COMMUNITIES EVOLVE

- Establish school-wide rewards for effort and excellence.

- Initiate a grading policy discussion that focuses on second chances. Confront groups with the research about the effect of commonly accepted practices such as averaging zeros into quarterly grades.

- Convene faculty study groups using books such as *Effort and Excellence in Urban Classrooms* (Corbett et al.) or *Bouncing Back* (Patterson et al.).

- Communicate your beliefs about effort and excellence.

- Interview students to determine what most gets in the way of their completing assignments and doing work at high levels and what most helps them to complete their work.

Check Which Goals Are Applied in the Classroom

Determine whose instructional goals and priorities are governing what happens in the classroom. Unlike communities that we describe as accountable, Collaborative Communities can engage in a fair amount of teamwork that is never applied in the classrooms and practices of members. Insights, materials, new ways of assessing, commitments to re-teach concepts or to provide certain kinds of focused practice and reinforcement may be implemented

[4]Corbett et al (2002) found that "two words separated the resilient [school] from those that are not resilient: 'no excuses.'"

only selectively. If that is the case, student experiences and opportunities to learn will still vary significantly from class to class, undermining the potential value of the collaboration. Elmore (2005) also points out that collaborative teams may be so focused on their own agendas and so comfortable working independently that they do not acknowledge shared school goals.

STRATEGIES TO HELP COMMUNITIES EVOLVE

- Clearly identify school-wide instructional improvement goals, establish criteria for implementing instructional and program changes, and ask teams to collect and analyze their own data on implementation, e.g., how many practice sessions on responding to open-ended questions students have completed, the caliber of the work produced during those sessions, the issues that are still a problem in most recent samples.

- Establish clear systems for getting feedback on implementation back to communities through the members of the Instructional Leadership Team.

- Involve the Instructional Leadership Team in identifying and communicating guidelines to help teams determine which problems they can solve independently of the ILT and administration and which require them to consult with or refer the problem to others.

- Brainstorm with groups "What problems do you anticipate occurring in your group?" Create a "T Chart" with problems identified and possible group solutions. Discussion should include in what circumstances they should seek help.

CASE 6.1 **Identifying the Stretch Points for Collegial's Teams**

Principal Mary Modest developed an entry plan that involved using several indicators to help her distinguish the collaborative teams in the school from the Accountable ones. She knew that she needed to get all of the professional communities working on math improvement if the school was to have a shot at helping some of its most vulnerable students. She also knew that only the 2nd and 5th grade teams had made significant changes in the way that students were assessed and taught while the other grade level groups had "agreed to disagree" rather than face some of the hard questions about what their members were accomplishing. In fact the 6th grade had spent a great deal of time and energy dodging hard questions about changes in math instruction.

Mary decided that if she created a high-functioning School Leadership Team (LT) to structure and spur the math initiative, it would boost ownership within the school and could be a model for what she hoped would happen at each grade level. She felt it was neither fair to students nor good for the school to tolerate isolated pockets of excellence when that excellence could be spread. She knew that stalled teams would not be able to move from "good to great" unless they confronted some hard truths about what their present instruction was missing. Mary was now part of Bonnie Able's Instructional Cabinet. It presented a potential model she could examine for effectiveness.

Creating Model Teams

What exemplars are available to faculty? If none are available, how do we create and monitor them? Developing excellent schools requires examining the alignment of efforts to improve learning, not only horizontally at the school level, but vertically throughout the district. When the organization needs mental energy and intelligence to be pooled in order for it to function as intelligently and efficiently as possible, working groups at each level—the superintendent's Leadership Team, the principal's Leadership Team, and the teacher teams—must serve as strong, effective models for others. Only if the district's or school's Leadership Team interactions are progressive can principals or superintendents reasonably expect *all* teacher teams to evolve into accountable ones.

The principle of vertical alignment says that leaders can learn from their own experience as a member of a progressive professional community. Thoughtful principals practice certain behaviors and take away strategies from what they see in the superintendent's instructional cabinet or at the assistant superintendent's task force and curriculum team meetings; teachers learn the possibilities and behaviors of powerful professional collaboration from their participation on school-based Leadership Teams (LT's) and in district-based problem-solving and planning groups. In many instances, that knowledge of how groups function to make everyone smarter finds its way into the classroom as well.

Attenuation of Implementation

Change loses strength the further it is from the initiating source. Listen to this lament from a superintendent trying to implement district instructional change with his Instructional Cabinet.

> We have agreed to focus on writing across the curriculum at all grade levels. It has been my assumption that all of you have been working with your teachers so that this focused initiative reaches every classroom. In the last few weeks Margaret (the assistant superintendent) and I have conducted some implementation checks in over 50 classrooms. We estimate that only 30 percent of the teachers are working for quality implementation—the rest are complying superficially, and at least 15 teachers are ignoring it entirely. What's going on here?

The further a change gets from the site of initiation, the weaker the implementation. Establishing effective teams that support classroom level change so powerful and significant that students feel the initiative is a challenge. Increasingly, schools are forming or trying to revitalize Instructional Leadership Teams in order to address this challenge. Forming the group is perhaps the easiest part of the effort. Next comes the task of transforming it into a collaborative and then an accountable professional community.

We asked a group of middle school principals to state their biggest struggle in building effective Leadership Teams (LT's). They noted that members have difficulty with the following:

- Assuming a "big picture" school or district perspective, i.e., balancing what is best for the school versus what is best for themselves and their colleagues.

- Abandoning the notion that they *represent* their department and that departmental agendas and personal goals should take precedence over collective goals.

- Listening and responding, i.e., communicating effectively.

- Preventing technical and logistical worries from overwhelming any possible focus on instruction.

- Holding individual LT members accountable to communicate and implement common agreements established by the School Leadership Team. Often agreements are communicated as principal mandates or ignored entirely.

Let's make this last, most frequently cited struggle, more concrete by listening to a middle school principal's response to the question: "What is your biggest struggle with your leadership team?"

I couldn't believe it: after considerable discussion, the Leadership Team (LT) had agreed to focus the next department meetings on the development of writing across the curriculum. The data were clear: the two sets of student work samples we looked at were pretty awful, and we had agreed that we had to bring the skill practice into each classroom. Before we left the meeting, we even filled in the Department Follow-up sheet we'd created so that all of us would be clear about what we had to do to follow up LT deliberations with action. When they reported back, only one team had a plan. The other teams said they had other more urgent things they were dealing with: a field trip and a discipline problem. This isn't the first time either. To be honest, I think I can easily name three or four other instances when various department leaders have not followed through. I know we're trying to decentralize decision-making, and I don't want to alienate people. What should I do?

Holding Leadership Teams Accountable to Follow Up

What would you do if you were the principal? What would your response be if you were the superintendent? If you are a laissez-faire leader, you might ignore failed follow-up; you would perhaps see it as an inevitable cost of "empowerment." If you are a more directive principal, you might be tempted to step in and mandate that departments produce a plan on writing across the curriculum immediately. The impatient superintendent might want you to make the second choice. But neither option is the probably the best one. Ignoring the behavior promotes low expectations for future performance. But asserting your authority does not place the responsibility in the right place—with the team and the individual team leaders.

Helping to equip teacher leaders and teams with the skills of recognizing and then managing their own dysfunction is the first priority. This is a case in which the Instructional Leadership Team had identified and made a commitment to a clear, school-wide goal but failed to hold each other accountable for implementation. Accountable teams place the needs of students at the forefront of consideration. If students cannot currently meet standards for writing and if the group has involved all its members in considering ways to tackle and improve that poor performance, then accountable teams will expect that every member's classroom will show that the new practices have been put in place and are being assessed. Members of such teams will raise the issue of failed or partial implementation with peers themselves rather than hoping that an administrator will eventually notice the discrepancy and take action.

The Instructional Leadership Team had collaborated effectively but had not yet taken responsibility for helping to see that its decisions are carried out. The challenge for skillful leaders is figuring out how to build that internal accountability. Part of the problem is experience; most members of a Leadership Team are likely to be more familiar with the behaviors and stances of Laissez-Faire or Congenial Communities than they are those of collaborative or accountable groups, and old habits are powerful ones. Another part of the problem is confidence; without prior models, prior experience, or training to imagine new ways of interacting with colleagues, it is difficult to believe that peers will listen to or accept what a Leadership Team member has to say. What follows is another toolkit of leadership team-building strategies that might form a partial answer the principal's question "What should I do? These strategies combined with the teacher leader development in the next section constitute the core work that will move communities from Collaborative to Accountable.

- **Consign responsibility for adult learning to the Instructional Leadership Team.** In many places, identifying the focus of professional development and designing training experiences is the business of a separate committee that may know little about the student learning issues that a group of teachers is trying to address. Eliot Stern, Principal of Boston's Thomas Edison Public Middle School (public), believes that the LT should drive both the student and adult learning agenda: "We [the LT] are responsible for adult learning in the school. We want our kids to become independent, rigorous, and reflective learners, which requires a different kind of instruction at the class-room level. We see a relationship here between creating independent learners in the classroom and creating adult independent learners. Independence does not mean doing your own thing but acting togeth-er in collaboration in solving difficult problems."

- **Present data that highlight a violation of a team agreement or norm to the entire team.** Raise your concern, not in your authority role as principal, but as a member of the team. If you have applied strategies from Community Building 101 (Chapter 4), you can link back to the publicly posted norms. You might even invite the group to do a norm check and see if the group can identify the issue by itself. You cannot ignore a norm breach, or it will give tacit permission to individuals to set their own agendas and violate agreements at will.

- **Do not take solutions away from the team.** Skillful administrative leaders assert themselves by defining group problems, if the team fails to do so, but do not determine solutions. These leaders coach groups who are accustomed to traditional lines of authority to assume shared responsibility. After presenting the data and defining the prob-lem, leave it to the group to establish or revisit a norm: "We have a problem here. We have a common agreement that is not being consis-tently implemented. If we are going to function on behalf of students we need to hold each other accountable and that includes me. If I agree to follow up, you need to hold me accountable."

- **Watch for indicators of dysfunctional behavior.** Sometimes adults under pressure to balance multiple priorities begin to lower standards for team performance incrementally. Everyone "understands" the iso-lated slippage until suddenly those single incidents have coalesced into an unhealthy pattern that threatens to undermine group effec-tiveness: meetings start late, members double-book themselves, peo-ple come unprepared, agendas are cursory and start to be over-whelmed by items that have little direct impact on student learning. All these behaviors can be signals that the group has lost its focus or that its commitment is waning. Most respond well to a combination of technical fixes (e.g., agendas focused on instruction with clear objectives) and posting and revisiting norms about attendance and preparation. Signals of more serious patterns that can ruin the effec-tiveness of an ILT include:

  All communication about team efforts runs through and is vetted by the administrators.
  Dissenters dissent in the hall or parking lot, not in the meeting.
  Roles and responsibilities for team functioning are not established or not shared.
  Team problems are not shared publicly.

Agreements and action steps are not shared publicly but are left to individual recollection; timetables and follow-up responsibilities are fuzzy or nonexistent.

If these behaviors are occurring, leaders must examine messages their actions or those of others have been sending to the group. Perhaps under the impulse to be efficient, an administrator has been "helping the group save time" by doing all the agendas and minutes. Perhaps enthusiasm for one particular initiative has led a person in power to "summarize" the group's deliberations by conveniently omitting any record of concerns or opposing ideas. Maybe a well-intentioned administrator has inadvertently fanned mistrust by holding side conversations or brokering deals between meetings in order to make sure the actual public discussions are harmonious and the agenda moves along. Or perhaps an individual who relies on bombast or sarcasm has reduced fellow team members to silent inaction. In any of these cases, the manifesting problem—from parking lot grumbling to passivity, a sense of being censured, or missed deadlines—needs to be exposed, named, and examined by the whole group. Members should follow a procedure that allows them to give honest and substantive feedback and to engage in problem solving once they have the data they need.

CASE 6.1 **Creating a Model Team at Collegial**

Principal Mary Modest worked hard to create an exemplary Leadership Team for her school. She modeled it after the superintendent's Instructional Cabinet, a group intentionally structured to let participating leaders practice becoming more accountable. It wasn't perfect; they didn't always summarize or always start exactly on time, but they spent the majority of their agenda time focusing on student learning and generally relegated low-level, technical questions to subgroups. Imitating what she had observed, Mary orchestrated her own process of norm development at her school. She focused the group on rotating roles and on taking responsibility for surfacing "elephants" (things never talked about in public) and raising concerns in the meeting and not in the halls. The Collegial Leadership Team (LT) adopted a variation of an objectives-based agenda and carefully allocated large chunks of time to working on student learning issues. Most important, she asked each team leader to establish parallel but not identical norms with their teams. She presented the capacities that distinguish a Collaborative from an Accountable Community to the LT and asked them to make a private, individual assessment of the group's current status. At a subsequent meeting, she presented the data from the individual assessments and asked the group to determine what goals they should set jointly.

As she watched her team struggling to learn new skills and let go of deeply ingrained habits and mindsets, however, Mary realized that in order to sustain collaboration and grow accountability she needed something more: the right people in formal grade level leadership positions and a way to nurture teachers who were clearly emerging as informal leaders for a variety of initiatives.

Selecting Teacher Leaders

How do we find a rich pool of expert teacher leaders who can spur improvements in learning and teaching across all classrooms? We know that improving student learning and closing achievement gaps is difficult work. Schmoker (2001), Dufour (2004), Reeves (2006), and others cite successful cases of improvement, but reform usually results in "islands of excellence" where less than one third of reform initiatives are even implemented (Reeves 2006). Building self-renewing communities that can sustain growth and improvement beyond the departure of the original change leader is even more challenging. Several researchers connect sustaining reform to the development of teacher leadership (Katzenmeyer 2001; Crowther et al. 2002; Donaldson 2006; and Reeves 2006). We must build a cadre of skillful teacher leaders if leaders want to sustain collaboration or build Accountable Communities.

We borrow our definition of teacher leadership from Katzenmeyer and Moller: "Teachers who are leaders lead *within and beyond the classroom*, identify with and *contribute to a community of teacher learners* and leaders, and *influence others* toward improved educational practice" (italics added 2001 5). Teacher leaders come in two varieties: formally appointed roles such as department heads or team leaders and informal leaders who derive their authority from "credibility, expertise, and relationship" (Patterson 2004). These two types of leaders can also be categorized as organizationally empowered "role-based" versus collegially empowered "community-

LEADER ALERT

A Panoply of Terms   "Decentralized leadership," "shared leadership," "shared governance," "shared decision making," "site-based management," and "teacher empowerment" are all names for getting more teachers involved in the decision-making work of the school. Unfortunately, too often these highly publicized "priority initiatives" of the year involve teachers in the more mechanistic or structural decision making of schools, e.g., in endless discussions of scheduling, restructuring the grading system, or designing a new report card rather than in substantive work that has a direct impact on student learning.

based" (Murphy 2005). Reeves (2006) describes informal leaders who play a "superhub" role because they connect many people through personal relationships and a willingness to share expertise—not through positional authority.

Initially leaders focus on selecting teachers for formal leadership positions that usually involve a stipend or compensatory time. These individuals are the subunit leaders needed to staff school and district departments, houses, teams, and School Leadership Teams (LT's). As we noted in the Congenial Community case in the last chapter (Case 5.7), when principals seek to fill formal teacher leader positions, they face limited a number of difficulties: absence of candidates practiced in real collaboration, pressure to reward the senior members of a faculty, the political agendas of various constituencies, and reluctance of the best candidates to step forward. The skillful leaders we watch begin their recruiting early and keep at it. They describe a long-term process that involves planting seeds about future ways to share knowledge and skills during supervisory interactions, naming and praising specific ways in which individuals take initiative to help others, sending people to local and national conferences, and asking individuals to provide their expertise to district committees, parent groups, or novice professionals. Strategic principals and Central Office staff also talk about making the criteria for the role public and transparent. They say that they often "think aloud" about how teacher leader roles have changed, about how the job is no longer a matter of distributing books or ordering supplies, in order to encourage those with a hunger for collaborative problem-solving to see the stimulating possibilities of being in a formal leadership role as well as the often-touted drawbacks.

Making the criteria for teacher leaders transparent and linked to the kinds of tasks the district will entrust to these leaders can help in frank conversations with individuals about personal goals and in offsetting political pressure to reward niceness, seniority, political connections, or popularity without substance. We propose some baseline criteria that can serve as starting points for discussion as schools or districts seek to be as explicit as possible about what they value. In the second part of this section, we look more specifically at ways to probe for the capacities that professional communities need in order to be effective.

The following attributes characterize suitable candidates. Effective teacher leaders:

- **Display a rich, substantive knowledge both of academic subject matter and of generic pedagogy.** Given their potential to influence practice, their authority needs to be anchored in expertise (Patterson and Patterson 2004). When available, teachers who have completed National Board Certification provide an excellent pool for selection.

- **Have a track record of seeking opportunities to collaborate actively with colleagues on teaching and learning challenges.** This practice stems from a mindset, not from a mandate. Even if the role is not explicitly described as requiring collaborative problem solving, these candidates will talk about making themselves available to support, advocate for, and even challenge colleagues.

- **Routinely reflect on practice and show indicators of having "expert careers."** There is clear evidence that these candidates regularly use data to inform their instructional decision making. They ask for help and seek answers from others when needed. As Bereiter and Scardamalia (1993) note, expert careers are characterized by reinvestment of mental energy in teaching and by a habit of progressive problem solving. Faced with complex problems, experts seek to widen their understanding and develop new competencies whereas "experienced non-experts" seek to reduce complex problems down to known routines or force fit them into established practices. Strong teacher leader candidates will always be looking for the next interesting challenge rather than a way to say "we do that already."

- **Seek growth, respond well to challenge, and accept the need for change when there is valid evidence that a practice is not working.** Because they often make quiet, unheralded adjustments that improve teaching and learning or set themselves new challenges to prevent feeling stale, such leaders usually know how to grab new programs and practices and make them their own rather than allowing themselves to feel overwhelmed and threatened by change.

- **Have a clear understanding of the school as a workplace and connect their classroom work to broader organizational goals.** They endorse and support the idea that classroom work needs to be aligned with school and district priorities and will show themselves to be well informed about district initiatives and questions that have impact on their students. There are many good (perhaps not great) teachers who limit their field of functioning entirely to their own classroom. They are less likely to make good teacher leaders.

- **Are not driven by egotistical needs to be the center of attention, the most dominant member of a group, or the person who gets external credit and praise all the time.** Individuals who have made a career out of competing with colleagues, getting various student and parent audiences to "love them," or dramatically proving their worth to the world are likely to end up using team initiatives to further their own personal agendas. The best teacher leader candidates should also signs of capacity-building leadership skills in the ways they have worked to bring out the best in their students and parents.

- **Understand the balance between individual autonomy and collective commitment**

This last attribute needs more explanation. We know that Toxic and Laissez-Faire Communities tend to produce individuals who place greatest value on their own academic freedom in the classroom whenever individual preferences come in conflict with group goals. We also know there is danger in forcing all decisions to be made collaboratively and in requiring that all teacher actions be somehow vetted by a group. Crowther found that [teacher] leaders "had strong convictions about individual values as well as a capacity to accommodate the values of others. Thus shared leadership was strongly associated with strong skilled autonomous individuals" (2002 41). The implication is that strong teacher leaders can help determine when energy should appropriately be spent on collective work and when it really should be spent on individual tasks. Evans (1997) names the danger of dissipating energy on jobs that do not need to be tackled collaboratively as "processitis … a preoccupation with procedure and interaction that affects many self-governing groups." Building powerful learning communities does not mean all work must be collaborative. Strong teacher leaders should be able to resist the call to "involve everyone in everything" that sometimes afflicts teams that have had early success.

Balancing autonomy with collective commitment has another face. Teacher leaders need to understand when it is appropriate to challenge administrative or union attempts to ensure conformity when that conformity is not in the best interest of students. Typically, teacher leaders need to be able to manage the demands of an overzealous administrator. The following excerpt from a letter to a union president, sent by a group of nine teacher leaders who were part of a new high school restructuring effort, illustrate this willingness to push back against colleagues.

> It is out of a concern for a union that seems to have lost its focus on kids and school reform that we write this letter. Whenever there is a meeting of union members here, we are told the union's position and that is the end of the discussion. There is no room for conversation; there is certainly no room for disagreement and when one of us dares to question the union's position on an issue, other union members make thinly veiled threats and condescending comments about our need to keep quiet in dissent. We are committed to changing our school and believe teachers should lead the way. That is why many of us have chosen to join our Instructional Leadership Teams. But we have been told by other union members that the "ILT" is a waste of time. Union members have said that it is the administration that is divisive and trying to divide the union. We disagree. It is other teachers who harass us and refuse to hear our voices. We want to work together as a school community—administrators and teachers for kids!

The teachers prevailed and together with their administrators have significantly improved the learning at this high school. We are not attempting to stereotype unions here. Supportive union leaders such as several of the members of the TURN network (www.turnexchange.net) do indeed support reform efforts, teacher collaboration, and appropriate collaboration with administration. We simply want to acknowledge that teacher leaders need to be willing to stand up to authority if they have good reason, whether that authority is admin-istrative or union.

Probing for Conviction

We also recommend that candidates be screened for their conviction. Beliefs are difficult to change; if they are in place we can more easily train for competence. To work with others in an Accountable Community, members need the kinds of convictions we outlined in Chapter 3:

- All adults and children have the ability to learn.
- Expertise develops as a result of continuous effort to find and tackle problems for which there is no currently known solution; it does not develop because individuals are able to force fit known technical solutions to new problems.
- Individuals must sometimes give up individual autonomy in order to pursue the collective good.
- Teachers must take ownership and responsibility for improving instruction.
- A strong sense of urgency and hope compels us to persist in trying to reach students even in the face of adversity.

Interviews or writing samples that address some of the beliefs cited above can help skillful leaders to sort out the teachers with the convictions needed to build Accountable Communities from individuals who have the loudest voices or longest lists of prizes and accomplishments. Please refer to www.ready-about.com for further resources on hiring teacher leaders.

Building Greater Teacher Leadership Capacity

Careful selection of teacher leaders often results in only a small pool of individuals who already possess the beliefs and skills needed to participate in an Accountable Community. Skillful leaders know they must build their own formal teacher leader pool through the use of their Leadership Team (see Creating Model Teams above). They also realize that to make deep impact on student learning they need to increase the leadership capacity of all teachers.

CASE 6.1   **Developing Teacher Leaders for Collegial Elementary**

Principal Mary Modest found, as a result of her screening, that none of the available candidates and only one member of her existing Leadership Team (LT) were ready to assume the type of leadership she wanted. No wonder building a model LT Accountable Community was going to take time, even with the good working exemplar of the Superintendent Able's cabinet. Although the LT was beginning to have progressive conversations, there was little transfer to the grade level units. Mary was committed to using the LT for leader training. She now realized that the only way to establish a truly distributed leadership community was to build a deeper pool of teacher leadership within her faculty so that all teachers began to think of themselves as contributing to leadership even if they did not want formal roles. Mary Modest believed that she must identify and grow as many teacher leaders as she could. Fortunately, she was willing to see the job through; she thought it might require as much as five or more years.

Informal Teacher Leadership

By implication every teacher a principal hires and nurtures is a potential role model; every teacher is someone who might nudge and inspire colleagues to create improved learning for students—or someone who can point the way to "just good enough" and "getting by." Not one of these teachers at the W school in the scenario that follows has a formal leadership role, yet each exerts significant influence over what happens there and the quality of instruction.

It was midafternoon in the teacher's room. One of the authors had just finished observing a 3rd grade social studies class with Mrs. V, a kindergarten teacher from the host school, and a 5th grade teacher visiting from a school across town. They were two of seven teacher leaders who had joined district principals and assistant principals in a course on observing and analyzing teaching. Within minutes, 3rd grade teacher Ms. K pulled up a chair. She explained that a colleague had volunteered to cover the last few minutes of the day and dismissal so that she could hear the discussion and "learn something new." As we probed the objective for the lesson and what the curriculum was "really after," Ms. K called a 4th grade teacher over and asked her to talk about what students would need as foundational concepts for doing research. Questions and speculation flew back and forth; it was clear that these three were not only comfortable pushing hard at one another's thinking but had also observed each other before. Finally, a visiting teacher asked if it was always like this at the W school. "For sure," Mrs. V said. "We had these great study groups and a peer observation program going 15 years ago, and it really changed this school. When the principal who started that stuff left, we decided we needed to take charge of our own learning because no one else was going to do it. We've had 4 different principals in 7 years; some of them got it and some of them didn't, but we just kept doing this because it's important to us. It's how we get better. We break the administrators in eventually—and the new people really love it."

In fact, almost every school the authors visit has such powerful informal leaders. In many places they are the glue that holds the school together either in relationship to one another or in opposition to something or someone. Informal leaders—sometimes called opinion leaders—are the people to whom others look for signals about how to respond to student learning problems, requests for action, or events that are in any way out of the ordinary. Their power, Donaldson (2006 120) notes, comes from their membership in the ranks and is the product of "naturally earned authority and credibility among peers." They know whereof they speak; they live with the same daily challenges; and they have immediate and repeated opportunities to shape problem solving and to help colleagues believe in their own potential for effective collective action (Donaldson 2006).

Taking too narrow a view of teacher leadership or assuming that a leader is someone with formal authority who marches at the head of a column, perpetuates certain misconceptions that can undermine learning. "Not everyone is a leader; you have to have some followers" or "Every building needs its foot soldiers" are often-heard assertions that represent this narrow view.

Informal teacher leaders show the way by example and affirmation. They lead through decisions to support or not support an initiative; they lead by contributing or not contributing in meetings; they lead by encouraging struggling colleagues or calling the question on laggards. Most important, they lead through their ability to reframe a problem and help others see a solution. They lead by shaping what a community is capable of doing; they mobilize effort to help a group of adults hold itself accountable for student successes and failures.

Skillful administrative leaders plan to improve teacher leadership capacity by continual attention to the following:

- Hiring with reflection in mind (see Chapter 10 "Improving Hiring, Induction, and Tenure Decisions")
- Communicating the vision of all teachers as leaders who shape and carry out the work of the school
- Anticipating barriers to teachers' considering themselves leaders and requiring new teachers to begin practicing leadership early
- Differentiating expectations for teacher leadership by matching to individual skills, personal circumstances, and career stages
- Making leadership part of individual supervisory conferences

Hiring Reflective Teachers

Failing to develop the habit and skill of reflection about experience significantly limits an individual's ability to learn and to act as a role model and catalyst for others' learning. Elliot Stern believes that great teachers and great leaders share the same skill of reflecting on practice. Because he finds it difficult to coach individuals who have never developed such habits, he looks for that capacity in every teacher candidate he considers seriously. After reacting to a series of case studies requiring reflective action, candidates teach a lesson. Next they meet with the screening team and are asked to respond to a series of questions:

- What was your mastery objective for the lesson (i.e., what did you want students to know or be able to do at the end of it?)

- How close did you get students to meeting that objective? What evidence do you have?

- What would you do differently the next time?

Stern looks carefully during the interview and in the first few years of employment for early signs of unreflective practice that can undermine both leading and learning. Such signs include automatically attributing poor student performance to students' innate ability and home life and getting too comfortable with the status quo too soon, sometimes described as having too many answers and not enough questions. He says he looks for "struggling learners," a term we usually use for unsuccessful students! Stern also assesses signs of defensiveness that teachers exhibit when their practice or decisions are challenged in order to find those open, curious individuals who will eventually induce others to behave the same way through example.

Communicating the Vision of All Teachers as School Leaders

Developing an ethic of shared leadership involves publicly inviting, expecting, and acknowledging leadership from all teachers. Principals need to be clear about what shared leadership means and what it does not mean. It does not mean that a teacher has to take a formal leadership position. It does mean assuming the presence of—and looking for—"the niche where each person's skill talent or passion can be tapped" (Katzenmeyer and Moller 2001 29). It does not mean that teachers' major responsibilities are outside the classroom; classroom teaching is still the priority. Sharing leadership means that teachers will be involved authentically and appropriately in work that has a direct positive impact on student learning. It does not mean that they will be asked to share responsibility for bus schedules.

Stern describes his vision as teaching and leading structured by the pursuit of common questions. Following are the questions teachers should be asking about their classrooms:

Why is this not working (impacting student or adult learning)?
What do we need to do?
What are the data telling us?
What does research say?
What are the ways we contribute to this problem?
What part of the solution do I own?

Questions such as these underscore a predisposition for intellectual curiosity and a willingness to "struggle and stumble" in search of answers to problems for which there is no currently known solution.

Anticipating Barriers to Practicing Leadership

Many barriers prevent educators from imagining themselves as formal teacher leaders. These include limited available time, personal considerations, commitment to the classroom, or membership in what Donaldson calls the "teacherhood." Some teachers don't want to be seen as "arms of the administration." Donaldson (2006) cites studies which found that "formally appointed teacher leaders can readily lose access and open communication with colleagues because of affiliation with the administration" (81). There are also mindset barriers to informal leadership including: "I am just a teacher," "I just want to teach," or "I am too new." Principals such as Eliot Stern anticipate these barriers by making informal leadership accepted and expected. "Every new teacher has to spend part of the first year rotating through the Leadership Team (LT), the pilot design committee, the content (subject matter) team. I know that some people say new teachers should only focus in the classroom—it's so overwhelming to be a teacher. I believe by participating immediately with more experienced teachers they accelerate their own learning. As they struggle in the classroom they gain confidence in other areas and most importantly they are redefining what we mean by being a teacher—which includes immediate contribution to their school community."

Another barrier to teachers acting as leaders is "phony consulting." One teacher told us: "Give me a break. We have so much to do in the classroom. He wants us to be leaders, but he doesn't even listen to our ideas. He role plays asking our opinion and then does what he wants. We don't like to be manipulated. I would be glad to share decision making if it was an authentic process." Administrators need to listen and often act on teachers' ideas to validate the teacher's investment in the larger school arena.

Differentiating Expectations for Teacher Leadership

The degree to which individuals can move beyond informal leadership to assume more official roles often depends on where teachers are in their career and in their personal lives. Teachers without pressing family responsibilities may step forward to chair an important committee or run a study group while people going through personal speed bumps may pull back, lead by example, and function primarily as a supportive team member for a period of time. Skilled principals know how to use and reward this informal leadership as well as they do other kinds: they consult by "running ideas by" informal leaders; they ask for feedback and "straight talk from someone whose opinion I trust." They ask a veteran to spend a few minutes chec/ring up a novice; they ask if they can send someone to observe or if the individual would be willing to provide a one-time consult for another group.

In addition to cultivating informal teacher leaders, principals and district personnel can help "build a deep bench" for a school and actively tap the expertise of its faculty by establishing a range of opportunities for leadership (see Table 6.2).

TABLE 6.2 Teacher Leadership Opportunity Pool

Committee Chairperson or Member
Curriculum committee
Policy review
Accreditation self-study
Professional development

Role Model
Mentor
Student Teacher Cooperating Teacher
Peer-assisted review (PAR) coach
Colleague Coach
Demonstration Classroom

Professional Development
National Board Certification
Masters in subject area specialty

Presentations
Regional/national conference
Faculty meeting
Team
In-service course

Union Officer

Resourcer
Grant writer
Researcher

E.T.I.D
TFA +
grantees

Making Leadership Part of Individual Supervisory Conferences

Currently little supervisory time is spent giving teachers feedback and setting goals related to their leadership or to their contributions to their professional communities even though most sets of teacher performance standards contain a category that addresses those areas.

Beginning with the hiring interview, the principal should immediately highlight the state or district's performance standard relevant to teacher leadership and/or contribution to professional community and give that standard "life and clout." Giving life means it becomes part of the informal and formal supervisory conversations. Giving clout comes later when supervisors collect data and report in more depth about this area of performance in the spirit of "We will inspect what we expect." We also recommend that every two years supervisors include a career discussion in their debriefing of teaching decisions. Part of that career discussion can involve asking individuals to cite examples of and set goals for their contributions to the professional community.

CASE 6.1 **A Last Look at Collegial Elementary**

When we first met Collegial elementary, we posed three questions: Is it stuck at good? Ready to decline? Or poised for greater growth? Many interventions and considerable messiness later, we think Collegial is well along on its journey from collaborative to accountable and well equipped to help all its students make the gains in math and literacy that had earlier seemed unlikely. Let's review what happened.

1. Superintendent Able and her team of Central Office instructional leaders assessed Collegial's evolution and recognized symptoms that said growth and learning had stopped and that a majority of teams in the building were stuck.

2. Superintendent Bonnie Able recognized that Collegial's highly successful charismatic principal (a Transition Leader) was no longer a good match for the next stages of growth the school needed, provided honest feedback and a statement of the problem, and helped the principal make a decision to leave for a position more matched to his skills and interests.

3. The selection process focused on hiring an individual (Mary Modest) with the conviction and competence to sustain progressive initiatives, distribute leadership, and mobilize the faculty for the next serious improvement push.

4. Superintendent Able was a good role model and provided clear support and structure for the new principal's entry. She helped Mary focus on building her Leadership Team (LT) as a top priority. Because the district's leadership team exemplified the beliefs, skills, and structures needed, Mary copied many of features of that group.

5. Despite her careful work with the individuals on her Instructional Leadership Team, Mary saw little carryover to the behavior and productivity of grade level teams. Eventually she concluded that she needed to communicate much clearer expectations for leadership and she needed to find new members with new competencies.

6. Mary's careful teacher leader selection process revealed how thin her "backup bench" had become and how little had been done to nurture teacher's sense of themselves as leaders within their professional communities. She needed time, a broader focus for hiring and supervision, and a commitment to recognizing and supporting both formal and informal leadership in order to build a school-wide accountable community.

Summary

Moving schools from collaborative to accountable requires creating conditions that can sustain and distribute growth. It involves making a transition from the personality-driven and leader-centered change often needed during early turnaround stages in school improvement to more distributed leadership. Hiring processes thus become critical. To "get the right people on the bus," we need rigorous screening for tenacious, disabling beliefs and for the particular skills that help to mobilize groups for successful problem solving. Skillful builders of Accountable Communities understand that organizations have few concrete models of highly evolved communities to draw upon. Such leaders try to build model Leadership Teams and to develop a deep reservoir of teacher leadership that can fill important formal and informal roles.

Selecting the right people and redefining the profession of teaching to include leading is perhaps the key to going from good to great schools. It creates a self-renewing energy source for Accountable Communities. Because leadership is no longer vested in a single person or committee, it protects improvement momentum from the potentially negative effects of individual ambition, political maneuvering, or sudden tragedies. As we shall see in Chapter 10, it also helps to keep high-functioning, innovative, and entrepreneurial teachers in the profession.

7 Collecting and Using Data: Vehicles

Why another treatise on using data to improve schools when so many fine ones already exist?[1] The failure to use data appropriately and effectively is one of the conditions that undermines learning. We have sometimes characterized the actions of data-free improvement efforts as the infamous "3 F's": flailing around, flaunting ignorance, and fogging up the mirrors so we don't have to take a critical look at the effects of our work. Or as the saying goes, "Don't bother me with evidence; I have my opinion."

Data are simply various forms of information, often facts or figures, used as the basis for making decisions about the link between outcomes and practices. This information can be a powerful tool to help us help students succeed. It enables people and organizations to work more intelligently and invest effort more effectively. Data also allow us to take on and change such unpromising practices as:

- **Strict adherence to standard operating procedures and business as usual without evidence that those procedures actually improve student learning.** For example, all math courses are the same length of time; only a certain percentage of students are allowed access to the most challenging reading books; and everyone must start at the same place in reviewing last year's material regardless of what they already know and can do.

- **Substituting attention to actions for attention to outcomes.** All teachers must be in the same place in the pacing guide every week; all teachers must write objectives on the board; or, "we have a project-based curriculum, so I tell my teachers they must do a minimum of two projects and a field trip a month."

---

[1]See for example Nancy Love et al. *A Data Coach's Guide to Closing Achievement Gaps: Unleashing the Power of Collaborative Inquiry.* Thousand Oaks, CA: Corwin Press in press; or Kathryn Parker Boudette, Elizabeth City and Richard Murnane, eds., *Data Wise: A Step-by-Step Guide to Using Assessment Results to Improve Teaching and Learning.* Cambridge: Harvard Education Press, 2005.

- **Willful, persistent disregard of the effects of actions and decisions on learners.** "I don't have time for pre-assessment, I have a curriculum to cover" or "True, he's pretty dry and a lot of the kids don't stick with physics, but they probably shouldn't be taking it in the first place. He's earned the right to pick his schedule. We're not running a kindergarten here; it's the real world now, and not everything is interesting."

- **A habit of focusing blame, explanation, and solution finding almost exclusively on external factors.** The students don't have the right parents; the department of education is making us test special education students; we lost our aides so we can't do hands-on science; I can't do error analysis because my class size has gone up to 26.

- **Large, random expenditures of effort (and sometimes funds) on activities and initiatives that are not clearly linked to data-driven learning goals or learning needs.** We're transforming ourselves into an arts magnet school to make students more motivated to read; we're having all our teams design at least two interdisciplinary units that engage the students with technology; we're having a pageant of all the Greek gods and goddesses as a culmination to our study.

- **Inability or unwillingness to ask hard questions about our own practice or resorting to "edubabble" in response to hard questions.** The new math curriculum is not skills driven but rather emphasizes investigatory experiences designed to engage students in metacognition and inform their capacity to utilize higher order thinking skills in non-traditional situations.

Note that many of the examples we offer above, such as the decision to use a project-based curriculum or to spend a year becoming an arts magnet school, are not necessarily inappropriate in themselves. The issue is whether those steps have been chosen because clear evidence shows that they fit an identified problem or improve learning for students. Otherwise, they belong to the category of flailing around.

Requirements of the No Child Left Behind Act have generated a "flailing" flurry of attention to analyzing external test data simply to be in compliance. To challenge deeply rooted beliefs and comfortable but unproductive practices, however, skillful leaders and skillful teachers need data that guide daily decisions about what actions will best help students, not just reams of test scores that arrive once a year. As Boudett and Moody note, educators are at a crossroads:

Across the country school leaders face the tough decisions about whether to take the relatively easy route of using data merely to fulfill external accountability [NCLB] requirements or the more challenging path of using data to help teachers [and administrators] become more accountable to each other and their students. (2005 12)

In the following pages, we consider what skillful leaders at all levels of the organization might do to confront the 3 F's and find the places where they have settled for mediocrity in learning and teaching. We examine ways to invest effort wisely by using data for:

- Learning-focused evaluation and supervision
- Collaborative problem solving and community accountability

Using Data for Learning-Focused Evaluation and "SuperVision"

Historically, teacher performance evaluation has involved assessing classroom practice against some agreed-upon set of teacher behaviors. The process is carried out more or less thoughtfully and comprehensively depending upon the

- Skill of the individual evaluator
- Willingness of the larger organization to invest time and effort in helping people produce credible assessments and ratings
- Degree to which the larger organization monitors the quality and impact of its performance evaluations.

Much of what passes for teacher evaluation in this country is a summary of one to three classroom observations; only minimal attention is given to other data sources that might shed light on the range of challenges teachers face and meet. The mirror on teaching is usually quite foggy!

Although rhetoric often calls for evaluation to be "growth inducing," few participants on either side of the desk describe it in that way. First, teacher evaluation is almost always contractually assigned to administrators; thus it is always in danger of becoming "something done by them to us." Second, traditional teacher evaluation usually produces a summative judgment; like a unit test, that summative judgment signals closure on the year and on the discussion of the data that were considered to determine the rating. No one is really expected to follow up on the information that 90 percent to 95 percent of each observed class was teacher talk, for example. Unless the evaluation rating is "failing," there may be no further formal discussion of practice for two to five more years. Finally, the object of the exercise, student learning, rarely enters the discussion or rating of teaching practice. As long as the target teacher behaviors are present, whether they worked well or not has usually been beside the point.

In contrast, learning-focused evaluation considers teacher actions to meet identified performance indicators and the impact of those actions on students. Both parties in the process, evaluator and evaluatee, have responsibility for gathering and analyzing data from a variety of sources. Whether they consider a lesson demonstration or an array of materials designed to support a unit, evaluators ask some combination of the following:

- What were the goals for the learner? Where did these goals come from?
- What choices did you make to help students reach those goals?
- What data did you use to pinpoint the relevant choices?
- How well did students learn? (How did you assess? What did your data show?)
- What will you do if they didn't learn? What will you do if they did?
- How will you monitor the next steps?

Learning-focused evaluation extends the assessment of teaching to include an explicit link between practice and appropriate student progress and products identified by the district. Results matter and require further action and discussion. Nonetheless, it is important to remember that they are only one source of data among many. Neither classroom observation nor student test scores should ever be the sole source of information for determining whether a teacher meets standards.

Supervision is more commonly considered to be formative and growth oriented. According to Jon Saphier, it is frequent, high-quality feedback provided by knowledgeable individuals for the purpose of stimulating teacher thinking and decision-making (1993 9-10). Sergiovanni and Starratt broaden the definition by explicitly including learners. The purpose of supervision, they write, is to "help increase the opportunity and capacity of schools to contribute more effectively to students' academic success" (6). The task of leadership is not simply to document the presence or absence of teacher behaviors but to engage members of the community in examining whether and how those behaviors work. Note that both these definitions do not say that supervision is the exclusive province of administrators. Finally, Glickman, Gordon and Ross-Gordon offer a shift away from more traditional activities of monitoring and determining compliance toward what they call "SuperVision" or acts carried out by a number of different individuals that spread a common vision of high-quality teaching and learning throughout the school (6-9). We have adopted that idea in looking at data use. To make sure we use data to make widespread improvements in teaching and learning, the teachers and specialists who are most directly responsible for helping students meet a performance target, not just administrators, must be involved in SuperVision.

Using Data for Collaborative Problem-Solving and Community Accountability

Until recently, data were considered to be things that administrators knew about, interpreted, kept secret except during annual public disclosures, and sometimes used to sort, select, and label students. Teachers had little opportunity to obtain timely, relevant information that could help them with decision-making unless they figured out individually how to gather such information from their own students. As recently as the 1990s, only a handful of leaders, teachers, and teacher groups would have considered the regular, ongoing examination of teacher-generated student performance data to be an appropriate focus for a supervisory conference or a meeting with colleagues.

Recently, teachers have been asked to look at the results of state and federally mandated testing, identify areas of weakness, and develop plans that will address those learning and performance problems. Depending on how it is structured, this activity can be a valuable undertaking or one that generates anxiety, finger pointing, denial, and resistance. Giving teachers or administrators an opportunity to react to test data or to someone else's "definition of the problem" will not, by itself, build Accountable Communities. Groups of teachers need immediately available, relevant data that let them put a name to a learning problem they care about: What is preventing 20 percent of our students from mastering multiplication and division of fractions? Why are our 8th graders not able to apply science concepts to new situations? What would help our 10th graders deal more effectively with the volume of reading demanded by the new social studies standards? Teams need to decide what data would help them investigate the causes of the learning problems and track the effects of their own efforts to solve the problem. As Nancy Love notes, "When teachers generate their own questions, engage in dialogue, and make sense of data, they develop a much deeper understanding of what is going on relative to student learning. They develop ownership of the problems they surface"(2007 6). Group analysis of data without ownership of learning problems is merely an exercise in compliance.

Expanding the Use of Data

We know that closing student learning gaps requires changing and broadening adult learning about data use. Table 7.1 summarizes some of these changes.

Two closely related questions about data use have guided our thinking and the organization of Chapters 7 and 8:

- How can supervisors and evaluators gather, process, and give meaning to data?

- What data might supervisors and evaluators use to illuminate student learning problems and assess the results of teacher practice?

Chapter 7 offers what we are calling vehicles, practical structures for collecting and processing data about student learning and teacher practice. Vehicles have organized formats. Some follow explicit rules and are highly prescribed models; others have looser guidelines. Chapter 8 considers potential sources of data. Sources are categories of data or places to go looking for information. Both vehicles and sources support learning-focused supervision and evaluation and the collaborative problem solving that help groups become more efficient and more accountable for student learning. Table 7.2 provides an overview of the vehicles and their relative utility for our three different purposes: evaluation, supervision, and collaborative

TABLE 7.1 Changing Data Use

NARROW FOCUS	BROAD FOCUS
Single Sources of Data	**Multiple Sources of Data**
Focus on summative tests	Summative tests balanced with formative measures
Externally driven, administrative applications	Internally developed teacher applications
Quantitative assessments	Qualitative anecdotal measures
Inspection, correction, and compliance	Ownership, trust, and deep problem solving

problem solving (CPS). Figure 8.1 provides an overview of the sources. Readers can select either entry point. If you already have the data or know exactly what data you need to collect, begin with this chapter. If you are uncertain what data to collect and where to look for information to fit your question, begin with Chapter 8.

Let us sound one cautionary note. Expanding data use in order to be more effective and more responsible in reaching students is not meant to be presented as "a new program we're starting this year" or a "cutting-edge" fad. The danger of menus is their invitation to engage in a frenzy of "sampling" or activity for activity's sake. Skilled leaders are strategic, selective, and committed to generating ownership as they broaden data use. Several general principles are worth keeping in mind:

- Practice complete transparency about the purpose of the data.
- Make data analysis the means to answering questions about student learning that teachers deem important and care about—not an end in itself.[2]
- Select multiple sources of data to allow cross validation (see Chapter 8).
- Initially, try to use new vehicles and sources for formative feedback (information), not for purposes of making judgments.
- Avoid proclamations and unexplained or unsupported mandates.
- Provide teachers with time, support, cheering, and opportunities to vent when the going gets tough.

---

[2]As Love, Stiles, Mundry and diRanna note, data "do nothing by themselves to improve teaching unless they spark a powerful dialogue and changes in practice" (7).

TABLE 7.2 Vehicles for Data Use

In the columns below, one check mark (√) indicates that the vehicle is a potentially useful way to achieve the particular purpose indicated on the column head. Two check marks (√√) signal that the vehicle is a powerful way to achieve that purpose.

VEHICLES	Learning-Focused Evaluation	Learning-Focused Supervision	Collaborative Problem Solving
Classroom Observation			
"Enhanced Formal"	√√		
"The Walk"	√	√√	√√
Room Tours[SM]		√	√√
Peer Observation		√√	√√
Non-classroom Observation			
Collaboration	√	√√	√√
Interactions	√	√√	√√
Conferences			
Videotape		√√	√√
"Reading the Walls"		√	√√
Student Interview	√	√√	√√
Assessment of Learning	√	√	√√
Student-led Portfolio	√	√√	√
Document	√√	√√	√√
Data-use	√√	√√	√√
Professional Learning	√	√√	√
Protocols			
Collaborative Assessment		√	√
Consultancy		√	√√
Collaborative Coaching and Learning		√√	√√
Lesson Study		√√	√√
Error Analysis		√√	√√

- Limit the volume of data examined in a narrow timeframe. Avoid "data dumping" to create urgency. "When too much data is released people are overwhelmed about what it means and what is most important" (Wagner et al. 2006 139).

- Strive for consistent practice among all school leaders. If only one principal or one school's supervisors ask to see unit plans or grade books, such disparate practices may result in the union charging a change of practice (see Legal Note 7.1).

LEGAL NOTE 7.1

Changing Past Practice

Even if the data vehicles and sources cited in these chapters have not been excluded from use by contract, many of them will not have been part of past practice in supervision, evaluation, or even professional development. "Past practice" has less relevance if new approaches are designated as a pilot or as a voluntary undertaking and are not part of performance evaluation. However, supervisors contemplating changes should consider whether it is necessary to establish uniform practice. If rejection or resistance is anticipated, the best way to implement new practices associated with the supervision and/or evaluation of employees or with making changes in work conditions is to give notice of contemplated changes prior to any efforts to implement them. Such notice should be given in writing, with sufficient detail to enable the employees' union representatives to understand what you want to do and why they should want to agree to your doing it.

To begin, consult with your school district's labor relations counsel to ascertain whether the laws in your states require you to notify the union of any new data-gathering procedures such as collecting data from students and parents, the "walkthrough," the use of videotapes, or the consideration of test scores. If your state law considers these practices to be mandatory subjects of bargaining, you are legally obligated to refrain from implementing any such practices without first bargaining the decision to do so and the impact of such changes. Failure to do so could lead to litigation that would result in returning to the status quo ante, i.e., restoration to the conditions that existed prior to implementation. This would be accompanied with a prohibition against using any of the information previously collected and an order to bargain over the proposed changes before any future implementation can occur.

| Evaluation | Supervision | CPS |

Vehicles for Collecting Data

To help leaders match strategy and purpose, we have inserted an icon in the margin with one or more tabs in boldface to indicate the most likely uses for this particular approach to data collection. Evaluation refers to assessment of teaching performance for the purposes of making employment decisions. Supervision refers to all activities carried out by various individuals that help to spread a vision of high-quality learning and teaching across an entire school (Glickman, Gordon and Ross-Gordon 6-9). It is meant to contrast with the "snoopervision" traditionally associated with building and district administrators). By collaborative problem solving or CPS we mean all the different activities that Collaborative and Accountable Communities use to determine how best to help students learn. In this section, we consider five types of vehicles for examining links between teaching and learning outcomes: classroom observations, non-classroom observations, conferences, protocols, and error analysis.

Classroom Observation

How can we shift and expand the way we use classroom observation to help us capture the connection between learning and teaching? Confronting conditions that undermine learning includes examining evaluation practices to determine whether they are helping or hindering improvement. We begin with the traditional practice of observation. With the rare exception of peer coaching or lesson study, observation has traditionally been the exclusive domain of administrators. Formal observation accompanied by "pre and post" conferences can provide data about how teaching is working to help students. More often, however, the observation process involves compliance with ritual rather than substantive, data-based feedback. Evaluations are made from single, 40-minute snapshots narrowly focused on a prescribed set of teacher behaviors. There is little attempt to determine the impact those instructional choices, or the lack thereof, are having on students. Typically, great teachers receive a few generic positive strokes ("keep up the good work") while less skillful teachers sometimes get a list of vague ideas for improvement. Follow-up is meager; there is little sense that teachers own either the process or the product that results.

Despite its imperfect history and limitations, however, direct observation remains the most common and immediately diagnostic source of information about the quality of teaching. In this section we offer ideas for more learning-focused observation practices. A number of the approaches also support collaborative problem solving and help a leader to model the idea that SuperVision or spreading the vision is a task that belongs to many different members of the professional community. We begin with the traditional, enhanced formal observation and then describe "walks" and "Room Tours^{SM}."

The Enhanced Formal Classroom Observation

Evaluation	Supervision	CPS

How can we make the observations that are traditionally required more effective? How might we use classroom observation to help spread a vision of high-quality teaching and learning across a school or district? Either announced or unannounced, formal observations must comply with collective bargaining agreements. Formal observations required by contract or evaluation agreement are findings recorded in formats ranging from minimal checklists to extensive, data-based analytical reports. Many districts require a final document that summarizes observational data along with other information about the teacher's practice. Whatever the agreements and procedures, leaders can go beyond compliance and maximize observation as a rich source of data by shifting the choice of lesson and the focus of the observation.

TIPS ON FORMAL OBSERVATION FOR TENURED FACULTY

✔ **Communicate early, often, and in multiple modes that you are widening the observation lens** from "Do you do all these teacher moves?" to "How are all these strategies and choices we make as teachers helping students?" Consider creating an activity (e.g., a brief, shared video or simulation) that allows the entire staff to experience what collecting and analyzing data about the students' responses will be like.

✔ **Carefully craft a beginning of the year memo outlining the purpose of observation and the ground rules and expectations for both participants.** End by explicitly inviting staff members to make suggestions and raise questions about anything that they find confusing. Before you send the memo, have a colleague or two read it critically to make certain you have been clear and perhaps to check that you are not violating any binding agreements. Send the memo to all staff and review it with each individual as you begin the process.

Note: In the early days of such a shift, there will be inevitable complaints about "not knowing" or "not being told" even when communication has been extensive. Veteran staff, assuming they "know how evaluation goes," may not look closely at the directions. By having expectations clearly laid out in writing, leaders can respond to the "you are picking on me" syndrome that sometimes develops if negative data surfaces as a result of the more stringent examination.

✔ **Start with an announced visit** despite the danger that the staff member will resort to a "dog and pony" show that does not reflect a representative lesson plan. If we can communicate the expectations clearly enough (see sample memo), giving teachers a chance to do their best has some value. The announced visit may not reveal what the teacher does on a day-to-day basis; however, it does show what she or he can do. Whether instruction is good, bad, or mediocre, the announced observation gives the supervisor a benchmark of performance. Comparing the data from an announced visit with that gathered from other sources such as learning walks or drop-in visits helps to validate judgments or highlight next steps. Note: In many cases, the desire to put on a show seems to go down in direct ratio to the frequency of the supervisor's visits.

✔ **Ask to see something from the heart of a unit (or a related series of lessons) that challenges students to apply or get better at a difficult skill or concept.** Emphasize that you prefer not to see either an introductory or "R and R" (recall and review) lesson but rather something complex that will allow both of you to gain insight into the demands that current programs are placing on students and teachers.

Note: We hear two points of view about the current lack of rigor in lessons observed. Skilled, insightful teachers sometimes complain that their supervisors only notice "stupid stuff" and miss critical decision points in the lesson. When we see an unremitting emphasis on easy-to-name classroom management techniques, rapport, engagement, and climate in a school's evaluation documents, we tend to agree that supervisors at least appear oblivious to unfolding lesson complexity whether they actually are or not. On the other hand, supervisors voice frustration that announced formal observations allow mediocre performers to present atypically well-prepared lessons.

✔ **Establish, communicate, and be consistent about upholding a "no penalties for a high-risk, rigorous lesson that doesn't succeed" policy.** Save any response that carries pointed consequences for people who continue to produce low-level demonstrations. In the pre-conference, emphasize that you want to be able to provide valuable data about a part of the curriculum that repeatedly confuses students or slows them down or that you want to help a teacher think through other ways to handle a complex concept when you meet to debrief.

Note: If the environment is threatening and the evaluator heavy handed or didactic, even good teachers are tempted to break out risk-free, carefully honed lessons that allow students to fly their hands, signaling complete understanding. One recalls the Madeline Hunter story in which she describes an apocryphal teacher preparing for an upcoming observation by instructing her students to raise their hands promptly in response to every question. She promises, however, not to call on them if they have their left hand up.

✔ **Collaborate with the teacher to identify what data on student understanding will be collected, by whom, and when before the observation begins.** The supervisor might collect a record of the kinds of questions students ask or answer incorrectly, the teacher might design and collect responses to a one-question quiz at midpoint in the lesson, the supervisor might interview students working in groups about their goal, the teacher would collect the problem set, essay, or lab report that results from several days of instruction.

✔ **Identify a clear mastery objective and some basic criteria for success before the lesson and have those statements ready to use when you begin to look at artifacts after the lesson.**

Data-Collecting Walks

How can we collect data in order to:

- Assess and monitor patterns of instruction and degree of program implementation?

LEGAL NOTE 7.2

Using Data for Teacher Evaluation

If you intend to use walk data collected by an employee whose position is part of the collective bargaining units but who has not collected data for teacher evaluation before, check with your local labor counsel first. Some state labor laws require that evaluation procedures must be collectively bargained with the local teachers' union before any changes in existing practice can be implemented. This does not mean that you can't go into a classroom for purposes of supervision, but it does mean that if you have not fulfilled any prior collective bargaining obligations, you will not be able to use the information you gather in your evaluation of the personnel involved.

| Evaluation | Supervision | CPS |

- Stoke community conversations on teaching and learning?
- Shift the emphasis from teacher behavior to student learning?

MODEL MEMO ON FOCUSING EVALUATION ON LEARNING

September 15, 2007

To: All Tenured Faculty Assigned to Formal Evaluation in 2007-2008
From: Frank Focused, Principal
Re: Formal Observations

Although I'll be in and out of your classrooms and getting to know your students
in other ways this year, I will also be conducting two observations as part of the
evaluation process. I want this to be a productive learning experience for both of
us and something that will move students closer to the kind of high-quality performance we want from them.

To that end, I want to be a useful "second pair of eyes" to help you with something that is hard for students to learn. Please invite me to a class where students will be challenged by having to work on a difficult concept or skill. Part of
the class could certainly be direct instruction, but I would like to see students
applying what you're teaching, either individually or in groups. That will give me a
chance to ask them a few questions we will agree upon at the pre-observation
meeting.

As a change from previous years when we would have held the "post" the very
next day, I would like to have the post-observation conference two to three days
later when you have had a chance to assess how students are performing in relation to your standards and objectives. You may or may not have final products,
but I will be asking you to bring sample work related to this observation. We'll
plan to look at the responses of one or two typically high-performing students,
two or three students whose work represents average performance for the task,
and a student who does not get it yet. We will make the progress of those students a topic of discussion as well.

Again, this shift is meant to have our discussions and the effort you put into
these observations yield worthwhile insights about our learners and programs.
We will talk in more detail as we set up appointments, but please don't hesitate to
catch me with suggestions and questions about how this might work.

Single-observer, single-lesson, single-purpose classroom visits have been
the observation data source of choice for a long time. Recently, however,
schools and school districts have been exploring the use of "walkthroughs"
because they allow examination of instructional patterns across several
classrooms in a relatively short period of time. Individual teachers, teams of
teachers, specialists, and administrators can now choose from a range of
protocols designed by different organizations to meet the different purposes
of a walkthrough. There are some common benefits. All types of walks
achieve the following:

- Provide an opportunity to collect diagnostic data on the degree of program implementation at a school, grade, or department level. While such data should not be used primarily to evaluate individual teachers, they can help anyone involved in school improvement select classrooms that should have additional supervisory and support visits as well as those likely to serve as models for colleagues to examine. Note: This guideline does not exclude giving feedback to and intervening with individuals when the data collected and verified in one or more return visits suggest misunderstandings, incorrect information, failure to meet program requirements, or other gaps in performance.

- Help build a learning community that is focused on teaching and learning and is aware of what is happening throughout the department or school. Most walks are structured around multiple visits to multiple classrooms. If properly structured, the post-visit conversation helps to develop more shared understandings of effective practices and their impact on student learning.

- Facilitate a shift in emphasis from observing teacher moves to collecting and analyzing different types of data about the links between student learning and instructional strategies.

- Increase the visibility of multiple adults in classrooms, which sends the important message to students that "we care about what is happening and what you are learning."

Some of the best-known walk protocols include the following:

Institute for Learning

Purpose: to build learning communities. An early version of the walkthrough was first used in the 1990s by administrators in New York City's District Two, a district that has since received national accolades for its improvements in student learning. The walkthrough protocol developed by Lauren Resnick at the Institute for Learning at the University of Pittsburgh was originally designed for administrators. It later evolved into the LearningWalk, which includes tools to be used by teachers and administrators for building professional communities (www.instituteforlearning.org).

Focus on Results

Purpose: to provide feedback on school improvement linked to teaching and learning. FOR defines a walkthrough as: "an organized tour through a school's classrooms and other instructional areas to collect evidence about how well school improvement efforts such as applying an instructional focus, providing professional development on specific instructional strategies and/or programs are being implemented school-wide. FOR defines a Reflective Walkthrough as an organized tour through a school's learning areas to provide feedback on instruction and learning in a particular area of focus. It is different from evaluation and is the least threatening approach to introduce visiting into the school culture." (www.focusonresults.net)

LEADER ALERT————————————————————————————

Verify Concerns with Additional Supervisory Visits Walks allow both teachers and administrators to collect data for supervision and collaborative problem solving rather then evaluation. However when persistent unpromising patterns are observed in certain classrooms, it is possible to use walk data for performance evaluation if it corroborates or adds to a pattern documented in other kinds of observations. Be careful. To avoid endangering the trust and sense of community built around the walks or violating agreements with the union, it is best to return and verify that a problem noted during a walk is actually something other than a one-time phenomenon. These visits to check out concerns then become either supervisory or evaluative in nature. Avoid using the term walk to describe the data gathering.

———————————————————————————————————————

The Three-Minute Classroom Walkthrough

Purpose: to collect snapshots of targeted teaching practices. This model stresses the importance of the walk as way to build a reflective culture, not as a vehicle for evaluation. "The Downey Walk-Through classroom visit is short in length—about 2-3 minutes in a classroom. It is like taking a short video clip of the moment. There is no intent to evaluate the teacher; rather it is time to gather information about curricular and instructional teaching practices and decisions teachers are making ... our experience is that in the 2 3 minutes we are in the classroom we typically observe 5-10 decisions being made" (Downey et al. 12).

Individual Supervisor WalkThroughs

Purpose: to monitor patterns of instruction and give feedback to staff. Developed by Margery Ginsburg and others, this variation is used by supervisors to collect data and give feedback to staff. It allows the supervisor to be more visible and, more important, can help the principal monitor agreed-upon instructional and learning priorities. In the "School Scan Variation," the supervisor quickly walks through the school to collect data on one or two focus questions. The resulting data is not reported out by individual teacher but by school patterns.

Ginsburg recommends that supervisors give brief feedback by email or by sticky note with a quick positive aspect of the visit. We would add that leaving a teacher a question to ponder is also a good approach for follow up.[3]

————————————————

[3]For a detailed description of this model see Lois Easton Brown, *Powerful Designs for Learning*. Chapter 8 "Classroom Walkthroughs." Oxford, Ohio: National Staff Development Council, 2004.

FocusedWalk[SM]

Ready About Consulting

Purpose: To train supervisors in learning focused supervision skills to elevate the quality of instruction. Ready About Consulting has developed the FocusedWalk[SM], which deepens leaders' skill in analyzing instruction and coaching teachers to use instructional strategies identified by research to have a positive impact on student learning. There are four phases to the FocusedWalk[SM] training: establishing a baseline, developing common knowledge, conducting the walk, and calibrating and processing (www.ready-about.com).[4]

EXAMPLE   Phases of FocusedWalk[SM]

Phase 1: The Baseline

As a pretest to establish a baseline, participants watch a 15-minute teaching video during which they capture data, identify events they consider significant, and rate the lesson. Inevitably people observe and capture very different things. Initially there is little or no inter-rater reliability and much disagreement about the important aspects of the lesson, the assigned ratings, and the potential impact on students. The object of the exercise is to demonstrate that defining teaching quality and its impact on learning, at least before training, varies with the eyes, ears, and biases of each observer.

Phase 2: The Knowledge

In a seminar setting, participants learn about effective instructional strategies that are aligned with the district's teacher performance standards. For example, they might examine elements for planning and implementing a successful lesson linked to the standard: Planning Instruction and Designing Learning Experiences for All Students (California Standards for the Teaching Profession). Next they would practice recognizing positive and negative applications on video or DVD. The goal is to create a common knowledge base,[5] reduce observer variation, and increase both reliability (consistency) and accuracy (validity).

Phase 3: FocusedWalk[SM]

Visiting two or three classrooms for 15 to 20 minutes each, teams of three to five participants collect specific data that has been identified ahead of time. Many walkthrough proponents advocate limiting time in any particular classroom to ten minutes or less. However, we have found these longer visits deepen leader understanding of the concepts linked to better learning for students. Longer slices also invite conversation about differences in expectations, academic rigor, or attention to high-level thinking—all of which are difficult to capture in shorter time bites. Rather than using checklists, participants are trained to gather multiple sources of data on the

[4]Ready About Consulting offers a variety of leader development programs under the title of Skillful Leader Training. FocusedWalk[SM] is a part of this training. Thanks to Shirley Stiles from Focus on Results for her assistance in developing this protocol. Thanks also to the Stupski Foundation for supporting the school reform initiative and the Elk Grove Unified School District for allowing us to pilot test this walk protocol.
[5]For a richly detailed resource on the potential contents of a shared knowledge base on teaching, see Jon Saphier, Mary Ann Haley-Specca and Robert Gower, *The Skillful Teacher* (2008).

identified focus: taking literal notes on teacher and student dialogue, interviewing students, reading the walls, and collecting artifacts. Observers are also encouraged to collect data on missed opportunities. These are key places in the lesson when the teacher has a clear opening to do something that will help improve the learning for students and does not take it. These gaps become important data for conversation.

Phase 4: Calibration and Processing

After the walk, participants convene a team meeting. Before discussion, participants rate the classes observed, organize their data, and prepare initial questions and feedback. This silent work builds individual accountability prior to group conversation and thus enhances skill development. The group discussion begins with each member signaling his or her rating in order to calibrate the team. Does each member rate the class in the same way? Is the lesson moving toward a worthwhile objective? Lively, data-based discussion ensues when ratings are at odds. The main event is to share data on the identified focus and consider what additional information or evidence would be needed, what questions would elicit this data from the teachers observed, and what coaching ideas might help teachers stretch their performance.

Suggested Schedule
Time: 2 ½ to 3 hours

- Orientation (20 minutes) State goal, explain focus, methods of data collection, and visiting logistics.
- Data collecting walks (60 minutes) Visit 2 to 3 classes.
- Individual processing (10 minutes) Before starting team discussion, individuals should organize their data and formulate feedback.
- Team holistic sharing (10 minutes)
- Group processing (30 minutes)

See web supplement "Running the Walk" (www.ready-about.com).

Room Tours^SM

How can the community use classrooms and classroom artifacts as data about the connections between learning and teaching? A Room Tour^SM is a modified walk; like other walks it usually produces a large volume of information in a relatively short period of time. Teachers lead a tour for any mix of colleagues and administrators during which they use items and arrangements in their room (or sometimes on their traveling cart) to stimulate a conversation about what they are doing and the decisions they have made to help students learn. Tourists collect data through observation, active listening, and probing questions. The tour can be used as an alternate to a traditional supervisory observation or a data source for the teacher's practice in relation to a professional standard such as Differentiating Instruction for All Students. A tour can be a way for a team to compare problem-solving approaches to a goal they are working on, e.g., how do we arrange the room and manage different kinds of learning stations so that a teacher can do targeted re-teaching three times a week? Most important, well-constructed and thought-provoking tours serve as community-building and professional development opportunities. Teachers guiding the tours often get to recognize their own competencies—steps they have taken, materials created, approaches to shared problems—through the interest of their colleagues. Tourists have opportunities to compare their own practices, expand their repertoires, and get immediate, practical information about something they might not have understood when it was presented in a larger session. Leadership team members may be able to determine the range of program implementation strategies in a building or identify places where agreements about practice are and are not being carried out at high levels.

Sample Questions

- What do you want to show us in your room that relates to helping students meet achievement targets or performance standards?

- What are the most important signs, models, or visuals in your room and how do your students use them?

- What would you like us to know about this student work?

- How do you decide what work to place on the walls?

- What criteria of success defined excellent performance on this assignment or project?

For web supplement, see www.ready-about.com

Peer Observation: Traditional Version

Evaluation	Supervision	CPS

For years, peer observation has been extolled as a way to reduce teacher isolation, make practice more public, and spread good ideas. However, scheduling challenges, financial woes, and the demands of planning for substitute lessons have limited its use. In most cases when peer observation has become a regular part of a department or school culture, it succeeds because of the specific personalities of group members or the support provided by leaders until the habit took root and became indispensable.

New and experienced teachers find that peer observation is a powerful tool for supervision and collaborative problem solving because it uncovers a wealth of valuable information with a relatively small investment of time (2 to 2.5 hours for conferencing, visiting, and conferencing again). Once a team has identified a learning problem or question, colleagues can study how students react to a particular program, new materials, or an assessment strategy; they can give one another feedback on experiments; they can help one another pinpoint a source of confusion or analyze causes of student misbehavior. They can also suggest modifications, monitor the degree to which agreements about practice are being faithfully implemented, and highlight innovations that need to be shared. Peer observation is supported by the habits of curiosity and openness and good communication about difficult issues developed in the team. Peer observation can also be part of an induction program for new teachers who learn about the value of transparent practice by having opportunities to see others at work.

Some district evaluation systems include a peer observation option as part of a multi-year professional growth cycle. In such cases, the person being observed specifies the data to be collected, analyzes the data, reflects on the findings, and may report his or her conclusions and further questions to a supervisor. An even smaller number of districts have Peer Assistance and Review programs such as Montgomery County, Maryland's. In Montgomery County, consulting teachers receive special training and then observe and critique new teachers and teachers who have been referred to the program for support.

Critical elements of a successful peer observation program include:

- Clearly communicating the purpose of the observation.

- Making the experience a requirement at some point in an evaluation cycle or induction program.

- Providing coverage or release time for the observation itself and the pre- and post-meetings of the visitor and visited. (A brief pre-conference meeting allows the teachers to plan the visit and talk about what the visitor wants to focus on. The post-conference meeting gives the teachers a chance to debrief the visit and reflect on their learning and how they will integrate their learning into their instruction.)

- Asking the receiving teacher to provide the observer with answers to two questions that can be sharpened during a pre-conference: What problem or learning challenge are you facing? What data would you like me to collect?

- Spending time determining exactly what data should be collected and the best way to record it.

- Training participants in how to conduct a collegial conversation based on data rather than on judgments and opinions.

Non-classroom Observation

Because student learning is affected by the quality of teacher collaboration, Dufour and others have advocated that, "Leaders must start by shifting their focus from evaluating and supervising individuals to developing the capacity of both teams and the entire school to work collaboratively" (2005 239). Building effective teacher and administrator collaboration creates a model for the kind of professional development that takes place in schools. It also requires us to consider how well we coach for or spread a vision of collaboration and whether we inspect that which we expect. Instead of focusing data collection and subsequent feedback exclusively on classroom instruction, we also need to assess two aspects of teacher performance outside of the classroom:

- Contribution to the professional community's efforts to improve student learning
- Interactions with students, parents, colleagues, and community outside of the classroom

Both desirable aspects of teaching performance commonly appear in sets of evaluative standards used by districts throughout the country but are rarely examined seriously. Documentation frequently consists of an elevation of the minimal ("Is punctual, shares materials, and is polite to all colleagues") or a cursory nod to an activity ("Represented the faculty at the PTO fair" or "Attends and participates in department meetings as required") unaccompanied by any link to organizational goals or student needs. Thus the message becomes "show up and comply with the superficial." Individuals who make significant, meaningful contributions to the life of the school may have more superlatives beside their names, but rarely do they see that there is any consequence for not meeting district expectations.

The data collected by administrators should be used mainly for providing supervisory feedback, coaching for improvement, and planning professional development. However, our mission is to confront conditions that undermine learning. When circumstances warrant, data can diagnose and document mediocre performance by individuals or by teams. If individual teachers are having a significant negative impact on a group's ability to meet its obligations, supervisors should carefully document the specific behaviors causing the problem, e.g., blocking decision making through a pattern of sarcasm, personal attacks, and negative commentary; not participating in problem-identification and later claiming disagreement with the group's analysis; or failing to carry a share of the workload. Specific evidence of a teacher's non-collaborative behavior, not just hearsay information, is important. Most individuals who engage in such behaviors do so across a number of different arenas from faculty meetings to inservice offerings to interchanges with parents and specialists. They often act noncollaboratively with impunity because supervisors are either afraid of the fallout from naming the behavior or unsure of how to go about raising something that is not part of classroom observation. A skilled leader simply begins to record and give feedback on each of the instances of behavior until the pattern reported by a team has been recorded in other public arenas. (See also Chapter 9 "Confronting Individuals Who Undermine Learning" for a discussion of escalated intervention and communication.)

In addition, supervisors might also need to collect data on a team's efforts and interactions when the school is trying to close significant gaps in student achievement. (For more detail on the subject of poor collaboration, see Chapter 5 "Challenging and Changing Malfunctioning Groups.")

Make the Purpose of Data Collection Clear   Practice full transparency about how meeting data will be used. Data can serve many purposes. Make the purpose of data collection clear. Is it for feedback and growth? Is it for evaluation of performance? How will it be shared and with whom? If you want to increase paranoia, do not follow this alert.

Evaluation	Supervision	CPS

Observing Teachers' Collaboration and Contributions to the Professional Community

Meetings offer rich sources of data on individual and team collaboration and contributions to the problem-solving work of the institution. Every teacher has a responsibility to take part in and contribute to a range of meetings on aspects of his/her work with students including curriculum meetings, special education plan meetings, grade level team meetings, data team meetings, department meetings, small learning community meetings, whole faculty meetings, parent conferences and information meetings, field trip and event planning meetings, to name just a few.

TIPS ON COLLECTING DATA FROM MEETINGS

✔ **Attend a meeting and observe contributions of a teacher identified as a blocker or team wrecker.** Details for this source of data are elaborated in Chapter 9 "Confronting Individuals Who Undermine Learning."

✔ **Collect team agendas and minutes.** With your leadership team, develop a template for meeting agendas and minutes. Have a timer record the exact time actually spent on each item.

✔ **Collect evidence for group growth.** As groups evolve, colleagues or supervisors can collect data and provide feedback on certain kinds of competence. What evidence indicates that teams regularly and skillfully use curriculum standards and data about student and adult performance in their deliberations?[6]

✔ **Ask teams to collect data on group functioning.** Here are some possible self-reporting questions:

How are we doing in relation to norms adopted?
In what ways have we examined as a group how our teaching is impacting student learning? What have we learned?
What is an example of a conflict and how we handled it?
How have we confronted difficult issues including the "undiscussable elephants?"

[6]For more on this topic, see Chapter 3 "Professional Communities and Mediocre Learning" and Chapter 6 "Moving Communities from Collaborative to Accountable."

How have we identified student performance problems, and what action have we taken? How do we balance individual autonomy with collective action?

How has our group handled issues of race, class, and culture?

Is there evidence of group members asking for help and admitting gaps in knowledge?

Observing Interactions Outside the Classroom

Evaluation	Supervision	CPS

Anyone in the business of visiting many schools most likely forms a strong impression of what that school is like and what its community cares about. A visitor is kept waiting without acknowledgement for five minutes while the school secretary and two teachers continue their conversation about a parent whose language "no one could understand," or a visitor is greeted warmly and promptly. A teacher, teeth clenched and voice loudly scolding, drags a student through the office door and announces in front of all present that the X can just "stay where he can't cause any more trouble for the rest of the day" or a teacher, accompanied by a student, quietly says "M needs a little time out and a chance to talk to Ms. P, and then he can come back." In the halls of a large high school, a teacher hollers to a counselor who is escorting a new student: "I hope you're not bringing me anyone new; I can't deal with the winners I've got already." The student shrugs his shoulders and hunches his head more deeply into his sweatshirt. A vice principal, feet on the desk, reads a newspaper at 9:30 a.m. while parents sit in the outer office waiting. When you walk down the halls of another large high school, you see pocket after pocket of teachers and students laughing together or engaged in spirited conversations at the classroom doors.

Although we think the most important actions to support student learning occur between teachers and students within the classroom, a school community's overall ability to make young people feel safe, known, welcomed, respected as individuals, and motivated to persist through difficulties can be significantly affected by the messages that interactions in its more public arenas send. Observations of interactions are particularly helpful for supervisory identification of places to improve or for community problem-solving. For purposes of problem-identification (an important part of problem-solving), school leaders, leadership team members, or clusters of teachers and specialists can try to collect data about the messages in their environment with outsiders' eyes.

TIPS ON COLLECTING DATA ABOUT ENVIRONMENTAL MESSAGES

✔ **Identify a question or set of questions about which a group would like data.** If you were a student of color in this school, how many messages would you get that indicated this was a place you belonged and a place you could influence? If you were a new student in this school, what would your first two days be like?

✔ **Agree in advance as a group on a set of indicators or questions that everyone will examine, a method for collecting the data, and a time interval.** Over a two-day period, how many times do we see adults greeting one another with a smile or by name? How many times do we see students greeted by name? If we walk all the halls of our school, how many examples can we find of students from diverse cultures being welcome? If we shadow (and act like) a new student for a day, what do we notice is particularly difficult?

✔ **Establish ground rules for recording and reporting out data.** Data will be identified only by gender or grade, or data will be only a set of tick marks under a particular descriptor with no other indication of the person who fit that descriptor.

✔ **Plan for groups to repeat or extend their collection activities.** After the first round of analysis, plan for new data collection as new questions arise.

Conferences

How can we use alternative conference formats to focus on data about student learning? Conferences traditionally have been sandwiched around observations. Teachers report little learning from these "pre and post meetings" if the sole purpose is to review what happened and get a signature on a document or for the supervisor to make a series of personal observations about what s/he "would prefer you do next time." Skilled leaders can do the following to make such mandated post-conferences more productive:

- Add the requirement that teachers bring evidence of student understanding.
- Spend time collaboratively analyzing student performance.
- Jointly identify next steps and next formative assessments.

Holding conferences in the teacher's classroom rather than the supervisor's office is also important. It allows ready access to lesson-related artifacts that will help both parties identify learning and teaching links. Finally, it creates a more collegial climate.

The post-observation conference based primarily on data from a single observed lesson is well suited for early career teachers and teachers in trouble. However, it may not be the best allocation of limited time for supervisors, highly skilled and thoughtful professionals ready to shape their own goals, or for experienced teachers who need a stretch. The alternative formats we offer on the following pages are intended to shift the focus of supervisory conversations toward what students are learning and how they are learning, what resources teachers need, and what steps should be taken next. In these alternative models, the primary purposes are problem-solving and creating a shared vision of high-quality teaching and learning; thus they should be introduced and implemented in an invitational, nonevaluative context. Three principles should guide leaders in their early efforts to introduce these formats:

- Explain the thinking underlying the conference format and model the approach with your own team or set of colleagues first.
- Seek voluntary teacher participation initially.
- Never use the new data to evaluate someone negatively.

The Videotaped Conference

Evaluation	**Supervision**	CPS

How can we use video technology to capture classroom data and anchor conversations about teaching and learning? Videotape has the benefit of being a preserved record that can be revisited in order to review teaching or leadership efforts. Staff members' discomfort about "seeing themselves on tape" and, more important, their concern about the use and distribution of taped performance examples make this an underemployed source of information. Collective bargaining agreements, in fact, usually protect teachers from unwarranted taping. Four principles may help build sufficient trust to help people use this powerful catalyst for discussion:

1. Make it voluntary.
2. Promise it will not be used for evaluation.
3. Turn the original over to the person or team who was taped.
4. Give staff members reflection time to review tapes individually before public sharing.

With these conditions, a staff member or team may decide to take the risk of being videotaped and of conferencing together about the tape; the goal of such an exercise should always be to analyze what helps or gets in the way of student learning or community productivity. If an individual agrees and if legal constraints can be met, arrange for a lesson or meeting to be videotaped for subsequent joint viewing. The supervisor or colleagues who will provide feedback may or may not be present during the taping.

Set the remote control in a convenient spot between teacher and audience or supervisor for easy pausing and play the segment. The staff member who was taped, the supervisor, or colleagues giving feedback can pause the video for conversation. In these "stop and reflect" moments, the conversation focuses on key decision points in the lesson or meeting. A sample supervisor stop might be "When you said 'Hold it gang, we are getting off course here; I may have confused you with the directions' what were you noticing that was impacting student comprehension of the directions?" These stop moments become conversation starters for teacher reflection and response. A sample teacher stop might be "You know I think I missed an opportunity there to fully clarify the criteria for success. The kids did not know what cre-

LEADER ALERT

Becoming a Role Model   To "walk your own talk" and make the intent and spirit of the process real, consider being the first person to volunteer to be taped leading a meeting, facilitating a group, or trying to lead a professional development session. Communicate your objectices or desired outcomes for the meeting; set criteria for success; and point people toward areas where you want feedback. Then conduct the conference with the leadership team members using the ground rules below. Model asking for and being receptive to feedback that will help you do the best possible job of reaching the audience or meeting your objectives.

---

ative meant. That's why they had so many questions." A staff member taped facilitating a team meeting might stop the tape to make an observation and ask a question: "This is where everyone started getting anxious, and the whole session started to spiral off track. What was the statement that created that? What could I/we have done to prevent that?" At the midpoint of the viewing and at the end, pause to have each participant summarize in writing insights, questions, and next steps for action or data collection so that the richness of the discussion does not get lost. Pool summaries so that each member walks away with a full record of the conversation.

Videotape can readily be used for collaborative professional development. Teachers can volunteer to be taped and to allow it to be shared with

LEGAL NOTE 7.3

Videotaping

Because of concerns that student images may turn up on the Internet or even on local access cable, both administrators and teachers need to proceed carefully. Videotaping in any setting that involves students and or their teachers may implicate legal issues of electronic surveillance and privacy rights. This note is not intended to discourage schools from using videotape internally because many districts have parents sign a general videotape release at the start of the school year to cover themselves for internal uses. Subsequently, if there is a need to place images on a website or release footage for other purposes, additional permission can and must be obtained. To be safe, review all relevant local policies and collective bargaining agreements and possibly have local school counsel guide you with regard to state and federal law dealing with privacy rights, copyrights, student records, and personnel records. It might be necessary to make parents aware that students may be taped in their interactions with teachers; they should be advised of what the intent and purpose of such taping might be. Special care should be taken in any circumstances that involve special education students since such videotapes may be used as evidence in special education hearings.

a group of colleagues who are working on the same student learning issues or who are trying to learn a new program.

Finally, taping and conferencing about the tape is a wonderful community-building strategy for groups like school leadership teams, instructional coaches, specialists, teams of special education and regular education teachers trying to improve their ability to implement inclusion programs, or administrative teams trying to get better at running meetings or leading work sessions. It models and supports sustaining transparency, an area of group capacity associated with Accountable Communities (see Chapter 3). Several protocols, including Collaborative Coaching and Learning (CCL), discussed later in this chapter, encourage observation of live teaching, but even with the easy technology, few use video for public examination of teaching.

The "Reading the Walls" Conference

| Evaluation | **Supervision** | CPS |

How does the teacher use visuals in the teaching environment to support instruction? Administrators can conduct a supervisory conference based on displayed data including student work on bulletin boards, expectation messages, and project artifacts. Such a discussion could be part of a post-observation conference taking place in the teacher's classroom or could simply occur in conjunction with the supervisor's effort to find out how a particular program is doing or what is happening with a particular set of students. Starting to talk about learning by looking at concrete objects helps give the conversation a focus and often reduces initial unease between parties. Teachers move fast and juggle many competing agendas. Put on the spot to describe something they did, they may gloss over important details because they are moving to the next unit or lesson. Wall peeping can reveal hidden treasures and prompt teachers to remember all the carefully structured ground work that led up to a particular student assignment.

Caution! Because room data are so visible, supervisors have sometimes attached too much importance to appearance over substance. We are not recommending a reversion to the 1950s when shades had to be lined up and bulletin boards were evaluated for neatness of printing. Instead supervisors can use the tangible products of teacher and student effort found on walls, tables, and in cupboards and display cases to examine the present nature of student learning and the teaching taking place to support that learning. Leaders should not assume such a process applies only to K-8 classrooms and dismiss the need to look at evidence on high school walls. We have observed some terrific high school "wall-supported" instruction as well as the more commonly bleak environments that signal that no one lives or works here. Finally, supervisors should avoid criticizing walls that are messy, naked, or dressed with yellowed, Houghton Mifflin laminated charts. Wall problems may not be the best entry point into a discussion to promote a student learning agenda. Avoid attaching too much importance to such a data source when teachers travel and share rooms.

Sample Focus Questions

- What are the criteria for selecting student work to be posted? Is there a clear connection with standards, rubrics, or performance checklists?
- Is there evidence of clear expectations for classroom discourse, e.g., criteria for active listening, guidelines for paraphrasing, or samples of clarifying questions?
- Is there evidence of thinking models or graphics such as Steps for Problem Solving, writing process charts, a word wall?
- Are content standards posted prominently in student-friendly language?
- Is there any evidence of housekeeping routines and expectations for student behavior?
- Is there evidence of effort-based "You can do it" messages?
- Are there any indicators of specific feedback on student work (not smiley faces or "Awesome" stickers)?
- Are there curriculum-relevant structures such as word walls or centers?

As a community-building idea, take digital pictures of some of the wall artifacts in different rooms, make into a quick slide show and show at the beginning of a faculty meeting.

Evaluation	Supervision	CPS

The Student Interview Conference

How can we gather data about the impact of identified practices on student learning through systematic questioning of students? The student interview conference focuses only on data collected from talking with students in their classrooms either as part of a supervisory observation or as part of a team's or department's initiative to understand their efforts from a student's point of view. At the pre-observation conference, agree on questions to be asked and what response the teacher would expect or want. The data is collected during a classroom visit and then reported back to the teacher in the post conference. For example, to find out how students are responding to the workshop model that requires them to work alone for extended periods, a visitor can ask them, "What do you do when you are stuck or confused? Their answers may vary from "I am never confused" to "ask the teacher for help" to a repertoire of strategies they can use before seeking the teacher's help (e.g., double check my work, re-read the problem, review the steps in direction, check the rubric or exemplar, check with my partner, consult with posted prompts or with notes taken in class). Contrasting answers such as these can give the teacher and observer(s) a sense of the student's perceived level of challenge, how well the teacher has done at helping learners apply effective effort strategies, and the degree of student ownership for learning that has been established.

Sample Questions

- Can you tell me the purpose or objective of this lesson? (Objectives/standards)

- Can you tell me the connection between the activities you are doing now and what you are supposed to be learning? (Context and connections)

- What do you do when you are confused? Or how do you get help to succeed? (Strategies)

- Are there practices and routines in place for you to keep track of your own learning? (Self-monitoring)

- What happens if you do not finish your work, your homework for example? (Expectations)

- How often does your teacher collect and comment on (your journal, notebook, etc.)? (Feedback)

- Does the teacher ever make a change in a lesson in the middle of class? Can you think of an example? (Modifying instruction based on data)

As with any other data point or vehicle suggested in this chapter, student answers should not be the sole source of information about an individual or team's practice. Such answers provide one point that can be cross-referenced against other evidence to pinpoint where improvement is needed.

Assessment Conference

Evaluation	Supervision	CPS

How can we collect and examine teacher-generated formative assessment data to understand how a teacher helps students meet important learning goals? Traditionally, supervisory conferences have centered on teacher performance data, (e.g., how many times a teacher asked a recall question, whether the materials were ready, how well the teacher did at modeling the skill, what was on the board) for one particular lesson out of an entire unit. For high-performing teachers, such experiences rarely provide new insights and information. What if systems allowed for differentiated experiences? What does it look like if supervisors, after having engaged in discussions with teachers and having acquired any necessary preliminary agreements from unions, are able to adjust timelines so that a conference can be held at the end of a unit? Instead of an observation of one lesson, the parties cover a table with papers and together look at:

- Unit goals and, if appropriate, some materials

- Assessment strategies or instruments

- Samples of formative assessment results from what students were doing in the middle of the sequence

- Samples showing the range of performance on the final assessment

- A data display showing the performance of all students on particular goals

The discussion begins with a close look at the overall performance in relation to the most important learning goals of the unit. The conversation might be framed by some of the following questions. Which skills or concepts did students master? Why do we think they were successful? Where did students have the greatest difficulty? What potential explanations do we have? How could we find out more? Throughout the conversation, the focus is on instructional decisions that helped student learning. An example would be, "I used, for the first time, a set of exemplars for poor to excellent history papers." Instructional decisions that appear to have hindered learning are also discussed. "The project directions put more emphasis on the form of the presentation than the content." The teacher, or perhaps even a team, guides the discussion and takes primary responsibility for drawing conclusions and identifying the next steps.

As with any other example we offer, matching the data collection strategy to the individual teacher and to the improvement goals of the school is important. Substituting an assessment conference for a classroom observation may not be appropriate if the supervisor does not know the teacher's classroom practice well, has concerns about that practice, or is unwilling or unable to suspend a directorial voice in order to be curious and open. That caveat offered, we think assessment conferences are a valuable and underestimated use of 90 minutes of supervisory time. Teachers we know who have participated in such conferences report that they often leave with "tons of good ideas for what to do next"; supervisors report gaining significant insights into the challenges both students and teachers face in trying to master a piece of content or a key skill.

Note: An easy, time-conserving alternative in districts that have common assessments or benchmark performances is the team conference. A supervisor meets with two to four people who teach the same course or grade level

LEADER ALERT

Assessment Conference   In schools with strong, positive professional cultures and good relationships between teachers and administrators, leaders can begin to replace the observation-based conference with an assessment conference for experienced teachers not in trouble. Or, if the climate is not yet ready for such a full substitution, administrators can create a hybrid by spending some part of the post-observation conference talking about an assessment of student understanding done as part of the week's instruction. In many instances, informally practicing this kind of conference with volunteers can lay the groundwork for later discussions or negotiations about making the practice consistent throughout the district.

to examine assessment results and artifacts. Call it supervision with a professional development twist. The model would work well to coach teachers around common assessments.

Portfolio-Based or Student-led Parent Conference

Evaluation	Supervision	CPS

How can we use student-conducted conferences as a source of data about teaching and learning?

An increasing number of elementary and middle school teachers conduct portfolio conferences where students take responsibility for presenting evidence of their learning to parents and teachers. Supervisors wishing to expand the ways in which they collect data about learning could observe one of these sessions either as a supplement to shorter periods of classroom observation or as one of the ways in which they differentiate experiences for high-performing staff. The post-observation conference about the student-led presentation then focuses on practices that produced this evidence of learning and issues with which the teacher or team is currently wrestling. This data source provides information not only on the learning of one student but on the type of feedback the teacher gives to all students.

The Document or Artifact Conference

Evaluation	Supervision	CPS

How can discussions about easily accessible "documents" be used to:

- Identify obstacles to student learning?
- Help a teaching team monitor their own expectations and practices?
- Assess teachers' non-classroom responsibilities, including outreach to parents, meeting professional responsibilities, or contributions to their community?

In the course of preparing an end-of-the year evaluation of a teacher, many administrators will look at a sample of documents or artifacts that an individual has produced. They then report that an activity has been carried out. Because such document examination takes place late in the year, it rarely has any impact on the community or on an individual teacher's learning or subsequent practice. A document conference gives a formal name and a learning goal to this behavior of looking at parent newsletters, course syllabi, tests, homework assignments, beginning of school letters to students, or guidelines for lab reports to understand the impact of teaching choices on student learning.

Rather than focusing on the contents of literal notes an evaluator has taken during an observation of a single lesson, a 30- to 40-minute artifact conference focuses on concrete examples representing weeks of practice. Those examples could include all the charts, rubrics, self-assessment prompts, homework assignments, learning center directions that an individual or a grade level team developed to support writer's workshop, or the packet of materials that the music department created to organize and support an upcoming trip to perform at a festival. Individuals or teams then reflect on the goals they had in creating the documents, what they learned as they used them, what worked and didn't work, how they modified the documents, and perhaps what they will do next. The process can be an informal give and take focused on what might help students. Or it can follow a formal protocol such as those used to identify problems or look at student work. (See Protocols later in this chapter.) The contents of the conference give supervisors and team members insights into the ways in which the teacher's efforts can be supported or perhaps give indicators of the need for school-wide professional development.

Document conferences can give collaborative and accountable communities insight into what helps or hinders student learning. For example, at one Maryland middle school we know, each grade level team collected all of the homework assignments given to its students over the course of the week to find out what percentage of their jointly assigned work was actually requiring students to use higher level thinking skills. At another school, all of the World Civilization teachers collected copies of their best and worst essays on a particular topic in order to analyze what skills they needed to teach more explicitly.

EXAMPLE   District-Level Examination of the Role of Homework

No one was happy about homework in this Northeastern school district. Depending upon the grade level involved, parents complained about too much or too little. Teachers felt it was impossible to keep up with students who were delinquent with homework. Principals saw a lot of busy work. Rather than beginning with homework policies specifying grade level time estimates, a skillful central office leader organized a system-wide collection of all homework assignments over a three-week period. She then had secondary departments and elementary grade level teams examine the quality of homework in relationship to learning standards and make recommendations. Each teacher shared his or her portfolio of assignments. It was no surprise that most assignments were only weakly aligned with standards. Groups then developed system-wide criteria that specified homework quality, purpose, and alignment. Teachers used those criteria to make significant improvements in the quality of homework assignments.

Document conferences provide a data point when a supervisor or evaluator receives complaints. Significant complaints could include the following: this teacher does not grade and return papers; the teacher makes many grammatical errors on communications to parents; this teacher does not do the reporting required by a special education plan. Document conferences also provide corroborating evidence if a supervisor thinks s/he has uncovered a potential problem as a result of some other activity. Potential problems could include no grade book or plan book available on the day of an observation, multiple misspellings or fragments on a project assignment worksheet, or no evidence of modifications for special education students during three different walk-throughs. In each case, the evaluator should name the problem and cite the specific evidence, provide feedback and recommendations for improvement, and follow up the conference with a written summary of agreements for changes and next steps.

The Data-Use Conference

| Evaluation | Supervision | CPS |

How can we assess team and individual effectiveness in using data to adjust instruction?

As its name implies, this conference focuses exclusively on how a team or individual is using external and internally generated data to "monitor student learning and adjust instruction," a common standard for teacher performance. When its primary purpose is either supervision or collaborative problem solving, the data use conference asks such questions as:

- What evidence do we have about what students are and are not learning and where we need to change our practice?

- How can we find out if our proposed strategy is making a difference?

- What data should we collect before we begin instruction?

Data-use conferences can be part of another kind of activity, e.g., 15 minutes of a grade level meeting, a high school department meeting, or a middle school team meeting; a brief meeting between two physics teachers who are redesigning a program; or an informal discussion that occurs as a result of two teachers' presenting their brainstorming about improvements for next year's science fair.

When an evaluator holds a data-use conference with a teacher to assess that teacher's ability to gather, analyze, and apply data to improve instruction, the evaluator will typically ask for evidence that the teacher is doing

LEADER ALERT

Name Is Less Important Than Practice   Regular conversations about evidence of student performance are essential if teachers are to believe the district cares about the performance standards of Monitoring Learning with Data. They are also essential if the practices of a school are to shift from unexamined activity to thoughtful problem solving. Naming this type of an exchange a "data conference" gives it dignity and signals that the school does not take the standard lightly. However, the name is less important than the habit of mind and practice. If using the name would make the process threatening or cause the intent to be misrepresented or overblown, simply make discussion of data a regular part of any post-observation conference.

those actions. The teacher should be expected to know what available external testing and internal benchmarking has revealed about students' skills and struggles and should be able to present evidence that the information has affected planning and instruction. Low student achievement scores coupled with a lack of evidence of formative assessment or modified instruction should trigger either large group professional development or direct recommendations and support to help individuals improve.

| Evaluation | Supervision | CPS |

Professional Learning Conference

How can we use conferences to improve the quality of professional development plans and choices so they improve student learning? A number of local supervision and evaluation systems and some state recertification provisions require teachers to prepare and implement individual professional development plans. Each fall principals ask teachers to submit their plans; each spring the parties meet to consider evidence of progress. These conferences can be treated as pro-forma check-offs or invaluable opportunities for thoughtful conversations about professional learning. Both the planning and the analysis conference allow leaders to connect the work of the individual, or in some cases the team, to the larger goals of the school and district. Underlying this activity is the assumption that teachers who feel a connection to a bigger purpose develop a greater sense of ownership and urgency about the results the school is getting and the changes that need to be made. These conversations serve primarily to clarify expectations about high-quality teaching and learning (supervision). However, the spring conference can also provide evaluation data to determine whether an individual has met the district's standard on professional learning.[7]

As we move toward effective collaborative work, leaders can also encourage team members to develop individual professional development plans based on the student learning problems that the team has identified linked to district and school goals. To improve the quality of such plans, references to data use should be required.

TIPS ON CONFERENCES ABOUT PROFESSIONAL DEVELOPMENT PLANS

✔ Clearly specify criteria for good professional development plans in advance; make sure proposed goals are measurable and arise, as much as possible, from previously identified gaps in student learning.

✔ Collect and annotate exemplars of appropriate and inappropriate professional development plans. Note: These serve to set a standard, guide teacher's work when they are new to the process, and stave off potential accusations of unfair treatment if a draft plan needs to be sent back for revision.

✔ Expand the focus of the conference to include career goals and professional long- term growth.

[7]For further information and examples of phrasing for standards on teacher professional development see Saphier (1993), Danielson, or the National Board for Professional Teaching Standards www.nbpts.org

✔ When contract provisions or prior negotiated agreements permit, allow collaborative plans from same grade level or from teachers of the same course who have analyzed data and identified a common, pressing problem they want to address.

✔ Do not accept poor quality, "do a project" type plans that require little or no stretch on the planner's part simply to get the process over with and "get on to a real need." Mediocre efforts will come back to haunt you. Be respectful and supportive, but send back for revision plans that are shallow, activity-based, or focused on the development of a minimal competency that the teacher should already possess.

Upgrading the Professional Learning Conference

Syracuse City Public Schools in New York wanted to upgrade both teacher professional development plans and the supervisory conversations about those plans. Principals brought samples and used them to develop criteria for success that would help teachers produce plans more clearly tied to student learning and help supervisors focus their required "Exchange Conferences" on links between activities and problems to be solved (see Example). During the work sessions, they role-played conferences around poorly written professional development plans.

EXAMPLE Syracuse City: Elements and Criteria for Professional Development Plans

Elements	Criteria	YES	YES BUT?	NO
Goals	• Identify the standard from the state or local curriculum documents, the topic or unit. • Frame a large question • Are SMART (measurable) • Based on data that show gaps in student learning • Are not teacher activity			
Impact on Learning	• Clearly state impact on students on student outcome form			
Action Steps/ Resources	• Have timelines indicated • Require collaboration or sharing with colleagues			
Reflections	• Focus on student learning • Highlight transfer of learning into classroom • Pose a new problem or goal based on findings • Show data-based inquiry			

What happens if leaders fail to upgrade planning and conversations around professional learning and instead treat the process as an exercise in form completion? Consider the example from a 4th grade teacher in Wishy-Washy District 2 who submitted this PD plan in the fall.

EXAMPLE Professional Development Plan—Wishy-Washy District 2

Name: Sally Friendly
Approved: November 1, 2007
Problem to be addressed: I am struggling with many preps and am finding my job stressful.
Connection to School Goals: Math initiative
Personal Goal: To round out my math teaching and extend my knowledge of various SS/Sci areas.
Data to be Collected: I will present a list of PD and complete the Reflection section.

The busy principal glanced at the form, stapled it to his own school plan, thanked Sally for meeting the deadline, and set out to track down laggards who had not yet turned in their paperwork. There was no conversation to elevate the quality of the thinking, much less the writing. Does this resemble your situation in any way? Leaders beware: compliance-driven processes with a focus on completing forms and meeting deadlines can create conditions that undermine adult learning.

In the spring, the teacher finished her plan and submitted the following:

EXAMPLE Ms. Friendly's Workshops and Conferences 2007-2008

Title	No. of hours	Date	Provider
So How is Your Self-Esteem?	4.0	7/20	Wellness Institute
Meteorology for Elem. Grades	2.5	9/10	HS Science dept
Storytelling Conference	5.0	9/30	US Storytellers' Assoc.
Costa Rica	1.5	10/15	Social Studies Coord.
Nonjudgmental Imagery	6.0	11/8	Wellness Institute
How to Teach Drawing	2.0	1/9	Community Education
Box It and Bag It Math	30.0	2/10-4/30	Inservice math training
Relieving Stress	4.5	3/7	In-service day

Statement of Reflection: I achieved my goal of filling in gaps in my learning and my desire to reduce the stress of the job. Next year I want to work on my literacy circles.

Once again the now frantic principal checked off Sally without a conference to discuss these results. So a poor, unmonitored plan with a nonspecific goal accompanied by low-level ideas for data collection translated into superficial reflection and little or no impact on students. The process was perfectly designed to get what it got!

Protocols

What structures will help teams monitor whether their effort is making any difference in terms of student learning? Protocols are data vehicles that help to structure collaborative problem solving. They have become popular tools to guide groups as they interact with data about instructional strategies and student learning. Protocols serve to protect team participants from time-wasting meandering or inappropriately judgmental interactions by helping groups to focus and monitor the flow of conversation.

> Protocols control transparency. By specifying, for example, who speaks when and who listens when, protocols segment elements of conversation … they make clear the crucial differences between talking and listening, between describing and judging or between proposing and giving feedback. (McDonald 5)

Monitoring and enforcing process is important to creating a safe climate. But ensuring substantive and productive analysis is equally important if teachers are not to leave a session with the sense that their time has been wasted.

Two drawbacks limit the promise of protocols. First, not all protocols work equally well for all tasks. Thus teams need to be careful to match the type of protocol to the problem that is to be solved or the question to be answered. Second, the highly structured nature of most protocols allows individuals or teams that are stuck in regressive interactions (see Chapter 3) to fulfill the technical requirements of the exchange without ever contributing much of value toward addressing student learning problems. The structures for focusing a conversation may accidentally lead to inauthentic and overly guarded exchanges. Or a protocol may prove too restrictive in the midst of problem solving as one of us noted while watching a group of teachers who clearly recognized an instructional problem they wanted to raise but could find no legitimate place in the process to insert the observation.

Protocols work best if they are used to help groups tackle data or a perplexing problem in which they have a clear stake: "Only 2 percent of our 8th graders were able to reach the advanced level on the persuasive essay despite the whole unit we did on it at the beginning of the year." An activity that does not address a current problem would be: "We're all doing 'looking at student work in small learning communities' this year." Here we provide just a few sample protocols and suggest resources for finding others. Teams may need to experiment with several different types in order to find good matches for their own contexts. Whatever the exact protocol selected to help a group do its work more effectively, participation in the process should not be voluntary. All group members, whether teachers with inside knowledge or administrators who come at the problem with a different perspective, need to take part in pooling their insights and questions to help the organization get smarter.

Collaborative Assessment Conference (Allen 1998)

The Challenge of Transfer Problems with protocols also surfaced when leadership teams used them. A study from the National School Reform Network found that administrative teams could become more collaborative using two protocols. Specifically they found that the group developed wonderful skills in clarifying, probing, listening, and even challenging each other about practice. However, what they learned as a team did not lead to organizational learning, i.e., a change in how the organization did business. Practices administrators had used in their own group were lost in the transfer back to school and department teams (Fahey). Finally, McLaughlin and Talbert report that:

> Well designed group activities and protocols are insufficient to spur change in teaching cultures toward teacher community practice … many schools used the protocol for data based inquiry in superficial ways that preserved teacher private practice. Similarly in a district initiative that required grade-level teacher teams to use a particular lesson study protocol, most teams made only ritual use of the protocol and few developed as learning communities through the lesson study process. Absent skilled guidance in using a particular protocol, a group's learning is apt to be procedural and shallow and cannot move teachers toward collaborative efforts to improve instruction. (2006 43-44)

Evaluation	**Supervision**	CPS

Purpose: This popular "Looking at Student Work" (LASW) model uses student writing as a source of data to derive insight into the instruction that preceded the text.

Steps

1. Reading the text. Presenting teacher shares a student-written text.
2. Observation and description. Members factually describe the work.

3. Raising questions. Members pose questions about the text, the author, and the context. The teacher is silent.

4. What is the student working on? Members speculate on what the student was working on as she wrote the text. The teacher is silent.

5. Presenting teacher responses. The teacher answers questions and fills in context.

6. Teaching moves and pedagogical responses. Both teacher and members consider instructional strategies that could challenge or support this writing.

7. Reflection. Everyone evaluates the conference and its usefulness and identifies implications for instruction for groups of students in different classrooms.

TIPS ON IMPLEMENTING THE COLLABORATIVE ASSESSMENT PROTOCOL

✔ Participants should withhold judgment about the text under examination.

✔ The presenting teacher reveals as little about the student writer as possible.

✔ The process requires a strong facilitator and a trusting group to ensure that the focus stays on instruction rather than on student flaws (Allen 1998 24).

Consultancy Protocol[8]

Purpose: To structure group problem solving around a presented dilemma. Here is one example offered by a principal to his professional community: "I have a real dilemma with my Leadership Team. We make agreements, but then I can't count on the team leaders to either communicate, or in some cases support, the agreement. As a result, there is little evidence that practice has changed when I visit classrooms."

Evaluation	Supervision	CPS

Roles

Presenter who offers the case for consideration
Facilitator who also participates

Steps and Timetable

1. Presenter poses a task or problem framed as a question. (10 minutes)

2. Members ask clarifying questions. (5 minutes)

3. Members ask probing questions. (10 minutes)

4. The group deliberates; they discuss the problem and offer sugges-

---

[8]This and other protocols were developed by Gene Thompson-Grove as part of the Coalition of Essential Schools and further adapted by National School Reform faculty (www.nsffharmony.org).

tions. The presenter is silent. (20 minutes)

5. The presenter responds and reflects on what was learned. (10 minutes)

6. Members debrief the process. (5 minutes)

TIPS ON CLEARLY FRAMING THE PROBLEM

✔ The facilitator must be rigorous about helping the teacher define the problem. We suggest writing it for public inspection. The authors have observed several cases of "solving" problems that were not clearly defined.

✔ Build in a feedback loop so that presenter of problem reports back to groups at the next meeting.

EXAMPLE   Combining Protocols with Study Groups

The Boston Middle School Principals Group wanted to increase their skill in developing and challenging their teacher leadership teams. Irwin Blumer of Boston College and one of the authors developed a hybrid model by combining a study group with a consultancy protocol. The idea was to model the kind of work that should be undertaken by the Instructional Leadership Teams (ILT's) at each member's school. Monthly sessions were 3 ½ hours.

Steps and Timetable

1. Chat and lunch. (30 minutes)

2. Study group: two chapters from Leadership on the Line (Heifetz and Linsky 2002) using Save the Last Word Protocol (National School Reform Faculty). (60 minutes)

3. Consultancy protocol: A principal and a colleague who have visited a Leadership Team Meeting (LT) present a problem of practice or a dilemma associated with his leadership team. (45 minutes)

4. New content: critiquing videos of LT's, examining new research. (30 minutes)

5. Assessing adherence to norms developed in first session. (5 minutes)

The well-attended sessions helped develop individual principal skills and build a strong model learning community.

Collaborative Coaching and Learning (CCL)[9]

Purpose: To support implementation of adopted literacy and math curricula across every classroom.

The Boston Plan for Excellence in conjunction with the Boston Public Schools has developed this powerful curriculum and staff development

---

[9]Source: *Plain Talk about CCL: A Guide for Teachers* (CCL) (www.bpe.org).

model. Guided by an expert coach in literacy or math, experienced and new teachers learn together by teaching and observing lessons. They then try out their new learning in their own classrooms and report back their experiences with artifacts of their students' learning. It replaces the one coach-consultant model with a peer team of colleague coaches. The teacher union has been very supportive of this work, and all teachers are required to participate during released time.

Asked to identify what initiative had made the most impact on the quality of teaching in his school over the years of his tenure, William Henderson, an experienced and highly skilled principal at Boston's O'Hearn Elementary School responded without hesitating:

> CCL has elevated practice more than anything else we have done. Giving teachers on a regular basis opportunities to observe their colleagues or coaches teaching literacy or math to their children or their colleagues' children—looking at the instruction then reflectively discussing what went well and what didn't go so well, and then focusing on what are some of the steps and strategies to make improvement. The collegiality is key. You are only going to learn so much from a principal who visits sporadically to evaluate you, but when you are spending up to 24 hours a year observing your colleagues teaching or they observing you, sometimes with an external coach and then having conversations about the practice, you are going to see things differently, you are going to see other possibilities and you are going to be encouraged and supported [and expected] to try out new techniques targeted to helping Mary or Rafael do better—we are talking about trying out specific techniques in specific content areas and coming back to improve what took place. We have definitely seen impact on student learning over the past few years. (personal communication 2005)

Steps and Timetable

1. **Inquiry Session** (40-60 minutes per week)

   The coach and a team of teachers meet weekly to review and discuss readings in its course of study and to relate them to each teacher's classroom practice.

2. **Lab Site** (60-90 minutes per week)

   Each week the participants, including the coach and the principal/headmaster, take turns watching and teaching a demonstration lesson that incorporates teaching practices related to the course of study and chosen by the team during the inquiry session. The person demonstrating meets with the coach beforehand to plan a lesson. During the lab site, the participants review the purpose of the lesson in a pre-conference. They then observe the demonstration and analyze the effects of the practice on students in a debriefing session.

3. **Follow Up and One-on-One Coaching** During the cycle and

between cycles, the coach and/or participants make visits to individual classrooms to support teachers as they implement workshop practices.

Lesson Study

Evaluation | **Supervision** | CPS

Purpose: Teams collaborate in order to elevate the quality of planning and teaching of selected "research" lessons.

This protocol comes from Japan through the work of Stigler and Hiebert. Similar in some ways to Collaborative Coaching and Learning (CCL) discussed above, Lesson Study asks teachers to select specific lessons to study in order to refine the instruction. Lesson Study stages include planning, teaching, observing, and critiquing the lessons.[10]

Steps

1. The team selects a goal or research question. It may be a lesson that all members find difficult or one unique to an individual teacher.

2. The individual, in consultation with the team, selects a lesson to serve as the "research lesson." Ideally all teachers on the team are teaching or about to teach that particular lesson. The research lesson is not a model lesson but rather one designed to explore or experiment with a way of approaching the topic.

3. The team responds to the teacher's lesson and suggests modifications.

4. The team and teacher select "goal-focused" data to collect; the data should serve as the focus for post-lesson discussion. Team members can specialize in collecting targeted data (questions asked, interviewing students about confusions, etc.)

5. The team observes the lesson or, if necessary, a videotape of the lesson.

6. The team and teacher conduct a post-lesson discussion. Members present data and reflect with the teacher about the implications for revision.

7. After the group revises the lesson plan, another teacher teaches the newest version of the lesson with the team observing. Note: It will not be always possible to have the team observe every lesson.

8. The team reports on what they have learned for future teaching of that lesson.

TIPS ON IMPLEMENTING LESSON STUDY

✔ Focus on difficult to teach concepts revealed by various types of student performance data.

[10]For additional resources see Lesson Study Research Group 2001 (lsrg@columbia.edu); William B. Ribas, Jennifer Antos Deane and Scott Seider (2005), and www.tc.columbia.edu/lessonstudy/.

✔ Let the presenting teacher lead off the post-lesson meeting with her reflections and questions.

✔ Record the learning so that future teachers can benefit from this action research.

✔ To assess the team's effectiveness, probe to determine how any questions or suggestions that were raised during the planning informed the teacher's instructional decisions.

✔ When teams share their feedback, it should be in the form of concrete evidence from the lesson (e.g., "I saw student X do this"), suggestions that draw upon members' own experiences (e.g., "When I taught a similar lesson, I did X differently because..."), and nonjudgmental questions.

Error Analysis (EA)

Evaluation	Supervision	CPS

Purpose: To analyze errors drawn from student work in order to identify which content and which students need re-teaching and how immediate instruction should be modified.

Because his experience suggests that student errors are a rich and revealing source of data about conceptual understanding or misconceptions, Jon Saphier has developed and begun experimenting with what he calls a "quasi-protocol" he has named Error Analysis. He uses the label "quasi" to differentiate EA from highly structured protocols that he believes can become overly restrictive and thus prevent teams from digging more deeply into the exact nature of the students' mistakes and the kinds of thinking or fragmented knowledge those mistakes reveal. Like lesson study, Error Analysis allows teams to deepen their understanding of content and to design immediate, timely interventions in the form of targeted re-teaching "tomorrow, not next year."

Paul Bambrick, Principal of the Northstar Academy[11] in Newark, New Jersey, believes that Error Analysis is one of the main reasons for the dramatic improvement in student learning at his school (personal communication 2005). While Error Analysis can be carried out on a quarterly basis using the results of common assessments, Saphier advocates using EA far more regularly so that teachers can take immediate advantage of what they learn from their data to re-teach students who still have not mastered a particular concept before they get too far behind. Once team members learn how to conduct Error Analysis, they can apply the process to virtually any assessment using the following guideline questions:

Questions to Guide Error Analysis and Re-teaching

1. What might the student have been thinking to make this error?
2. How can we find out which of these hypotheses are right?
3. What different teaching strategies could we use to "fix" or undo

---

[11]For more information on Northstar Academy, see www.uncommonschools.org/nsa/home/.

whatever led to this error and help the student solidify his/her skills and concepts?

4. How are each of us going to plan and manage tasks and time during the instructional period so that we will get 15 minutes to re-teach skills and concepts at least three times a week for those students who made errors?

5. How can the team help?

Saphier claims that when Error Analysis is part of an assessment and immediate re-teaching loop, the impact on learning will be substantial. He acknowledges that some management planning is necessary to free up time to work with kids who don't get it yet... but will![12] The Conviction belief in "ability to learn" is critical to motivating the participants. Participants in Error Analysis must believe that all students are able enough and that the content is important enough to be worth re-teaching.

TIPS ON IMPLEMENTING ERROR ANALYSIS

✔ Leaders of the process should be rigorous about keeping the exchange focused on the questions listed above.

✔ In order to support teacher teams, principals should use their own Leadership Team (LT) to practice the process and should periodically sit in on and participate in Error Analysis sessions.

✔ LT members should over time be trained to carry our EA with their teams.

✔ Teams must share subject matter and ideally be teaching the same course. (In small schools where only one individual teaches a course, members can rotate cases from each of their disciplines for analysis by the entire group.)

✔ Individuals who benefit from team thinking should always report back on what they did in re-teaching, how it went, and what they learned.

SUGGESTED RESOURCES

Allen, David, *Assessing Student Learning, New York*. Teacher's College Press, 1998. [Especially helpful in working with teacher communities.]

Garmston, Robert J. and Bruce M. Wellman. *The Adaptive School: A Sourcebook for Developing Collaborative Groups*. Norwood, MA: Christopher-Gordon Publishers, Inc., 1999. [For building collaborative groups, this reference stands above the rest. This must be in your professional library.]

McDonald, Joseph P., Nancy Mohr, Alan Dichter and Elizabeth C. McDonald. *The Power of Protocols: An Educator's Guide to Better*

---

[12]Thanks to Jon Saphier for his assistance on this topic (personal communication 2007).

Practice. New York, NY: Teachers College Press, 2003. [A wonderful bible of protocols.]

Nelsen, Jeff, Joe Palumbo, Amalia Cudeiro and Jan Leight. *The Power of Focus: Lessons Learned in District and School Improvement.* Focus on Results, 2005. [This tidy little text gives examples of protocols in action.]

HELPFUL WEBSITES

Center for Performance Assessment, www.makingstandardswork.com [This is a rich set of resources for everything about standards and data and for additional resources for Data Teams.]

Critical Friends Group (CRG) (www.cesnorthwest.org/cfg.php) [This provides many of the same protocols at the National School Reform Faculty with some tweaks and modifications.]

National School Reform Faculty www.nsffharmony.org [Highly recommended, this permission-ready, copyable website is a rich source of protocols for examining work, solving dilemmas, and for learning from student work and from school and classroom visits.]

Summary

This chapter specifies methods of collecting and using data by providing vehicles ranging from rule-driven protocols to more loosely structured RoomTours^{SM}. Leaders are invited to select vehicles that match their own context. However, vehicles are not ends but means to using data to focus energy on student learning. In the next chapter we enumerate data sources rather than the structures as another entry point into collecting and using data.

8 Collecting and Using Data: Sources

In Chapter 7 we presented vehicles or structures that supervisors and evaluators can use to gather, process, and give meaning to data. In this chapter we consider what sources of data supervisors and evaluators might use to illuminate student learning problems and assess the results of teacher practice. To keep the organization of the two chapters parallel, Table 8.1 lists the sources or categories with the same three applications: evaluation, supervision, and collaborative problem solving.

Teacher-Generated Data

Grading and Progress Reports

Evaluation	Supervision	CPS

What do grading and reporting practices tell us about the teacher's expectations for student learning? Teacher's grading and reporting practices undermine student learning and sap community conviction when they:

- Do not provide accurate information about performance in relation to an agreed-upon standard
- Are not based on valid and varied assessments of students' work
- Are based upon the teacher's beliefs about a student's innate ability, attitude, or effort
- Send messages that the teacher does not expect or require most students to reach mastery

TABLE 8.1   Sources of Data

In the columns below, one check mark (√) indicates that the vehicle is a potentially useful way to achieve the particular purpose indicated on the column head. Two check marks (√√) signal that the vehicle is a powerful way to achieve that purpose.

Source	Learning-Focused Evaluation	Learning-Focused Supervision	Collaborative Problem Solving
Teacher-Generated Data	√√	√	√√
Grading and progress reports	√	√	√√
Formative assessments	√	√√	√√
Artifacts	√	√√	√√
Reflection on and modification of instruction	√	√√	√√
Supervisor-Generated Data			
Student Placement	√	√	
File notes	√	√	
Attendance patterns	√	√	
Arrival and departure times	√	√	
Discipline referrals	√√	√	√
Surveys and Interviews Teacher surveying students	√	√	√√
Student focus groups		√	√
Student interview to document a complaint	√√		
Student interview to monitor implementation	√	√√	√√
Teacher self-evaluation		√√	
Student Achievement Data	√√	√√	√√
Teacher's Collective and Individual Use of Data to Influence Decisions	√√	√√	

Grading Patterns for Supervision and Evaluation

Supervisors should examine grading patterns whenever there is concern about fairness or comprehensiveness in the teacher's evaluation of students or when grade distributions vary considerably between individuals teaching the same curriculum to similar students. Teachers working in isolation or under great stress can easily fall prey to leniency error (grade inflation) or severity error in ranking their students. Grading leniency or severity are particularly acute in schools that do not have:

- Common assessments or benchmarks based on state and local standards
- Criteria for success identified and adopted by all teachers of a particular grade or course
- Jointly developed and field-tested rubrics or other grading tools

LEADER ALERT ————————————————————————

Using Grade Books   Looking at grade books to assess a teacher's priorities fulfills the maxim "you inspect what you expect." However, before you begin, read and pay attention to any provisions regarding data sources in your contract and evaluation agreements. Because of past practice, shared mythology about who owns the records, or a collective bargaining agreement in a particular contract, alarms and objections may be raised when supervisors start asking for grading records. Underlying this reaction, Reeves notes, is a "pervasive belief that teaching is a private endeavor and grading policies are the exclusive domain of those private practitioners" (2006 113). As with many alternative sources of data, use grade books cautiously, always accompanied with other sources of information. Avoid rushing to superficial judgments about completeness or neatness. Instead, use the grade book as an opportunity to probe a teacher's thinking and understand the way s/he makes decisions.

——

What teachers choose to grade is a statement about what they consider important. The grade book thus provides an entry point into a discussion about assessment. Scanning an actual grade book or computer display gives a supervisor an overview of the teacher's assessment practices for an entire marking period and provides valuable data such as:

- How many assignments and what types of assignments are given
- How different types of assignments are graded
- How assignments are weighted (i.e., whether trivial assessments like true-false quizzes are given the same weight as demanding writing assignments)
- Completion rate for students
- Extent of make-ups by students
- How many students do the homework

- Extent of grading of homework
- Student turnover in the class
- How assignments/assessments are connected to important standards
- What, if any, role extra credit[1] plays in grading

The ensuing conversations often uncover practices that conflict with findings of research on closing achievement gaps (Corbett). For example, a common practice that has been found to undermine learning is that students who want to be retested on a concept they missed the first time and who earn a higher grade on the second test cannot be allowed to keep that grade; the conventional thinking is that would be cheating other students who got it the first time. Those conversations may also expose the need for professional development or raise difficult policy questions that ought to be considered in whole faculty groups and small professional communities (e.g., the advantages and disadvantages of standards-based grading versus norm-referenced grading).

Standards-Based Grading

There is growing interest in adopting standards-based grading to counter the limitations of traditional grading systems. Marzano (2000), among others, cites three problems for "100 year old" grading practices.

- Teachers can include non-achievement factors in the assignment of grades.
- Teachers can differentially weight assessments.
- Current systems mix different types of knowledge and skills into a single score.

We would add that frequently grades are not referenced to explicit criteria for success; thus different teachers assign different grades for the same performance on the same task. Traditional grades rarely represent consistent (reliable) and accurate (valid) measures of student achievement. Furthermore, there is little alignment between teacher grading and external measures. Experts agree that grades end up evaluating a subjective basket of qualities including: cooperation and compliance, effort, work habits, extra credit, and academic progress. We strongly encourage leaders to begin to move in the direction of standards-based grading that has three key characteristics:

- It clearly distinguishes what is being assessed and graded.
- It requires clear criteria for success to be communicated so students know how to be successful.

---

[1]Extra credit is often the enemy of reliable grading! Extra credit should be carefully monitored and should not supplement regular credit (see "Grading to Communicate" by Tony Wagner in *Educational Leadership*, November 2005 Vol. 63(3): 61-65).

• It reports progress toward mastery of a standard based on identified sources of data.[2]

Even though there are some wonderful, isolated examples of standards-based reporting, as of late 2007 few schools have implemented these methods, and we have yet to find a high school that has abandoned traditional GPA grading systems. That should not prevent leaders from initiating conversations about grading and standards with teams.

Grading Information for Collaborative Problem-Solving and Internal Accountability

Discussions of grading should be public; teachers should share and compare their ratings against those of their colleagues. In addition to supervisory examination of individual grade books, teams can examine grade distributions and grading practices to determine what effect they have on the caliber of student work or students' motivation to learn. Teams can also use grade distribution data to identify potential problems and to define and monitor common goals. Linda Hunt, math teacher at the Bonnie Eagle High School in Hollis, Maine explains how her 10th grade team uses grade targets as a common goal.

We have developed a team goal of expecting and helping all students to have a minimum grade of 85. At the end of the semester, we have a chart where each of us put all of our grades based on our progress reports. We then calculate where we are on our mean and will share our grades in relationship to our goal. We do a lot of questioning about other teachers' grades. If someone says "this is pretty good for that student," we say "what do you mean pretty good for him? What criteria you are grading that on?" Sometimes it hard for the teacher to take, but we have a community when the teacher is more likely to reflect and think "I have to back up and look at this." This also allows us to surface how different teachers reach different students and why certain students are doing so well in one class but are floundering in my class. We might question: "are you making it too easy for the students?" We have grading discussions about allowing make-ups and not averaging. Not everyone agrees on this; we have not reached a common agreement, but at least but we are having the discussion.

Making grading a team discussion shifts accountability for student progress to the team and away from the individual teacher. It is a powerful strategy for building Accountable Communities that impact student learning.

---

[2]Teachers or administrators who wish to influence grading practices should begin with Bob Marzano's *Transforming Grading Practices* (Association of Supervision and Curriculum Development, 2000).

Student Progress Reports

Theoretically, quarterly or midterm progress reports should provide students and parents with useful feedback about how the student is performing in relation to the curriculum standards or benchmarks and should note what the student needs to do next. However, school or district expectations for progress reports and the forms those reports take vary widely. Often, the practice has been in place without monitoring or critical examination for so long that few members of the school community can remember why it started and what it was supposed to accomplish. If providing progress reports or "warning notices" has become a pro forma exercise of checking off blocks with little connection to student self-assessment or little opportunity to provide individualized feedback, this data source is not useful for evaluation. Nor would it be helpful for individual supervision. To make substantive progress reports part of a vision of high-quality teaching and learning, skilled leaders might:

- Raise questions about the impact of progress reports
- Gather data about progress reports from parents and students
- Ask teams to examine the value of the practice critically and to suggest ways of making it more effective for students.

If the district has engaged in a critical examination of progress reports and communicated clear expectations for their content and rigor, then such reports can provide supervisors with data about the overall patterns and quality of teachers' comments to students. Persistent patterns of mediocre feedback (e.g., trite refrains such as "a pleasure to have in class" or "not working up to potential") can be an indicators of low expectations, lack of clarity about outcomes, or poor assessment practices, all of which affect student learning.

Special notice should be given to midterm warning notices. Failure to notify poor performers in a timely manner can be a characteristic of mediocre teaching. (See *The Skillful Leader: Confronting Mediocre Teaching* 2000 80). High-functioning Collaborative or Accountable Communities can exchange warning notices as a source of data for collaborative problem solving. To turn their collective commitment to student success into actions, teams or subgroups within a department can use the warning notices as the starting point for:

- Analyzing the causes for poor performance
- Forming hypotheses about the obstacles to performance faced by different groups of students
- Proposing ways to collect data about present obstacles for groups of students
- Jointly designing interventions targeted to different types of obstacles

Often warning notices are closely linked to assessment practices and the ways in which teachers communicate their expectations with non-performers. Thus, examining practice on midterm warning notices leads groups deeper into discussions of other critical issues related to helping students stay connected to school and persist in the face of difficulties.

Formative Assessments

Evaluation	Supervision	CPS

How can we use teacher-generated assessment data to develop internal accountability and build ownership for monitoring student growth? This category of data is about assessments for learning in contrast to assessments of learning whose primary intent is summative evaluation (Stiggins). It includes interim measures such as quarterly assessments, writing tasks, and projects that teachers use individually or collectively to assess student progress. Designed and scored by teachers, these internal, curriculum-specific assessments give teachers, administrators, and, most important, students data to track progress in meeting academic standards. In some cases they also help students prepare for external higher stakes examinations, competitions, and exhibits or other public and norm-referenced assessments of learning.

When formative assessments have been thoughtfully and collaboratively developed, they also contribute to teachers' sense of accountability and ownership for student and school success (Reeves 2004). Common formative assessments are powerful tools for helping schools and communities determine whether instruction is working and where improvements need to be made quickly. However, districts have been slow to commit time and resources to identifying or creating them. The absence of such a resource contributes to "flailing around syndrome" described in the last chapter, that is, to large amounts of effort expended in ways that make little immediate difference to whether students learn.

Formative assessment artifacts (e.g., project rubrics, writing prompts, quizzes, challenge problems, lab reports) and their results can serve as important starting points for supervisory conversations (see Assessment of Student Learning Conference in Chapter 7). When assessments have been individually created, they provide information about the:

- Depth and range of content knowledge being demanded
- Alignment of skills and content being assessed with curriculum frameworks and state standards
- Degree to which students must use higher level thinking skills to produce responses
- Match between the means of assessment and the learning goals
- Assumptions about students' background knowledge or prior concept attainment

Supervisory examination of formative assessments and the range of student work they produce might propel the supervisor into planning for school or department-wide professional development. If almost all samples from teachers are quizzes and tests requiring low-level recall or if textbook-provided tests are being used for convenience and do not match the school's curriculum, this is clearly a condition that undermines student learning and requires further discussion. Examining formative assessment sources of data might cause the supervisor to send the findings to the leadership team for serious deliberation. Individuals may be working hard to create assessments in isolation from one another with the result that each sample has strengths and weaknesses and no one measure is asking students to produce high-level results. This requires school-wide intervention and discussion. Finally, the data might allow the supervisor to do a more careful and comprehensive job of documenting an individual's performance under the appropriate standard in the evaluation instrument.

If a team, school, or institution has invested significant effort in designing formative assessments and analyzing the resulting data, then teachers who are failing to live up to those agreements appropriately should receive direct feedback and structured recommendations for change. If the pattern persists even after feedback and support, then the evaluation rating must reflect that unsatisfactory performance.

Using formative assessments as a data source can also support collaborative problem solving to address impediments to student learning or even to figure out how to stretch a high-performing group of students. Looking at assessment samples, for example, allows groups to compare what they emphasize, which learning goals they actually check, and what assumptions they make about students' prior knowledge opportunities. Individuals can use an outside perspective to fine tune their individual measures so that each one is as clear and well matched to the learning goals as possible. This source of data can also be the foundation for engaging in specific error analysis and pooled expertise to plan re-teaching when students are struggling with similar concepts and skills (see "Error Analysis" in Chapter 7).

| Evaluation | Supervision | CPS |

Artifacts of Practice

We use the catch-all term artifacts here to refer to all the tangible representations of different aspects of teachers' complicated work. Artifacts range from word walls, journal guidelines, and writing rubrics to parent newsletters, web pages, homework help sites, study guides, lesson plans, reminder charts, and activity center materials. Some artifacts, like lesson plans or criteria for success lists, are outward manifestations of inward activities such as planning and designing. Others, like editing checklists, reminder signs for math problem solving, or a formula "cheat sheet" for physics, show evidence of problem solving in response to an identified need. Still others—an encouraging note in a child's homework notebook, a letter to a parent, a detailed syllabus, or a social contract hanging on the wall—reveal efforts to communicate and reinforce expectations. Artifacts are valuable starting points for conversations about complex issues and student learning needs. They are readily available and should always be part of the data considered in documenting an observation or preparing a final evaluation. We will consider a sampling of the most easily accessible artifacts in the next section.

Lesson and Unit Plans

How do planning documents help us to uncover teacher's thinking and to identify areas where individual and group effort needs to be better aligned to external standards? Judith Boreschek, recently retired Director of Curriculum for the highly respected Wellesley, Massachusetts, Public Schools, notes that far too much supervisory focus is on single-lesson plans. She believes that unit plans give much more insight into the quality of teaching because such plans reveal whether a teacher:

- Understands and can communicate the big ideas and essential understandings of his/her discipline

- Can identify the prerequisite knowledge and skills students must have to master the content of the new unit

- Knows how to design activities that will get students actively involved in thinking about, communicating about, and using the big ideas of a unit of study

- Can design pre and post assessments to determine what students are bringing to the unit of study and what they are taking away

Written plans, and perhaps intensive discussions about the structure of a unit, can provide key insights into causes of substandard performance. They are essential when a supervisor is trying to follow up on classroom observation data that suggests a lack of coherent planning or poor understanding of the subject matter.

Many districts now require that lesson and unit plans be keyed to state and district frameworks. These plans become a data source for teacher groups if, for example, they are trying to determine why students consistently do poorly on an external accountability measure. Comparing the plans to the actual implementation to test items often helps teams uncover vocabulary discrepancies between the test and the unit, concepts not given adequate time or attention, or materials that are not rigorous enough. Once the problems have been identified, unit and lesson plans can become a focus of joint curriculum work or provide the research questions for teams engaged in Lesson Study (see "Protocols" section in Chapter 7).

Student Work Samples, Criteria for Success, and Teacher Feedback

How can we use teacher-developed work samples and criteria to collect information on the clarity and rigor of expectations for student work? Only recently have supervisors begun asking teachers to bring samples of students' work to post-observation conferences or to specific meetings devoted to examining evidence of learning (see Chapter 7). Supervisors and teachers may jointly examine graded and annotated work products by students to determine the characteristics of different levels of performance (e.g., what does A, B, or D work look like?). They may look at the products of a lesson to determine what students did and did not understand and to identify how those outcomes were connected to teaching choices the teacher made.

Initially, the focus of such conferences is supervisory, to identify places where teaching and learning could improve. In some instances, however, student work may be used to corroborate supervisor's judgments about teaching that is not yet meeting standard or about problems in an observed lesson that are likely to have led to the results.

Because researchers have increasingly linked standards-based feedback to improvements in student learning, it is important for supervisors to ask for and examine samples of teachers' feedback to students (Marzano 2001). If most members of the school community do not understand how to give standards-based feedback, then the supervisor can use this skill gap to plan professional development where teachers can learn to distinguish effective feedback from squishy responses such as "awesome" and happy faces. However, if the data samples show that most teachers are using principles of good feedback, then the supervisor can make specific recommendations to individuals or design an individual MiniPlan^{SM}.

Artifacts such as rubrics and criteria checklists are helpful in answering the question "What does it take to get an A?" When combined with examining grade books as described, artifacts provide powerful data about conditions that undermine or promote student learning. They also reveal the degree to which an individual or team of teachers has been able to think through and communicate subtle gradations in performance that will help students assess their own work.

Student work samples, criteria, and rubrics all become important data sources for teams to consider when they are attempting to:

- Determine what is helping students improve
- Clarify expectations or develop shared high expectations for students
- Identify where students do not yet have adequate information and tools to meet standards

Looking at one another's graded papers is a high-risk activity requiring trust. It tests team commitment to do whatever it takes to help improve learning. Accountable Communities may be able to be forthright with one another about the caliber of feedback being provided and thus make maximum use of that particular data source. If communities are evolving from congenial to collaborative or collaborative to accountable, they can begin with the lower risk activities of looking at anonymous work samples by using one of the vehicle protocols described in Chapter 7 that help evolving groups to structure the interaction. The key is to pick protocols that encourage participants to focus discussion on modifying instruction in light of the analysis, as opposed to those that allow participants to talk endlessly about individual student performance.

Homework and Practice Assignments

Homework assignments, worksheets, and handouts all become sources of data that reveal what teachers emphasize and how they have students spend

LEADER ALERT————————————————————————————

Rubrics Are Not a Panacea Keep in mind that merely having a rubric or criteria list is not enough. Scrutinize samples carefully and make sure they are substantive and user-friendly. Most of us are imperfectly trained in creating such tools, so bad rubrics and criteria lists abound. One of the best ways to determine whether a rubric is likely to help students understand what is required of them is to attempt to use the document on real work samples without allowing any intervening explanations or modifications from its author(s).

————————————————————————————

classroom and independent practice time. The spirit of collecting homework and practice assignment data is not meant to be "gotcha" but rather to stimulate reflection about how such tasks best support student learning. However, when necessary, these samples can be offered as one type of corroborating or contradictory evidence for a judgment that an individual is not:

- Modifying assignments according to special education plans
- Providing students with carefully crafted practice and application tasks
- Specifying the purpose of homework and the kinds of competencies exercises should be developing
- Providing scaffolded practice for complicated skills

Teams can take stock of the kinds of skills being practiced, the level of rigor, and important messages being conveyed through projects and assignments by asking each member to place any material given to students over a specified period in a box for team examination.

Teacher Portfolios and Web Pages[3]

In *The Skillful Leader: Confronting Mediocre Teaching* (2000), we wrote enthusiastically, "Portfolios are perhaps the most promising source of performance data because they present authentic views of contextual learning and teaching over time. The hope is they can more accurately reflect the teaching-learning processes we want our teachers to use with their students" (Platt et al. 186). We must confess that our enthusiasm for increasing the role of portfolios ran into time and quality monitoring constraints. National Board Certified teachers report an expenditure of 200 to 400 hours to prepare their portfolios. It is unrealistic to expect this level of commitment from a full-time, already accredited teacher.

_____
[3]For an intelligent discussion of teacher portfolios, see *Evaluating Teaching: A Guide to Current Best Practice,* editor James H. Stronge 1997, especially the chapter "Portfolios in Teacher Evaluation" by Kenneth Wolf et al.

We continue to support teacher portfolios as a valuable source of data for hiring or as a work product in a professional development course or an alternative certification program. For leaders considering expanding the use of portfolios, the National Board Certification Standards has created excellent guidelines for selecting and evaluating material to be included (see www.nbpts.org). For most purposes, however, we favor more organic and ongoing "minifolios" where professionals assemble small artifact collections focused on targeted student learning.

We are rapidly approaching an era when all teachers will be developing and maintaining web pages for their classes. This also becomes a voluntary artifact for supervisory conversations (see www.ezedia.com).

Evaluation	Supervision	CPS

Reflection on and Modification of Instruction

How can we capture the ways in which teachers modify instructional practice to improve students' opportunities to learn? In order to obtain better results for students, expert teachers apply learning gained through professional development or private reflection in a variety of ways. They experiment with different strategies and report results informally to colleagues; they implement new models and examine how well those models work with their own students in local contexts; they reallocate class time or reorganize space to accommodate needs of particular students, or seek coaching and feedback when they have youngsters who are not making adequate progress. This commitment to continuous improvement is rarely documented except in the most superficial fashion, yet it is a critical characteristic that distinguishes expert from mediocre teaching. Some districts have begun to experiment with journals or professional learning records in an attempt to capture the nature of teacher reflection and problem solving; others build in a conference about new ideas that teachers are implementing as part of the independently directed activities in a multi-year cycle of teacher evaluation.

The tangible products of reflection and modified instruction are likely to be the easiest pieces of data to collect and discuss. To tap into this wealth of information about a teacher's ability to reflect on the success of instruction and direct his/her own learning, supervisors can ask for two or three artifacts that the teacher believes best represent substantive improvements s/he has instituted over the course of a term (see "The Document or Artifact Conference" in Chapter 7). Because this practice is likely to be unfamiliar in many schools, supervisors can begin the process informally by asking teams or grade level groups to bring them up to speed on innovations or modifications that team evidence shows to have made a significant difference in student learning. The discussions then become data to help a leader determine whether more professional development and whole faculty discussions are needed or whether an individual intervention is needed. During such low-key, whole-group discussions of teacher learning, supervisors can also begin to model the process of capturing reflection and innovation. If both qualities are lacking, supervisors can send the first signals that what is expected will be inspected.

Here we've suggested that data on a teacher's ability to reflect on and modify instruction be used primarily for supervisory purposes. However, this data source can be used in conjunction with classroom observation, where artifacts related to the observation and evidence of student learning can also become one of multiple sources used to diagnose causes of performance problems or to acknowledge efforts that have helped students make significant progress.

Feedback from Colleagues

Feedback from colleagues is another largely untapped data source. Despite lofty hopes, peer observation has taken cultural root in few schools. Dogged by the challenges of finding and planning lessons for substitutes, administrators and teachers find little incentive to use traditional peer observation. But short-term visits (walks) and protocols such as Collaborative Coaching and Learning (CCL) and the videotaped conference offer new possibilities for colleague feedback (in Chapter 7 see "Moving Beyond the Traditional Post-Observation Conference").

To spread understanding of what high-quality teaching and learning look and sound like, administrators want to support teachers' commitment to using feedback from skilled colleagues to improve what they do. Encouraging teams or individual teachers to share with supervisors the time they spent on a problem jointly identified with a colleague, the strategies they implemented, and the preliminary impact on student performance all help to focus effort and build favorable conditions for learning.

Supervisor-Generated Data

While rarely used and certainly not a source for collaborative work, supervisor-generated data are useful in documenting poor performance on standards associated with meeting professional responsibilities outside of the classroom. We have provided several Legal Notes to guide the skillful leader through the considerable legal traps.

Placement of Students

Evaluation	Supervision	CPS

What information about teacher and school values and practices can we get from placement decisions and records? Placement referrals made by grade level groups and placement requests for or against teachers often create summer headaches for principals. For example, 4th grade teachers may protect all their special education students from a 5th grade teacher who refuses to honor educational plan modifications by placing those students in only two of the three available sections. Decisions for or against placement requests, initiated by parents or high school students, can result in unequal class sizes, inequitable student loads, unhappy parents and students, or any combination thereof.

Rather than protecting individual teachers by withholding data about such requests, administrators should give the affected teachers direct feedback on these "voting with feet" patterns. Once the data is out in the open, supervisors can then work with the teacher to identify the reasons for the negative perception and diagnose the causes of the problem. In one high school, for example, social studies teachers had total student loads ranging from 50 to 140 because students perceived particular teachers to be less effective and the system selection allowed them to act on their perception. The low-load teacher was accurately portayed by students as low demand and by the school as having low impact on student learning. Higher performing teachers essentially were punished for their effective effort with more work. Based on these data, a new principal worked with the union who had raised the inequitable loads as an issue of fairness. The data about inequitable workloads and the perceptions creating those conditions was presented to the "low-load" teacher, and both union and administration applied joint pressure for improvement. With coaching and continuous

LEGAL NOTE 8.1

Supervisor Notes

It is critical to know whether teachers will be entitled to access to supervisors' notes pertaining to their work before collecting information and writing it down or recording it in some other retrievable form. The disposition of supervisor notes depends upon your state's laws with regard to public records and/or personnel records. In some states all records, in whatever form they are kept, i.e., paper or electronic records, are considered to be public records to which anyone can have access unless there is a specific exemption for the type of information contained in the record. Additionally, other statutes, regulations, policies, contract language, or past practice may regulate the development and maintenance of records that are deemed to be personnel records. You should assume that anything you record in whatever way you record it is subject to access by the individual employee involved. In most circumstances there is no legally recognized privilege that would insulate personnel records from having to be shared with the employees identified therein. This is particularly true in those circumstances in which the records are subject to lawfully issued subpoenas.

Supervisors should consider how the information about to be memorialized in a record would play if it were published on the front page of a local newspaper, aired on the 6 o'clock evening news, or perhaps even discussed while townspeople shop at the local supermarket. This should not discourage recording important information and outcomes but rather should highlight the importance of doing it carefully so that it does not come back to haunt you when the information becomes known to the supervisee.

demand, the teaching became more consistent across all sections, and the workload inequities were reduced.

Supervisor's File Notes

| Evaluation | Supervision | CPS |

How should supervisor notations be used for documentation? In order to make an accurate judgment about performance, acknowledge extraordinary contributions, or have a record of interactions with a teacher about a controversial issue or a potential performance problem, supervisors keep notes and information about teachers in desk files. These files often contain:

- Notes from parents
- Letters of complaint or, more rarely, compliment
- Notes from parent/student conferences attended by supervisors
- Observation notes from professional meetings

All of these items on file may be used as part of performance evaluation if appropriate procedures are followed in their collection and in informing the teacher of their existence. The disposition of parent letters is typically covered in contracts. The best practice is to immediately inform the teacher of a complaint and provide him or her with a copy. All letters of complaint or compliment should be kept on file.

Teacher Attendance Profiles

| Evaluation | Supervision | CPS |

How can attendance patterns be used as a source of data about teacher performance? If teachers' presence in school made no difference to students, robots and computers could provide instruction. Students need their teachers. When attendance issues begin to affect learning, administrators need to pay attention. Attendance patterns can be analyzed by checking on the use of allotted sick days, especially Fridays and Mondays. A new principal noticed the suspicious attendance pattern of a 15-year high school teacher who was out two months because of a serious snowmobile accident. After a week, the teacher had used up all his sick days and needed to call on the sick leave bank. This new principal wondered why a veteran teacher would need to go into the sick leave bank. He should, the principal assumed, have had almost 300 days to his credit. When the principal examined 10 years of attendance data, he saw that the teacher had taken all of the system's remarkably generous 20-day allowance each year and that 75 percent of the time the teacher was out on a Monday or Friday or both. He felt that he was entitled to these days since they were in the contract. The new principal discussed the data with the teacher and put particular emphasis on the effect such absenteeism had on students. The attendance pattern improved, and the teacher confined his snowmobiling to weekends.

LEGAL NOTE 8.2

Informing the Employee

Many contracts contain strict timelines for notifying personnel of complaints; failure to follow them can compromise the ability to use the information for any personnel action. When an employee should be informed of a complaint should be a function of the nature of the complaint and whether the supervisor should carry out some investigation first.

LEGAL NOTE 8.3

Dealing with Absenteeism

There is a built-in tension between tolerance for the personal circumstances of the employee and legitimate concern for the quality of instruction that children receive when their teacher is absent. Teacher absenteeism clearly undermines learning and is one of the most sensitive issues that supervisors must address. While schools have not always been able to be generous with salary compensation, they have been quite generous (some would say over-generous) with sick leave and a variety of other paid absences. Fifteen days of annual paid sick leave coupled with the ability to accumulate sick days without limit and, if exhausted, to draw upon "sick leave banks" to which other employees have contributed, makes sick leave one of the most generous benefits offered in any employment setting. Effectively, many public school employers have become income guarantors and self-insurers when it comes to offering very generous sick leave programs.

It really doesn't make any difference why an employee is absent (e.g., legitimate illness, family illness, personal day, professional day). When a member of a team is absent, it can disrupt the workplace. The central issue is when does absenteeism become excessive so that that the teacher is no longer effective or qualified to continue to hold his/her position. The issue is sensitive because other employees and their unions watch carefully to see how the employer responds to absenteeism because everyone has the potential of someday using extensive sick leave. At the other end of the spectrum is how students and parents view absenteeism. They know that each day that a child's teacher is absent potentially disrupts the learning process.

Determining when absenteeism is excessive and actionable depends on the circumstances of each case. It requires thorough and accurate record keeping with respect to each employee's attendance. It also requires centralized record keeping so that patterns and practices can be scrutinized from a system-wide perspective and reacted to where appropriate. The issue is further complicated by the interaction between local policies, contract language, and state and federal laws pertaining to disabilities (e.g., the Americans with Disabilities Act) and medical leave (e.g., the Family Medical Leave Act).

Unless you have irrefutable evidence of abuse, all absenteeism should be approached with caution, compassion, and a positive frame of mind on how supervisory personnel can obtain valid information regarding the cause of the absenteeism and the impact it is having on the goals of the organization. Developing an appropriate response may be further complicated by the private nature of the reasons why an employee may be absent and the constraints of various privacy laws relating to medical records. Counseling, employee assistance programs, formal investigations, warnings, progressive discipline, and, ultimately, if justified, dismissal are all part of the options available to the employer. The facts of each case will ultimately determine the appropriateness and the legitimacy of the employer's action(s) in response to employee absenteeism.

Arrival and Departure Times

Evaluation	Supervision	CPS

When and how should time on-site patterns be documented? Rigorous attendance taking should not dominate an admistrator's time. Establishing a punch clock mentality does not support conditions for adult learning. However, administrators must pay attention to this source of data when teachers' arrival and departure patterns regularly violate the contract. Ignoring minor contractual breeches repeatedly can become part of the tacit institutional agreement that violation will be tolerated. A quick oral "I have noticed that you have been 10 to 15 minutes late the last few weeks. Can you help me understand what is going on?" can set the stage for written reprimands later, if necessary. Leaders should distinguish between isolated incidents and patterns that regularly violate contract agreements. (See Chapter 9 "Confronting Individuals Who Undermine Adult Learning.")

Discipline Referrals

Evaluation	Supervision	CPS

How and when should referral discipline patterns be used to document a teacher's performance? Assistant principals claim that student discipline problems are more associated with teachers than with students. Certainly a handful of kids are equal opportunity disrupters across many classrooms. More often, however, there are certain teachers who can control the kids and those who cannot. Administrators can use the patterns of discipline referrals as a source of data to identify students who are being sent to the office and make comparisons with the same students in other classes. The following anecdote illustrates how referrals can be put into the context of other available data to give fuller meaning. A teacher wrote a behavioral referral to the assistant principal, "John is destroying the atmosphere in the class. If he does not shape up, I am going to request that he be transferred." The assistant principal pulled out the midterm report forms where "good effort" and "good conduct" had been checked off. In a three-way meeting with the parents, the teacher admitted that he might have sent mixed messages. Confronted with the midterm report data, the teacher assumed responsibility for poor communication and took action to give more precise feedback on performance.

Collaborative teams can use this data source to support a colleague having trouble with discipline by establishing a "Case of the Week" with priority given to students who regularly were removed from class.

Surveys and Interviews

How can teachers and administrators use surveys and interviews to get information from students? If we make surveys and interviews only one point of data, they can be very useful. New Internet tools make the construction and administration of surveys much easier (consult www.zoomerang.com). In this section we will examine the possibilities and pitfalls for using surveys and interviews as we seek to create conditions that support student learning.

The Coping with Change Interview

Susan Loucks-Horsley and her colleagues have developed a "Concerns-Based Adoption" model that allows program evaluators to collect data about evolving "levels of concern" about implementing change:

> The model holds that people considering and experiencing change evolve in the kinds of questions they ask. In general, early questions are more self-oriented: What is it? and how will it affect me? When these questions are resolved, questions emerge that are more task-oriented: How do I do it? How can I use these materials efficiently? How can I organize myself? and why is it taking so much time? Finally, when self and task concerns are largely resolved, the individual can focus on impact. Educators ask: is this change working for students? and is there something that will work even better? (Bybee 1996 www.nas.edu/rise/backg4a.htm)

Surveys such as these can help monitor adult concerns and responses to change as leaders seek to harness energy to improve student learning.

| Evaluation | Supervision | CPS |

Teachers Surveying Students

How could anyone argue against using data from students as one source of information about teaching performance? In the words of one high school student, "We are the ones who observe teachers every day. Why don't they ask us for our opinions?"[4] We believe that teachers should use student responses to carefully crafted instruments and interview protocols as a source of data about their teaching, as opposed to administrators using those same student responses to evaluate teachers. Students should have opportunities to respond anonymously, and instruments should allow teachers to obtain specific examples in response to questions rather than simple statements of preference or opinion (e.g., Please give two examples of actions the teacher does that help you learn and two examples of actions you think are not helpful to you as a learner). Analysis of results should focus on finding patterns of responses that can guide future choices. Many successful, student-oriented teachers routinely use student survey data to inform their decisions. As part of their supervision and evaluation system, districts such as Montgomery County in Maryland expect secondary teachers to give and analyze student surveys and to be ready to talk about how they use the information they get from those surveys. We also believe it should be a required source of data for teacher use. Supervisors signal the importance of this data

---

[4]Some may be concerned that teacher popularity unduly influences ratings, but findings show that students are very accurate in their ratings. Ebmeier, Jenkins, and Crawford (1991 cited in Stronge 1997) compared high school ratings of "meritorious and nonmeritorious" teachers and found that students were as accurate as qualified evaluators.

source by asking teachers: What did you learn from the data you collected from the students and how will that affect your future practice?

Communities that are working on questions of student motivation, safety, engagement, or understanding of different types of programs may be able to use survey data to help determine what is and is not effective. Teachers' willingness to put their own student survey data on the table for group analysis signals high levels of trust and openness to new ideas that are strong indicators of an Accountable Community.

LEADER ALERT

Rate My Teacher.com   We are suspicious about web site ratings such as RateMyTeacher.com that provide outlets for complainers and invite stuffed ballot boxes and skewed responses. In one case a slew of positive ratings showed up toward the end of the semester for a teacher generally conceded to be a mediocre performer. No one could prove it, but colleagues thought the teacher might have inflated the data!

Student Focus Groups

Evaluation	Supervision	CPS

Student focus groups can be used to help teachers and leaders determine where they might best target further data collection or what other sorts of data they should examine in order to identify barriers to learning. If the data from focus groups is positive, it should be readily shared with the faculty. Negative information should also be shared but only after it has been cross checked with other data sources in order to get a reliable picture of a weakness. For example, as part of his entry plan, a new high school principal decided to hold a focus group with students to gather their ideas about ways to improve the school. In the process he picked up some interesting data about a teacher and the school. Two young women suggested that the new principal establish rules requiring teachers to grade and return tests and papers before the end of the marking period "so that we could learn something from doing the assignments." They pointed out that in one of their classes, work was never returned and that the teacher routinely "got terribly sick" three or four days before grades were due each quarter. She stayed home for several days, the students speculated, to catch up on her correcting. After their grades had been submitted, the teacher would return some of the student papers with few comments. One or more sets of assignments usually disappeared, but when students complained, the teacher told them to "stay focused on getting into college, and don't sweat the small stuff." The students accurately predicted the teacher's next set of days out of school.

LEGAL NOTE 8.4

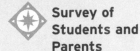

Survey of Students and Parents

Unless the subject of collecting data from students and parents has previously been bargained for with the teachers' union, any effort at implementation is most likely to precipitate allegations of unilateral implementation, which might be considered a prohibited labor practice and/or a grievance and demand to bargain.

Examination of a second data source, the teacher's attendance patterns, revealed that this teacher had been following the same practice for at least six years. The issue had never been mentioned in her evaluations, which were based solely on classroom observations and self-reported professional development. The principal wondered whether this teacher was simply following practices accepted throughout the school. Further data gathering helped him to determine that:

- There was, in fact, little evidence of consistent timely feedback on performance provided to students school-wide.
- The individual case represented the most serious example of "feedback fraud," and no other staff member was abusing sick days in this way.

Understanding the power of feedback to raise academic achievement and developing methods for giving feedback more efficiently became a focus for cross-department problem solving in year one. The more pointed information about patterns of absenteeism went only to the single teacher. The skillful leader had confronted a negative practice that was undermining learning.

Student Interviews

In the last chapter we cited student interviews during classroom observation as a vehicle for conducting systematic student learning data. These interviews could be conducted either by teachers or administrators. There are two additional times to use interviews as sources of data: to document a complaint (collected by administrators) and to monitor implementation of school, grade level, or department decisions (collected by either teachers or administrators).

Evaluation	Supervision	CPS

Student Interview to Document a Complaint

Where there are a significant number of parent or student complaints or where issues have surfaced that need further investigation, administrators should interview a random selection of students from a class in order to get a further picture of the issue. Inappropriate behavior by teachers is rarely observed directly as teachers can often edit their behavior in front of an evaluator. In this situation we need students to shed light on patterns of behavior that signal mediocre performance, such as failure to collect, read, critique, grade, and to promptly return work. Students can also let supervisors know about confusing assignments and about treaties and deals around submission of work.

TIPS ON STUDENT INTERVIEWS AND SURVEYS

✔ Many researchers advise against giving too much importance to student data below grade 4.

✔ Student data are more reliable when collected from a large number of students over long periods of time, which helps establish patterns.

✔ Tell the teacher you will be collecting additional data and explain how you will select the students. Make sure you interview a mix of complaining and noncomplaining students.

✔ Let the teacher know the questions you will be asking. Make sure the questions are open-ended rather than leading.

Below are sample questions in response to parent complaints about Mrs. Smith's lack of respect for students. Administrators take literal notes during the interviews and write a summary of the data connected to each question with their conclusions and recommendations.

Poor example:	Do you have any complaints about Mrs. Smith?
Better examples:	Tell me about your relationship with Mrs. Smith.
	What do you think I should know about Mrs. Smith?
	What do you like the best about Mrs. Smith?
	Is there anything about Mrs. Smith that you would like to change if you could?

Student Interviews on Implementation of School/Grade Level/Department Initiatives

Evaluation	Supervision	CPS

The Breakfast Interview   Skillful leaders should monitor the impact of structural and instructional initiatives on student learning. For the past thirteen years, principals at Silver Lake High Regional School, Massachusetts, have held weekly breakfast meetings with students. Through a random drawing of two students from each grade level, principals Richard Kelley and, previously, Dr. John McEwan probed beyond the perceptions of the Student Council or eager student volunteers. Mr. Kelley provides a light breakfast and gathers feedback on the school. He tells the parents the purpose of the breakfast invitations, "The purpose of the meeting is to discern from the students how the year is going. It is a way to find out their concerns and to address any issues before they become problems. Students have an opportunity to make suggestions and to voice any ideas they might have, directly with the principal."

Mr. Kelley is systematically collecting data from a representative sample of students in his school of 1200 students. In recent years, using a protocol of questions the breakfast invitations have revealed as particularly useful, Mr. Kelley has identified a range of problems, for example:

• Girls avoided Bathroom 112 because of smoking.
• Students felt that the honor role had been inflated by allowing students with a C balanced by an A to attain honor role status.
• Students felt that no one should be exempt from a final exam

because of high grades in the class. They argued that it is an important assessment to create a complete picture of student performance and teacher instruction.

- Students requested restoration of midterm exams because school-wide measures should not just be at the end of the year.
- Teachers were not teaching "bell to bell" during the long block.

Students from all subgroups within the school raised these matters initially before the teachers did. They noted problems of school climate (smoking in the bathroom), but they also began to identify issues of standards and expectations related to learning. They questioned policies that appeared to dilute rigor (honor role averaging and final exam exemption). The "bell to bell" instructional issue required that Mr. Kelley collect confirmatory data. He did so systematically through a series of walks at key times over several weeks and was able to confirm the student perception ("much busy work and getting ready for transition in the last 30 minutes"). He communicated the "bell to bell" data to the faculty. Collectively, they decided to modify the block from 90-minute to 1-hour classes.[5] In effect they admitted some inefficiency had been allowed to develop with the 90-minute block. Kelley summarized the outcome:

> We found the optimal instructional time was 60 minutes. This allows teachers to appropriately frame the lesson, check for understanding, and provide activators without belaboring. We also feel that since students will be attending their classes every day as opposed to every other day in the long block schedule, that student retention rates will rise and continuity be enhanced in the lesson.

Mr. Kelley also used the breakfast meetings to monitor the school climate priority: whether students perceived that teachers cared about them enough to challenge them. Together with other data, principal Kelley was able to confirm that the "care index" was very high. While he does not seek data directly about individual teachers and discourages specific complaints, he does pick up personnel questions that may need further investigation and intervention. Not only is he able to collect useful data, he is also creating conditions that support learning by giving students a powerful voice.

TIPS ON PRINCIPAL "BREAKFAST" SURVEYS

✔ Take action. If students don't see themselves as change agents, then the "breakfast data" do not impact the school culture.

---

[5]Block scheduling invaded many high schools in the 1990s. It is important to examine new structures to see if they are delivering on the hope of improving the instruction or if they are really undermining learning. It may be a case of slipping back to old ways or that the old ways never really changed. Zepeda and Mayers reported, "research failed to provide the evidence necessary to declare unequivocally that teachers' practices and student learning had changed and, therefore, that block scheduling was a real reform" ("An Analysis of Research on Block Scheduling" by Sally Zepeda and Stewart Mayers in *Review of Educational Research*, Spring 2006 Vol. 76 (1): 137-170).

✔ Regularly update the staff as whole, as well as individual teachers, on the data collected.

✔ Maintain a notebook with a page for each week to properly log and track student concerns. The page should list the questions, students in attendance, and data collected. Note repeated themes.

✔ Consider expanding this practice to hold monthly breakfasts with parents selected at random.

✔ Serve food! It nurtures participation and creates a congenial atmosphere.

✔ Use a similar set of questions in consecutive years so comparable data can be collected across time.

LEADER ALERT————————————————————————————————

Context Is Everything   This data-collecting strategy works well here because Richard Kelley and previous principal John McEwan have built a culture of respect and trust with the teachers' union. The principal sets the tone. In the words of the Silver Lake Education Association President Ted Gallagher, "The principal has an open door policy. He is a people person. We meet several times a week both formally and informally to address topics before they become an issue. The teacher's association is an active partner with all stakeholders in the school to provide quality instruction and rigorous teaching practices." It is clear that honest, open communication is an institutional value, so the breakfast meetings are accepted as one more way for the principal to stay in touch with his school and not as a "get the goods on the teachers" meeting.

——

The 5-Minute, All-Students Interview

One superintendent has scaled up student interviewing to collect data on the impact of district-wide instructional decisions. After identifying performance gaps and identifying school-level initiatives, teams of interviewers do 5-minute implementation surveys with every student in the district. For example, if the priority is math problem solving, then interviewers ask students to identify problem-solving strategies or explain strategies they would use. Data are then presented at faculty meetings, and new or modified priorities are adopted ("The Most Important Data" by Lesley Abrutyn in *Educational Leadership*, March 2006 Vol. 63, no. 6 54-57).

Evaluation	**Supervision**	CPS

Teacher Self-Evaluation

Mediocre performers tend to rate their performance significantly higher than do supervisors, parents, or students; good teachers tend to be overly critical and give themselves poor ratings on self-evaluations. Therefore, teacher self-evaluation has little validity as a source of data for performance evaluation. However it serves admirably as a starting point for professional development and goal setting. Data collected by teachers as part of their reflection on their own practice (or as a part of peer observation or collaborative problem solving) can be used to identify areas of professional growth.

> **TIPS** ON TEACHER SELF-EVALUATION (ADAPTED FROM AIRASIAN 1997)
>
> ✔ Rating criteria should be referenced to the established district evaluation criteria or goals that have been set.
>
> ✔ Self-assessment must always be compared with another source of assessment such as peers and the supervisor.
>
> ✔ Teachers should predict what ratings and feedback the other sources would show.
>
> ✔ Data from self-evaluation exercises can be combined with other survey data that focus on the same criteria, in a similar fashion to 360-degree feedback where personnel receive structured feedback from of peers, supervisors, parents, students, and subordinates.[6]

Evaluation	Supervision	CPS

Student Achievement Data

What are the appropriate uses for student achievement data? Political pressure is growing to use student achievement results as a significant point of data for teacher performance evaluation. NCLB is moving the focus for accountability to individual classroom teachers by reporting classroom level results. While most people agree that comparative student achievement data should be part of collaborative problem solving, misconceptions and controversy swirl around the use of student achievement results in teacher evaluation. The ways in which results get used depend in large measure on the amount of reliable and valid longitudinal data about individual teachers and

---

[6]In The *Skillful Leader: Confronting Mediocre Teaching* (2000), we quoted then superintendent of the Danvers Massachusetts Public Schools, Richard Santeusanio, as saying about 360-degree feedback "I think this process has helped administrators and teachers come up with better action plans, which presumably improves teaching. It is still too early to tell," In a follow-up conversation in 2006, Superintendent Lisa Dana commented on "360" as having some reliability problems—especially in peer rating. When asked about the impact on achievement, "Can't say [re 360 feedback]… but critical friends groups have helped, especially at the Middle School." Our recommendation is that time be spent on protocols that build collaboration rather than on complicated data collection structures such as 360. That does not mean that it could not be instituted in a particular context. See Manatt (http://workhelp.org/Performance_Management/360/more2.html).

students that a district has readily available. We think a productive approach for dealing with test results is to provide leaders with potential answers to questions raised each time the topic comes up for discussion:

1. **Should poor student test scores on high-stakes external measures cause teachers to receive poor ratings on their evaluations?**
   No. Not if the poor results are a one-year phenomenon and were significantly influenced by factors beyond the teacher's control.
   No. Not if other data sources indicate that students have made, or are making, appropriate progress from the year's starting point.
   No. Not if other data sources reveal a wide range of strategies being used by the teacher and the school to help students meet the identified standards.
   No. Not if the school and district have not pointed out the gap between desired and actual achievement to the teacher in supervisory conferences, offered recommendations for improvement, and provided support in changing practices.
   Yes. If three or more years of reliable achievement data combined with other sources such as classroom observation, examination of student work, and formative assessments indicate that the caliber of instruction is not sufficiently skilled to help students meet performance targets.

2. **Should supervisors bring up and discuss comparative achievement results with teachers and ask them to be accountable for implementing changes to improve student learning?**
   Yes. Lesson designs, practice assignments, and rubrics should be influenced by the kinds of results the teacher is trying to get. Teachers should be able to identify how their design decisions have been shaped by students' prior achievement and by the performance targets they need to meet.
   Yes. Achievement results are an important criterion for examining whether instruction is working for students or programs are being appropriately implemented. Teaching is not just "doing moves" regardless of their impact on students.
   Yes. Teaching is an isolated activity, and it is sometimes difficult to get perspective on how effective one's actions are. If there are reliable comparative data available, individuals need to know how they are doing in relation to others in similar circumstances.
   No. Not if the so-called "results" are drawn from measures that do not match district curriculum or from measures that test background knowledge, natural talent, or other capacities not likely to have been influenced by the year's instruction.

3. **Should information about student achievement results appear as a data source in an observation report or summative evaluation?**
   Yes. If the information about performance was one of the multiple data sources jointly examined and discussed and there are no

secrets about the next steps resulting from that discussion.

Yes. If the information either highlights the teacher's accomplishments or illustrates the kinds of challenges s/he is handling and the progress being made.

Yes. If reliable longitudinal data indicate the teacher has a pattern of helping children make significant progress or if reliable longitudinal data indicate that there are problems with inconsistent or poor results.

No. If there has been no substantive discussion of the data between the teacher and supervisor and the reason for its inclusion is not clear.

Student results data are critical for charting instructional improvement. The experiences of schools that have been successful in raising student achievement suggest that teachers should regularly consider data about student performance on benchmark assignments and teacher-generated assessments as well as outside measures as part of their collaborative attempts to improve student learning. Supervisory conferences should signal that results matter by including discussions about:

- How well students are currently doing at mastering important skills and knowledge
- What performance targets the teacher, or team of teachers, have set and how they are currently using performance data to help students meet those targets

If students are not making adequate progress, both supervisory and collaborative problem-solving discussions then focus on how to help the teacher address the obstacles to learning s/he has identified. When supervisory or evaluation conferences reveal evidence that the teacher is not using results to aid decision-making, then the failure to "monitor learning and adjust instruction appropriately" in response to poor results should be addressed as part of the teacher's evaluation, not the poor test scores themselves.

If evaluators can document that an individual teacher shows a multi-year pattern of poor student performance on benchmark assessments in comparison to the performance of similar groups in other classrooms, then that information should become a point of data for individual evaluation. At the same time, leaders should be careful not to undermine building collaborative learning communities by using test results as an implied evaluation threat.

What is the appropriate use of student test results in performance evaluation? There are two significant measures for student achievement: one is the current level of proficiency as determined by standardized tests and the other is the degree of improvement from the previous assessments whether the latter are standardized or homegrown. Many state tests are too removed from individual classrooms and with the reporting lag time are not very useful sources of data. A different type of student data, however, common benchmark assessments, is an excellent source of data. This following sample provides an example of one way to use student achievement results as an information source for teacher evaluation when the data collected reflect performance on established curriculum benchmark assessments. Classroom data are reported for all teachers, not just ones who are getting poor student performance. Conferences are held for individuals or groups who have students not meeting grade level.

Using Test Results in Teacher Evaluation

The example below shows how one supervisor included student results from a district-designed benchmark assessment as one data source among several. The supervisor rated an underperforming teacher as not meeting the district's standard for Assessing Student Learning and cited the disconnect between what the teacher was planning and delivering as lessons, her failure to check whether students had mastered the prerequisites before they moved on, and what students were accomplishing.

EXAMPLE Standard 6.1—Assessing Student Learning

Results from benchmark assessments show that many students are not achieving the standards outlined in the grade level benchmarks. As a result, the written expression of almost 50% of the class (11/23 total students) has not progressed as expected.

Results for ELLI Benchmark Testing: Hearing and Recording Words 2005-2006		
	October Assessment	February Assessment
Class Average	17.5/39	18.5/39
No. students not meeting benchmark	14	11
No. students meeting level 1	8	7
No. students meeting level 2 (grade level expectations)	4	6

Ms. Grey and I discussed the implications of the student achievement results cited in the "Benchmark Data" section of the evaluation. We developed a sequence of next steps:

- She will develop an intervention strategy for each student not achieving grade level.
- She will set up a series of meetings with the literacy coach to help plan for these interventions. Ms. Port will help with direct instruction with two identified students.

- Ms. Grey will use the consultancy model to request specific case assistance from colleagues during grade level common planning time.
- We will meet every three weeks for Ms. Grey to update me on progress.

The data citation incorporated in the interim evaluation becomes a supervisory conversation starter and serves as the foundation for helping the teacher set performance goals for each student. The emphasis at this stage is on next steps and on solving the problem. However, the supervisor has put the issue and supporting data on the record. If after three years the pattern of underperformance continues, this information could become part of the documentation for dismissal.

Value-Added Measures

Value-added student achievement data measure degrees of improvement. Emerging from the work of the very prolific William Sanders, this methodology calculates achievement gains based on expected outcomes predicted by a pre-test. If actual class average gain is above or below the predicted gain, the change can be largely attributed to the teaching. Supporting their mission of increasing the number of quality teachers especially in poor and minority districts, the nonprofit Education Trust has become a strong advocate for the use of value-added measures (see www.edtrust.org). Citing the research of Sanders, they recommend that each state adopt a Tennessee Value-Added type system as the most promising approach to assessing teacher impact on student learning. Education Trust believes that value-added data can assist principals with meeting the demands of NCLB. We adapted the following example from the Education Trust web site.

A hypothetical elementary school principal whose school failed to meet Annual Yearly Progress (AYP) analyzed school data using the value-added model. She found that Grade 3 students only made 50 percent of the expected progress that year. Grade 4 students made 125 percent of their expected progress. The Grade 4 gains actually made up for some of the losses in grade 3, but the value added allowed the principal to break out the differing impact of the instruction. Value-added data show that the issue is in Grade 3, not Grade 4, so the principal knows where to focus efforts for professional development and instructional improvement. In schools that are making AYP, principals can use value-added data proactively to ensure that they are on target for continuous improvement. Absolute measures of performance, such as those under NCLB, are essential for identifying not just progress, but whether students have the skills and knowledge they need to succeed.

The limitations of value-added measures for evaluation should not prevent skillful leaders from using this source of data for supervision and collaborative work but should prevent them from using the data in isolation to make merit pay or other financial decisions.

LEADER ALERT

Value-Added Statistics and Teacher Evaluation   Most teacher evaluation experts are not yet recommending the use of value-added measures to evaluate individual teachers. Ken Peterson gives a careful analysis of the contributions and gaps of Tennessee Value-Added Assessment System and concludes that it significantly limits its use for teacher evaluation (146). The limitations include: the requirement for three years of data, which excludes primary teacher data and teachers in subject areas than vary by year (e.g., high school biology, chemistry). Value-added methods are impossible to use when the teaching subject does not have a standards-based test. Thus literacy and math might lend itself to value-added measures, but social studies or art teaching may not (147).

Teachers' Collective and Individual Use of Data

Evaluation	Supervision	CPS

How can we monitor the extent to which teachers use data to inform their decisions? Data should anchor classroom decisions, supervisory conversations, and the work of communities (see Chapter 3). Thus leaders need to assess the extent to which teachers are actually using data to influence their decisions. Although we are cautious about using student achievement to evaluate individual teachers directly, we believe teachers and teams should be evaluated on how well they adjust and modify instruction based on student performance data. This is the essential skill of "continuous improvement" efforts: schools and teams systematically collect data to check the effectiveness of instruction to find where changes need to be made and what kinds of changes will best help students. Asking teachers about their data use and giving appropriate feedback and support when the practice is not in place is a key part of developing internal accountability. Faculty members who balk at being held accountable for this standard of monitoring learning and adjusting instruction may have overly restrictive or fearful ideas about what constitutes acceptable data. Many with whom we have worked worry about "using math and graphs to reduce an art to a science." Leaders must convince teachers of the importance of gathering and analyzing data to pinpoint where effort should be invested (see Chapter 3). To effectively use this source of data, evaluators and teachers need to ask and answer the following questions:

1. What sources of data about student performance in meeting (agreed-upon) standards are currently available for the team to examine together? How have we done so?

2. How has that information from those data sources been used thus far to generate goals for students, to document progress, and to shape instruction?

3. What are the planned next steps or changes the teachers will make in order to help each student make gains?

EXAMPLE   Principal's Memo to Faculty on Using Data to Plan Instruction

August 28, 2008

We are all committed to get the best performance from all of our students by using a range of data to check and modify instruction. This is a lofty goal, and we are both still learning how to do it well. This year, as part of my formal supervision and evaluation and hall chats, I will be trying to push our thinking through with framing questions: *What data, either provided to you or your team or collected by you, have influenced you to modify your instruction? What are some examples of those modifications? How will data influence your future instructional decisions?* My purpose is to create a conversation around data-based decision-making. I will devote some time in faculty meetings to try to answer a parallel question as I use data to inform my leadership for student learning. Stayed tuned and have a nice start to the school year.

This kind of communication sends several important messages about alignment of focus, the leader's learning, and the priority use of data to inform decision-making.

Summary

This chapter and Chapter 7 provide teachers and administrative leaders with a variety of vehicles and sources for data gathering and making meaning from data for three purposes: evaluation, supervision, and collaborative problem solving. Strategic use of data sources can help administrators make more valid judgments in performance evaluation by including more student-focused measures. Supervisors should expect to review and reward evidence that teachers are holding themselves accountable for what children know and are able to do. Collecting and using evidence drawn from a variety of data sources (1) increases an evaluator's competence and credibility, (2) reduces the impact of bias and judgment errors, (3) allows the evaluator to develop a more complex and precise profile of the teaching performance, (4) eliminates drawbacks associated with using classroom observation alone, and (5) provides clear guidelines for goal setting and improvement plans.

Creating conditions that support rather than undermine learning goes beyond using better data for supervision and evaluation. We seek to build communities that support excellent learning. We should put collecting and processing data at the center of collaborative work of leaders and teachers. Thus examining grading patterns, designing and implementing assessments, and reviewing homework assignments become public activities. Using data effectively is central to developing high-functioning Accountable Communities to ensure better learning for students.

Confronting Individuals Who Undermine Learning

Research indicates correlations between high-functioning professional communities and high-performing students (Schmoker 1999 1; Dufour 1998 4; McLaughlin and Talbert 2006). Leaders expect professionals to work effectively with colleagues, not because collaboration is an end in itself, but because they know it has the potential to spread improvements in instruction and student learning across many classrooms in ways that single, sequential change efforts cannot. Becoming a high-functioning professional team, however, is easier to proclaim than to accomplish. In Chapter 5 "Challenging and Changing Malfunctioning Groups," we considered some of the factors that interfere with a professional community's ability to pool intelligence and act effectively in concert. There our focus was on the capacity and the behavior of the community as a whole. Sometimes, however, the critical impediment to progress is just one or two individuals.

This chapter focuses on confronting people who undermine collaboration or fail to use it to continue their own learning. Teams that find themselves unable to pursue important student learning goals because of a member's mediocre teaching, refusal to honor promises and agreements, or inappropriate behavior typically need administrators to intervene. Although performance evaluation is not the primary tool for building powerful learning communities, it is a legitimate way for leaders to indicate and protect what they care most about. Judging by the hundreds of evaluation documents we have read over the last five years, it currently requires little effort for a teacher to "meet standard" for professional collaboration. One just has to show up on time at a meeting.

Confronting group wreckers requires that leaders have both the conviction and the competence to change supervisory practices. If we want excellence on the teacher or administrator performance standard of "contribution to professional community," we need to collect data, give feedback, note negatives as well as positives in evaluation reports, and demand changes when behavior is inappropriate. Just as quality standards for teaching are set by the lowest level of teaching tolerated without intervention, quality standards for community work are judged by leaders' and groups' tolerance for low-performing contributors. Without intervention in the form of clearly communicated expectations, skilled supervision, and honest evaluation, such individuals will continue to erode a group's efficacy and a school's ability to raise student achievement.

Finally, leaders sometimes absolve themselves of the responsibility to intervene with individuals who are poor collaborators either by saying that they trust a community's ability to "work things out without help," or that one cannot expect difficult people to get along with others. Administrators are responsible for communicating and upholding high expectations for performance in all areas; they must make include assessments of an individual's collaborative or uncooperative behavior in their ratings of performance.[1] In a few instances, leaders who assume that everyone will want to work together on important questions may be surprised and dismayed by unexpectedly negative responses from people who have been supporters thus far. When communities that value autonomy and anonymity are asked to change their practice, strong "status quo protectors" materialize. How leaders deal with people who resist collaboration sends messages about whether there is a real expectation and therefore accountability for contribution to the professional community.

For practical help with the challenge of confronting group underminers, we turn to Patterson et al., *Crucial Confrontations*. Taking on unmet expectations or behavior that undermines the group's effectiveness is, the authors note, the heart of accountability. They define *confront* as "to hold someone accountable face to face" (2005 4). The profiles that follow present different symptoms and different types of challenges for leaders. However, the context and starting point for confronting individuals is the same. The effort begins with communicating the vision and expectations before defining problems in terms of individuals' "broken promises, violated expectations, and bad behavior." Crucial confrontations require leaders to follow four steps:

1. Privately and publicly identify the non-negotiable aspiration for student achievement and the role of collaboration in reaching that vision. Get the vision of where students should be performing and what they ought to be able to do clear in your own mind. Be able to articulate it simply, without jargon, and in a way that everyone in the school can picture. Connect it to research cited in this and other books.

2. Specify the standards and expectations for carrying out the vision

---

[1]Even expecting collaboration, however, may not be a top priority. Over the last six years, we have asked participants in our skillful leader training sessions to describe what criteria they use to judge teacher excellence. In less than 50 percent of the cases, now numbering over 3000, do leaders cite collaboration or an equivalent term as a criterion for excellence. Administrators talk about "PLC" and often implement basic support structures such as common planning time, but, barring egregious behavior, they often fail to monitor even basic participation, much less contribution.

of collaboration.[2] Be able to answer the following questions: Do people know what the relevant performance standard is and what meeting an expectation would look like and sound like? Can they translate the standard into indicators of what they need to do to be successful? Do they understand what evidence would indicate success?

3. Describe the gap between the individual's contribution to the professional community and the stated expectations using the language of the performance evaluation as necessary.

4. Jointly develop a series of gap-closing interventions specifying what needs to be accomplished in order to keep the promise embedded in the vision.

Although this chapter deals with Steps 3 and 4, we caution leaders not to jump prematurely to identifying performance gaps in others. Skillful leaders must stop and conduct an honest self-assessment: Have I, and others charged with improving student learning, been clear, inclusive, and candid in setting forth what the expectations will be and how they will be supported? Have the goals and ground rules shifted without people's knowledge? Are there genuine structural and resource barriers to collaboration that I have not acknowledged? Chapter 4 "Community Building 101" examines ways to create the conditions that will support effective group collaboration. In addition to those stage-setting strategies, schools can also offer team leaders training in how to work with difficult team members and can create support and case study sessions for individuals who must lead groups. If Steps 1 and 2 have been effectively carried out, the expectations are clear and the supports are in place, then the leader can move to the intervention steps.

LEGAL NOTE 9.1

Performance Standards

Leaders must understand their district's performance standards and how they are to be measured. Depending upon state laws, you may have considerable discretion in adopting performance standards or you may be required to negotiate with the teachers union over all aspects of performance standards including the permissible data-gathering procedures you can use to determine whether the performance standard is being met. Be sure to check with the appropriate Central Office personnel and the district's legal counsel to avoid costly missteps in this area.

Types of Non-collaborators

This chapter presents profiles of individuals who undercut group effectiveness and strategies skillful leaders could use to address each specific type of case. The profiles fall into three categories of behavior that impair collaboration: active undermining, detracting from group competence, and failing to lead.

---

[2]In hundreds of performance evaluations we have found few examples of teachers being cited for lack of effective collaboration. The collaboration standard, usually called Professional Responsibilities or Professionalism, contains a hodgepodge of non-teaching responsibilities: carrying out routine duties, record keeping, and parent and community communication. These tasks are given equal weight with "Contribution as a Member of a Faculty" or "Professional Collaboration." A harried, deadline-driven supervisor may cite occasional attendance problems or failure to be punctual for playground duty but not lack of contribution to the professional community.

Teachers Who Actively Undermine Team Functioning

PROFILE 9.1   **Shirley Temple Block—The Stopper**

Shirley, in her 12th year in Grade 5, is considered a good classroom teacher. Most of her students score well on state tests, and she meets her professional responsibilities. Over the years, supervisors have focused their evaluations entirely on Shirley's classroom teaching. Reports have always highlighted her rich repertoire of standards-based teaching techniques. She has, however, become a "stuck competent" teacher and is resistant to the collaboration that would help her reach the small group of struggling students who test her patience because they "mess up her schedule" each year. Routinized in her planning, she can predict exactly how much time to allocate to teaching so she can balance the rest of her life. Shirley complies with administrative mandates and attends required team meetings. She is not a complainer like 3rd grade special education teacher Myrtle Bender who talks endlessly about traveling south. Nor does she emulate the 6th grade math teacher Ralph Settle, who corrects papers and reads newspapers during meetings. She is not, however, a team player and actively blocks team ideas for change that might cost her time in her well-balanced life. She sits quietly through protocols examining student learning data and then drops blocking responses when ideas for modifying instruction are discussed: " We have tried that before," or "That would never work because…," or "If it ain't broke don't fix it…" and other refrains intended to stop change. She rarely volunteers to take on additional work. The frustrated "Teamvener" (the name for the grade level leader) spoke with Shirley, who responded politely "I see little value in wasting my time in meetings when I need time to plan lessons. My classroom is what is most important." True to some extent, this serves as a convenient cover for keeping her workload in check.

Challenges for Leaders

Shirley presents the dilemma of the reasonably good but routinized classroom teacher who cooperates with administrative mandates but balks at ideas that might create more work. Her naysaying behavior is not because of deeply held beliefs against collaboration but more about protecting her self-interest in preserving a predictable workload. In fact she has a reacted in this way since year seven, only now she directs resistance to the team as well as the administration. It is tempting to celebrate her good teaching and ignore her poor collaboration. Principals worry that confronting Shirley will negatively impact her teaching; therefore they struggle to frame communication, resulting in "sounds of leader silence." They may also worry about how confronting Shirley will impact school climate if Shirley goes public with the feedback and her peers side with her and alienate themselves from the administration. Leaders need to confront their own silent, complicit behavior. Questions for leaders to ask themselves include: Am I behaving in ways that signal my dissatisfaction so that my silence is dishonest? Are peer pressure, social pressure, or external forces causing me to be silent when ignoring the problem goes against my values and better judgment? Am I downplaying the cost of not speaking or exaggerating the cost of speaking? Block's growth as a professional has slowed, and she is not using the team to continue her learning. In addition, she actively undermines the group functioning and so reduces the group capacity to analyze errors and design re-teaching experiences for students who need a bit more help. Let's examine how ineffective leaders respond and compare those responses with effective leader interventions.

Ineffective Leader Responses

- Excuse team-blocking behavior in light of good classroom performance with expectation reduction statements: "Shirley does a nice job in the classroom; can't expect everything" or "She's left over from the days when teachers had more autonomy; she will come around in time" or "Shirley's so focused on her students and developing her own classroom; I don't want to upset that."

- Fail to collect and use data to document and give feedback on Shirley's poor collaboration.

- Lapse into cliché-ridden written suggestions on evaluations such as: "She gets the job done in the classroom even if she could beef up her work on her team" or "Shirley *might* want to consider increasing her collaboration with her colleagues" or "Shirley should *continue* to develop her contributions to the team" or "Shirley needs to contribute more in meetings." These "softball" suggestions do not change teacher behavior.

- Transfer Shirley to another team without feedback. This is an internal "dance of the lemons." Sometimes transfers make sense, but they should be accompanied by reasons for the transfer and expectations for change in behavior.

- Blast Shirley in writing on her final evaluation, claiming that formative observations deal only with classroom performance.

- Make negative personality attributions regarding Shirley's motivation: "She really is so selfish and never considers the team."

Skillful Leader Responses

- Collect the data and identify Block's gaps in collaboration.

- Invite her to tell her story about what forces influence her not to collaborate. A probing question might be: "Talk to me about where you are in your career and how collaboration might be impeding your goals." This does not focus on the symptom of the naysaying but on the underlying cause of her undermining behavior.

- Acknowledge differences in priorities but affirm mutual purpose. "Shirley we may differ on where to put energy, but we agree on focusing on doing everything we can to improve student learning."

- Link gaps in performance to professional development goal setting. Acknowledge Shirley's previous success in the classroom and her desire to balance her life, but reframe the gap as a "stretch" to help her become a complete professional. Work to enlist Shirley in jointly setting a measurable goal.

- Match improvement steps to Shirley's needs and strengths. For example, if Shirley is concerned with how time is spent in meetings, assign Shirley the leadership role in selecting and directing a Looking at Student Work (LASW) protocol. If Shirley desires more recognition for what she does in the classroom, request that she organize a workshop for colleagues on standards-based instruction. Sharing professional knowledge is a form of collaboration.

- If there is no change in behavior from clear direct feedback, escalate the communication and, if necessary, implement a MiniPlan^{SM} intervention (see Chapter 12).

PROFILE 9.2 **John W. Collabnot—The Toxic Lone Ranger[3]**

John Whiner Collabnot is a good high school English teacher. He has taught 12 years, is passionate about his subject, is well prepared, and challenges his students. He is very academically qualified

[3]Thanks to Ruth Lynch and the administrators of the Duxbury Public Schools (Massachusetts) for the original conception of this case cited in *The Skillful Leader: Confronting Mediocre Teaching.*

and is ABD (all but dissertation). All John's evaluations have been positive. He has grown as a teacher during these seven years but views his job narrowly; some might say he suffers from "hardening of the categories" as he believes that anything other than classroom teaching is an inappropriate demand on his time and detracts from academic work with his students. He has developed several interesting approaches to teaching literature but is reluctant to share with colleagues and unwilling to be part of curriculum committees whose charge is to revise and upgrade the program of literature and language studies for the entire school.

Students who invest effort in school are generally positive about Mr. Collabnot. He is especially successful with, and prefers, high-achieving and highly motivated students, those who are attracted to his passion for his subject. His advanced literature classes are challenging and similar to college seminars. A few years ago when he complained about "low-quality" students he had been "sent," the department head granted Mr. Collabnot's request to teach only 11th and 12th grade honors. Last year newer department members complained that it was not fair that Collabnot taught most of the high-level courses. The department head defended the decision by observing, "John is much better with the higher level students and has earned selection priority through seniority."

Collabnot believes that his job is limited to classroom responsibilities. Unlike Shirley Block who complies with administrative requests, John gives routine duties low priority. Paperwork is incomplete or misplaced; deadlines are ignored; duty assignments missed; and communication with parents is minimal. He has isolated himself, is not part of a broader community of teachers and students, and feels no sense of collective responsibility. For example, if a group of 9th graders whom he does not teach are shouting in the hall outside his room, he will complain to the 9th grade team leader about "your kids making noise" rather than solving the problem or saying something to the students himself.

John also feels little responsibility to participate in school and department deliberations. He is a constant complainer and regularly portrays himself as a victim. Administrators are always "theys" and "thems": "They're always adding new things for us to do. How do they expect us to do all of this? Why didn't they tell us about this sooner? Whose idea was it? They just want us to do their work for them. They're not treating us as professionals. Why do they get the new copier and we get the 1980s Xerox? They don't appreciate us." In department discussions, if John does speak, it is to convey his disapproval of anything he has not suggested himself: "This is a really bad idea. We tried this five years ago. I don't have time to modify the curriculum for that student."

Challenges for Leaders

Supervisors who focus on management would think that failure to cooperate with basic administrative routines is the biggest problem. Indeed, lack of compliance with housekeeping expectations does undermine the community and needs to be addressed. But, more important, by failing to collaborate, Collabnot has missed the opportunity to learn how to succeed with all types of students. If Collabnot chose to collaborate, other members of his team could challenge his fixed ability-based beliefs about student learning and share their strategies for helping students who are struggling.

Supervisors appropriately give more weight to classroom teaching than community participation. However, because a healthy professional community strongly correlates with high-performing students, we cannot ignore the "Toxic Lone Ranger."

Collecting useful data can be problematic. A starting point is capturing concrete data about attendance, covering duties, and submitting paperwork. Unfortunately, often noncollaborative behaviors are subtle and difficult to detect because they occur outside the view of the supervisor, for example, in the faculty lunchroom or in a parking lot conversation with a parent.

In cases like John Collabnot, people watch to see if supervisors will do anything. A few diligent souls may attempt "for the good of the students" to compensate for Collabnot's lack of cooperation. Certainly, after a while they will likely resent the inequity that causes them to contribute more than he does. Finally, even if the Collabnots are few, they have a disproportionately large, negative effect on efforts to build a growth-oriented school culture. Supervisors need to realize that other teachers assess an administrator's and an institution's commitment to certain principles by scrutinizing responses to these individuals.

Diagnosis of Collabnot's poisonous behavior presents a further challenge. As Patterson et al. put it, there is a danger of leaders making an attribution error and "assuming that others do contrary things because it's in their makeup or they actually enjoy doing them and then ignoring any other potential motivational forces" (2005 60). The cost of this belief is that leaders assume that he is an unchangeable personality and allow him to remain an unchecked culture killer.

Ineffective Leader Responses

- Accept John as a maverick or one-dimensional teacher, e.g., "John's heart is in his classroom; he doesn't do . . ." (implying that the other areas are optional) and not hold him accountable for being a member of the school community.

- Make yearly mild suggestions of the "needs to" or "should work to" variety (e.g., "John needs to share more of his curriculum ideas" or "John should work to become a more contributing member of his department") without identifying any follow-up action for John to implement.

- Enable the behavior by not assigning John to duties or by not asking

John to serve on any committees and accepting his entitlement to retain his hold on advanced courses.

- Criticize Collabnot publicly without giving him any vent time, which may be necessary to enlist his tacit cooperation.

- Wait until the next evaluation to confront John with his lapses of routine duties.

- Punish him by assigning him low-level classes or forcing him onto membership on the School Spirit Committee.

- Jump to judgment and attribute Collabnot's behavior to his disposition, not his skills.[4] "John is just plain negative" or "Collabnot has a difficult personality" or "John had been nasty with adults for years" or "He is one of the most recalcitrant individuals I have ever met." These attributions spare the leader from any responsibility for attempting to influence Collabnot's behavior.

Skillful Leader Responses

- Separate the problem of missed duties from noncollaboration and make it a discipline not an evaluation issue. Use contractually specified procedures to require compliance.

- Let Collabnot know you respect him. Get his story to help diagnose why Collabnot is exhibiting toxic reactions. Ask how he built his skills as a teacher. Explore if he has had colleagues who helped him along the way. Try to learn the culture in which he developed as a teacher. This may help you understand his behavior better. Does he have a history of poor team experiences? Has he no models or experience of good collaboration? Does he feel undervalued? Does he feel disrespected?[5] Does he have problems on the home front?

- Request all teachers, including Collabnot, to submit self-assessments on nonclassroom areas of performance. Review this as part of the evaluation or goal-setting process. Add leader perceptions to the self-perceptions to round out the assessment and explicitly address teacher assessments that are very different from your own.

- Ask the teachers to set a goal around collaboration; use self-evaluation benchmarks and follow-up conferences. Become a support person, "How can I help you reach your collaboration goal?"

- Match the benefit resulting from collaboration to his compelling interest. Sometimes collaboration can be nurtured in paired or small group work in the subject area. For example, Collabnot might be motivated to help a new teacher to design and implement his curriculum. Another incentive might be access to professional development that Collabnot is vested in.

---

[4]In *Crucial Confrontations*, Patterson et al. write about attribution error where people leap to explanations about observed behavior that focus on personality variables rather than situational forces (2005 60).

[5]"People feel unsafe when they believe one of two things: (1) you don't respect them as a human being (you lack mutual respect); (2) you don't care about their goals (you lack mutual purpose)" (Patterson et al. 91).

- Give Collabnot a leadership role in addressing one of his most common complaints (Some complaints may be legitimate institutional impediments.) Support John in taking responsibility for developing plans to resolve issues he complains about.

- Share high school relevant research that highlights the impact of collaboration on student learning and the achievement results gained from common application of certain strategies (Newmann and Wehlage 1995; Schmoker 2001; Marzano 2001).

PROFILE 9.3   **Nadia Knowital—The Novice Who Knows it All**

Nadia is 25 and midway through her second year of teaching science at Central Middle School. She has become a controversial focal point in a battle between the director of secondary science and her principal who share supervisory responsibility for her. The former believes that Nadia is bringing much-needed intellectual rigor and excitement to a tired department. The principal, who believes strongly in collaboration, finds her not to be a team player, but arrogant, self-centered, and unwilling to be coached or to accept feedback from someone not in her discipline.

The product of a noted liberal arts college with a major in chemistry, Nadia is described by her graduate school professors as "possessing a fine intellect, capable, and an asset to the discipline." Nadia was considered one of the best "catches" in her highly publicized experimental state program to funnel content area specialists directly into middle and high school classrooms. Nadia sees herself as someone who "really gets what's important" and someone who could be a catalyst for change. In her interview she referred to herself as a "catalytic converter." At her orientation she told her experienced colleagues at Central Middle School that she had found the state's six-week summer orientation to classroom practice "boring, academically empty, a waste of time." She complained of endless icebreakers and warm-ups. Some of her colleagues found the remark offensive; others initially saw it as a welcome sign of a "return to rigor."

The director's first semester evaluations gave Nadia glowing reviews for her materials and challenging lesson plans and closed by asking her to present at the spring K-12 articulation meeting. Feedback and first observation reports from the middle school principal were considerably less positive. He praised Nadia's commitment to excellence but raised questions about her early behavior in team meetings and cited a comment when she brashly claimed that she would be able to show students just how exciting science could be with someone who "was smart and cared, someone who wasn't just waiting for retirement." Several of her colleagues found the remark offensive. When Nadia questioned the feedback, the assistant principal suggested various strategies that Nadia might use to change the perception that she was not a team player. The AP began to drop in to team meetings once or twice a week for a few minutes. Nadia felt that she was being subject to unfair attention by "someone who doesn't know the first thing about science" who was unfairly focusing on teamwork when she was hired to primarily to teach science. She complained to both her director and the union, thus raising the ante.

By December of year 1, Nadia's growing disillusionment with certain students and colleagues who "didn't get it" showed itself in displays of temper outside the classroom. She described herself as "betrayed and furious" when a number of her 7th graders did poorly on their first unit tests; she sent home failure warnings to 40 percent of her students. Colleagues' efforts to help were rebuffed. When the math teacher on the team suggested that Nadia might consider offering students retakes after they attended extra help because some might need a little more time and a slightly different approach, Nadia responded that she wasn't a babysitter and "besides it penalizes the students who could do things the first time." She clashed with the veteran English teacher on her team by repeatedly insisting that she would never be able to cover the required material unless students were regrouped by math ability. When her mentor suggested she observe in a class being team-taught by a special educator and regular educator to pick up strategies for adjusting her instruction, Nadia rejected the idea. She told her mentor the issue was the students' general laziness and poor preparation in the elementary schools, not learning disabilities.

After the rocky first year, the principal required that Nadia attend a summer program designed to increase her repertoire of strategies for reaching students through creating cooperative classrooms. The principal connected her inflexibility in the classroom with her problems with her colleagues. He also assigned her to teach 8th grade in the hopes that older students would be better able to respond to her rapid-fire delivery, bouts of impatience, and sporadic sarcasm while benefiting from her interesting curriculum. At the end of 6 weeks into her second year, 17 families had requested that their children be transferred from Nadia's team to "get away from the Demander," as one parent put it. More than half the families reported that they had consulted with Mrs. Knowital who had informed them that she would be unable to slow down the curriculum for children whose limited ability did not allow them to keep up. Nadia told parents they were better off putting their children someplace where they would be less frustrated.

Nadia is efficient and controls her time carefully. She completes all paperwork requirements promptly, carries out her hall monitoring and dismissal duties faithfully, and is present at all mandatory meetings. She does not attend after school events unless they are required or Friday afternoon socials at the local bars and is out the door as soon as the contract allows it each day. District policy excused her from participating on committees her first year; this year she volunteered to be on the Discipline Committee but contributes little.

Challenges for Leaders

At first glance, Nadia seems like an early career edition of Collabnot, and indeed they share some profile similarities. They are both smart and competent in the classroom; both know their subject matter; both want to be effective. But John has developed his skills to a level of competence while Nadia is a new teacher who brings an unpromising overconfidence together with debilitating beliefs about student learning. Her current inability to empathize with her slower students seems echoed in her seeming inability to find any worthwhile qualities in her colleagues. Nadia's profile also represents the dangers of competing supervisory views and either-or approaches to supervision. Nadia has potential and real problems. Nothing constructive will happen with Nadia until both supervisors sing from the same song sheet and require that she use and build upon her clear strengths while addressing her limitations. Neither should decide that Nadia's brilliance and commitment to excellence (not to mention the scarcity of good science teachers) excuse her unwillingness to teach all students or to interact constructively with colleagues. Neither should determine that her current belief system, prickly personality, and limited repertoire mean she will never be able to change (see Legal Note 9.3). Finally, the case introduces the difficulties administrators face when they are trying to decide what to do about new faculty members who are certified in "hard to hire" areas.

She wants respect for and acknowledgement of her ideas and ability to contribute to positive change but appears not to know how to present those ideas. Supervisors must thus make the importance of positive interactions within a professional community a key part of Nadia's evaluation.

Ineffective Leader Responses

- Engineer group composition so that either Nadia gets to teach all of the top students or students with learning difficulties are always placed with other teachers.
- Give her satisfactory evaluations and ship her off to the high school in return for an opening to be filled with a more friendly, child-centered person.
- Accept Nadia as a maverick and allow others to label her and ignore her.
- Tell Nadia that she needs to "tone it down" or to "stop showing off and start fitting in."
- Assume that Nadia's intensity will eventually wear out under real-world pressures and indulge her until then.
- Attribute the other supervisor's assessment to a lack of understanding of "what really matters" and tell Nadia so.
- Counsel Nadia to bide her time and try to get into an administrative role where she can use her talents.
- Decide that the "devil you know with a good content background" is better than "the devil you don't know" or someone with little or no

science background and not make Nadia aware of the seriousness of the concerns.

Skillful Leader Responses

- Communicate a clear expectation that all teachers in the building need to be able to give and receive feedback and coaching; provide Nadia with specific evidence that signals an unwillingness to meet that expectation; then check to make sure that that signal is what she intends to send and not an accidental byproduct of her intensity.

- Seek to understand Nadia's motivations and what factors in her background most influence her decision-making. Have one or more career coaching sessions that ask Nadia to identify her hopes, goals, fears, and the degree to which her present strategies are getting her what she wants. Provide specific, concrete evidence of what she says and does that would be helpful to her in meeting her goals, and what she says and does that is getting in the way.

- Ask Nadia if she has had times in her learning when she has felt well nurtured and supported. Have her describe the actions of the person who was supporting her. Then ask her to reflect on to what extent she used these strategies and how she might increase her use of them.

- Ask Nadia to observe the behavior of a member of her team who has strong collaboration skills. Have her note specific things the person does and says, including a focus on the language and tone the person uses. Ask Nadia to pick three of these behaviors and practice them. Set up a structure, pairing Nadia with the teacher or yourself, to give her feedback on her practice.

- Ask Nadia to collect, analyze, and interpret data about what her students say is most and least helpful to their learning.

- Confront her beliefs in fixed ability by explaining the consequences of such beliefs on student progress. For example, share excerpts from *Effort and Excellence in Urban Classrooms*, *Expecting-and Getting-Success with All Students*, quoting students about the impact of differing expectations on their motivation and success.

- Highlight that high expectations for all students is a core value, central to decisions to grant permanent appointment.

- Be aware that no level of the school district needs a teacher who gives up on and blames students as Nadia currently does. Resist any pressures to give her good evaluations and allow her to transfer to the high school.

- Communicate and follow up on a clear expectation that Nadia must demonstrate effective effort in trying to reach all students with a variety of strategies if she is to remain employed in the school district.

- Make the decision to let Nadia go and not grant her tenure (see Legal Note 9.2).

LEGAL NOTE 9.2

Awarding Tenure

After an intervention period, the skillful leader must be prepared to make the tough personnel decision re submitting a recommendation on the renewal of a contract. The law in most states provides for a probationary period, commonly three years, after which the teacher receives "tenure" and can then only be removed for "cause." Mindful of the fact that Nadia has subject area competency in an area often characterized by shortages, the real test at the end of her second and third year is whether the supervisor is convinced that her strengths outweigh her limitations and that she can reach excellence without consuming scarce supervisory time. If you can't answer that question affirmatively, don't renew her contract.

PROFILE 9.4   **Cary R. Changer—The Overconfident Career Changer**

Cary, age 38, spent 10 years as a software engineer at AnimalSoft before a downsizing that left him out of a job and free to pursue a long-time interest in "giving back to society" as a teacher. He enrolled in a fast-track career transition program that gave him the basics for a provisional license and was hired almost immediately to a teach Physical Science at High Aspiration High School (HAHS). Although the principal was slightly bothered by Cary's lack of teaching or coaching experience, he was awed by his credentials, pleased with his enthusiasm for the content, and realistic about how few options were available.

No one questions Cary's knowledge of Physical Science and his hard work. He does however have problems in four out of his five classes. His steady diet of "Chalk and Talk" copied from the university classrooms where he got his own training, bore and confuse the math- and science-challenged students who have been assigned to these low-level sections. A successful and diligent student himself, Cary has great difficulty understanding and relating to what he perceives to be a lack of interest and effort on the part of students. His students do recognize that he cares about his material and is trying hard. Thus their disruptions tend to be low-level: passing notes, sharpening pencils, whispering, yawning, or sleeping in class. As one student commented, "Mr. Changer makes things more difficult. I just cannot follow him. He never stops to see if we are with him or if we have, like, questions. I mean, I think the guy is smart. He knows his material. When is he going to help us learn it?" Students also complain about his confusing speech patterns, for example:

> This lesson **might** enable you to understand a little more about some things we usually string theory. **Maybe** before we get to **probably** the main idea of the lesson, you should review a few prerequisite concepts. **Actually** the first concept you need to review is Newton's Law of Falling Objects. **As you know** this work predated String Theory.[6]

Cary is guilty of "assumptive teaching;" that is, he makes unwarranted assumptions about what students know, fails to check in with students, and presses onward even in the face of behavioral signals that should tell him students are having problems. Because he grades on a curve, actual achievement is masked. State testing, in place for only one year, cannot help either Cary or his principal. Results come too late for Cary to adjust his instruction, and it will take a number of years before the supervisors have a clear pattern of performance that they could examine with Cary. To further complicate the picture, Cary is having success using the same methods with what he fondly calls his "best class," a senior AP Physics group of eight students who

---

[6]Adapted from an illustration of vagueness terms in Saphier and Gower (1997 204).

are likely bound for the industry Cary has just left; those students are willing and able to fill in the holes in his speech and instruction in return for his insights and ability to tell stories of real problems. This one bright spot in his day allows Cary to blame the students in his other four classes for being unable or unwilling to take advantage of his expertise.

HAHS had a cohort of 12 new teachers; each was assigned a mentor. Cary's mentor told the principal that Cary requested material in early meetings but not instructional support and has preferred to "go it alone." He does not seek, nor is he offered, assistance from colleagues. Unfortunately, the laissez-faire culture of the science department influences Cary. There is no expectation to collaborate beyond logistical planning, so he is isolated from his colleagues by choice and structure. Finally, district supervisors are tied down with a new math adoption in the middle school, and department head Pascal Triggy has only one released period for supervision. Triggy's teaching schedule conflicts with opportunities to observe Cary; thus he is unable to lend much monitoring or support.

LEADER ALERT————————————————————————

Speech Sidebar   Hiring qualified math and science teachers may mean putting non-native speakers into classrooms. This can create communication problems. During one interview a student told us, "We can't understand him. He knows his math, but he has this accent. We are seniors taking advanced math. I know it's hard to get math teachers, but if you can't understand him you can't learn" (Tamika, H.S. senior). It is important for leaders to arrange for English proficiency classes and not be satisfied by simply filling the position.

Challenges for Leaders

Career changer Cary is knowledgeable in subject matter but relates poorly to students and adults. Building relationships was not part of the success requirement in his first profession. Cary worked alone in a cubicle for long periods of time or contributed his knowledge to small, task-oriented teams when he was asked to do so. He has little experience with motivating or leading groups. He does not yet have the background experience to articulate what he does not know about teaching a range of students, so he falls back on blaming his classes for lack of performance. He is not inclined to seek help, a predisposition that is reinforced by the laissez-faire department structure and that is likely to add to his sense of frustration. His case also illustrates the problem of providing adequate attention and support when a school is dealing with an influx of new teachers who have been inadequately prepared for the demands they face.

As with Nadia, this case highlights the difficulty of finding competent teachers in high demand–low supply subject areas such as science and mathematics. Cary is struggling, and no one is taking charge of Cary's growth, including Cary. He exercises his option of blowing off his mentor, and his inadequately trained mentor has no choice but to accept Cary's decision. The department head has little time or skill to supervise; this is a weak, laissez-faire department with no common assessments or history of collaboration to address learning problems. Finally, shortages in the field almost guarantee a reduced standard for continuation.

Ineffective Leader Responses

- Practice wishful thinking and assume Cary will settle in and learn how to relate eventually.

- Assign Cary only the top students and leave him alone as long as there are no parental complaints or requests for transfer.

- Privately label Cary as a "loner" and blame him for his personality deficits without thinking about ways to help him grow.

- Write supervisory suggestions that generalize about what Cary needs to do but provide no implementation steps:

    "Mr. Changer needs to improve his explanations."

    "Cary has made a good start and is settling into the department. It is suggested that he seek more assistance from his colleagues."

    "As Mr. Changer transitions into the high school he should seek to improve his planning in order to better frame his goals."

Note: Recommendations for novices that contain language such as "needs to" or "it is suggested that" or "should seek" without telling the beginner how to do something and what specific good practices the supervisor is looking for are usually useless. They provide neither a clear goal nor ways for the novice to assess whether an effective change has been made.

Skillful Leader Responses

- Have a face-to-face meeting to privately re-communicate the vision of how the school works to reach all students and the role that collaborative problem solving should play in that effort. Skillful leaders have already communicated this publicly.

- Use specific data to give the teacher feedback on his performance relative to the vision.

- Connect to Cary's larger purpose by asking him why he made the career change. See if you can tie the answer and his core values to the vision for the school. If you can, celebrate that and shift attention to how to support him to be successful in embodying and applying his core values in his teaching (Patterson 127).

- Audiotape or vidcotapc a class for the teacher to review guiding questions identified by the supervisor that focus on the problem areas.

- Understand that the main issue for Cary is not his lack of collaboration per se but his unwillingness to seek or accept assistance, which predicts poor adult learning.

- If there is no improvement in two months, identify Changer as a teacher at risk and develop a MiniPlan^{SM} of support (see Chapter 12). The plan should include an opportunity for Cary to observe exemplary classes for targeted areas such as teacher explanations and then summarize what was effective and what he will apply. Cary and his mentor could also videotape and critique a lesson in which Cary attempts to use what he has been learning.

- If there is no improvement after 18 months, decide not to renew Cary's contract even in the face of anticipated teacher shortages.

LEADER ALERT

Mentoring Career Changers   Picking, training, and matching mentors to individuals who make career changes is critical to their successful transition into teaching. Using experienced mentors who have particular skill in connecting to students and knowledge of pedagogy is more important than subject matter expertise. One idea is to bring back recently retired expert teachers who might want to continue to polish their legacy without a major time commitment.

Teachers Who Detract from Group Competence

The following two profiles are different from the active team wreckers described above. These people do not seek to undercut groups; rather they lower the ability of groups to do high quality work on behalf of students. Both these teachers are poor classroom teachers as well as poor collaborators.

PROFILE 9.5   Louis Lesliterate—Mr. Can't or Won't?

Louis Lesliterate, a 37-year-old special education teacher, was recruited twelve years ago to "connect with" under-motivated, struggling students. During the hiring interview, Louis was honest about his own learning challenges including a slight auditory processing problem and a "touch of ADHD," as he put it. His honesty, enthusiasm, and strong advocacy for Special Education (SPED) students allowed the search committee to excuse his poorly prepared application documents, rambling and sometimes ungrammatical interview, and the stark contrast between his abysmal "on-demand" writing sample and those of other candidates. The principal who hired Louis sought an individual who would contribute to school life to replace a traditional SPED teacher who went home at 3:00 free of student papers. Louis has worked at both the middle school and the high school as enrollments have shifted. An exuberant and outgoing individual, Louis gives the district hours of unpaid time each year by chaperoning functions, sponsoring clubs, attending sports events, and otherwise pitching in to be a solid male role model. He believes in "going to the mat" for his students, a stance often played out as advocacy for less demanding standards, relaxed rules, and third chances to "protect his kids."

During the first five years, Louis had his own SPED classroom giving "pull out academic support." Louis's "teaching" was more about good humor, cheerleading, and patient persistence than direct instruction. Because he worked with small groups in less formal settings, he delivered one-on-one support and encouragement without the need for formal lesson plans. He "talked kids through" their assignments or he got classroom teachers to explain what they wanted and then translated their expectations but rarely provided alternative materials or approaches. Nothing was ever written on the board; the overhead projector was unused; and bulletin boards were filled with purchased posters and photos of his students. His classes were relaxed and appeared to have little structure to an outsider, but he expected and got respectful, on-task behavior from students.

All Louis's heavily impacted students love him, seek him out for advice, and exert enormous effort for him. Students with learning disabilities who are enrolled in challenging academic classes and need help with papers and reports note that Mr. L is "great, but he can't help you much with writing or reading science and stuff." They tend to use Louis as a sounding board for personal worries or as an advocate when they become overwhelmed in a particular class.

About five years ago, NCLB Adequate Yearly Progress (AYP) results were beginning to show that the special ed subgroup was falling behind and not meeting standards. In response the district moved to teaming and inclusion. New demands for collaboration meant giving up some autonomy, but Louis agreed to "be positive" and work with regular ed colleagues. He now brings the same loud cheerleading and encouragement to the inclusion class but also little substantive instruction and feedback. Always congenial, his contributions during joint planning sessions are superficial, focusing on "fun activities" and not on student outcomes. His team participation is equally shallow. In the once a week "kid meetings," Louis keeps putting the same kids back on the agenda. When the team seeks to solve student learning problems, he reduces solutions to short-term fixes and reports back that they failed to make a difference. He brings vigor but little rigor to his classroom work and to his work with colleagues.

Louis is a drain to the community in other ways. His mandated IEP reports are always late and often incomprehensible; the prior department director enabled his behavior by having him dictate his thoughts to her. Secretaries often cover for and clean up after Louis when he must write something; he thanks them with flowers, tickets, and home-cooked goodies, but no one ever names the deal explicitly.

The new SPED director is beginning to hear complaints about Louis's performance coming from teachers under pressure to improve test scores. She begins to observe him and becomes concerned.

Challenges for Leaders

Louis's poor skills reflect badly on the profession, stoking unfair "Those who can't… teach" insults. More important, the very students who desperately need skillful teaching to help them achieve are losing out. The year they spend with Mr. Lesliterate is a lost year that can never be recovered.[7] The demand for more collaboration and the pressure to raise NCLB scores have highlighted Louis's skill gaps to his colleagues. Despite being an embarrassment to the profession, he has been the beneficiary of 12 years of administrative "free passes." His hard work, enthusiasm, and charm have shielded him from direct, honest feedback. Inflated positive evaluations over the years have given Louis false confidence in his performance. New administrators searching the file would find a preponderance of glowing evaluations.

Mr. Lesliterate's personnel file has letters from grateful parents and even administrators for whom he went "above and beyond" in his work outside the classroom. None of Mr. Lesliterate's evaluations contain any reference to his problems with written communication or to problems with grammar and syntax. None of his evaluators has recommended that he seek help in this area. Only one supervisor ever documented the pattern of late and poorly prepared paperwork; that notation by a Central Office supervisor occurred during his first year in the district. In Louis's second and tenure years, the assistant principal completed his evaluations; the latter was a close pal and football buddy, someone who, in Louis's estimation, "had his priorities right," and all questions of paperwork problems were presumably resolved. Furthermore, even as the district moved to inclusion and teaming, no one captured data that suggested a need to improve. Louis's new supervisor had a clean slate to overcome!

---

[7]For research about the lingering effects of a poor teacher see W.L. Sanders, *Cumulative and Residual Effects of Teachers on Future Student Academic Achievement*, University of Tennessee, Value Added Research and Assessment Center, 1996. See also *The Real Value of Teachers*, Education Trust 2004 (www.edtrust.org).

Where to begin? Andrew Grove, Founder of Intel writes: "When a person is not doing his job there can be only two reasons for it. The person either can't do it or won't do it; he is either not capable or not motivated" (157). Capability has two components: native capacity to do the work and the requisite skills or knowledge. Leaders need to find out whether Les *can't* perform or *won't* perform or some combination. The skillful leader diagnoses the cause of poor performance and sets a course of intervention. Let's examine leader response patterns.

Ineffective Leader Responses

- Continue to cover for Louis with a litany of inflated statements "Louis does a great job with 'the hard to reach student'" or softball suggestions such as "Mr. Lesliterate should work to expand his contribution to the team." Or " Louis should be more careful with his written communication."

- Hide behind the tenure excuse "Can't do much; Louis has tenure."

- Fail to use NCLB student results that focus specifically on Louis's students who are classified as "Needs Improvement."

- Give up on Louis and surprise him with a negative evaluation.

- Decide that Louis does not have it and won't have it and therefore turn attention elsewhere.

Skillful Leader Responses

- Assume Louis can improve, realizing that he has never received the direct feedback and support to test whether his poor performance is because of native inability or lack of skills and knowledge.

- Collect very specific data to define the problem. Being explicit will be important to give Louis the best possible chance to acquire skills and knowledge if those are the domains of his deficits.

- Be concrete with Louis about expectations: the steps for him to take, the support, the performance measures, and the timeline.

- Recognize that confronting Louis's performance will contradict previous inflated messages and therefore is likely to engender resistance.

- Consider the possibility that Louis could be fired for incompetence in three years so begin to carefully document each step of intervention. (Leaders must accept the idea that dismissal of a tenured teacher who has an "Everything is beautiful" record requires about three years of work.)

- Base interactions on standards and hold him accountable for the same standards for lesson planning as other teachers.

- Observe and write up Louis co-teaching in the inclusion classroom.

- Plan a series of conferences where the supervisor:
    Acknowledges Louis's past effort and motivation

Clarifies the standard and the gap
Establishes clear targets for improvement
Enlists Louis in specific goal setting for improvement
Captures agreements in a MiniPlan^{SM}.

PROFILE 9.6   **Sara Sickasudden—The Absentee**

Note: Sara presents a two-problem profile that describes a mediocre teacher who develops an abrupt absence pattern in response to increased supervision. One principal called this "supervisor-induced absence syndrome (SIAS)." It really does not make any difference why an employee is absent (e.g., legitimate illness, family illness, personal day, professional day). When a member of a team is absent, it can disrupt the workplace for students and adults. The central question is when does absenteeism become so excessive that the teacher is no longer effective or qualified to continue to hold a position. The issue is sensitive because other employees and their unions watch carefully to see how the district responds to absenteeism; everyone has the potential of someday using extensive sick leave. The authors' do not intend to disparage genuine physical or mental illness requiring extended sick leave. We wrote this profile because numerous principals have reported a sudden outbreak of illness for teachers whose performance was beginning to come under scrutiny after years of slack supervision.

Sara, in her late 40s, has taught 7th grade math for 18 years. Her record has been unremarkable and so has the record of her three previous supervisors who chose to ignore her rather mediocre performance both in the classroom and with her colleagues. Sara had not merited attention from busy administrators as she has been compliant with all demands, attended faculty and department meetings, and prepared functional lesson plans for her classes based on the Hunter model she learned in graduate school. She is the quintessential "just OK" teacher as evidenced by recent state test scores that were mediocre not terrible.

Evaluations from previous administrators are uninformative and full of neutral phrases that signal a record of "doing the basics" and "getting by:" Her evaluations exhibit low-octane descriptor "A words" such as "accommodating," "agreeable," and "amiable" and no mention of "R words" such as "resistant," "reluctant," and recalcitrant." Supervisors used neutral fillers like "Mrs. S successfully implemented the new math curriculum" (without a mention of quality or impact on students) or "The teacher should be complimented for attending all meetings on time" (omitting all references to whether she contributed). Two recommendations were especially low level. "Mrs. Sickasudden should continue to be punctual." A summary statement read "It is a pleasure to have Mrs. S as a member of the Hopeful Middle School." No performance gaps were identified or addressed.

Sara's classes are organized, predictable, and routinized; in the shorthand of students, they are "same old, same old." A typical class agenda might read:

Today October 3

Standard 4.1 Add, subtract, and multiply polynomials
Warm-up
Homework review
Model problem
Guided practice
Independent practice
Summary and HW assignment

Activities vary little. With the exception of some occasional pairing, group work is usually non-existent, and opportunities for student participation are minimal. Students sit in rows and usually interact with the teacher in a traditional "tripartite" recitation model: (the teacher asks a question; the student responds; the teacher responds and asks another question). Mrs. Sickasudden clearly communicates expectations for work procedures and drill routines. Students impress their parents by dividing using three digit divisors. Sara spends so much time on computation she rarely gets to problem solving, and state test scores on that subtest were very low two years ago.

Sara attends all meetings. At department or team meetings, she does contribute to scheduling and discussion of school routines and is seen as compliant rather than cooperative. Her contributions often take the form of laments: "We need more time for individual preparation," "6th grade teachers are not adequately preparing students," and "program materials do not emphasize practice on basic skills."

Challenges for Leaders

Mrs. Sickasudden presents several challenges. Historically, "Saras" tend to be "off the radar screen." Principals, usually not math experts, observe during rare visits that the teaching is perfunctory but appropriate and competent. Lesson plans, while basic, connect to the state standards. Though not a good collaborator, Sara is a compliant participator. She benefits from poor communication between the math supervisor and the principal and counts on math initiatives to be focused elsewhere, for example, on new adoptions at elementary. Sara has built an effective wall around her teaching and lives in the unnoticed gray zone of mediocrity. So the first challenge is for an administrator to notice her poor performance and plan for intervention.

In light of recent poor test scores on the state test, the principal decided to call for help and ask the new math supervisor to examine the causes for poor results (see Legal Note 9.3). Astounded by the low scores, the supervisor began to attend middle school math meetings and ask probing questions

LEGAL NOTE 9.3

Multiple Evaluators

Commentators generally look favorably on the involvement of multiple evaluators in circumstances involving unsatisfactory evaluations due to inefficiency and/or incompetence.

> The school district's evaluation procedures are a model of how a professional employee should be rated. The evaluations occur at two levels. At the first level is the principal; if he rates a professional employee unsatisfactorily, the matter is referred to the second level, the superintendent, for further evaluation. While a teacher might object to being rated so often in a short period of time by different persons, such a procedure is clearly in the employee's best interest since it brings into the evaluation different viewpoints thereby lessening the influence personal bias can have ... with respect to teaching methods. (Rosso v. Bd. of School Directors, 380 A.2d 1328 Penn. 1977)

See also Cliff v. Bd. of Sch. Comm. 42 F3d. 403 (1994); Spry v. Winston-Salem 412 S.E. 2d 687 (1992).

about how the teachers, including Sara, were using the data to inform their teaching about problem solving. Other teachers were open to the conversation and were ready to address problems of student performance. At one meeting she asked teachers to bring examples of student work. All but Sara brought the requested work. Sara, not welcoming this extra work, spent the bulk of the meeting finding opportunities to complain about the intrusion on her schedule and planning time that this activity had created. Finally at midyear, the math supervisor observed the three 7th grade teachers targeting problem solving. Sara's lesson was mediocre at best. The supervisor told Sara that she thought Sara needed some extra assistance and that she would be returning frequently to her class with coaching meetings to follow each visit. She enlisted the principal as well to do some walkthrough visits. The math supervisor informed Sara of the plan on a Friday to begin the next Tuesday.

Sara did not take well to supervisors collecting data not only in the classroom but also during meetings. In fact she took sick, claiming stress caused by having her supervisors "ganging up on her." Raising the stakes to change her performance had appeared to cause a sudden pattern of absence. Mrs. Sickasudden reframed the supervisory challenge into a territory that makes intervention more difficult (see Legal Note 9.4). Her absence creates a problem not only for her students who are now getting an even more fragmented curriculum but also for her colleagues who are trying to engage in an improvement effort.

The principal and the math supervisor are caught in a dilemma. Should they continue to visit and increase the stress and "cause" more absence or let up and put attention elsewhere? Part of the challenge is practical. Absences reduce the opportunity for observation. Timelines stretch out.

Vacations come and go. Predictably, even though her colleagues are also losing out, Sara receives support from the staff "sympathy orchestra": "Poor Sara, she has had a tough year health-wise. The principal should get off her back and let her recover. She is under a lot of stress with those poor math

LEGAL NOTE 9.4

Absenteeism

As a general rule employers have the right to expect reliable attendance patterns from employees. However, the specific facts in each case will determine whether the employer's reaction to excessive absenteeism is reasonable and/or lawful if reviewed by an arbitrator or a judge. Most public school employees have relatively generous sick leave policies, including 12 to 15 sick days per year, coupled with personal leave days. Contract clauses that allow some or even unlimited accumulation can create an atmosphere of entitlement that makes it difficult to deal effectively with absenteeism that increases in the context of heightened supervision and concern about performance.

Past practices in many school districts have resulted in avoidance of confrontation around attendance issues. If an employee with 150 accumulated sick leave days selectively calls in sick and totally frustrates the supervision and evaluation process, it distracts from the original problem of poor teaching. Moreover, though such cases require a thorough understanding of local policies, practices, and contractual requirements, they must also be approached with an informed understanding of the legal obligations imposed by a complex web of federal and state laws and regulations regarding unlawful discrimination. Among the most important laws to be aware of are the Americans with Disabilities Act (ADA) and the Family and Medical Leave Act (FMLA). Most states also have some form of similar legislation with unique provisions that may apply in your state. Be sure to consult local counsel before taking any action.

Labor arbitrators will generally excuse absenteeism that results from circumstances beyond the control of an employee, especially if the employee's contract provides for such contingencies. After all, benefits have been negotiated to provide for an uninterrupted stream of income when an employee is sick, without regard to the cause of the illness. Employees cannot be disciplined for taking advantage of benefits their union proposed and the employer agreed to incorporate into its policies and collective bargaining agreements. As such there is no precise litmus test as to what will be considered "excessive absenteeism" in the facts of each case. Nonetheless, the right of an employer to discipline employees for excessive absenteeism is "generally recognized by arbitrators." (See *How Arbitration Works*, 6th ed. BNA Books, 2003 822.)

The problem with an employee who is repeatedly absent from work may be characterized as "job inefficiency." It is reasonable to expect an employee to be an effective member of the staff and contribute to the efficient operations of the district. This problem could be translated into the following rule. Your employment with the district necessitates that you be present and perform your job so as not to unduly disrupt or adversely impact the efficient operations of the district (Andelson 1994 38).

scores. It isn't her fault." The supervisors are in a low-win situation as well as a legal quagmire.

Legal Note 9.4 certainly raises caution flags about the absenteeism landmine. (See also legal notes on attendance as a source of data in Chapter 7 "Collecting and Using Data: Vehicles.")

The careful reader may be tempted to give up and put energy elsewhere. But to give in is to yield to Sara's strategy of getting you to lose interest in her poor performance.

Ineffective Leader Responses

- Cease all effort to collect data on Sara's teaching or team participation.
- Stop making appointments to conference with Sara.
- Fail to keep a notation log of appointments made and broken with notations of reasons and actions taken.
- Fail to continue supervisory collaboration especially around math team supervision.
- Assign students to Sara who need a strong teacher but do not have adults who will forcefully advocate for them.

Skillful Leader Responses

- Continue the collaborative supervision by the principal and the math supervisor.
- Continue to schedule observations and appointments for assistance and keep a log to document attempts to meet. Record when a meeting or observation is rescheduled. Start and keep a written record of each missed meeting/observation and its stated purpose in helping Sara.
- Develop a "refrain" and continue to communicate verbally and non-verbally that the work is important, Sara's students need her to do it well, and the school believes she will be able to make the necessary changes given the planned support.
- Be explicit about the system of support you are recommending, the support you are providing, Sara's responsibilities in this regard, and the timeline for improvement.
- Provide a written notice (email or quick memo) of each potential meeting or observation and its purpose in relation to student achievement. Keep the focus on the impact on student learning.
- Discipline yourself to observe a class or meet with Sara on a day after she has been absent rather than to establish the expectation that she will be granted leeway each time she misses school.
- Inform the personnel or superintendent's office of the potential problem and seek legal advice.

- Engage Sara in designing a MiniPlan^{SM} and timetable to help her make necessary improvements.

Note: It is no secret that part of the supervisors' goal is to keep pressure on the teacher. If a supervisor prematurely turns attention elsewhere, the teacher will have won the encounter.

LEGAL NOTE 9.5

Point and Counterpoint on Absenteeism

The skillful supervisor should be mindful of the following "points and counterpoints" in responding to Sara Sickasudden's absenteeism:

Point   Employees are entitled to a presumption that their use of authorized sick leave is legitimate, absent the employer's ability to establish that they have falsely claimed illness.

Counterpoint   The supervisor will be able to take disciplinary action if there is credible evidence to establish the misuse of sick leave. Many arbitrators consider misuse of sick leave to be "theft of time"; employees have sustained severe penalties, including termination on a first offense, if the employer produces credible evidence to prove the offense.

Point   Supervisors are entitled to expect employees to function efficiently.

Counterpoint   The employer will have to prove that Sara's intermittent frequent absences are having an adverse impact upon the delivery of the instructional program. This could be difficult when a substitute carries on effectively or if the employer chooses not to provide a substitute.

Point   The law of employment discrimination protects "otherwise qualified" handicapped employees. It is well established that an employee who is "excessively absent" is generally not an "otherwise qualified" employee. See *How Arbitration Works*, 6th ed. BNA Books, 2003 (824).

Counterpoint   Even in cases in which arbitrators have found an employee guilty of excessive absenteeism so as to make them inefficient or unqualified to hold a position, they have found them to be entitled to all of the benefits of paid sick leave plans, sick leave banks, long-term disability policies, and, in some case, workers' compensation and disability retirement benefits.

In summary, carefully consider a response to Sara's absenteeism before reacting to the frustration it can create.

Leaders Who Do Not Lead

These two profiles describe in-house applicants who were promoted to leadership positions: a teacher to department head and an assistant principal to principal. Whether because of political realities, availability of candidates, or misplaced optimism about their job skills, the wrong leaders were selected. Our purpose here is to not discourage considering inside candidates. On the contrary, we advocate careful consideration of people who have come up through the system (see Chapter 5 "Moving Communities from Good to Great" for specific information on hiring teacher leaders). However, with insider candidates there are forces that can contaminate the processes and lead to selection of poor candidates.

PROFILE 9.7   **Frank Steel—The In-House Department Head**

Frank, the newly appointed department leader, is known for his sarcastic edge. In *The Skillful Leader: Confronting Mediocre Teaching*, we introduced Frank Steel, a mediocrely performing teacher who was preoccupied with coaching. A very traditional teacher, he was also a poor collaborator. "At faculty meetings Mr. Steel sits in the back of the library facing sideways. Sometimes he corrects multiple choice quizzes; at other times he leafs through a textbook or swaps golfing tips with Bill, his golfing buddy" (2000 46). Over the years, he applied for department head and was turned down three times. When Frank turned 58, there were few alternative candidates; he was finally promoted to department chair on the basis of seniority. Although the principal had reservations, he was hopeful that giving Frank additional responsibility and a "bump" in retirement pay, might help him become "more positive." He had already softened a bit as golfing buddy Bill had retired, and he clearly had organizational skills from coaching that would come in handy in the management aspects of the position. During the hiring interview, the principal told Frank that had great confidence (surely wishful) that he would be able to turn the department around to focus on student learning.

Frank's department, five teachers plus Frank, is a very traditional, change-adverse group that exhibits many of the Toxic Community elements described in Chapter 3 "Professional Communities and Mediocre Learning." Right out of graduate school, Julie New is the only young teacher; veteran Larry Flint is a routine-driven teacher with an edgy sense of humor and low expectations for students; Amy Granite, a quite unhappy and at times unpleasant but competent teacher, complements two others who will retire within five years. They all do their work but limit their commitments. Let's listen in on a department meeting.

Frank begins the bimonthly department meeting. "Today we are supposed to look at our assessments, so I have brought some copies of my tests. I mentioned that we might be doing this today. Did anyone else bring anything to glance at?"

Julie, the new teacher tentatively raises an arm, right angle at the elbow, arm not above her head.

Frank: Great, Julie. Why don't you go first?"

Julie: "Frank, what would you like me to share?"

Frank offers, "Just hold them up and reflect on them. Reflect, that's what we are asked to do these days. Did anybody bring a mirror?" (Chuckle).

Julie begins, "Well, during my graduate program, I learned to develop rubrics and drafted one for my World History General Level. [New teachers in this department are routinely assigned to lowest level sections.] I share them with the students to be clear about what standards I am expecting." She holds up a sample.

Larry Flint interrupts defensively, not rudely. "Wait, no offense, Julie, I thought we were talking about tests. This rubric stuff makes me nervous. I got stuck with a low-level section this year and hope no one is expecting me to create these rubrics. Frank, you said this was a one-year assignment cause Julie couldn't cover all the sections but that I didn't have to create a new curriculum. Since most of these kids are limited, pretty unmotivated, and won't do well on the state test anyway, I was figuring videos should get them through." Then he adds with a little smile, "Just joking."

Julie responded pleasantly, "I would be glad to share what I did. I'd love to get your thoughts; these are far from perfect."

Frank senses a need to lower expectations for Larry but does not want to discourage his newcomer. "No problem Lar. Any modifications are totally up to you. Julie, why don't you make a copy for Larry, and that would be great if you want to talk about it with him. I also brought in some tests. Here is my term test that I just administered—honed over the years to get at the key ideas." Frank, pleased at the nascent collaboration, distributes the one-page short answer test and proceeds to detail how it works for him. The hour is close to contract departing time, so Amy Granite, a veteran who had not participated, gets up and announces that she has a dentist appointment and must leave "a few minutes early."

Frank chortles, "No problem, you won't miss much."

As she goes out the door Amy calls back, "You know I was just told I am not highly qualified—I am sick of the NCLB stuff—I may retire in ten years!" All but Julie chuckle.

Frank wraps up, "We will continue this conversation in two weeks. I am trusting that the rest of you will bring in something. We can make some decisions, and then I can report back that the department has addressed assessment. Julie, could I see you for a minute after the meeting?"

Frank is not really nasty, and his sarcastic banter is the product of years spent in a toxic department and the male coaching culture. He wants to do a decent job but has no skill or experience that prepare him for such a role. Readers may want to speculate what he says to Julie.

Challenges for Leaders

Getting the right people in leadership positions is not easy (see Chapter 5

"Moving Communities from Good to Great"). Especially at the department level, the pool is often thin. Unfortunately, seniority rather than qualification often determines who gets appointed. Not so long ago, department head was a more managerial role, and schools could function smoothly with nuts and bolts leaders. With demands for student learning-focused collaboration, however, leader selection becomes much more critical. It magnifies the importance of getting the right people in leadership roles. It is clear that Frank is ill prepared for leadership and hiring him was a poor decision.

Any leader would struggle with this department, which practices behavior that undermines the learning of adults and consequently students. Frank leads a "3R" team characterized by routine, ritual, and resignation. Absent is the focus on standards and data as well as urgency and aspiration on behalf of students. There are no expectations for quality collective work although the department "led" by Frank is complying minimally with the principal's request. The new teacher, Julie, is tolerated but not supported. A year from now she will likely be gone. (An exaggeration? See Chapter 10 "Improving Hiring and Induction.") Frank sets a low expectation for teamwork, and the department is more a collection of teachers than a team. Unfortunately, toxic groups have strong cultures; they are very hard to change, especially with Frank as the leader.

The challenge is whether the principal can help Frank succeed or can help Frank out of the position if he fails. It is not Frank's fault that he was appointed. When decision makers mess up, they are quick to shift the blame. Nothing in Frank's past suggests that he has the skill, knowledge, or disposition to handle the position.

Ineffective Leader Responses

- Make the initial mistake to promote Frank to department head, ignoring the caveat that without strong intervention that alters behavior "the best predictor of future behavior is past behavior."

- Compound the questionable hiring decision by not establishing expectations for the job or escape clauses if Frank does not work out.

- Let Frank believe the leadership position is his because of seniority and that he can assume he has a sinecure until he retires.

- If stuck to hire Frank, fail to give clear feedback about past behavior and share reservations about the demands of the position.

- Communicate unwarranted confidence in place of warranted skepticism: "Frank will be fine once he learns the ropes" rather than "Frank will need much support and coaching if he is to succeed."

- Blame Frank and claim surprise about his poor leadership when it was the principal who made the decision to appoint him.

- Turn the mistake into low expectations for change. "We have to make the best of it. He'll be gone in five years. The administrative union would go nuts if we moved him out."

LEGAL NOTE 9.6

Dismissing Department Heads

Though the laws of each state differ, courts and arbitrators generally give more leeway to employers when they seek to make changes in leadership roles, e.g., department heads, team leaders, directors, and coordinators. Usually these are the assigned leaders of formal groups in the schoolhouse setting. Often state tenure laws and the procedures associated with the suspension and dismissal of instructional personnel do not apply in the same way to these positions. Unless otherwise established by state law or collective bargaining agreements, supervisory positions are often annual appointments subject to renewal each year. In such cases, unless the reasons for nonrenewal are unlawful (e.g., age or racial discrimination), as long as the employer does not act in an arbitrary or discriminatory manner, the public employer can appoint whomever they wish to leadership roles if the applicant meets the minimum requirements set for the specific role (e.g., state certification or license).

LEGAL NOTE 9.7

 Seniority and Department Heads

While seniority can make it more difficult for employers to dismiss supervisory employees, the employer can usually make changes as long as the mandated procedures for nonrenewal and demotion are carefully followed. Some commentators have described the standard as the difference between "good cause" and "just cause." "Good cause" is something more than an arbitrary rationale whereas "just cause" requires that the decision maker justify the rationale for a demotion to a judge or arbitrator.

Skillful Leader Responses

Before hiring, skillful leaders will:

- Communicate clearly reservations about past performance as a predictor for success.

- Construct the interview to make Frank prove he is worth hiring. This is useful even if there are no alternative candidates. (See "Leader Selection Questions" in Chapter 6 for suggestions on interview questions.)

- Have Frank visit other successful departments and report back on what he sees that he would like to emulate.

- Assuming no alternative candidates, hire Frank if he agrees to be interim until his performance can be assessed. If this is not politically feasible, indicate that this is not a tenured position and that he will be evaluated during his first year.

- Specify performace standards for the job in writing; ask Frank to address each standard and discuss his ability to carry it out.

- Have Frank participate in a realistic assessment of the department culture and identify the challenges he will face.

- Frame position in terms of "finding the right match," giving both the principal and Frank a chance to assess the fit. This also builds in a "face-saving" opportunity year by letting Frank "voluntarily" step down under the "not the right fit, wasn't what I had expected" scenario.

- Be very clear about the leadership expectations and that he will be monitored, coached, and assessed on a regular basis. "I will be visiting your team meetings on a regular basis."

- Be accountable to their superintendent for leadership appointments. This means that principal leader hiring decisions are explained and justified to the superintendent. With inside candidates the superintendent should be especially rigorous in questioning the principal nomination.

- Resist automatically appointing the senior applicant. Though most collective bargaining agreements designate seniority as a tiebreaker if all other facts are equal, skillful leaders will not make seniority the sole determining fact.

After hiring, skillful leaders will:

- Consider chairing a few meetings to model for Frank expected behaviors and skills or minimally coach Frank on how to establish group norms.

- Observe and collect data on performance such as the meeting described above.

- Schedule regular feedback meetings with Frank and give directed recommendations.

- Establish a model Leadership Team (LT) that demonstrates the kind of interaction Frank and others need to emulate. (See Chapter 6 "Moving Communities from Collaborative to Accountable.")

- Dismiss Frank after one year if performance is very poor (see Legal Note 9.6).

LEADER ALERT

The Wrong Match   Watch using the "wrong match excuse" for poor hires. It is the leaders job to carefully select and make the right match. Occasionally, we find cases of individuals who really don't fit the context. But most often it is a face-saving euphemism for the leader who hired the wrong person because they did not properly assess the skill and knowledge set the candidate was bringing to the job.

PROFILE 9.8   Peter Principle—The AP Promoted to Principal

See Chapter 11 "Principal Hiring and Recruitment" for more information on promoting Assistant Principals.

Peter was a successful high school assistant principal who built his reputation on scheduling, discipline, and reliability. As a consummate organizer, he was a good complement to the visionary, but random, principal. When the principal retired, a group of faculty supporters urged Peter to apply for the position. After a disappointing search process turned up an inferior pool, the search committee recommended and the superintendent promoted Peter to principal. Clichés ruled the deciding conversation: "It is a poor pool," or "He's a known," or "Peter is a safe bet," or "You know what you have," or "He has earned his stripes and deserves a shot," or "Peter is very even handed," or "He knows the system. He knows the players." One parent member supporting Peter's candidacy said wryly about the outgoing principal, "We've had enough vision around here. We need a little peace and quiet."

Peter had been a very traditional English teacher whose assignments featured format over substance. One student had said: "He is demanding. He just demands the wrong things—stuff not related to our learning." Whether that assessment was totally fair, even Peter would have described himself as an "average teacher." He often told colleagues that he had never tried to be a superstar and that he thought there was a lot of room in schools for people who could just "soldier on." Once he became an assistant principal and had to observe these same colleagues, his attention focused largely on whether there was order and apparent attention in the classroom.

As assistant principal, Peter put in full, busy days. He arrived before the first teacher and departed in the evening after all athletic events were completed. He had his "finger on the pulse" of every discipline issue, every problem with the facility, buses, or cafeteria, and every event that involved parents or the community. He was always willing to try to meet faculty requests and gained special credit for his clever scheduling of common-planning time. Less comfortable with instruction, however, he rarely attended meetings involving curriculum and programs, left data analysis and planning sessions to his department heads, and privately professed himself bored beyond belief by the Central Office sponsored "conversations on teaching and learning" that were required professional development for all building administrators. Finally, Peter disliked doing teacher evaluation and hated having to observe classes. If faculty members' paper work was complete and on time and their attitudes were generally positive when he asked for something, Peter gave them inflated ratings without commenting on instruction. Thus all but the "deadline challenged" received glowing evaluations. In spite of all of these negatives, Peter was flattered at being recruited by his peers and attracted to the concept of being principal.

The teachers initially welcomed Peter, which made a smooth transition. They were pleased by early moves to streamline and simplify processes. He did what he knew best, and he did it well. For example, Peter made a quick hit with the faculty when he established a "5 minutes late and you can't attend class" policy—something resisted by his predecessor and applauded by teachers.

In his first leadership team meeting, he signaled preference for a laissez-faire culture when he said, "I expect you to run your departments and deal with the curriculum problems at your level. I'm here to solve problems if you need me, but I don't want to be in your way." Department heads were delighted as the 90-minute meeting was completed in 47 minutes. Peter had said "I value your time so we will meet every other week. Hold the time in case something comes up. Just one request—no surprises. I don't want to hear bad news from downtown. Keep me posted."

The first faculty meeting followed a similar formula: business was over in 20 minutes and teachers were pleased by the lack of demand. Peter emphasized the importance of being on top of kids and developing a respectful, orderly climate for learning. There was no mention of the need for academic rigor or of the value of working together to solve learning problems. The former principal had begun to emphasize collaboration, especially with the newly available common planning time. The opening meeting delighted individuals who had resisted the idea of working in small learning communities, while others who had pushed the initiative were deeply disappointed.

Peter was the ultimate responder. He reacted quickly to quell situations. He saw conflict and uncertainty as problems, preferring fair weather terms such as "smooth sailing" "calm waters," and "clear skies" to characterize successful days. He was a complaint-driven leader who responded to situations as they arose. If a parent complained about a teacher he would speak to the teacher but recorded nothing ever in writing even if complaints were quite serious. The trains ran smoothly, but there were few stops to reflect about student learning.

After a few years, Peter's preference to manage, not lead, began to be a problem. A small delegation of parents objected to the poor caliber instruction in honors classes and brought samples of out-of-date materials, low-level tests, and what they called "infantile" projects that students had been assigned. New testing data for math and science revealed a growing achievement gap between the performance of the 18 percent Hispanic and 23 percent African-American population and white and Asian students. Peter's way of dealing with this gap was to distribute the data to department heads: "Talk to your departments and come up with some ideas." He missed the opportunity to lead a school-wide, focused inquiry. Instead he assumed departments would solve the problem despite their uneven skills and varying degrees of ownership.

Challenges for Leaders

The Peter Principle is the theory that employees within an organization will advance to their highest level of competence and then be promoted to and remain at a level at which they are incompetent (Peter and Hull).

Though more mediocre than incompetent, Peter clearly fits his name. He was promoted from assistant principal, a position for which he was well suited, to the position of principal, for which he had no preparation or skill. Bad promotion decisions arise when there are uncertain alternatives (an inferior pool of applicants) leading to unwarranted hope that the best available candidate will "rise to the challenge." No one should be surprised by his failure to become a leader principal; Peter was a known candidate with well-established strengths and weaknesses. The problem is that Peter will likely remain principal for many years in a career marked, not by disaster, but by mediocrity. Superintendents and school boards need to confront the conditions that cause them to appoint under-qualified, (especially internal) compromise candidates without a pre-established back-up program of coaching, benchmarks, feedback, and rigorous supervision.

Ineffective Leader Responses

- See Peter's appointment as a function of outside forces and fail to create better hiring protocols with clearly identified standards for leadership (see Chapter 11 "Principal Development and Support").
- Over-rate Peter's management strengths and fail to communicate expectations for leadership of instructional improvement at the time Peter is hired.

- Fail to focus Peter's professional development, supervision, and evaluation on building the skills that Peter needs to develop to be an effective principal.
- Defend a poor decision by reiterating the hiring clichés "Peter is very even handed," or "He is well organized," or "He is better than most people out there."
- Wait to find Peter the mentors and outside support he needs to develop competence until he has been in the role for several years and either feels secure about his chosen course of action or has lost all credibility with key faculty.
- Try to keep up Peter's morale and give him encouragement by excessively praising the things he does well and communicating the areas where he needs to change so vaguely and with so much sugarcoating that Peter misses the message.

Skillful Leader Responses

- Develop an individualized professional development plan in collaboration with Peter that supports his development in instructional leadership and community building.
- Pair Peter with a successful principal who has strong skills in the areas Peter needs to develop to provide support.
- Collaborate with Peter on preparing his key messages and signals re instructional improvement, designing his first meetings, and building his leadership team; then attend selected events to observe how Peter carries out his plans and give him feedback.
- As a Central Office team, jointly identify the directions Peter should not take (e.g., giving over all decision making to subunits within the school) and explicitly communicate those guidelines.
- Invite Peter to participate in a study group with this book, focusing on Chapter 4 "Confronting Malfunctioning Communities."
- Have regular supervisory meetings with Peter with short-term, 4-6 week goals with agreed-upon action steps, adapting the MiniPlan^{SM} model.
- Provide an interim position for assistant principal with the idea that Peter could bump back into his old position if his trial as a principal does not work out or make both principal and assistant principal positions interim so that Peter could save face if he finds the principalship is not a fit.
- Equip Peter with an assistant principal for instruction who will take major responsibility for teacher evaluation. Caution: this could be viewed as an enabling strategy but is a possible alternative leadership structure.
- Conduct a Central Office "What went wrong?" mistake analysis to determine how future hiring procedures should modified.

- In advance of the next job opening, adopt a set of standards and ways to assess them.

Summary

Leaders must communicate their vision of student learning improvement and how collaboration will help the entire school achieve that. Skillful leaders communicate explicit expectations for professional collaboration, train teacher teams in how to achieve it, and establish structures to support it. Even as teams develop their capacity to monitor their own functioning, they need administrators to intervene around sticky issues of collaboration. We examined eight profiles of individuals who undermine teams or their community and laid out specific strategies for intervention.

10 Improving Hiring, Induction, and Tenure Decisions

Personnel decisions are a good place to look for and change conditions that undermine learning. Schools and school districts need teachers who can deliver engaging, rigorous lessons and reach out to learners with a wide variety of backgrounds, knowledge, and skills. They also need individuals who show the promise to become strong collaborators and to make valuable contributions to Accountable Communities. In this chapter we consider three phases of personnel decision making that are critical to getting students the best possible teachers and specialists: hiring the right people, building strong induction programs to support and retain excellent teachers, and making the tenure decision.

Hiring

The ability to hire and retain the right people is a key characteristic of a high-performing organization. The need for excellent teachers has never been greater as escalating demands are placed on schools to reform their structures and practices, improve student achievement, and narrow the achievement gaps between white and non-white students. Yet research and models of outstanding teacher selection systems remain relatively scarce (Peterson). Hiring is frequently rushed, competing with end-of-the-school-year activities or summer vacation plans. There are costs associated with poor hiring decisions and the mediocre learning that ensues. Bolton notes, "The cost of hiring the wrong candidate can be higher in terms of supplementary training, wasted salary, adverse public relations, and lost productivity than the cost of more extensive recruitment" (10).[1] Clear standards and procedures must be set for recruiting and hiring promising new teach-

[1]See also Darling-Hammond and Berry (2006 19): "A recent study estimated the cost of replacing new teachers who leave at between $8000 and $48,000 each, depending on whether we consider student learning costs (Benner 2000)."

ers if we are to build and sustain cultures of excellence. As you read the following cases, look for the missed opportunities to make better hiring decisions.

CASE 10.1 **Alicia Nativeson**

Bill Wills, chair of the English department at Midtown High School, has a position to fill. While there are numerous applicants, Bill has top-listed Alicia Nativeson who is a graduate of Midtown High. Nearly 60 percent of the teachers attended Midtown as students. Alicia was very popular as a student, performing in many of the school musicals and serving on the varsity cheerleading squad. Her father, a long-time middle school guidance counselor in the district, is Bill's good friend. Alicia also did her student teaching at Midtown. Vivacious and sociable, she quickly became popular with teachers in the department and formed close, peer-like relationships with many of her students. While not a strong student, her letters of recommendation from several of her college professors highlight her interpersonal skills and dynamic personality.

Shortly after the new school year begins, the principal expresses some concerns. "You know Bill, I've been by Alicia's room a few times, including one formal observation. She is great with kids, but I don't see rigor. The content seems a long way from the challenge we need for our kids." Bill reassured the principal that she would grow into her role as a teacher as she "becomes more familiar and comfortable" with the curriculum.

CASE 10.2 **Margaret Reader**

It is early June, and Principal Russell Lowell at the Wilson Street Elementary School has a very busy Thursday ahead. He has a meeting at the superintendent's office in the morning, and the 6th grade awards ceremony is scheduled for later in the afternoon. In addition, he will also sit in on a grade 3 meeting to facilitate looking at student work. Despite nearly an entire school year of common planning time and training, the four grade 3 teachers just cannot work productively together. Lowell sees one particularly resistant teacher as the problem but is relieved that she will be retiring at the end of the school year. In fact, interviews have been scheduled early that afternoon for two candidates whose resumes were sent down from the Central Office. Lowell reviews the resumes while having a quick sandwich. By midafternoon, Lowell has completed the interviews and there is little doubt in his mind whom he wants. One of the candidates, Margaret Reader, interviewed extremely well. An articulate, poised young woman, she graduated from a nearby private university and appears to be an avid reader of journals and books on education. Just what that grade level team will need to give them a shot in the arm, thinks Lowell, as he lifts the phone to make a reference call to her faculty advisor. The advisor is effusive about what a solid student Margaret has been and how she will no doubt be an outstanding teacher despite her bumpy experience at student teaching. Inquiring about the bumps, Lowell is told that the supervising teacher was a poor match for Margaret's energy and intellect. Looking at his watch and remembering the awards ceremony, Lowell thanks the reference and heads to the gymnasium.

Two months into the following school year, the grade 3 teachers are still struggling to collaborate, and now several of the teachers refuse to meet with Margaret. Comments such as "Who does Ms. Reader think she is?" and "Where does she get off telling us what we should or shouldn't be doing!" are beginning to surface in hall conversations around the building.

CASE 10.3 **Larry L. Day**

The new school year begins next week, and Andrea McDuel, principal of Pacifico East Middle School, is anxious to fill a special education position created by the incumbent teacher's decision to move to another city over the summer. Certified special educators are scarce, and her school is moving to full inclusion. Shortly after advertising the position, she is relieved to find a resume in the mail from a certain Larry Labor Day, who has three years of experience as a special education teacher at an elementary school. He was laid off at his previous school due to a budget-driven reduction in staff (a more senior classroom teacher with special education certification "bumped" him). In that school, Larry ran a self-contained resource room with a caseload of ten behaviorally challenged students. Pleased to have a candidate with the appropriate certification, Andrea schedules an interview with Larry for the next day. They talk about special education in general terms, and Larry impresses Andrea with his knowledge of special education law and procedures. After the interview, Andrea quickly calls Larry's former principal and is told in a short conversation that while Larry was "a bit of a loner," he did a "nice job of keeping a handle on the kids." Thanking the principal for his time, Andrea promptly offers Larry the position.

As the school year begins, it becomes clear by October that Larry was more comfortable in the isolated pull-out class than in the collaborative inclusion setting. The principal had hoped that Larry would become an inclusion leader, but instead he assumed more of a teaching assistant role.

Perhaps one or more of these scenarios is familiar. Viewed from afar, it is tempting to troubleshoot each case with a quick suggestion: to clarify the criteria for the position, to use more data in making a hiring decision, or perhaps to invest more time in the process through an advisory committee with teacher input. Rushing to fix the problem, however, may miss an opportunity to build the 3 C's (Conviction, Competence, and Control). Putting effective systems in place will require re-thinking existing beliefs, skills, and practices. Three questions organize the work of this chapter.

- What beliefs drive the actions we take in recruiting, hiring, and supporting new teachers? (Conviction)
- What can we do to build our competence to recruit, hire, and retain the very best possible people? (Competence)
- What institutional deficiencies—systems policies and practices—must be confronted and replaced in order to improve the selection of promising new teachers? (Control)

Conviction in Recruitment and Hiring

Beliefs strongly influence the decisions that leaders make and the actions they take, but how frequently do we examine them? Leaders can begin the process of building an effective system for hiring new teachers by challenging debilitating beliefs that lead to poor hiring decisions and replacing them with beliefs that drive excellence and lead to good hiring decisions.

LEADER ALERT

Where are Your Biases?

A solid interview performance?
A glowing recommendation?
A known quantity, the inside candidate?
A high grade point average?
A candidate with a parent, relative or spouse in the district?
A coaching background or other co-curricular strength?
A transcript from a prestigious college?
Appropriate certification, particularly in a high-needs area?

Debilitating Belief 1

"I base hiring decisions on quick impressions and pretty much know a good teacher when I see one."

Consider the three previous case studies. Each principal locked into quick favorable impressions based on limited data. Hiring on a hunch, going with the known entity, or hiring a certified body to quickly fill a vacancy led to poor hiring decisions. Rarely are one or two sources of data sufficient to make a decision to ensure that each student will receive expert instruction or that professional community will be strengthened and expanded.

Mr. Wills, the department chair in Case 10.1, relied heavily on Alicia Nativeson's inside candidacy and her glowing recommendations to make his decision. Absent was any real consideration of how hiring a candidate with a parent (or relative or spouse) on staff or in the district will translate into effectiveness in the classroom. Alicia's outgoing personality and positive relationships with students and peers obscure her mediocre teaching and lack of academic rigor. Wills also relies heavily on the favorable letters of recommendation. Such recommendations typically provide little in the way of useful information in discriminating among applicants.

In Case 10.2, Principal Lowell was swayed by Margaret Reader's strong interview performance, graduation from a prestigious college, and familiarity with current research. The interview itself was insufficient to predict Margaret's capacity to collaborate effectively. In addition, he placed significant weight on the recommendation from Margaret's faculty advisor who may not have observed Margaret in the classroom and interacting with other teachers. In rushing to conclude that Margaret may be just what this team needs, Lowell ignored important information about Margaret's working relationship with her supervising teacher. All of these factors conspired to create a false favorable impression, resulting in a poor hire.

Andrea McDuel, the principal in Case 10.3, made a rushed decision based on Larry's certification and his interview performance, which assured her he was well versed in special education regulations. These are important factors but insufficient to fully determine Larry's suitability and potential to support the school's major initiative of full inclusion. The principal ignored a reference that raised a red flag about Larry's capacity to collaborate with classroom teachers. Larry is, however, a known quantity by virtue of holding the appropriate certification; combined with the Labor Day hiring challenge, he was the beneficiary of a hasty process.

It is not surprising that, in the absence of clearly established criteria, favored biases become the default for selection. For example, are you likely to put pre-service education and a traditional certification path at the top of your list of criteria? If so, your thinking may be challenged by several recent studies that do not find traditional certification to be a predictor of effectiveness in the classroom.[2] When building one's portfolio, the conventional

---

[2] A six-year study in the New York City schools of 10,000 new teachers identified them in three categories: (1) traditionally certified, (2) alternatively certified, or (3) uncertified. Researchers found that variations in student achievement were much wider within each of the categories than among them. Of particular interest is the fact that the second two categories were primarily New York City Teaching Fellows and Teach for America candidates. Thomas Kane of the Harvard Graduate School of Education, one of the study's authors, concluded that when hiring new teachers the traditional route of university pre-service certification is not the best thing to look for nor are strong academic credentials, which are primary selection criteria in both Teach for America and the NYC Teaching Fellows program. He further noted that strong academic credentials were not highly correlated with student achievement. His recommendation is for districts to establish a "rigorous hiring process based on known characteristics of good teaching, watch each teacher's learning curve for two years, and then decide who should stay in the classroom" (Keller 10). A study by the Brookings Institution points to recent research that despite the stringent, credentials-centered measures of the No Child Left Behind Act, "certification of teachers bears little relationship to teacher effectiveness (measured by impacts on student achievement)" (Brookings Institution 2006 5).

wisdom is that one should not buy a mutual fund or stock based solely on past performance. Similarly, extremely high pre-service academic performance is not necessarily a valid predictor of success in the classroom.[3] We will explore ways of reducing individual bias when we look later in this chapter at setting clear criteria for the position to be filled.

Driving Belief 1

"I need to consider several sources of data to make good hiring decisions."

In hiring we are attempting to match the best candidate to the available position. New teachers will be expected to plan lessons, select instructional materials, assess student work, collaborate with peers, reflect on their practice, and grow professionally. Additional sources of data, beyond the traditional interview, allow us to better predict a candidate's capacity to perform these tasks effectively. Multiple data sources also help to keep hiring decisions objective, fair, and out of the political arena. We will examine specific features of data-based systems when we look later in this chapter at competence in recruitment and hiring.

Debilitating Belief 2

"Not every prospective candidate is destined to be a star in the classroom, and that's okay."

The urgency to fill a position must be placed in the larger context of an institutional urgency that every child deserves a teacher who can help all students achieve at high levels. Diminished expectations for new hires will translate into diminished expectations for students in the classrooms. Hit-or-miss hiring and settling for second best may be rationalized in a number of ways. Do any of these sound familiar?

Warm Body or Half a Loaf Syndrome

"We're lucky to find someone to fill this position. She wouldn't necessarily be my first choice, but she does have the correct certification, and the school year starts in a week."

Devil You Know Complex

"Here's someone we can work with. There's no telling what you might find out there these days. We've seen her in action and know what she can do. The staff loved her when she student taught in our school. Her mother is a fine teacher in the district, and we're a family here. We want to create opportunities for members of our community."

Bridesmaid Selection

"Not much of a pool out there, so second choice will have to do. We'll be

---

[3]"There is some evidence to suggest that teachers with very low GPA's fare more poorly than those with moderate to high GPA's. There is little evidence suggesting that candidates with extremely high GPA's (over 3.7) fare better than those with modest GPA's (3.0 to 3.7)" (Title 12).

sure to give him plenty of support in the beginning of the year to get him up to speed."

Endangered Species Anxiety Disorder

"Where on earth are you going to find a certified physics teacher these days or, for that matter, someone who can teach calculus or is a licensed speech language pathologist? If I get an application from someone with those credentials when I have a vacancy to fill, I'll jump on it!"

One Size Fits All Mindset

"He's not quite as strong in the classroom as the other candidates, but teaching is only one of the many jobs we need done here. He has a good coaching background and won't shy away from lunchroom duty; in fact he's even filled in for the principal during emergencies. He could be good assistant principal material."

Catch and Release Game Plan

"We'll give her a shot and see how she manages with those kids. The worst that can happen is we'll have to let her go. That will at least buy us some time to look around for someone better."

The Team Will Ensure Greatness Strategy

"He's not as strong academically as we'd like, but I'll be placing him in a good team that really has its act together. They should be able to get him on an even keel."

Dues Paid in Full Account

"He's been teaching driver education here for years and faithfully keeping his math certification renewed. We owe it to him to give him the math job that opened, particularly when you consider all of the things he's done around here over the years."

Each of these rationalizations signals a missed opportunity to find the best possible person for the position. They communicate resignation and "settling for" rather than a resolve to confront conditions that undermine learning.

Driving Belief 2

"It's our job to find the very best teachers we can—our students deserve nothing less. The short-term inconvenience is worth the long-term investment."

The short-term inconvenience of not filling a position and actively pursuing a better candidate or pool of candidates to choose from is well worth the long-term gain of making a quality hire. Leaders signal their belief that we will not settle for short-term solutions when they:

- Develop a pool of internally trained substitutes who can fill in for short-term openings as well as planned and unplanned leaves.

- Establish a Substitute Academy that provides focused training in instructional and classroom management strategies as well as district policies and procedures.

- Institute an Excellent Maintenance Teacher (EMT) program of qualified substitutes and instructional assistants with short-term contracts for challenging, unfilled positions.

- Maintain an active pool of recent retirees for short-term support, training, and coaching of fill-in personnel.

- Establish relationships with higher education teacher preparation programs as a source of reliable substitutes.

- Connect with local businesses to provide short-term substitutes. Nationally, two large employers, IBM and State Farm, have begun programs to support schools. Nearly 900 State Farm employees have been state certified as substitute teachers in a program that supports 185 schools in 54 districts. IBM has recently begun a program to facilitate veteran employees with a math or science background to pursue coursework to become teachers; nearly 100 employees are participating in this pilot program (*businessweek.com*, June 2006; www.businessweek.com/magazine/content/06_26/b3990014.htm?chan=search).

- Resist second- or third-best hires and keep looking for the best, holding themselves accountable to answering this question: "Is it possible that someone out there is better than this person?"

Debilitating Belief 3

"Salary is the only viable incentive for attracting and keeping strong candidates."

The migration of teachers from urban or rural districts to higher paying suburban districts has certainly contributed to this belief. Bargaining stances during contract negotiations in many lower paying districts frequently include the refrain that remaining competitive with salaries in better paying districts will stem this flow. Though new-teacher attrition in such districts may be in part due to better paying districts and professions competing for talented young employees, there are other causes. Believing that one can't compete with other districts because salary is the only thing that matters sets the stage for accepting "second-best" candidates. This can result in a missed opportunity to tout challenge, professional growth opportunities, improving student achievement levels, and quality induction as recruitment tools. Many new teachers we have interviewed have been quick to cite such features as pivotal in their decision to teach at a certain school or transfer to another school.

Tara, an elementary teacher talked about her decision to leave her school for another after her first year of teaching:

In my first year of teaching experience, I was so excited and enthusiastic about getting hired and doing what was best for kids; I was bubbling and that's what got me the job. When I got there I learned very quickly the other teachers weren't doing what I was doing in my classroom. I was very naïve, and I tried to figure it out. The mentor teacher and first year teacher thing was missing, the mentor kind of went away, and she kept saying, "Cool off a little, cool off, don't be too loud, too excited around these people, you need to wait a few years." That was the constant message, and I was confused. There just wasn't a sense of that professional development atmosphere I thought was supposed to happen.

Melissa, second year high school teacher, spoke about her decision to leave for a different school after her first year of teaching:

Professional development opportunities are really important, and it's necessary for new teachers to have access to them. But often there were only a few slots available, and professional status teachers usually get them. As for mentoring, well, if you're going to have it, it should be done thoroughly; my new school is committed to it. And make sure the department collaborates—in my first school I felt isolated, I didn't know who to ask for help. I was drawn by the department support in the new school. The salary was a little better too, but that was not my main motivation [for changing schools].

Driving Belief 3

"Intrinsic incentives can be powerful recruiting tools."

The lack of support to grow professionally was a determining factor in Tara's and Melissa's decisions to leave for other schools. Skillful recruiters look at what might be the sellable features of their district or school that will set it apart from the competition. They highlight a package of compensation, curriculum, colleagues, and community. How would you answer the following questions?

- Are there ongoing, accessible, and high-quality professional development opportunities available?
- Do teachers enjoy a high degree of collaboration to support their daily decision-making? Is there a clearly articulated curriculum?
- Is there a real professional community in place with a strong sense of mission?
- Are staff interactions productive and professionally satisfying, built on trust, a high regard for one another's competence, and a focus on student achievement?
- Are effective supports in place to induct new teachers such as quality mentoring, frequent de-briefing sessions for new-teacher peer groups,

clear orientation to key school and district priorities, and opportunities for peer observations?

Source: Recruiting New Teachers (www.rtn.org)

Closely paralleling our notion of the Accountable Community is what Scardamalia and Bereiter call knowledge-building communities, i.e., communities that support both individual and group expertise in advancing beyond current limits of competence. They note a number of motivations among members of such communities that are easy to spot (199):

- Desire to grow professionally
- Desire for recognition and respect from peers
- Desire for impact
- Desire to participate in significant discourse

We are struck by the passion and clarity with which these desires are expressed by leaders and teachers we have read about and visited in high-performing/high-poverty schools and how they can influence the recruitment and selection of new teachers. As you read the following interview quotations, note the clear articulation of mission, the sense of urgency and challenge, and the opportunities to join a team committed to making a difference in the lives of children.

A teacher in Washington D.C. explains why she chooses to work in a parochial school consortium where she earns $10,000 less than she would if she were still working in the D.C. public schools:

> I like that the standards for teachers in the consortium are high, and they are continually raising the bar. We are given the tools and the support to be effective instructors and to allow our students to be successful as well. (Mathews 2007)

Mary Skipper, Principal of Tech Boston Academy, Boston, describes what sets her staff apart:

> It goes back to the first sentence of our mission statement that every child can learn and what that means is that you have to have high expectations for every student that walks through the door. No matter if it's the first or the last day of the year, there's no giving up on kids. If we expect these kids to be lifelong learners, then we, as the adults in the building, have to be committed to do that as well…. The criteria for becoming a teacher here set these teachers apart. Everything here is about the students. It's not about your subject. We're here to teach kids. Yes, you need to know your content very well but also be committed when the kid doesn't get it the first, second, third time to evolve as a teacher until the kid does get it. (Personal communication 2005)

An additional incentive lies in opportunities teachers may have to move into leadership roles. We are not talking about the traditional career ladder of moving out of teaching and into administration, but rather the availability of teacher leader roles. Moller and Katzenmeyer help to expand our thinking about teacher leadership: "Our definition of teacher leadership proposes that teachers are leaders when they are contributing to school reform or student learning (within or beyond the classroom), influencing others to improve their professional practice, or identifying with and contributing to a community of learners"(5). Opportunities to lead committees, facilitate a team looking at student work, coach colleagues, or possibly take the lead role in introducing new curriculum or units of instruction can be attractions that set a school apart from others. Eliot Stern, principal of the Edison Middle School in Boston, sees teacher leadership as a defining feature of his school and an essential ingredient in its success. He notes that teacher leaders in his building are "not necessarily experts or a duplication of the principal but folks mobilizing other folks to do good work" (personal communication 2007). He begins looking for qualities of leadership in the hiring process and communicates to prospective hires that all teachers have opportunities to assume leadership roles in the school. (For more on teacher leadership see Chapter 6 "Moving Communities from Collaborative to Accountable.")

Are incentives such as these alive and well in your school community? These are the features that will appeal to the candidates we most wish to find and keep. Strong school communities collectively engaged to move beyond mediocrity in teaching and learning may well be the best advertisement for high-quality new teachers.

Competence in Recruitment and Hiring

What can leaders do to build their competence to recruit, hire, and retain the very best possible people? What skills and strategies will maximize leaders' competence to recruit and hire the best possible teachers? Building competency includes developing skills in setting clear criteria, collecting multiple sources of data, and engaging the school community in the process. Hiring should be guided by defined standards of good teaching. Here are some key strategies to get us on the road to competency in hiring the best possible people to teach in our schools.

Strategy 1: Establish Clear Criteria for Positions

What qualities must a candidate have in order to succeed in the position to be filled? When we ask this question, we are operating like effective teachers who are clear in their thinking about what a successful student product or performance will look like. Criteria give us a clear picture of the desirable candidate and will shape the types of questions we will ask applicants in an interview. In short, criteria describe the qualities, attributes, and skills necessary for success.

Defining criteria will depend on the context and the position to be filled. One urban high school principal shared with us his school's criteria for a social studies position he was seeking to fill:

- **Experience.** The candidate has urban teaching experience or, if new, student teaching in an urban school.
- **Persistence.** The principal specifically asks candidates: "Please recount a time when you were initially unsuccessful at an important task and tell me what you did to improve."
- **Articulateness.** The candidate can communicate clearly and precisely. A 10-minute writing sample is administered answering the question: "What will be your biggest challenge in this position?"
- **Capacity to collaborate.** Since his school is structured around small learning communities, the principal wants candidates to share specific ways they have worked on a team or in a collaborative venture. "Please share with me a time you have been part of a team other than an athletic team. Tell me the role you played and what we can expect from your participation in your department."
- **Enthusiasm for and knowledge of content.** The principal asks candidates: "Please share the two most recent books you have read in your content area and how they influenced your thinking."

Criteria can be drawn from school improvement plans and data on current student achievement patterns. In a district where one of the authors previously worked, an elementary school planned to move to a multi-grade structure. A grade 3 teaching position needed to be filled. The school added prior successful experience teaching in a multi-grade classroom to other criteria identified for the position. Similarly, a district or school goal of raising achievement levels in math at the elementary level may well require criteria that include a strong background in teaching math and strong collaborative skills in sharing that expertise with others. Hiring for a position on a middle school team that shares students will likely call for criteria describing a candidate's capacity to effectively collaborate, i.e., to actively listen, communicate clearly, and to acknowledge the value of group decision-making norms in working productively with others.

Many criteria are job-specific; yet there are two that should be part of every hiring process. These are the ability to learn (Conviction) and the ability to work in diverse cultural settings (cultural proficiency). We have written about ability to learn as a core conviction for high-performing teams. Beliefs are very difficult to change even with on the job training, so we need to hire teachers who make decisions based on strong beliefs about students' capacity to learn. Prospective teachers need to have internalized and acted upon the threshold belief "All can achieve; there are no excuses." Questions to probe beliefs about ability to learn include: "How might you explain your of lack success with a particular group of students? What might you do when you are not successful with an individual learner or group of learners? Describe specific steps you took to address this situation."

Because we believe in creating equitable classrooms where all kids succeed, we advocate for a second criterion: cultural proficiency so we can hire teachers who work well (or want to learn about working) with culturally diverse students. Lest readers from suburban or rural settings skip this section, thinking "Oh this is an urban criterion," diversity exists in all schools, and issues of race, ethnicity, class, culture, gender, sexual orientation, and other differences must be addressed directly in supporting the learning of all students. At the same time, leaders face urgent needs to close achievement gaps among African Americans and Latinos, so that will be our primary focus. Martin Haberman has spent over 40 years studying the specific demands placed on teachers, especially those who work with students at risk of failure in public schools. Having cultural proficiency means understanding the specific needs of students from diverse backgrounds and being committed to closing the achievement gap for these students.

Lindsey, Roberts and Jones describe cultural proficiency as "a way of being that enables people to successfully engage in new environments"(13). It is this level of engagement, a new sensitivity to cultural and racial differences, that can inform the work of groups intent on higher levels of collaboration and accountability in supporting the achievement of all students.

Haberman's work (2005) has led him to identify the ideologies of "star teachers" who succeed in making a difference with low-income and culturally diverse students. Decades of research and development have resulted in pre-screening and interview instruments to identify potentially successful multicultural teachers. For additional information regarding the Haberman Selection interviews see www.Habermanfoundation.org. The criteria assessed in the pre-screening instrument are listed below.

1. **Persistence** predicts the propensity to work with children who present learning and behavioral problems on a daily basis for the full 180-day work year without giving up on them.

2. **Organization and planning** refers to how and why star teachers plan, as well as their ability to manage complex classroom organizations.

3. **Values student learning** predicts the degree to which the responses reflect a willingness to make student learning the teacher's highest priority.

4. **Theory to practice** predicts the respondent's ability to see the practical implications of generalizations as well as the concepts reflected by specific practices.

5. **At-risk students** predict the likelihood that the respondent will be able to connect with and teach students of all backgrounds and levels.

6. **Approach to students** predicts the way the respondent will attempt to relate to students and the likelihood this approach will be effective.

7. **Survive in bureaucracy** predicts the likelihood that the respondent

will be able to function as a teacher in large, depersonalized organization.

8. **Explains teacher success** deals with the criteria the respondent uses to determine teaching success and whether these are relevant to teachers in poverty schools.

9. **Fallibility** refers to how the teacher plans to deal with mistakes in the classroom (www.habermanfoundation.org).

The follow-up studies of the instrument's effectiveness are compelling and address the problem of attrition of teachers: "Studies have shown that the retention rate for teachers who have been hired using the Haberman 'Star' Teacher Selection Interview is about 95% to 98%. The Milwaukee schools, for example, showed a 95% retention rate eight years after the 137 Haberman-interviewed teachers were hired" (*The Education Innovator* #7, U.S. Dept. of Education, February 23, 2004).[4] Clear criteria can thus help predict success of a candidate while also reducing individual bias. Our next strategy also counters individual bias by building collaboration and accountability into the hiring process through the use of a school-based interview committee.

LEADER ALERT

Speed Hiring Despite many advantages of committee hiring, there may be situations when the use of a school-based interview committee is ill advised. Leaders engaged in turning around Toxic and Laissez-Faire Communities must gauge whether such communities can effectively contribute to interviewing candidates without hindering the process or attempting to hire in their own likeness. Speed hiring may also be a viable alternative where there is little time for meaningful collaboration. A recently retired principal noted his use of "speed hiring": moving quickly to fast track the hiring process when a strong candidate is available early in the hiring season. Richard Schaye says that there are a limited number of exceptional candidates who can "write their ticket." Making a quick decision in the case of these candidates to get in front of the competition can indeed be a skillful leader strategy (personal communication 2007).

---

[4]A recent study in Buffalo (Frey 2004) compared retention data with national research in the field. The study concluded, "Use of the Haberman interview results in statistically significant increases in teacher retention as compared to data collected nationally" (http://www.habermanfoundation.org/research/research.asp?page=Research&article=dissertation).

TABLE 10.1 Benefits of School-Based Interview Committees

Multiple areas of specialization
Greater legitimacy of group assessment
Fuller recall and more comprehensive records of interviews
Reduction of individual bias through consensus
Opportunities for members to challenge each other's observations, assumptions, and decisions
Multiple areas of specialization

(Source: Peterson 73)

Strategy 2: Build Teacher Ownership and Responsibility for Hiring

Ownership and responsibility are basic convictions of Accountable Communities. How might leaders apply this belief to the hiring process? In many schools and districts, the opportunities for candidates to interact with school personnel other than the principal remain infrequent. A four-state (California, Florida, Massachusetts, and Michigan) survey conducted by Edward Liu of the Project on the Next Generation of Teachers found that though the vast majority of new teachers interview with the principal, "less than half interview with other teachers, and fewer than one in six with department chairs, students, or parents at the school"(Johnson). There is a missed opportunity here not only to build investment in the hiring process but also to offer prospective candidates more information about the school and so increase the likelihood of an effective match. In addition, a school-based interview committee can reduce individual bias by offering multiple perspectives on prospective candidates. It is an opportunity for a community to reflect on its standards for membership and regenerate itself through collaborative effort.

When a school-based interview committee is used, it should serve in an advisory capacity to the principal both to establish the criteria for the position and to interview candidates. Training is critical to committee success (see the Tips on preparing the committee).

TIPS ON PREPARING A SCHOOL-BASED INTERVIEW COMMITTEE

✔ **Clearly communicate committee roles and responsibilities.** The committee is advisory, but as leader you will give much weight to their recommendations.

✔ **Remind the committee to avoid asking inappropriate questions.** Don't ask about marital status, sexual orientation, and political affiliation.

✔ **Develop and field test questions.** Good questions are those that are likely to obtain the information you want based on the criteria for the position to be filled.

✔ **Avoid questions that clearly signal a particular answer.** "Do you believe all students can be successful?" or questions that can be answered with a simple yes or no: "Do you use technology in your classroom?" More can be learned about a candidate by asking "Share some of the ways you support all students in your classroom to be successful," or "Describe specific ways in which you incorporate technology into your instruction."

✔ **Let the candidate do most of the talking.** Be concise and clear in questioning and allow candidates time to fully answer the question. If the response is not complete, cue the candidate and allow him or her to keep talking. The 80/20 rule should prevail with the interviewers talking 20 percent of the time and candidates 80 percent.

✔ **Allot time for the candidates to ask questions.** Some advise that candidates have an opportunity to ask questions near the end of the interview, but others encourage questions in the middle to allow modification of remaining questions. The committee can get important information from the questions and should not short cut this two-way interchange. The type of questions candidates ask may also communicate their interests, concerns, and feelings about the position as well as their values and beliefs.

✔ **Avoid rushing to judgment before completing all of the interviews.** Conduct a full review of each candidate's strengths and weaknesses relative to the criteria after the interviews are done.

✔ **Project the positive image, professionalism, and respect that you believe characterizes your school community.** Be aware that perceptive candidates will be gathering information about your school and its potential to be a good fit for them. In particular, they may be looking at the committee's level of preparation, quality of questions, courtesy, attentiveness, and how committee members interact with one another.

✔ **Create a relaxed environment.** Nervous candidates tend not to reveal much of real substance about themselves. The principal can speak with the candidate briefly before the interview, describe who is on the committee, and, when beginning the interview, have members introduce themselves and tell their roles in the school. Having water available for the candidates and otherwise ensuring their comfort can also help. Consider a U-shaped seating arrangement that allows eye contact and a sense of inclusion for the candidate rather than seating him or her alone and across the room or conference table from the committee.

After the interviews are conducted, the principal facilitates the committee discussion of strengths and weaknesses of each candidate, *relative to the criteria*. The goal is to provide the principal with input from the multiple perspectives of committee members. The final decision will rest with the principal or possibly a Central Office administrator in consultation with the principal. For this reason, committee ranking of candidates or voting on candidates should be avoided. This can potentially set up conflict over candidates and denigrate the work of the committee. Principals who have used interview committees in the hiring process note the value of identifying clear criteria for the position and of the important community-building role the committee can play.

> With regard to an interview committee, to get buy-in and acceptance by a team or the teachers the new person would be most closely associated with, it is important to include teachers in the process. Our most recent hire came down to experience vs. fit. I felt strongly the fit was going to go to the teacher without experience but who had great potential (a 36-year-old career changer). The experienced teacher was a bulldozer and wasn't in my mind a clean fit with the team. Everyone on the committee decided to react to my concerns and call the two back for a second interview. On their own they concluded that the inexperienced teacher was the best fit and had the potential to be a good match for that team, and they continue to support that. (Bonnie Poe, former Principal, Edmunds Middle School, personal communication 2005)

In summary, when conditions allow, a school-based interview committee can provide a level of collective engagement that builds ownership and responsibility in the hiring process. The process builds community capacity for meaningful collaboration while also building membership in that community.

Strategy 3: Use Multiple Data Sources in Making Hiring Decisions

Though a thorough review of credentials, an interview, and reference checking are essential, they simply cannot yield enough data upon which to make a hiring decision.[5] Collecting additional data permits a more holistic view of the candidates and helps determine who might be the best match for the position. Several approaches allow a more authentic assessment of candidates.

Ask Candidates To Bring a Portfolio

Experienced teachers and even student teachers seeking their first positions should be asked to bring teacher-generated artifacts to support their candidacy. These could include:

- Formative assessments/tests and quizzes.
- Lesson and unit plans.
- Professional development plans.
- Web pages.

[5]Title notes that the use of a traditional interview as the primary means of selection may not be sufficient (1995 5). He cites variables such as interviewer bias and competence as challenging the reliability and validity of the interview data.

Reference Checking Letters of recommendation can be helpful when we look carefully for specific evidence of outstanding performance or the use of superlatives in describing the candidate (e.g., "in the top 5 percent of student teachers I have supervised"). Vague, less precise comments such as "a solid, all-around student," "a good teacher," "a very engaging personality," or "has some real potential" are of little value. In fact, their vagueness begs for alternate sources of data. We strongly recommend "Googling" candidates prior to hiring.

- Student work samples with feedback. An alternative would be to provide a sample of student work and have candidates analyze it relative to district standards (Reeves 2007). (See also Chapter 8 "Collecting and Using Data: Sources.")

Observe Candidates Teaching a Lesson

Having final candidates teach a sample lesson can offer a rich pool of additional data with which to compare candidates and make the best selection; yet it is rarely done. In Edward Liu's survey cited above, he found that only 7.5 percent of the teachers in the four states he researched taught a sample lesson as part of the hiring process. Final candidates for a position can be scheduled to teach a 30-minute or longer grade-appropriate lesson of their choice. The classroom of a teacher on the interview committee can be used for the sample lesson, and, for summer hires, a summer school class or summer recreation program could be used. In cases where distance or timing is a problem, videotaped lessons could be substituted. Keep in mind that teaching his or her own students might allow the candidate an unfair advantage. Here are some things to look for in observing candidates teach sample lessons:

- How effectively does s/he establish a rapport with the students?
- Does the candidate engage all students or a subset of the class?
- How does s/he activate students' current knowledge or otherwise get the class engaged?
- Are they maintaining student attention in a variety of ways beyond simple verbal reminders? How do they handle a student who is off-task or disruptive?
- Are they using explanatory devices such as visuals, models, analogies, or simpler language to make their instruction more vivid and accessible to the class?
- Are there opportunities for student involvement?

- Does the candidate practice wait-time, checking for understanding, or allowing students to summarize what they are learning?
- Does the candidate ask questions beyond recall? (It is unrealistic to expect too many higher level questions, but some application questions might be appropriate.)

Interestingly, teacher experience has not been found to be a predictor of a successful sample lesson. Though a more experienced candidate may be better prepared to anticipate student confusion and respond to a wider variety of unexpected student behaviors, novice candidates, having just completed their student teaching practicum, may feel more comfortable being observed (Title).

Additional adaptations can be made depending on the position to be filled. Candidates for a school guidance counselor position can conduct a small group session on topics such as bullying, community building, or college application strategies. School librarians can teach a library skills lesson, and so on. Again, the primary interest here is to look beyond the interview to actually see how the candidates interact with students, the level of rapport they build, their level of enthusiasm in teaching the lesson, the general appropriateness of the lesson for the student age or grade level, as well as the instructional decisions that were made. We are not simply interviewing candidates but hiring them to be teachers and learners.

Assess Candidates' Capacity for Reflection

Hiring people who are learners is one way to confront conditions that undermine learning! Our work in looking closely at mediocre teaching reminds us that teachers do not become more effective by accumulating experience but rather from processing their experience. We look at a candidate's capacity to reflect on her performance as an important indicator of her potential to grow professionally.

Eliot Stern, Principal of Edison Middle School, Boston MA, shared his approach to assessing a candidate's capacity to reflect. After observing a candidate teach a lesson, he conducts a conference in which he asks the candidate to share with him "what your mastery goal for the lesson was, how close you got to it, what's the evidence of that, and what would you do differently next time. Feel free to stumble, thinking is messy... I want you to be as rigorous as you can in reflecting on this lesson with me" (personal communication 2007).

After completing a sample lesson, candidates should be asked to submit a one-page, handwritten reflection on the lesson in which they express how they feel it went, what worked well, and where they would fine-tune or improve the lesson. The purpose of receiving a candidate's reflection in handwritten form is to look for clarity and legibility in their written communication. After all, this is what students and parents will see from the teacher. Principals receiving reflections frequently note that the stronger performing candidates were often more self-critical and reflected more deeply about their practice. Additional things to look for in reflections include the following. Can the candidate:

- Assess how the lesson went based on what students were able to do or likely to be able to do?

- Precisely describe the strategies s/he chose and why s/he chose them?

- Attribute the causes of a successful or unsuccessful performance to internal factors? Own the outcome or point to factors outside of his or her control?

- Produce reasonable ideas for improvement?

- Cite additional assessment data s/he would seek if given an opportunity?

- Analyze the possible causes for failure (lesson autopsy)?

The cumulative value of these skills is to assess the individual's ability to learn and conviction that his or her effort to motivate and engage students will make a difference.

Taking Control of Recruitment and Hiring

What institutional deficiencies—systems policies and practices—must be addressed to improve the selection and retention of promising new teachers? What prevents your school from taking control of recruiting and hiring good teachers? The best efforts of building leaders are often stymied by unpromising district practices, policies, and structures that undermine hiring. District leaders can provide the necessary control to select the right people by actively collaborating with building leaders to identify and reform unpromising practices.

Unpromising Practice 1

Policies and procedures are not in place to conduct teacher hiring in a timely and effective fashion.

Too often fragmentation of major district policies and procedures contributes to losing promising candidates. Getting to the market late guarantees a pool of candidates diminished in both quantity and quality. Consider, for instance, how often a district's annual budget approval date is set weeks or even months after the teacher notification date for contract renewal. Facing the possibility of a budget defeat, districts are often compelled to issue lay-off notices to new and less senior teachers who then migrate to other districts, leaving their positions vacant until a budget is eventually approved.

Schools often end up getting teachers who undermine efforts to improve student learning. In its study of five large urban districts, The New Teacher Project found "on average, fully 40 percent of school vacancies were filled by incumbent teachers over whom schools had little or no choice in hiring" (www.tntp.org 2005 4). Not surprisingly, the study also found that nearly half of the principals surveyed indicated that they would seek to conceal vacancies in their schools to avoid hiring either excessed teachers or voluntary transfers. The implications for leaders striving to build accountable school communities are painfully apparent here: "You cannot hold principals accountable for student achievement and not let them pick the team to get the job done. No CEO could run a company that way. These rules no longer work in an era of high-stakes accountability" (Michelle Rhee, CEO and President of The New Teacher Project, TNTP release, November 16, 2005).

In large urban districts, a teacher shortage is often identified as the reason for hiring difficulties. In addition, it is commonly assumed that the poor working conditions in many of these districts and stiff competition from better paying suburban districts or other professions will leave them with second- and third-rate candidates. A 2003 study conducted by The New Teacher Project (www. tntp.org) counters this conventional view and instead points to institutional deficiencies as the significant challenge for urban schools. The study found that urban districts are getting quality applicants but are not able to hire them in a timely fashion. The four urban districts in this nationwide study received many more applications than there were vacancies, largely due to targeted recruitment strategies. In addition, the study reported that nearly 37 percent of the applicants applied to teach in high need areas such as mathematics, bilingual education, special education, and science. However, slow and inefficient hiring practices, delays in state budget timetables, and seniority contract provisions were seen as the chief impediments to effective hiring. When these districts eventually did make formal job offers in mid- to late summer, 30 percent to 60 percent of the applicants had withdrawn, many of them accepting positions in suburban districts that had made appreciably earlier offers. The report's authors state that this process of late summer hiring and applicant attrition occurs in large urban districts nationwide. What is particularly disturbing about these findings is the extent to which these institutional practices contribute to perpetuating mediocrity in the classroom, as evidenced by profiles of the "lost" candidates.[6] In the wake of these missed opportunities, urban districts scramble to fill positions with less qualified and less committed applicants.

Promising Practice 1

Systematically address institutional deficiencies.

Three significant initiatives can be undertaken. First, identify teacher notification requirements that impede timely hiring and make their revision a priority. Given the large initial investment in training that districts make in new and early career teachers, preventing their displacement will offer cost benefits. Second, reform collective bargaining transfer provisions with a clear resolve to eliminate the automatic granting of voluntary transfer requests.

---

[6]Withdrawers had higher GPAs and were 40 percent more likely to have a degree in their teaching field than the eventual new hires. In addition, between 37 percent and 69 percent were candidates for hard-to-fill positions. The majority of withdrawers—50 percent to 70 percent—cited the late timeline as a major reason for taking other jobs, although almost half said they definitely or probably would have accepted an offer from the urban district if it had come earlier. In addition, four out of five applicants said that despite the problems, they would like to be considered again for an urban teaching position (Levin 2005).

LEGAL NOTE 10.1

"Bumping" Rights

Several recent studies that have addressed the impact of collective bargaining agreements on education reform call for an elimination or modification of transfer and "bumping clauses" based upon seniority because of the constraints such clauses place upon a principal's discretion in filling vacancies in their schools. In many cases current contract language allows multiple criteria and cites "seniority" as a tiebreaker in important personnel decisions regarding transfers, bumping, and promotions. These clauses can provide a balance between the traditional discretion afforded to principals and the recognition that should be given to employee preferences. However, most administrators have been reluctant to use the discretion that many collective bargaining agreements now provide because of the fear of grievances and the cost of proving their cases to the satisfaction of labor arbitrators. Look at your contracts and consult your personnel office about your degree of discretion in filling vacancies.[7]

[7]See *Collective Bargaining in Education–Negotiating Change in Today's Schools*, Harvard Education Press, Cambridge, MA (2006); *A Better Bargain: Overhauling Teacher Collective Bargaining for the 21st Century*, at http://www.ksg.harvard.edu/pepg/PDF/Papers/BetterBargain.pdf and *Teacher Contracts: Restoring the Balance*, The Education Partnership, 2006 at http://www.edpartnership.org/?id=1104

Teachers wishing to voluntarily transfer can thus be given the same consideration as external candidates so that schools can select the best candidate for the position. Though state law and ethics usually recommend giving excessed teachers prior consideration for vacancies they are certified and qualified to fill, when possible you should shorten their priority period. For an example of how one principal managed to navigate his way through the maze of voluntary transfer provisions see the Leader Alert on Replacing Retirees. Finally, streamline district human resources procedures for receiving and processing applications by connecting applicants to schools with the potential for a good fit. In large districts, closer coordination between human resources departments and individual schools is essential; when human resources personnel have a clear understanding of individual school initiatives and improvement efforts, they can begin saving time by conducting a paper screening and targeting specific applicants to particular schools.

Unpromising Practice 2

Unsettled contracts and imposed salary ceilings impede effective hiring.

Unsettled contracts not only cause diminished morale and, in many cases, work-to-rule environments, they can also result in sizable teacher migration to increasingly better paying, nearby districts. The prospects of filling vacant teaching positions with the best possible candidates become daunting. In addition, a spoken or unspoken salary ceiling placed on new hires where hiring is based not on data gathered, but rather on pre-determined financial parameters, is a sure formula for selecting inferior candidates. Short-term

LEADER ALERT

Replacing Retirees An urban principal with a successful track record in turning around a previously under-performing school describes his effort to take control of the hiring process in his new school. The teachers' contract in this urban district permitted teacher transfer from other schools based on seniority, not performance. The transfers were often the unwanted "lemons." However, if a principal could obtain a 60 percent vote of the school's faculty, it would allow within-school open posting of new or vacated positions so that young new hires could be retained. Addressing the staff early in his first school year, he acknowledged that they were likely aware of his reputation in moving ineffective teachers out (he had never lost a dismissal case). He made a deal with the aging faculty. "I will work with you (won't hassle you with tough evaluations) if you let me pick your replacements. He got the 60 percent faculty vote, and over a period of five years the school has become one of the city's top-performing high schools. He attributes this in large part to the new teachers he has hired and, more importantly, retained. Leaders, however, should tread carefully in this potential age discrimination territory. Announcing the "going easy" policy in exchange for control of hiring replacements might shock some readers. This anecdote is not a recommendation but a commentary on how principals may have to work the system to get the control to hire the right people and keep them.

> **LEGAL NOTE 10.2**
>
> **Step Salary Ceilings**
>
> At least one court case in Connecticut has held that a school district's policy of limiting new hires to step 6 of the salary schedule to effectuate budget economies was unlawful because the plaintiff proved that such a hiring practice had a discriminatory impact upon teachers over the age of 40 who were statistically more likely to have more experience than teachers below the age of 40, (*Geller v. Markham*, 635 F.2d 1027 (1980). All hiring criteria should be based upon "bona fide occupational qualifications" or at least should avoid a discriminatory impact upon applicants based upon a protected characteristic such as race, ethnicity, age, sex, marital status, and, in some states, sexual preference. See "Federal Laws Prohibiting Job Discrimination Questions and Answers" at: http://www.eeoc.gov/facts /qanda.html.

staff turnover savings may have longer-term implications for student achievement, not to mention possible age discrimination problems. An unsettled contract and/or a ceiling on placement create very poor conditions for recruitment.

The example of one regional high school is a case in point. Working without a new teachers' contract for four years, the principal noted 30 of 170 teaching positions became vacant. Some teachers retired, but the bulk of them moved to higher paying neighboring districts. Adding to this predicament, a cap was placed on new hires on the salary schedule; the ceiling was BA column, step 3. Though replacing higher salaried retiring and departing teachers with lower salaried new hires was viewed with delight by the district's business manager, the principal was increasingly troubled and demoralized by the quality of the new candidates available to hire. "Not a pretty picture for improving student learning" was his summary remark.

Promising Practice 2

Address contract negotiations and budget barriers to hiring the best possible teachers.

Though there is no easy solution to speedily settle prolonged contract negotiations, the full impact on staffing must be acknowledged. Good communication between negotiating parties and a sense of urgency over the impact on staffing and student achievement should be a critical focus of ongoing bargaining. The cost/benefit ratio of hiring only new teachers with limited experience must be examined when looking at turnover savings. The intact skills and training of candidates with more experience, though more expensive on the salary schedule, may offset in-service training and staff development costs associated with inexperienced teachers.

Creating a system for hiring requires (1) confronting debilitating beliefs that undermine hiring and committing to replace them with driving beliefs (Conviction); (2) expanding hiring to include strategies for using multiple sources of data and involving the community (Competence); and (3) confronting practices, structures, and policies that support poor hiring decisions (Control). We know that leaders cannot wait for the perfect candidate. We know that forces, distractions, and constraints work against that every day. Still, when we put standards in place for excellent hiring process and procedures, we have a better chance of the getting the best teachers. Now we need to examine how to retain the newly hired teachers and improve them or, if necessary, get rid of them.

Induction

Induction is about retaining the right people and making important decisions about who should not be retained. In *Good to Great and the Social Sectors*, Jim Collins notes:

> In the social sectors, where getting the wrong people off the bus can be more difficult than in business, early assessment mechanisms turn out to be more important than hiring mechanisms. There is no perfect interviewing technique, no ideal hiring method; even the best executives make hiring mistakes. You can only know for certain about a person by working with that person. (Collins 2005 15)

Working with new teachers is part of a comprehensive induction system to ensure that they receive the necessary support and that sufficient data can be gathered for making tenure decisions. The critical variable throughout this induction process is that new teachers are confronted with a dual challenge: "They have to teach and they have to learn to teach" (Feiman-Nemser in Chauncey 65). To effectively grow new teachers and prevent mediocre learning, leaders must develop induction programs that provide useful feedback to novices on how they are teaching and also support their ongoing growth and skill in learning to teach.

New teachers typically arrive on the first day of school with butterflies in their stomachs and wonder and worry about the new year. Leaders send important messages by the way they communicate with new hires before the start of school, especially during the first few days. While the process of induction happens over two to three years, before tenure decisions are made, the power of those first days to define the work of teaching for new teachers is profound.

Here are some common experiences new teachers have in schools across this country every fall and the accompanying implicit message to teachers each experience holds. See what connections you can make between these messages and the type of communities they might characterize.

A recent college graduate who majored in English and was hired to teach secondary English Language Arts reviews the schedule she is handed on the first day of school and realizes she is teaching a remedial math class for eighth graders. She took one math class in college because it was a requirement, and she can barely remember what she learned in her own middle school math classes.
Message: Being qualified to teach a subject is not important. Since we didn't give you any advance notice of this change, we don't expect you to be prepared. The class and the students in it are not important, and not much is expected of you.

The orientation for new teachers is a 15-minute tour of the school that highlights the teachers' room, the adult bathrooms, the room with the copier, the book room, and the main office. The teacher who leads the tour offers advice as the group walks the corridors, commenting, "We don't like to talk about teaching in the teachers' room. We teach all day and need a place to chill out and relax. The secretary runs the school. She's the one to count on. She can be a bit moody so watch your step. If you ever cross her, your life will be hell. The most important thing for a new teacher is to keep her students quiet. If you do that, you will be fine and no one will bother you by visiting your classroom."
Message: Teachers don't talk to one another about teaching in this school. Getting support and help is based on relationships. The person with the most power is unpredictable and has the least expertise and ability to help you improve as a teacher. Learning is secondary to controlling your classroom, so focus on control first and foremost. Administrators only visit classrooms where they think there is a problem, and the goal is to keep administrators out of your classroom.

A group of teachers are in a meeting with the principal the day before school starts. The principal announces that to honor a late summer class change request of a veteran teacher, a newly hired teacher will go from teaching a regular education 2nd grade class to a special education 5th grade class. The new teacher, 22 and fresh out of college, looks visibly stricken by this news and starts to cry. The principal continues with her announcements, and the teachers either don't notice or choose to ignore their colleague's distress.

Message: You can't trust the principal to keep her word. New teachers are not important and veteran teachers' interests rule. It does not matter if you are prepared to teach your class. You will be treated poorly here; how you feel about things isn't important; and don't expect your colleagues to support you. You will not be taught what it means to be a professional and how to act appropriately.

At the end of November, a new teacher finds a completed evaluation of her teaching in her mailbox with a note from the principal that she needs to sign the evaluation and return it to her by the end of the day. As the new teacher reads the evaluation, she is surprised by what she is being evaluated on though she vaguely remembers getting a blank copy of the evaluation in the 6-inch pile of materials she was handed on the first day. She is confused by the whole process because the principal has never been in her classroom and the assistant principal has visited two or three times but never for more than 5 minutes. The evaluation is very general and says the teacher is doing a "good job." There is nothing in the evaluation that will help the teacher improve her practice. *Message: Your evaluation isn't important. There is no transparent process by which evaluations are done. It is something that will be done to you instead of your taking an active role in the process. Evaluations are not intended to help teachers improve their practice.*

These images are painful and tell just the beginning of the story of new-teacher attrition, an issue that is particularly troubling in urban districts where close to 50 percent of new teachers leave by the end of their third year of teaching. Each of the messages expresses the cynicism, resignation, and lack of standards that characterize regressive communities (toxic, laissez-faire, and congenial) where mediocrity is perpetuated and learning is undermined. Each of the scenarios conforms to the pessimistic assessment of Johnson and Kardos that, "Despite the range of demands placed on new teachers, few schools deliberately and thoroughly introduce new teachers to their work or their workplace" (Johnson 193). What passes for induction is often a welcoming breakfast, a one-day, district-wide new-teachers' meeting, and possible assignment to a mentor who likely has had little training in that capacity. If schools are to become places that nurture adult growth so that new teachers can thrive, then skillful leaders need to create conditions that support new teachers and engage other teachers to join in the effort. Let's turn to a vision of new-teacher support that illustrates what nurturing conditions look like.

CASE 10.4 **Merry Young**

Merry Young, a first-year teacher, was hired in the spring to join the staff of Bellevue Elementary in September as a 3rd grade teacher. Enter the mentor. The same day she received her contract letter, Merry received a phone call from Keisha, a member of the 3rd grade team at her school who was calling to welcome her to the school. Keisha will serve as Merry's mentor in her first year of teaching, which will include many opportunities for Merry and Keisha to observe one another teach, plan together, and review student performance data to inform their instruction. Keisha is an outstanding teacher who has assumed an important leadership role on the grade 3 team. Her students consistently demonstrate more than a year's growth under her leadership, and she has been trained to work with new teachers, helping them to develop their skills and problem-solving strategies. Keisha invites Merry to visit her classroom before the school year ends to observe 3rd grade and to receive a set of curriculum materials Merry can use to prepare over the summer.

Message: New teachers are not isolated and left to "sink or swim." This school has high expectations for its students and teachers, and there is a well-planned support system for new hires to ensure the expectations are met. Relationships among teachers are collegial.

Within a few weeks, Merry has been invited to a summer institute offered by the district that will introduce her to the English Language Arts and math curricula the school uses. She has also signed up for a three-day classroom management seminar that is being taught by teachers from her school. Before the end of June, Merry's principal emails her to make sure she has received the information about the summer professional development. She also asks Merry to save the dates of the new-teacher orientation the school will host at the end of August and the two-day, all-staff professional development meeting that will address strategies to support English language learners. Merry emails back information about her summer professional development plans and the principal replies, "Fabulous, I think you will enjoy the sessions, and they will help you kick off the year well with your students. We're so happy to have you as part of the Bellevue team."

Message: New teachers in this school will not spend the summer worrying about what and how to teach in the fall. This is a community that values learning and wants students and teachers to succeed. The administration emphasizes this priority by making personal contact with new hires about professional development before school starts.

After all the summer activities, Merry feels quite at home in her school. She spends the day before students arrive setting up her classroom and organizing the complete sets of instructional materials that the assistant principal made sure she had in her classroom. In setting up her classroom, Merry applies some of the ideas she and Keisha discussed earlier in the summer as well as ideas she gleaned from the professional development sessions. At noon she joins her 3rd grade colleagues for lunch, and they spend the afternoon sharing their plans for the first week of school. She has a couple of last-minute questions and is looking forward to hearing their ideas. As Merry leaves the afternoon meeting, she starts to imagine meeting her students the next day. She also reminds herself of the first new-teacher support meeting the principal will host after school on Friday. Reviewing the teaching standards and the teacher evaluation instrument are also on the agenda of this first of a yearlong series of biweekly meetings the principal will hold for new teachers. Merry makes a mental note to review both documents that are in her new-teacher orientation binder before the meeting.

Message: New teachers are not alone. They are members of a team that devotes time to sharing ideas and answering questions. They have new-teacher orientation binders. Once school starts, the support will continue. Meeting agendas help new hires focus on their teaching standards.

Merry's first day gives us a vision of a school and district committed to ensuring the success of all new teachers. Merry's example shows that a strong support system for new teachers begins as soon as the teacher is hired. Merry's interactions with her mentor, Keisha, and the opportunity to meet with her 3rd grade colleagues to discuss plans for the first week of school are early experiences in collaboration that not only support Merry's planning and confidence for the upcoming school year but also begin the process of acculturating her to the norms of this school community.

In thinking about how to build an induction program for new teachers, we return once again to the three C's framework: Conviction, Competence, and Control.

Conviction and New Teacher Induction

What beliefs about teaching can help leaders build high-quality induction programs? In schools that operate as Collaborative or Accountable Communities, there are beliefs that guide every action and decision in the school. These same beliefs guide the support new teachers receive and encourage community building.

Belief 1

Teaching is a profession that has standards for adults just as it has standards for students. All teachers are responsible for exploring every imaginable resource and opportunity to find the best way to teach their children. It is not acceptable simply to say, "I don't know." Such a statement must be followed by all the ways the teacher intends to learn what she needs to know to serve her students well.

Belief 2

All students have the ability to learn to the level of high standards. There is a sense of purpose and urgency about ensuring students meet the standards. It is understood that realizing this potential is the job of teachers, and that student performance is as much a reflection of teaching as of study.

Belief 3

Becoming a great teacher is very difficult and takes support and time. Truly great teachers never realize their full potential because as they gain knowledge and skills, they are simultaneously humbled by how much more there is to learn. Because of these challenges, it is important to help especially new teachers to focus on teaching, removing as many administrative and non-instructional responsibilities from their plates as possible. Expert teaching takes many years to develop, and teachers are made, not born!

Belief 4

The more great minds you apply to a problem, the better the chance of solving it. Isolation is the death knell for teaching excellence. Time needs to be dedicated for teachers to communicate, including time to talk to one another, watch one another teach, and look at their students' work together.

Even though we observed only the very early phase of Merry's induction, all of the above beliefs are embodied in her interactions with colleagues, her principal, and the school. But beliefs need to be translated into Competence (skill and knowledge) so that skillful leaders can design appropriate professional development for new teachers.

Competence in Inducting New Teachers

What can we do to build our competence to train and retain the very best possible people? The most common problem schools and districts face is that they can't articulate the elements of good teaching. They pass out the performance instrument on the first day but rarely give exemplars of the embedded standards. Supervisors rely on the "I know it when I see it" belief, which leaves new teachers doing their best with little guidance. Schools that are characterized as toxic, laissez faire, and even congenial are unlikely to have shared standards for excellent teaching. On the other hand, Collaborative and, especially, Accountable Communities know what good teaching looks like and continually strive to perfect it in daily practice. Focus on standards prevents new-teacher induction from becoming a stand-alone program disconnected from the larger business of the school and district. "No longer does the induction program depend on the initial enthusiasm of a few dedicated administrators or teachers for its survival. It becomes institutionalized as an integral part of the professional development of the district" (Saphier, Freedman and Aschheim 25).

TABLE 10.2 Multi-year Goals for Supporting New Teachers

Year 1 Goals
Help the new teacher stay a step ahead of her students.   Support her first year of teaching by focusing on building and expanding her repertoires of classroom management and instructional strategies.   Build skills in group collaboration and problem-solving skills (e.g., grade level planning teams, looking at student work with colleagues).   End the year with a sense of efficacy and connection to colleagues and the school.   Encourage the capacity to reflect on all she has learned and to plan for next year based on this learning.
Year 2 Goals
Focus on deepening the new teacher's skills and working on effective instructional strategies that are useful across content areas.   Continue planning and collaborating with colleagues.
Year 3 Goals
Demonstrate her growing ability to address the learning needs of all the students in her classroom.   Demonstrate her capacity to reflect on her practice and then use it and student performance data to inform instruction.   Demonstrate a strong record of success in collaborating with her colleagues.

Based on what we know about the struggles of new teachers and their development over their first three years, we recommend a three-year, standards-based induction. We have included both a chart on goals (Table 10.2) and a list of topics for study (Table 10.3). Both the goals and the list of topics appear overwhelming. Skillful planners weave together several of these topics, e.g., a training series introduces the elementary math curriculum and helps new teachers plan their lessons to include learning objectives, aligned activities, and assessments to measure student learning. It is important to realize that any strong curriculum for new-teacher support is spiraled, meaning that topics are seldom addressed completely and then abandoned. Instead, the skill building becomes more sophisticated over time, e.g., classroom management in year 1 may focus heavily on establishing rituals, routines, clear expectations, and a system to address inappropriate behavior. In year 2 the focus will deepen to building students' self-management skills for cooperative learning and giving students meaningful roles in managing class behavior. Year 3 might focus on learning strategies to meet specific underperformance. A third-year teacher being considered for tenure must meet all of the goals for years 1, 2, and 3, which are listed in Table 10.2.

To make the induction plan manageable, skillful leaders need to work with their new teachers to develop an individual professional development plan. This plan should be aligned with the district's priorities, the school's priorities as outlined in its school improvement plan, and the demonstrable knowledge and skills of the new teacher. Through a process of teacher self-reflection, classroom observation and discussion with the principal or supervising administrator, and review of district and school priorities, the teacher

TABLE 10.3 Topics of Study for New-Teacher Induction

Year 1
Classroom management. Standards-based lesson planning. Curriculum and associated instructional materials and assessments. Content knowledge: literacy and math are starting points for elementary teachers; content training for secondary teachers, with an intensive focus if the teacher is teaching in an area in which s/he is not certified to teach. Looking at student work and analyzing assessment data to inform instruction. Introduction to district and school priorities such as differentiated instruction, culturally competent teaching. Strategies to meet the needs of special populations, e.g., English language learners, students with special education needs. Norms for collaboration with colleagues.
Year 2
Deepening of topics in year 1 plus: Foundations in effective pedagogy: a 30- to 40-hour course that builds a common understanding, set of strategies, and vocabulary about the elements of effective teaching. Development, use, and analysis of a year-long assessment system that measures student growth and guides instruction. Introduction to classroom-based action research. Cultural proficiency.
Year 3
Deepening of topics in years 1 and 2 plus: Completion of a yearlong classroom-based action research study that addresses a question the teacher has about her practice or a question that the teacher and her supervisor have developed together. Development of the tenure review folder, which documents the teacher's instruction, students' learning, and the teacher's growth and development in her first three years of teaching.

develops an annual professional development plan that outlines two or three learning goals, the activities s/he will engage in to meet learning goals, the support s/he will need, the benchmarks s/he is expected to reach, and the process the supervising administrator will use to assess progress. This tool can then be used to guide the teacher's work and to organize the support and feedback the supervisor provides.

Taking Control of New-Teacher Induction

What institutional systems, policies and practices need to support induction? Acting on core beliefs to build new-teacher competence requires processes and resources that support leaders to translate those intentions into reality. The specific structures we highlight below, many of them relying on teacher leaders, are driven by needs that new teachers have for:

• One-on-one time with a support person

- Opportunities to work and share experiences with other new teachers
- Opportunities to learn with more experienced colleagues
- Meaningful learning experiences from their supervision and evaluation

One-on-One Support

Interest in new-teacher developers or coaches has grown over the past few years through the work of the New Teacher Center at the University of California, Santa Cruz (www.newteachercenter.org). This model assigns successful, experienced teachers who have been trained as mentors to each new teacher. The developer meets with the new teacher for several hours each week and works on the targeted topics listed above. The power of this work lies in the relationship and trust established between the developer and the new teacher and the fact that the new teacher's needs drive the work. The developer's first commitment is ensuring the new teacher's success. Though the developer's work is guided by the district's teaching standards, the new teacher defines the focus of each visit and works with the developer to identify what would be most helpful. The developer also keeps track of deadlines the new teacher has to meet for everything from administering formative assessments to submitting grades at the end of the marking period.

Mentor programs can also provide one-on-one support. Developers have specific skills and responsibility for guiding new-teacher growth; mentors provide new teachers a safe place to share their concerns with someone who has nothing to do with their evaluation. Care must be taken, however, in the selection of mentors to ensure that new teachers are being matched with effective teachers. In many districts the opportunity to become a mentor is based on years of service or contractual provisions that distribute a stipend or release time for mentoring based on seniority. Experienced, older teachers ostensibly can show rookies the ropes. Mentor status may be granted to reward non-academic contributions to the school or to blunt or buy off opposition. Either practice will do little to help new teachers and may well perpetuate limiting beliefs and ineffective practices in the classroom and in the school. Leaders should look for important professional qualities that mentors can model for novices such as:

- Collaboration
- Problem-solving orientation
- Learning from others' and one's own experience
- Critical thinking
- Reflection
- Goal setting
- Self-assessment

Here are some key questions to guide your thinking in building an effective mentoring program:

LEADER ALERT ————————————————————————

Teacher Leaders and Mentors We believe that experienced teacher leaders should not be encouraged to become mentors. With the demand to find teacher leaders to build our professional communities, we wonder whether the one-on-one assistance is the best allocation of our best teacher leader resources. Instead we recommend making mentoring an early career leadership opportunity for teachers with about five to eight years of experience. This makes them closer to the challenges encountered by new teachers. For more discussion of the role of teacher leaders, see Chapter 6 "Moving Communities from Collaborative to Accountable."

———

- Are there clear and adequate criteria in place for selecting mentors based on expert teaching behaviors rather than seniority or veteran status?
- Do mentors and novices teach at the same grade level and content area in nearby classrooms?
- Is training available for mentors with clear standards and expectations for their role and responsibilities?
- Is sufficient time made available during the school day for mentors and novices to observe one another teaching and to meet and conference?
- Are oversight and accountability for the mentoring process in place at the school and/or district level?

New-Teacher Peer Group

There are few things more comforting to a new teacher than sitting around a table with a group of fellow new teachers. Hearing other novices lament the late-night planning, the students who seems to exist for the sole purpose of haunting their every waking (and sleeping) hour, and the lesson that falls apart most unexpectedly is deeply reassuring. Such an exchange is healthy if the conversation does not disintegrate into complaining; new teachers should leave the meeting with strategies to try back in their classrooms. Structures must be set to ensure that that the meeting is productive.

TIPS ON NEW-TEACHER PEER GROUP MEETINGS

✔ Develop a calendar of the year that aligns the focus of these meetings with significant work underway in the school. September is a good time to discuss rituals, routines, and classroom management. In October literacy and mathematics instruction should be discussed after the first formative assessment data in literacy and math are received.

✔ Use protocols for problem solving (see Chapter 7 "Collecting and Using Data: Vehicles").

✔ Some schools establish weekly, bi-weekly, or monthly seminars for new teachers (often before or after school) that are facilitated by an experienced teacher who is skilled in working with adults and understands the challenges new teachers face.

✔ The principal can facilitate the group to signal her commitment to the new teachers and to keep in touch with what is going on in classrooms.

✔ Meetings must be a safe, confidential, and nonevaluative place for new teachers to share their experiences without fear of reprisal.

Learning with More Experienced Teachers

There are a wide variety of ways that new teachers and more experienced teachers can engage in learning together. The more experienced teacher may guide the learning. Or the new teacher may bring ideas from her preparation and prior experience that are new to her more experienced colleagues. The goal is to learn together and share practices and ideas. Certain structures are often used to limited effect because they are mismanaged. Here we outline the structures, common pitfalls, and best practice.

Grade Level Team, Department, or Cluster Meetings

Scheduling time for teachers to meet who teach the same grade, the same subject, or the same students is critical to sharing practices, introducing new ones, and ensuring consistency for students. It can also be a powerful vehicle for new-teacher support and growth by reducing isolation and promoting collaboration. The effectiveness of these meetings hinges on whether there is a clear agenda for this time, support provided as needed, and expectations for outcomes that are reviewed by an administrator. Several strategies can be implemented to maximize the benefits of meetings for new teachers. (See Chapter 4 "Community Building 101: Setting the Stage" for more information on setting up groups.)

Peer Observation

Peer observation is a tool that can generate wonderful results for new and experienced teachers with a very small investment of time (2 to 3 hours/visit). This is a way for teachers to share promising practices and a way for teachers to invite colleagues for feedback on a practice or dilemma that they are working on. (For more on peer observation, see Chapter 7 "Collecting and Using Data: Vehicles.")

Collaborative Work with Instructional Coaches

There is a growing interest in instructional coaching, particularly in literacy and mathematics. Skillful coaches have deep content knowledge and demonstrated success as classroom teachers and can help new teachers build their skills in content and pedagogy. The most powerful way a new teacher can participate in coaching is to do it in collaboration with her colleagues. One-on-one coaching in literacy and math is useful, but it reinforces the isolation of teaching. Bringing a group of teachers together to learn, guided by a coach, can be very productive because teachers share ideas, build their understanding together, demonstrate lessons and observe together, try out their new learning in their own classrooms, report back their experiences, and share artifacts of their students' learning. Teachers come together around a topic of common concern. Practice is made very public, support is readily available, and review of relevant research is made easy. Here is an example of how this might look using the Collaborative Coaching and Learning model. (See Chapter 7 "Collecting and Using Data: Vehicles.")

CASE 10.5 **Collaborative Coaching and Learning (CCL)**

A 3rd-grade team meets with their coach weekly for 90 minutes. They have identified vocabulary development as their learning priority because their review of students' comprehension assessment results suggests that students are struggling to understand many of the words they read. Last week, the coach introduced the book *Bringing Words to Life* by Isabel Beck, which is full of strategies that the team can discuss and practice together. Supplied with the book by the principal, the teachers read the coach's assignment for their second meeting. At the second meeting, following the coach's agenda, the team starts with a discussion of the chapter they read, the strategy outlined, and any questions they have. Anna, the brave teacher who has volunteered to be the first to try the week's strategy in her classroom, in front of the group, preps the teachers for their observation. She describes what she is going to try to do and what she wants them to watch for. The coach facilitates these discussions, interjecting as necessary to make sure teachers are focusing on the most important aspects of teaching vocabulary.

Soon the team heads to Anna's classroom to observe her teach. They take notes on an observation sheet provided by the coach, focusing on what Anna and the students are doing, questions they have, and Anna's "please watch for" requests. Several teachers ask students questions to assess what they are learning. After the lesson, Anna turns the class back to the substitute who is covering for her while she meets with her team and coach to debrief the lesson. During the debriefing, Anna shares her experience and the teachers present their observations. Together they address questions that have been raised. By the end of the meeting, the teachers are prepared to go back to their own classrooms to try the strategy with support from the coach. They will report back on the results of their efforts at the next meeting. The coach assigns the next chapter of the book for reading, schedules times to visit each teacher in her classroom, and another teacher signs up to demo the new strategy. As teachers collect their materials and head back to their classrooms, the conversation spills out into the hallway; the energy from the session is palpable. (For more on Collaborative Coaching and Learning (CCL) see Chapter 7 "Collecting and Using Data: Vehicles.")

For any teacher, but particularly for a new teacher, this kind of learning is transformative. In this setting, a new teacher learns from the ideas of her colleagues, she observes colleagues teach, she reads about the practices she is trying to develop, and she has access to an expert in the subject. The messages the new teacher gets about her work, her learning, and the profession are powerful and acculturate her to a community that supports continuous learning.

Supervision and Evaluation

At first glance, it may seem odd to have "supervision and evaluation" listed as a new-teacher support structure. Such a reaction is more a commentary on current practices in these areas than it is about the potential of supervision and evaluation. We use the same definitions of supervision introduced in Chapter 7. Saphier defines supervision as formative and growth-oriented "high quality feedback on practice from someone who knows what he/she is talking about" for the purpose of stimulating teacher thinking and decision-making (1993 9). Glickman suggests that good supervision spreads the vision of excellent instruction as colleagues and administrators engage with new teachers (43). Peers and supervisors can provide feedback through visits followed up by a note or a quick conversation about things that that went well in the class as well as at least one question aimed at encouraging the teacher to reflect on practice. A new teacher thirsts for this kind of feedback and, if done systematically, it creates conditions that sustain adult learning.

In comparison, evaluation is a more formal process that pulls together the data from supervisory visits and longer formal observations and makes a judgment about the performance of the teacher. It is less interactive than supervision, but when it is well done, it facilitates important conversations about effective teaching, expectations, and supports for teachers. The keys to effective evaluation, especially of new teachers, are:

- **Engage the new teacher in the process as an active participant.** This can be done by asking for a review of learning goals and requesting the teacher to write a reflective self-assessment to be used as part of the evaluation process.

- **Provide a written evaluation of the new teacher's performance that is evidence-based.** Describe specific teacher behaviors and cite their impact on student learning.

- **Include concrete recommendations and areas for growth.** Recommendations should be framed as goals, not just "consider" or "continue" suggestions. Formulate goals for improvement and discuss what implementation would look like and how the teachers would know if they are successful.

Final Thoughts on Induction

Overwhelmed yet? Here are two things to remember to make this all seem more manageable and worth the investment of your time and resources. First, the hiring guidelines offered earlier in this chapter support you to make strong hires that will have an immediate positive effect on the retention of new teachers. Second, the induction system outlined above will, within a year or two, further reduce the number of new teachers you need to serve each year. The goal is to nourish the development of a mindset—a way of acting and thinking as a learner within a community of learners (Darling-Hammond 1995 95).

LEADER ALERT

Pre-tenure Transfers In *The Skillful Teacher: Confronting Mediocre Teaching* (Platt et al. 2000), we spoke of the "dance of the lemons" where poorly performing teachers are transferred within a district to a different school. Districts should avoid transferring any teachers during the years before tenure is granted and should never transfer poorly performing teachers. Though it is tempting to see this as largely a big district issue, we have seen it replicated in the smallest of rural schools and districts where even newer teacher are re-assigned out of the classroom to perhaps a Title 1 or resource room position. Over time the practice becomes institutionalized with excuses for not confronting mediocrity embedded in rationales such as:

"Maybe a fresh start in a new school is what she needs."
"It's mostly a personality conflict with the other teachers in his
  department."
"The chemistry is just not quite right."
"We think she'll do much better in a school with less demanding
  parents."

Regardless of the rationale, student learning is clearly undermined by not having the best possible teachers.

Making the Tenure Decision

Induction is about supporting and growing our new teachers. Conferring tenure, the culmination of the induction program, is about making a critical judgment about a teacher's competence. Failure to carefully weigh this decision is a missed opportunity to confront conditions that undermine learning. Often principals and districts underestimate the importance of tenure and routinely grant it to everyone except the truly incompetent teachers. The standard becomes automatic tenure after three years. As a result, the district has the burden of employing mediocre teachers for as long as they want to work—teachers not bad enough to fire nor good enough to positively impact student learning. The debilitating belief that "Not every prospective candidate is destined to be a star in the classroom and that's okay" may be the first step in making the granting of tenure routine.

Difficulty in making tenure decisions or automatic granting of tenure to nearly every new teacher may signal inadequate or nonexistent induction programs. This is a supervisory and institutional contribution to mediocre teaching and learning. The two questions you should ask yourself are:

1. Does everything I know about the teacher involved clearly indicate that s/he is or has the capacity to become excellent without an unreasonable amount of supervisory support?

2. Would I want my child to have to spend a school year with this teacher?

If you cannot answer yes to both of these questions, don't award the teacher tenure!

Tenure should be something teachers actively pursue through a clear demonstration of their competency, commitment, and capacity to collaborate effectively with others. Ideally, if public schools were operating as Accountable Communities, our system of granting tenure would more closely resemble that of universities where the tenure-seeking professor compiles work products to be presented to a group of colleagues. High bars for tenure should be set. When teachers receive tenure, there should be a formal, public acknowledgement to indicate that it is meaningful and a celebration of their skills and accomplishments. Listen to one principal first describe her own experience as a teacher getting tenure and then her current thoughts about granting tenure:

> She (my principal) set a very high standard, and I had such respect for her. She never simply said, "You're great" or something like that but gave very specific feedback. For three years I worked very hard to be a good teacher. In this district it was a three-year process for tenure, and they had a ceremony when teachers were given tenure. The superintendent spoke about each teacher. It was very formal and a wonderful opportunity to celebrate what had happened. And I really feel it was something I earned.
>
> In this state a teacher receives tenure in two years, and when they reach that point in the process, I want them to know they meet the standards for this district. I don't want them to think it just happened. (Sandy Weist, Assistant Principal, Elk Grove Unified School District California, personal communication 2000)

LEGAL NOTE 10.3

Tenure

The following points are culled from the voluminous case law regarding tenure decisions.

1. Tenure is a creature of state law; you must have a thorough knowledge of your state's law to understand what you must do and when and how you must do it.

2. Requirements of your state law are supplemented by your local policies and collective bargaining agreements with regard to teacher evaluation and personnel decision-making.

3. Courts and arbitrators will generally allow employers broad decision-making authority so long as your decisions are not motivated by unlawful discrimination, are not a violation of statutory or constitutional rights, and follow whatever procedures the law and your contract requires.

4. Missing notification deadlines in most states will result in automatic reappointment for at least another probationary year, if not tenure.[8]

[8]An old but still useful reading on the law that governs this most important decision is "Seeking Excellence: Not Reappointing an 'Average' Teacher in Order to Employ a Better Teacher," *School Law Bulletin*, 13 (4):1,15-19 (Oct 1982).

The message here to new teachers is unequivocal: tenure, i.e., membership to a professional community, is not a given, but is earned through meeting clear standards. Skillful leaders, bent on confronting the conditions in their schools that undermine adult and student learning, grant tenure as recognition of achievement and not as a matter of course. No teacher should be reappointed or given tenure if a better teacher can be hired!

Getting the Wrong People Out of the Classroom

Throughout induction, leaders focus on supporting new teachers. There is parallel responsibility to remain vigilant to early warning signs that might distinguish predictable novice practitioner problems from indicators of potential and ongoing mediocre performance. If induction does not work, it will be necessary to help mediocre new teachers out of the district. As leaders work hard to support new teachers in their first two years on the job, they can be alert to these red flags.

- **Failure to manage routines and discipline.** Beyond the rookie year with its predictable, on-the-job learning of classroom management skills, new teachers should demonstrate growing and credible capacity to effectively manage their classrooms. Failure to do so in their second year should be grounds for moving them on.

- **Absence of desired skills and attitudes predicted during the hiring process.** Look back at the data gathered during the hiring process outlined earlier in this chapter; after comparing that to the current performance you are observing, ask if the initial prediction of likely success was inaccurate. If so, make the tough decision early while you still can. This is also an important way to assess and fine-tune the hiring process to improve future hiring decisions.

- **Failure to plan a coherent, thoughtful lesson.** Operating effectively in a standards-based environment requires skilled and rigorous planning. Under no circumstances should tenure be granted where doubt exists as to a new teacher's skill and willingness to consistently plan for student mastery.

- **Little or no capacity to collaborate.** We are hiring teachers not only to teach but also to productively engage in a professional community. Throughout the second year we should be observing evidence of growing communication and interpersonal skills as well as a track record of working effectively with colleagues. Beware of "lone rangers" who prefer to focus solely on their own classrooms and otherwise remain detached from the larger community.

- **Limited problem-solving skills.** Novices often solve problems using an existing repertoire of routines. As teachers gain experience, supervisors need to look for evidence of progressive problem solving where teachers "construct new concepts and methods for unfamiliar cases versus force-fitting them to existing routines" (Bereiter and Scardamalia 99). We need skillful problem solvers in the classroom and in our school communities.

- **Evidence of limiting beliefs.** Limiting beliefs are extremely difficult to change and will not drive a new teacher to make good decisions on behalf of students. Letting the person go is the only effective response when a new hire communicates and acts on limiting beliefs and shows little capacity to accept feedback and direction to change. We provide a review of limiting beliefs from *The Skillful Leader: Confronting Mediocre Teaching* below.

Limiting Beliefs

Mediocre performers do not believe in constant learning. As a result, courses and workshops are more for the purpose of acquiring recertification points, and there is little evidence of transfer of learning into the classroom.

Mediocre performers do not believe that learning is a risky business. As a result, they model learning that is linear, predigested, and rote.

Mediocre performers do not take responsibility for their students' learning. As a result, they blame the parents and the students for lack of progress.

Mediocre performers do not believe that students will have questions or are confused. As a result, they teach by "mentioning" and assume all the students "got it" or all the students "should get it."

Mediocre performers do not believe all students can learn. As a result,

LEADER ALERT ────────────────────────────────────

Accountable Administrative Community We can use hiring and induction issues to help build an accountable leader community. Though it is has been widely recognized for some time that teachers work in isolation, the debilitating effects of administrator isolation warrant much greater scrutiny and action. Here are some concrete tips that may help build more accountable administrative community practice around hiring and induction:

Share hiring results after the first quarter of the school year—what hires have proven to be good matches, what are the "possible hiring mistakes," and, in both cases, what might be the reasons why. Sometimes these are called "autopsy meetings."

Share observation write-ups of new teachers for feedback on strengths and areas to stretch.

Organize swap shops about strategies that help induct new teachers.

Present difficult supervisory cases and use group expertise to identify appropriate responses to those cases.

────────────────────────────────────

they accept low performance from certain groups or individuals as all that can that can be expected (Platt et al. 177).

Summary

It is all too easy, particularly in large districts, to think about recruiting, hiring, and supporting new teachers as discrete functions, often conducted by different school personnel. This fragmentation and lack of collaboration creates numerous cracks for promising new teachers to slip through and frequent opportunities for unpromising hires to stay on staff. "In a sense, hiring is the first step of induction, the beginning of a dialogue between a school and the new teachers about what it means to teach at the school" (Johnson 191). Granting or denying tenure is the culminating event of that dialogue. It is when skillful leaders advocate strongly for students and hold themselves accountable for making the best possible decisions on behalf of students.

These challenges are opportunities to rethink current hiring practices and find better ways to hire teachers who will add value to the organization. The stakes are high, and for students who only have 3rd grade or 10th grade once in their lives, the urgency is great and the time is short.

11 Principal Development and Support

Research tells us that school leadership matters. Strong, capable, committed leadership increases a school's ability to ensure high levels of student learning and achievement for all of its students (Sebring and Bryk 2000; Hallinger and Heck 1998). Many of the preceding chapters focus on what principals must do to build and support high-functioning professional communities. Yet nationwide we hear that skilled community builders, indeed skilled school leaders in general, are rare. We hear that the pool of principals is "thin on quality" and "shrinking." Economically disadvantaged school districts struggle to find and retain high-performing principals. Who, then, will do the work outlined in this book? Where do we find excellent school leaders? How do we prepare aspiring principals to be such leaders and support them in their growth once they are in the field? Finally, we need to consider what we should guard against. We need to address institutional practices that undermine leadership development and sustain mediocre performance at the school and the institutional level.

In districts that have successfully transformed schools and raised student achievement, leadership excellence is never a matter of luck. Superintendents and Central Office staff are driven by the conviction that good leaders are made, not born, and that it is the district's responsibility to ensure a steady flow of knowledgeable, skilled principals for its schools. That conviction shows in the carefully designed selection and development processes districts use and in the way they marshal resources to support goals. It is also apparent in the way districts confront forces that undermine adult learning and leadership quality. This chapter examines the most important elements of a strategy to ensure excellent leaders in every school. These strategic elements include:

- Competencies for practice that reflect the research base on effective school leadership
- Thoughtful, comprehensive recruitment and preparation that expands

and strengthens the pipeline to the principalship

- Hiring and placement that put the best people in the principalship and match their skills to school needs
- Support for new principals that responds to their immediate needs and fosters a vision for their work

Along the way we also contrast these approaches with some of the unpromising practices that can lead to or sustain mediocre leadership. Short case studies featuring four aspiring principals help us illustrate decision points and their implications.

The selection of school leaders is one critical decision point. During the selection process, districts signal what their top leaders value and envision for their schools. Intentionally or accidentally, they reveal whether they are committed to excellence or willing to settle for business as usual. Unfortunately, the selection process is the only step some districts take to ensure strong school leadership. They expend no thought or effort on a differentiated recruitment strategy and development programs for aspiring leaders. Instead they begin to pay attention only when they must choose from applicants who happen to see their advertisement or who have a personal connection. As you first meet our four new principals, consider how the selection process for each one communicates that the district is not committed to, or competent in, finding the best possible leadership for its schools.

CASE 11.1   **Steve—The Vice Principal Who Paid His Dues**

Steve has just been hired as a new elementary school principal in the district where he attended school and spent his entire professional career. He knows all the principals in the district have served as assistant principals (AP's) before getting their schools. Steve has "paid his dues as an AP" for five years as well, and that knowledge gives him confidence as he joins their ranks. After all, he has spent years refining the procedures for buses, lunch, discipline, and operations in the building; he knows running a school like the back of his hand. Everyone—teachers, students, and parents—loved him at his old school. He's heard he has a reputation in the district as a nice, solid guy, and he's proud of it. He figures the fact that he knows everyone in the district will surely help him in his new role.

What are the messages here? Assistant principals, who often have primary responsibility for operations, are the people the district intends to hire as principals. In this district AP's have little experience in leading instructional improvement efforts. Either instructional improvement isn't really the most important work of a principal, or Central Office thinks it is easy and believes AP's learn those skills quickly on the job. It would also seem that putting in time as an assistant principal is a stepping-stone to being given a school and that knowing the right people is critical for success. Maria's district, however, has a different idea of what is most important.

CASE 11.2 **Maria—The Data-Savvy Curriculum Coordinator**

Maria is excited to parlay her expertise in curriculum, instruction, and data analysis into her new job as a middle school principal. In her last job as curriculum coordinator in a K-8 school, she worked behind the scenes to ensure a strong, well-aligned instructional program. She was known across the district for her beautiful charts and graphs of student performance data and had impressed the superintendent at a district meeting. In her previous role, Maria struggled to get teachers to see the power of student performance data and to use it to inform their instruction. She also had a hard time dealing with student discipline issues when they arose. In hiring Maria, the superintendent noted that she was thrilled to have a "real instructional leader" in the job. Although she heard about Maria's challenges in moving groups of teachers and in managing discipline, the superintendent assumed the teachers in Maria's old school were resistant and difficult. She also assumed that Maria's assistant principal could deal with student discipline and that Maria would be able to do a wonderful job of teaching her principal colleagues what she did with data.

Maria's district wants principals to be experts in curriculum, instruction, and assessment. Those in charge of principal selection seem to believe that strong technical skills in the organization and analysis of student performance data will ensure that the individual can lead instructional improvement. Note that their definition of "instructional leadership" seems to emphasize instruction rather than leadership. The implicit message is that a candidate's success in working with groups of teachers and with students is not important. The superintendent who chooses Isabel, however, doesn't agree. He wants peace and order and a warm body in place immediately.

CASE 11.3 **Isabel—The Head Teacher Who Knows the District**

In the middle of August, a veteran elementary principal, eligible for retirement for the last three years, informs the superintendent that he is "taking the plunge" and plans to retire on September 1, five days before students return to school from summer vacation. Panicked, the superintendent calls around looking for someone who can start in the next two weeks. He is prepared to offer a two-year contract just to get the position filled. He has two potential candidates. First is Isabel, a head teacher from a neighboring school who ran a "tight ship" during her principal's two-month medical leave. She isn't certified, but the superintendent is willing to work around that. The other choice is a principal with two years of experience who was fired by a neighboring school district in the spring. The superintendent heard there was a personality conflict between the principal and her supervisor, and he figures a new opportunity in a different district may be just the thing. Relieved to have two viable choices, the superintendent stops his frantic calling and decides which of the two candidates to hire. In the end he chooses Isabel because she knows the system and is older; thus she is more likely to garner respect immediately.

The way in which Isabel was selected suggests it is not important to plan for the succession of a principal. In this district identifying a strong pool of candidates prepared for the principalship in case of a vacancy is not a priority. In a pinch, you need to take who you can get, and you can't look too closely or be too picky. Filling the position is more important than getting the best possible candidate to maintain the momentum of teaching and learning at the school. The superintendent who chooses Alvin has some of the same concerns.

CASE 11.4 **Alvin—The Sacrificial Lamb**

Alvin left his principal interview with the superintendent feeling a bit worried. Two months earlier he had applied for the principalship of Park Street, a new, small high school. His application was the culmination of careful career planning that included working for seven years as a high school math teacher, completing a principal certification program two years ago, and working as an assistant principal with one of the district's strongest principals for the last two years. He had pushed his principal to give him responsibilities for teaching and learning as well as operations; as a result he felt ready to lead his own school. The interview had lasted only 20 minutes. It seemed to go well, but he met only with the superintendent. That surprised Alvin; he had hoped to meet teachers, parents, and a student or two. The superintendent focused his questions on Alvin's willingness to work long hours and manage a tough parent constituency. As Alvin was standing up to leave, the superintendent patted Alvin on the back and asked if he was interested in leading Washington High School. The district's largest high school, Washington was known around town for chewing up and spitting out principals, particularly inexperienced ones. Hence the superintendent was looking for the school's fourth leader in five years. Alvin had specifically not applied for that job because he thought he wasn't experienced enough to take it on. The superintendent ended the interview saying, "You might be just the person for Washington."

What are the implicit messages in the way Alvin was hired to lead Washington High School? Hiring a principal is something the superintendent does with no input from the school community. Screening a potential principal can be done in 20 minutes by asking a series of questions. The skills, expertise, and experience required of principals do not differ among schools. Give a young principal candidate who shows promise a really hard assignment, rather than one that includes support, maximizes the likelihood of success and job satisfaction, and builds skills for increasingly difficult assignments.

We define leadership excellence as the ability to lead a school community (teachers, students, families, and partners) in creating an environment that is relentlessly focused on helping all students achieve at high levels. In this environment all stakeholders are supported, and all assume responsibility for student success. As our cases highlight, principals are often hired in ways that are more likely to ensure mediocre leadership than excellence. Note the apparent absence of district competencies for principals. Leader selection is idiosyncratic and depends on the competencies a current superintendent or personnel director values:

- Steve's skills in operations and student discipline and his general likeability
- Maria's knowledge of curriculum, instruction, and data use
- Isabel's availability, age, and familiarity with the system
- Alvin's ability to work long hours and take on a difficult assignment

Combining these strengths provides a list of some characteristics of effective principals. Yet, this list is incomplete. Without clarity about what we value in a school leader, we are hard pressed to make good hiring decisions.

Identifying Competencies for School Leaders

Over the last decade, the movement to standards for student performance has fundamentally shifted public education in this country. State, local, or nationally developed standards to define what students should know and be able to do have shaped curriculum, instructional strategies, and the assessment of student learning. Standards also have had a profound effect on students. Promotion from one grade to the next and often graduation from high school depend on ability to meet academic standards. Imagine if that same level of accountability existed for school principals:

- Districts would establish and communicate competencies for what principals should know and be able to do.
- Principal applicants would be assessed against these competencies.

- Principals would be supported through professional development and supervision to reach the competencies.
- Principal evaluations would be aligned to the competencies, and they would get regular, clear feedback on their performance.

The current, competency-free approach to leadership selection, development, and evaluation that characterizes practice in many American school systems makes it hard to provide guidance and career-planning to aspiring leaders. Without standards, it is difficult to diagnose strengths and weaknesses and plan improvement strategies. It is difficult even to distinguish principals who are stellar performers from those who are barely getting by. And without defined competencies, it is hard to design activities that will provide ongoing support and training to principals with a wide range of knowledge and experience.

A lack of clearly defined competencies for principals reinforces existing cultures of distrust. Without clear competencies, any differentiated treatment is perceived as favoritism or harassment. Such interpretations make building a supportive, Accountable Community among principals impossible and make efforts at supervision and evaluation of questionable value.

If high performance is not clearly defined in public and transparent ways, behavior that gets rewarded or encouraged often reflects little more than the personal biases of the supervisor, the principal's connections and popularity, or the principal's ability to "keep the lid on and the heat off" in a difficult building. Like outstanding teachers in toxic cultures, principals who hold themselves to higher, internally dictated expectations are often isolated and dismissed by both their peers and their supervisors as know-it-alls and prima donnas. Professional development and other forms of support are seldom differentiated to respond to the specific needs of the individual principal, and most evaluations read like a list of general platitudes. As a result, mediocrity becomes accepted as the norm and is reinforced in district practices.

District-based preparation programs are an interesting source of information on principal competencies. Because such programs have been created in response to an overwhelming need for principals and dissatisfaction with traditional principal preparation, they are explicit about what principals should know and be able to do. The Interstate School Leaders Licensure Consortium (ISSLC) standards are important to consider because they were developed by representatives from state and professional associations and have been adopted by 41 states.[1] Three sets of competencies currently in use to design and assess principal preparation programs reveal clear priorities:[2]

1. **Interpersonal skills**: communication, negotiation; conflict resolution; ability to collaborate, delegate, empower, and nurture leadership in others
2. **Leadership**: vision, courage, resilience, ethics, reflection, continuous learning, humility, and self-monitoring

[1]http://www.csso.org/projects/Interstate_Consortium_on_Leadership/ISLLC_Standards/
[2]NYC Leadership Academy, Boston Principal Fellowship, Interstate School Leaders Licensure Consortium (ISSLC).

3. **Effective instruction**: alignment of curriculum, instruction, and assessment with standards; elements of effective instruction across content areas, deep understanding of district curricular/instructional initiatives, specific strategies to close the achievement gap as well as serve English Language Learners and students with disabilities effectively

4. **Alignment of resources to instructional improvement priorities**: time, people, money, professional development, supervision and evaluation, tenure decisions, family and community engagement

5. **Data collection, organization, analysis, and use to inform practice**: student performance data is first priority with other qualitative and quantitative indicators of school performance included as well

6. **Understanding of organizations, culture, change processes, and strategy**: how to analyze a school as an organization to understand the values, structures, and norms and then reshape the culture as needed, all with an understanding of the support that the adults and students in the building need to engage in change

These standards suggest that to be an effective principal you have to know teaching and learning; strategic planning; organizational leadership; mobilization of adults to high performance; and modeling of the kind of leadership, ethical behavior, and resilience that everyone working in schools needs to possess.

LEADER ALERT

Community Builders Needed Interpersonal leadership and managing oneself top the list of principal competencies for the Boston Principal Fellowship, the NYC Leadership Academy, and the ISLLC. On-the-ground training programs tend to lead with these standards because program participants often learn firsthand about the challenges of managing adults, remaining calm in the eye of the storm, and communicating in ways that build rather than erode community. Students in traditional educational leadership programs often do not get deeply enough involved in leading work in schools to fully understand the importance of interpersonal leadership. They learn this lesson, often painfully, on the job.

The list of school leadership competencies is daunting. Nobody comes to the principalship with all of these skills in top form. Given the breadth and depth of skills required, few leave the principalship at the top of their game in all these areas. Instead, candidates bring natural aptitudes in certain areas and hard-won skills in other areas. If they are fortunate enough to be hired in a district that has a differentiated and comprehensive leadership development program, principals acquire new capabilities instead of being stuck with the baggage they brought in initially. Some competencies come easily; others are hard to build and require ongoing reflection and fine-tuning. The clear articulation of expectations enables the district to be equitable and transparent in its response to leaders' work.

Recruiting Principals

Skillful Central Office leaders and committed boards recognize that finding and nurturing the next generation of school leaders is a key part of the legacy they leave a district. Unfortunately, few districts have a robust strategy that will ensure a pool of talented applicants for principalships. Driven by political pressure, habit, or tight timelines, they tend to pluck new principals from the ranks of APs. Because they are not part of a district with a development strategy, many of those AP's are likely to have worked in narrowly defined roles with little or no opportunity to practice or acquire the full range of competencies demanded of school leaders.

Developing a Strong Pool of Potential Candidates

Districts organized for excellence know they need a renewable pool of prospective principal candidates and that they must be resourceful and proactive in seeking them. These districts look for key beliefs and attitudes that are critical to principals' success. Aspiring principals should:

- **Believe in adults' ability to learn and like working with adults.** Many people enter the teaching profession because of their love of children. If they later become principals, they are often startled by how taxing adults can be. Although adult misbehavior may not be much different from kid misbehavior, it is often more veiled. For some aspiring principals, failure to keep promises or meet expectations is much less tolerable in adults than in children. Leaders who enjoy working with adults tend to lead schools that have a warmer school culture and are more fun to work in. If they see working with adults as a less enjoyable part of the bargain, their school culture often reflects that.

- **Have a clear, sustaining vision for and commitment to children's success.** Effective principals are compelled by what they are trying to create for students. They understand that realizing their vision for students requires an artful balance of engaging, supporting, coaxing, cajoling, and demanding significant accomplishment from their staff.

- **Have strong convictions about the potential of specific subgroups of children.** Most aspiring principals will speak about a generic vision for young people and mouth the oft-repeated line that all children can learn. Suppose candidates have spent the last decade in a school culture that believes certain students need to be controlled and that their learning is of secondary importance. Suppose these same candidates have been trained in keeping order above all else. They may not emerge from that experience with deep-seated conviction about students' ability and need to do challenging work. Nor will they have models for the ways in which the most powerful schools and teachers draw out even seemingly hopeless students' potential.

• **Have a sense of urgency and hope and be able to convey it.** In recruiting prospective principals, skillful leaders need to examine the context of candidates' past experiences and the attitudes they bring to the system's goals and core values. Good models from past experiences and a positive attitude contribute both to resiliency and the ability to manage all the challenges associated with leading a school.

Adult beliefs can be changed over time, but it is a difficult task. Most school districts are ill prepared to help people make such changes. Thus it is wise to make sure the individuals you recruit have those key beliefs in place.

The prospective principal pool can be divided into four main feeder groups: (1) assistant principals carefully chosen for a constellation of skills, (2) teacher leaders, (3) experienced principals from other districts, and (4) non-educators with leadership experience. We can identify clear advantages and disadvantages of drawing principals from each of these experience groups.

Selecting Assistant Principals

Table 11.1 summarizes the relative merits of appointing assistant principals to principalships. If a school system selects its assistant principals with deep understanding of effective instruction and leadership potential, the strategy can be a good one. It also works well if the system has a substantive, well-designed program such as Montgomery County Maryland's for developing the leadership skills of aspiring and/or sitting assistant principals. However, many districts regard the assistant principal position as a way to divide up a heavy workload or to allow a principal to "dump" parts of the job that s/he either does not like or does not do well. Few school systems carefully consider what it would mean to build assistant principals' competence and ensure their readiness to lead a school; most assume that competencies will be acquired through observation and osmosis. Additionally, many school systems choose assistant principals who do not see the job as a stepping stone to higher administration. Such individuals prefer to have someone above them taking the responsibility and the hits. They like comfortable hours and well-defined expectations. If districts want their APs to be the pool from which principals are hired, they must have an explicit strategy to build APs' instructional and leadership skills.

Steve, the AP introduced in Case 11.1, possesses many of the strengths and limitations outlined in Table 11.1. His impression that his years of managing operations made him ready for the principalship suggests that Steve isn't fully aware of the range of principals' responsibilities and doesn't appreciate the importance of understanding and leading instructional

TABLE 11.1 Strengths and Limitations of Assistant Principals

Strengths of AP's	Limitations of AP's
Understand the operational elements of the job, e.g., buses, lunch, facilities, test administration, and student discipline	May think operations management is the most important element of the principalship
Know the culture of schools and people in the district and the community and how to get things done	May not have had much opportunity to learn about and take responsibility for the teaching and learning aspects of the school
May have assumed some leadership of instructional improvement	May not have the big-picture perspective and the ability to think strategically
May have good working knowledge of the school's curricula if teaching experience is recent	May have limited experience in simultaneously managing the teaching and learning and operational components of the job
May be popular with faculty because they handle daily irritations efficiently	May not respond well to conflict or stressful situations.

improvement. Support in this area before he assumes a principalship would surely increase the likelihood of his success.

Selecting Teacher Leaders

In school systems that have differentiated roles for teachers and a variety of teacher leadership opportunities focused on instructional improvement, teacher leaders are another pool of potential principals. Mentors, instructional coaches, grade level/cluster/department leaders, student performance data managers, or members of the school's leadership team often receive training and develop leadership skills as they carry out their roles. They also develop an understanding of the power of teacher collaboration, gain a school-wide perspective, build their understanding of the elements of effective school leadership, and have the chance to practice in arenas beyond their own four classroom walls. These leadership skills and opportunities complement their deep knowledge of instruction and talent as classroom teachers.

Isabel, the teacher leader who took over for her sick principal and was hired to fill a late principal vacancy, possesses both the strengths and limitations of teacher leaders listed in Table 11.2. She was a good teacher and understands how to help students learn in a variety of ways. Her experience beyond her classroom helps her understand the larger picture of a school. Yet the leap from teacher-in-charge to school principal is huge. Isabel is moving from a role where she was filling in to one in which she is charged with setting the vision for the school and putting the structures and systems in place to realize the vision. When she covered for her sick principal, she had the backing and additional support of her fellow teachers who were happy to pitch in during a difficult time and wanted to ensure her success.

TABLE 11.2 Strengths and Limitations of Teacher Leaders

Strengths of Teacher Leaders	Limitations of Teacher Leaders
Are experienced in using standards, effective instructional strategies, and data analysis to support student learning	May find the transition from teacher to administrator challenging as they mourn the loss of peer colleagues and struggle with the isolation and responsibility for adult performance that principals face
Understand the school and all of its dimensions more broadly than many teachers	May not have much experience with the strategic aspects of the job and how to fit together all the pieces of leading a school
Have a clear understanding of the work of teacher colleagues, including the range of skills and experience among teachers and the skills required to work effectively with adults	May be unfamiliar with the operational responsibilities of the job
Understand the power and possibility of teacher collaboration	May not respond well to conflict or stressful situations
Might have had the opportunity to build skills in differentiating support to teachers	

Leading a school of her own will be a lonely experience for Isabel and something for which she needs to prepare herself.

Selecting Experienced Principals from Other Districts

Table 11.3 contrasts the benefits and drawbacks of hiring experienced principals. Assuming they are in good standing, experienced principals from other districts bring school leadership know-how that can be powerful and can increase the likelihood of a smooth transition. However, the environment from which they come shapes the way they view the role and their own capacities. If they have been highly successful, lone rangers, or much revered in another district, they may have difficulty in adapting to a new culture and set of expectations. Or they may be stunned and dismayed by the level of dysfunction in their new environment. It is important to ensure that their beliefs and style of leadership match the district's vision and that the standards and expectations of the hiring system are both transparent and clearly communicated. Relying on this outsider group to fill principal vacancies has a potential downside. By poaching, a district gains a principal at the expense of another system. The result does not expand the principal pool.

Selecting Non-educators with Leadership Experience

To be competitive, non-educators must bring strong leadership and managerial experiences, a fundamental understanding of the work of public K-

TABLE 11.3 Strengths and Limitations of Experienced Principals

Strengths of Experienced Principals	Limitations of Experienced Principals
Know the transferable "nuts and bolts" of the job	May not know how the district works
May have firsthand experience with other programs that would enhance the hiring district's repertoire and success with students	May not know the priorities and initiatives of the district
May bring standards and expectations that will help receiving district push for excellence	May not have contacts within the district
Bring another perspective on how to lead a school	May bring an attitude of complacency from prior work
Are likely to have learned to stay calm in stressful situations and to respond to crises	May be homesick or unable to move from "how we did it where I came from"

12 education, a willingness to learn all they do not yet know about schooling, teaching, and learning, and a sense of humility about what they do not know. Equally important is their ability to work within the existing culture of schools and the district. Outsiders are often hired with the idea that they will change the culture of the school or be part of a district culture change effort. While this may be a reasonable long-term strategy, it is crucial that these hires can thrive in the current culture. One of the greatest assets outsiders bring is a broad perspective on how things can be done and a tendency toward more innovative and entrepreneurial thinking than is often represented in schools. Table 11.4 summarizes the relative advantages of this group.

Districts committed to building leadership excellence must be prepared to help aspiring candidates and newly hired principals develop existing strengths and create new ones. School leadership competencies are comprehensive and challenging. Each of the experience groups making up the pool is likely to need skill building in at least one competency. Table 11.5 suggests likely development requirements. There are always exceptions to these generalizations, such as the assistant principal who has facilitated grade-level data analysis sessions for two years or the lead teacher who has learned conflict management skills in a former job as a school counselor.

As the chart suggests, certain skills must be built across all groups, but each role group also has distinct needs. Customized support for new and aspiring principals, mapped to competencies and based on individual assessments of skills is not the norm in most education leadership programs, much less in districts. Yet that is what is required. To meet that goal, a district needs a multi-pronged strategy that includes good assessment tools, district-sponsored learning opportunities (courses, professional development sessions, school visits, authentic work assignments set in the context of schools) in each of the standard areas, and mentoring support.

TABLE 11.4 Strengths and Limitations of Non-educators with Leadership Experience

Strengths of Non-educators	Limitations of Non-educators
Have experience in another sector that may allow transfer of promising leadership and management practices into the schools	May not know the core work of teaching and learning
Bring a fresh perspective	May not understand the culture of schools and school districts and how to lead effectively in this environment
May have a driving and appealing conviction that has caused them to make sacrifices others understand	Lack credibility
Bring another perspective on how to lead a school	May bring an attitude of complacency resulting from the perception that the new place has greater status
May have connections to resources outside the school	May become disillusioned by the inertia and political complications they encounter

Professional Development

Well-designed training can be a powerful recruitment and screening strategy for aspiring principals. It can offset negative stereotypes about the role and give those who think they are not interested in moving to administration a new perspective on its possibilities. For example, a process that highlights instructional leadership may attract teacher leaders who have discovered they enjoy problem solving with adults. Often some of the most knowledgeable members of the community, these teacher leaders nonetheless shy away from the principalship if they see the job as primarily managerial. Having the opportunity to hear the district's commitment to student learning and to see principals who are strong instructional leaders can be compelling to passionate individuals who are seeking ways to maximize their impact on students. Such a focus might also inspire and energize an assistant principal who has grown bored with the operational requirements of her job. Professional development allows prospects to learn more about the district's expectations for principals and enables them to make informed decisions about the match between the actual role and their own interests and talents.

Professional development programs that build a strong pool of principal candidates pay attention to two things:

- **Vision-setting and career management to build conviction:** Programs educate staff about the position, gauge their interest, help them

TABLE 11.5 Competency Development Needs by Experience Groups

Role	Competencies					
	Interpersonal Leadership	Leadership	Effective Instruction	Alignment of Resources	Data	Organizations, Culture, and Change
APs Veterans hired to manage operations and discipline			✓	✓	✓	✓
Specialists transitioning from non-academic areas	✓	✓	✓	✓	✓	✓
Teacher leaders	✓	✓		✓		✓
Principals from outside district*	✓	✓	✓	✓	✓	✓
Leaders new to education			✓		✓	✓

*Focus of the learning is on the context of the district, special programs, procedures, cultural issues, etc.

decide what roles they are most interested in pursuing, and then direct them to the next steps that will best prepare them.

- **Skill development to build competence:** Once people understand the role and responsibility of principals and choose that career path, the focus shifts to building their skills to ensure they are well prepared for the role and positioned for success.

Vision-Setting and Career Management

Vision-setting activities have several goals. They should force the district to develop and articulate a common vision for the principalship. Effective activities will help people better understand the district leadership, its vision for the work in schools, and the role of principals and other school administrators in implementing that vision. An important goal is to recruit a diverse and talented group of candidates who might not otherwise be interested in becoming principals.

School systems can organize vision-setting activities in a number of different ways. The different approaches all offer aspiring principals the chance to hear from the people leading the work and to see the work in action. Vision-setting experiences for new and aspiring principals include hearing from the Central Office, getting a sense of a day in the life of a principal, and making a career plan.

Hearing from District Leadership

In populous or spread out districts, people working in schools are often isolated from top leaders in the Central Office. Hearing the superintendent talk about the district's vision and the role of the principal in realizing that vision is inspiring. Participating in a discussion with the superintendent makes people feel much more closely connected to the district and its leadership. The superintendent's choice to spend substantive time with aspiring leaders helps them to feel valued. Depending on the size of the district and the complexity of its improvement strategy, learning from district leadership can be accomplished in a few after-school sessions or it can extend to six to eight sessions.

Experiencing a Principal's Workday

Many educators spend their careers working in a single school. As a result, they assume that the way things are done in their school is the way things are done in every school. For this reason, half-day to daylong visits to other schools are a small investment that reaps tremendous benefits for aspiring principals. Participants regularly come back from visits marveling at everything from how differently lunchtime is managed to the consistency of classroom set-ups or the way teachers compare notes on their lessons and student progress in common planning time. After one or two visits of this sort, participants' thinking about the role of the principal, school culture, the potential impact of a principal, and different strategies to help a school improve broadens and deepens.

Career Planning

This aspect of vision setting helps aspiring leaders make conscious, well-informed decisions about their careers and pursue their goals wisely. Because careers in education are often defined by decades in particular roles, educators are unfamiliar with the idea of career planning and districts do little to promote the idea. Such a mindset supports mediocrity. It suggests a career is static and repetitive, rather than dynamic and changing as adults develop and learn. It is problematic for the people already in the field and lethal to recruiting highly capable individuals who are committed to their own growth and advancement. Career planning should help aspiring leaders know what their choices are, understand the expectations and opportunities associated with each choice, and identify the supports available to assist them in the steps towards their career goal.

Districts that have a variety of administrative roles can offer a career pathway for people interested in leadership. A career pathway is as important to the teacher with 20 years of experience who has taken on numerous teacher leadership roles but cannot imagine stepping directly into the principalship as it is to the "young whippersnapper" who intends to pursue leadership opportunities after five to seven years of teaching. Their needs and interests may be quite different, but a district's ability to retain and assign the best candidates to administrative roles is critical to its success. A session that highlights the work of and career pathways taken by the best curriculum coordinators, department heads, assistant principals, and principals broadens people's perspectives about the possible routes into administration and toward the principalship.

Once people have learned about the work of school administration and the possible paths to those positions, it is helpful for them to understand how the district will support them to get to where they want to go. Some will need to earn their principal certification. Others will have the certification but need additional skill building in specific areas. Some will want to pursue a non-principal administrative position as an interim step towards the principalship. Others will be ready to pursue the principalship but will need guidance in navigating the screening and hiring process.

LEADER ALERT

Someone Like Me Make sure individuals who lead vision-raising activities reflect the people you are trying to recruit. Panelists at a session for example, should include the races and ethnicities of the students your district serves. If you want to entice excellent veteran teachers out of the classroom and into administration, make sure there is someone who fits that profile who talks to the group about her work and her pathway to the principalship. The same principle would apply if you seek rising young stars.

Presentation Skills

This strategy could equally have been placed under vision-building or competency building. It is an important one for districts that want to increase the diversity of their applicant pool and to attract talented individuals from all members of the educational community. Watching applicants for principalships or even educational leadership programs weeded out because of how poorly they present themselves can be painful. Reviewers have no idea what the knowledge, skills, and accomplishments of these applicants are because nothing in their resumes communicates their capabilities. Problems include vague resumes (see Example A) not accompanied by a cover letter or vague cover letters that do not explain the resume or the applicant's interest in the position or program.

EXAMPLE A—Weak Resume Entry

1987-2007: Teacher—Franklin Elementary
- Taught first, third, and fifth grade
- State of Michigan certification in elementary teaching

Resumes of many career public educators tend to reflect the narrow perspective their work life has afforded them. The idea of using their resume to celebrate their accomplishments is foreign. They seldom change schools or apply for new positions, so they don't have experience with resume writing, interviewing, and navigating the system. They may work in a culture marked by parochialism or a toxic pressure to avoid any behavior that might distinguish one teacher from another.

Younger professionals often have an advantage over their more experienced colleagues in knowing how to present their accomplishments. People entering the profession now expect to change jobs regularly and understand how to present themselves. The ability of younger educators to package themselves reinforces stereotypes about young go-getters and tired veterans that are unfair to everyone and can lead to districts making bad decisions about who should be recruited or encouraged. In every district, strong people present themselves in self-defeating ways simply because they lack easily acquired skills. To make sure such candidates get fair consideration, districts need to offer resume and cover letter writing workshops that help people communicate their experience as Example B does. Interviewing poses the same challenges to career educators. Interview role-plays with feedback can be enormously helpful in raising candidates' awareness of standards and expectations and general interview "know-how."

EXAMPLE B—Strong Resume Entry

Teacher Leadership Experience

2005-present   Co-chair, Student Support Team

- Developed system for tracking students who are at risk of failing academically and providing individualized social, emotional, and academic support.
- Serve as school liaison to community-based organization that provides counseling to students.
- Partner with tutoring and after-school program to provide supplemental education services to identified students.

Teaching Experience   Mary Bright Elementary

2000-present   Teacher, Grade 4
1995-present   Teacher, Grade 2

- Implement Readers and Writers Workshop and TERC Investigations math curriculum.
- Use Responsive Classroom curriculum to build strong climate that gives students responsibility and develops their conflict resolution skills.
- Use project-based learning to teach big ideas across curricular areas.
- Serve as a model classroom for TERC Investigations curriculum, hosting teachers who visit to learn how to implement the curriculum.
- Completed introductory, intermediate, and advanced Investigations curriculum training. Serve as a trainer.
- Serve as team leader for Grade 4, facilitating grade level team meetings and serving as the grade level liaison to the administration.

Skill Development to Build Competence

Skill development is the second part of a strategy to recruit a strong pool of candidates for leadership positions. Through vision-setting, a group of aspiring principals surfaces. Some may be ready to apply for principal positions immediately; others demonstrate great potential but need additional training and support to get them ready. The training and support the latter group receives affects the future of school leadership in the district. The focus and the delivery send key signals about what the district values. As Table 11.6 indicates, mediocre training focuses on keeping the trains running and things under control. Participants are not asked to do any critical thinking, problem solving, or application of learning. They might well conclude that the district believes effective professional development is talking at people, giving them things to read, and assuming they know how to use what has been covered.

In the high-quality training, participants study teacher performance standards, view videos of teacher practice, and define good practice. The activities demonstrate the importance of recognizing instructional strategies and analyzing their impact on students. Through the process, aspiring principals build their skills to work effectively with all teachers. The interweaving of skill building and application in this course helps participants internalize the concepts. Through their own experiences as learners, they see the power of professional development that engages learners, gives them opportunities to practice, and expects them to problem solve and build good judgment.

Certification Programs

Districts must decide to what extent they want to get into the business of preparing principals. Do they want to offer support at the stage where candidates have already gained certification? Or do they want to start earlier, thus influencing who gets certified and how aspiring candidates gain the credential? Options include:

LEADER ALERT ───

Building Your Farm Team Vision-setting activities give district leadership valuable opportunities to scout potential talent. Watch closely! Participants in these activities distinguish themselves through the questions they ask, the observations they have, their level of synthesis of readings and presentations, their presence, or their warmth and ease. District leadership can encourage and nurture the most promising people in the programs and become aware of people who may not be well suited to administrative work.

───

- Developing an internal educational leadership program that includes certification
- Collaborating with a professional association or consortium of districts to pool resources and develop a program, link up with a university-based educational leadership program, or add elements to an existing program
- Providing post-certification leadership development offerings tailored to the specific needs and priorities of the district

Size, annual need for new principals, the internal/external capacity to oversee a program, and specific challenges the district faces all affect the decision about which option to pursue.

Whatever choice the district makes, careful program design, implementation, and oversight are critical. Every aspect of the program expresses the district's beliefs, values, commitments, and interests to the participants and everyone watching. Just as the principal's behaviors are observed by every-

TABLE 11.6 Characteristics of Mediocre versus High-Quality Training

High-Quality Training for Aspiring Principals	Mediocre Training for Aspiring Principals
Content: elements of good teaching, teacher supervision, and evaluation	Content: how to "run" the school: operations, discipline, legal issues
Pedagogy: watch videos of teacher practice and discuss; role play conversations with teachers focused on supporting the improvement of their practice	Pedagogy: passive, "sit and git," listen, regurgitate, and leave unsure how to apply the learning
Homework: observe teachers of different levels of experience and expertise and come to class with an observation write-up, prepared to talk about three things you learned about teacher practice through your observations and two questions you have	

one in a school to interpret what is important, a program that prepares principals is scrutinized. Training for aspiring principals will affect many schools and will be highly visible because it will be interpreted as the route to the principalship (whether that is true or not). People will talk about their experiences in the training, and that will create the program's reputation. In the best scenario, the program will send a powerful message about the principals the district is trying to nurture, the schools it is trying to develop, and the district it wants to be. This reputation will affect who applies to the program, how seriously it is taken, and how graduates are perceived.

Hiring and Placing Principals in the Right Schools

Succession planning, by which we mean projecting anticipated principal openings years in advance and developing and implementing a specific strategy to fill those positions, is an unfamiliar concept in many districts. Districts tend to operate from retirement eligibility lists and the rumor mill to project openings. Central Offices sometimes treat principalships as if they are interchangeable; they debate between putting a novice principal in a 300-student elementary school with a significant Spanish bilingual student population or a 700-student K-8 with a special education program. Of course, it is unlikely that the new principal under consideration has expertise in both bilingual education and special education. This haphazard, semimagical approach reinforces mediocrity in several important ways:

- It undervalues the significant opportunity for improved student and adult learning that every personnel vacancy presents to a district or school.

- It disregards the planning, care, and individual attention that should be given to each building's leadership.

- It does not demonstrate to principals that different constellations of skills and leadership styles matter in different schools.

- It serves as a warning sign, making the district less appealing to candidates who do understand the importance of planning and matching.

Hiring

To make good hiring and placement decisions, district leaders need to get to know principal applicants. Not the "Yeah she's great, reliable, a solid performer" kind of knowledge but knowledge of:

- What she would look for when observing a teacher teach and how she would support the teacher to improve her practice

LEADER ALERT

Writing Matters Be very wary of hiring a principal whose writing under time constraints and without assistance (real conditions under which principals often have to write) is weak. That person's inability to communicate effectively will become apparent to the entire school community and will surely lead to substantive concerns on the part of staff, parents, and the community as information is miscommunicated or unclear. Promoting an adult who can't communicate effectively in writing undermines any message you are sending to students and teachers about the importance of high expectations.

- How she would work with an upset parent
- What she believes in her heart about the reasons for the achievement gap and what she thinks her responsibility is to address it
- How she would build the elements of a healthy school culture
- How she would design a year of professional development for teachers based on student performance results and teacher needs

This depth of knowledge cannot be acquired in a 45-minute interview in the superintendent's office. Nor can it happen through a letter writing campaign by parents and teachers on an applicant's behalf or a call from a school committee member or a city councilor. It happens by spending time with an applicant in an unfamiliar school, visiting classrooms, interacting with adults and students, watching closely, listening, and asking questions. The people who screen principal applicants need a deep understanding of the competencies for principals and what they look like in action. Screeners should be experienced and successful school leaders who have mastered improvement challenges and participated in district-sponsored sessions that helped them to calibrate their responses. They should know how to observe principal applicants, collect data, and then ask questions to understand the applicant's behaviors and beliefs. They should present scenarios that require applicants to apply their knowledge and solve real-life problems and should require on-the-spot writing samples.

Let's return to the four new principals we met at the beginning of the chapter. What might we have learned about each of them had a selective screening process been in place?

Case 11.1 Steve's affable nature and knowledge of operations would surely have stood out. His relative inexperience with leading instructional improvement would have become apparent once he was asked to talk about the practice of a teacher he observed.

Case 11.2 Maria's skills of observation and analysis of instruction would have been impressive. Her less well-developed social skills would also have been revealed as she met new people and spent time with her interviewer.

Case 11.3 Given Isabel's limited experience, such a screening process would have been invaluable because it would have revealed raw talent and potential.

Case 11.4 It would be telling to see how Alvin reacts in a new school setting, given his relative youth in education, especially in school administration. How does he interact with students and staff? What does he focus on in classroom observations, and what questions does he ask teachers?

What does a screening process that uses the authentic work of principals look like? Do you traipse every principal candidate through a school for a day? Perhaps. Are there ways to simulate some of the experiences a candidate would have if she visited a school? Yes. Can you have a team of people review a single candidate to provide multiple perspectives on her candidacy? Absolutely. To provide one concrete example, consider the screening process for the Boston Principal Fellowship. The process has four steps, is memorably rigorous, and is as much a learning experience as it is an assessment for applicants. Most important, it shows applicants what the district values and the high standards to which it holds principals. Though this process is designed for people who want to participate in a yearlong principal preparation program, most of the components can either be used as is or adapted to principal screening.

EXAMPLE   Boston Principal Fellowship Screening Process

Step 1: Paper application that requires transcripts, resume, references, and two essays. The essays are designed to surface applicants' core beliefs as well as their ability to analyze a school, diagnose problems, and develop appropriate responses.

Step 2: A half-day performance assessment in a school that consists of four activities that approximate the roles of a principal:

- Review of a video of a teacher in action, analysis of her performance, and articulation of a strategy for debriefing the observation with the teacher
- Group problem-solving activity
- On-demand writing of a letter home to families on one of three current and relevant issues
- Classroom walkthrough followed by a presentation of what the applicant learned about the teachers and the school from the classrooms

Step 3: Final interview that focuses on standard interview questions directed to all finalists as well as specific questions that grew out of the applicants' performance assessment. Before the interview, district staff check references and talk to the applicant's current supervisor; this information also informs the focus of the interview.

Three to five screening team members drawn from sitting principals, senior level Central Office staff and supervisors, certification program staff, and higher education partners follow applicants through the three-step screening process. They read and discuss applications, observe the performance assessment, and review related artifacts. Finally, they identify individualized final interview questions and conduct the interviews. After each step in the process, screeners reduce the number of applicants by roughly 50 percent.

The Boston Principal Fellowship screening process is labor-intensive for the district and exhausting for the applicants; yet the dividends it pays are tremendous. Screening teams of district leaders from schools, the Central Office, and key partners calibrate their observations and talk about what matters most in the principalship as they review candidates. The conversations about instruction, leadership, and the standards for principals are a powerful capacity-building activity for the district. Exchanges are often spirited as small teams try to reach consensus, and everyone on the team leaves the experience thinking more broadly about the attributes of effective principals. As they watch a prospective principal navigate the process, screeners gather valuable information about how s/he will handle the stress of the job. The candidates themselves learn more about the expectations for principals and their readiness for the job.

LEADER ALERT—————————————————————————

Notice Group Behavior   Take heed if a principal applicant's behavior in the group activity of the screening process raises red flags. Applicants who don't listen to the others in the group and dominate the group problem-solving sessions may well have trouble listening to their staff. The white applicant who turns her back to the black candidate on her right and then directs all her remarks to the two other white applicants, ignoring the other applicants of color in the group, has some conscious or unconscious biases that should make you very concerned about her ability to lead a school that will serve all students well and close the achievement gap.

Placement

Intensive, multi-faceted screening processes allow a district to make thoughtful placement decisions. At the outset, the district knows what potential new hires are ready for, what they will need help with, and how they can be best supported. This information is invaluable in ensuring strong matches as new principals are assigned to schools. For example:

- The candidate in the group activity who demonstrates strong consensus-building skills and an impressive ability to include everyone in the conversation may be best placed in a school where there are divisions among the staff and a history of antagonism between the principal and teachers.

- The candidate who demonstrates thoughtfulness, deep understanding of instruction, and strong questioning in her review of the teaching video and the walkthrough may be placed in a school where instruction improved significantly several years ago but seems to have plateaued. Her skills might help the faculty push to the next level of instructional improvement.

Bad placement decisions are as common and damaging as bad hiring decisions, but they are rarely recognized. After placing someone in a position without thought to matching skills and style to school needs, systems commonly choose to muddle through years of ineffectiveness or to move the

LEADER ALERT

Data-Driven Talk among Administrators When gathering feedback from stakeholders, be clear about the goals (assessing the school and its needs) and the norms for how impressions are shared. For example, any statement made about a school or its current leader must be objective and data based. It is not acceptable to make a broad statement like, "The school isn't focused on instructional improvement." Instead participants must cite data such as:

- "Only 5 of the 15 eligible teachers have participated in the mandated math training the district offers."
- "Two instructional coaches have asked to be transferred from the school over the past two years because the principal has not set up a schedule that allows them to work with teachers."
- "There are no teacher evaluations on file in HR for this school for the past two years."

Requiring these kinds of data is a powerful culture builder and a way to confront conditions that undermine organizational and individual learning. It holds adults accountable for what they say. It forces the district to make data-driven decisions, and it squelches a culture of decision-making based on relationships and hearsay.

principal from one position to the next in the hope that something will improve.

Small, compact districts have distinct advantages in matching decisions. Central Office staff generally know a great deal about a school's culture, current performance, and future needs. To make good placement decisions in large school districts, district leadership must develop accurate and substantive profiles. Sources of information can range from demographics and current student performance data to teacher and parent surveys and assessments from curriculum staff who interact with the school regularly. If the district is large, the current principal's supervisor and Central Office staff are good sources of data. Feedback from these stakeholders can be gathered in writing or through focus groups where the relevant people are brought together to talk about each school with a principal vacancy and to determine the characteristics of a leader who would be a good match.

Intensifying a district's focus on principal preparation, hiring, and placement forces the organization to perform at a higher level. It shifts the district's vision from business as usual to a long-term commitment to excellence. That commitment is further exemplified by the level of support a system provides to its newest principals.

LEADER ALERT

Too Much Support Is No Support at All   New principals are inevitably overwhelmed in their first year. The induction system is supposed to lessen that feeling rather than exacerbate it. District support must be strategic. Don't bury new principals in volumes of information that they cannot possibly process. Without clear signals in the form of well-winnowed basics, new principals make their own interpretations of what is most important and the district loses the opportunity to set the direction for their work.

Supporting New Principals

The first year of the principalship and the first year of teaching share much in common: the same sense of being overwhelmed, the frustration of trying to juggle all the responsibilities of the job, and the feeling of not yet being comfortable in the role. The goal for first-year principals is enlightened survival: completing the first year without a disaster, emerging with a clearer picture of the needs of the school, making initial steps towards improvement, and feeling clearer and more comfortable managing the multiple demands of the role. Table 11.7 illustrates the roller coaster ride of a principal's first year.

TABLE 11. 7 Common Lifecycle of First-Year Principals

Month	Emotions
August	Energetic and hopeful
September	Overwhelmed
November	Exhausted; doubting the decision to become a principal
January	Renewed
February-March	Weary, slogging through hard work
May-June	Confident, feeling like a principal

In addition to these predictable stages, new principals struggle with particular aspects of the job. Some of the struggle is the result of doing technical tasks for the first time such as writing and submitting teacher evaluations, developing the school's budget, hiring new teachers, or meeting district expectations for reports, updates, and other kinds of paperwork. Other needs are broader and less technical; they involve the most important and complicated parts of the job such as: establishing a healthy school culture, building teams, forging communities that can address the school's most daunting problems, and forming meaningful relationships with parents. A support system for new principals is most effective if it addresses these broad issues as well as technical tasks.

Good support systems do more than provide information and establish a network; they also build high-functioning professional communities for administrators. This community helps to offset new principals' loneliness, ensures novices have a safe place to talk about the hardest parts of the job, and provides an opportunity to build competence. The network of experienced principals and Central Office colleagues they create will sustain them long after the first year is over. One example of a first-year support system includes:

- Summer orientation
- Peer mentoring by an experienced, excellent principal or retiree
- Technical support by Central Office staff in critical functional areas
- New-principal network meetings held monthly to build skills, problem solve, and provide general support
- Professional development, provided sparingly, focused on specific skills new principals need
- Growth-oriented supervision

This combination of supports addresses most of problems of new principals and sets the tone for the future. Especially in large or spread-out districts, the support system for new principals signals that many people care about them and will provide help. Introducing the new principal to a variety of colleagues increases the likelihood that the new leader will make a personal connection with one or more of these people. That connection means the new principal has a trusted confidant to whom she can admit that she needs help. Let's take a closer look at each of the elements of a new principal support system to see some of the pitfalls to avoid, and what can be accomplished when each element is implemented well.

Summer Orientation

When new principals are hired, there is a long list of things and people they need to know. Anyone who has endured an eye-glazing, brain-numbing parade of department heads reading slides of bullet points can identify mediocre orientations. District leadership must set priorities and determine what gets covered at what depth to signal its priorities and vision. Consider the messages offered in the partial orientation agendas in the Example that follows:

EXAMPLE   Contrasting Orientation Agendas

A new-principal orientation should address the most important issues, dig more deeply into them, and provide resources for the other need-to-know information. Imagine the impact of our classic orientation, agenda A. By 11:00 a.m. the audience's attention has shifted to what they will be doing after the orientation or their brows are furrowed and their hands are cramped from note taking. Stultifying quiet has replaced the bubbly enthusiasm that permeated the room when the new principals arrived. By the end, the eager novices barely remember their own names, much less anyone they met. Trying to figure out how to retain everything coming at them, some participants start to panic. Agenda A's focus on minutiae erodes the new principals' confidence; it also suggests that fire safety and food service, not student learning, community building, and vision, are their most important tasks.

In contrast, Agenda B signals the district's priorities by focusing on building professional community among the new principals and between them and their Central Office colleagues. Participants leave with individualized entry plans based on their vision for their school and their understanding of the current conditions. They also leave with a clear understanding of the district's expectations of them and the supports available to them.

Because they have planned their entry strategies, including outreach efforts, new principals are likely to meet many of the school staff before their first day together. They may meet individually with teachers to hear insights about what is going well in the school, what needs improvement, and any advice they have to offer. The new leaders use the teachers' feedback to shape time with staff on the first day. They focus on building community and setting the tone for the year. They identify one or two critical areas, such

New-Principal Orientation – Agenda A	New-Principal Orientation – Agenda B
Duration: 1/2 day Only Day Welcome and Introductions (15 minutes) **Facilities Director and Fire Chief** Fire safety: what can't be posted on school hallway walls (15 minutes) **Director of Food Services** Lunch menus, food delivery, and lunch monitors (15 minutes) **Legal Counsel** Legal responsibilities of principals (15 minutes) **Director of Curriculum and Instruction** Review of district's standards, curriculum, instructional materials, and assessments in all content areas (60 minutes) **Director of School Safety** Code of discipline (15 minutes) **Budget Director** Process for ordering materials and supplies (15 minutes) **Summer School Director** Information on promotion decisions new principals will need to make about students from their school (whom they have never met) who are participating in summer school (30 minutes)	**Duration: 2-5 days** Day 1 Team building among new principals (60 minutes) **Superintendent** Welcome celebration and interactive vision discussion (60 minutes) Small Group Meeting with Supervisor Expectations for new principals and support provided (60-90 minutes) **Mentors** One-on-one at lunch **New Principals w/ Facilitator** Working session focused on entry planning, summer outreach, first days of school with staff and students (3 hours) Day 2 Team building (30 minutes) **Director of Human Resources** Review of staffing process and status in each school and supports available (60-90 minutes) **Director of Budget** Review school budgets and procurement processes; meet budget liaison and schedule appointments (60-90 minutes) **Director of Curriculum and Instruction** Review district standards, curriculum, instructional materials, and assessments; receive year-end school performance data (3 hours) **New Principals w/ Facilitator** Working session focused on developing instructional leadership strategy (60-90 minutes) Day 3 **Director of Operations** Need to know info. (90 minutes) Staff assignments and their supervision How to get mailing labels and phone numbers for staff and families, stamps, keys to the school, cell phone, etc. Summer programs in the school Lunch **Technology, HR, and Budget Staff** Training on HR/Financial Software (3 hours)

as how to use formative assessment data to improve instruction or how to make the most of common planning time. The day is largely devoted to getting teachers developing a plan for implementation. Teachers have time to examine, understand, and plan for the year's priorities. Moreover, this welcome to the new school year models how the teachers will welcome their students into their classrooms on the first day, help the children get to know one another, and signal the most important behaviors for being successful students.

While the characteristics of effective new-principal orientation are constant, the way it is implemented varies based on district size and the number of new principals hired annually. In a small district much of this work may happen one-on-one in individual meetings and working sessions. Larger districts may schedule several days of new-principal orientation during which many of these topics are addressed and lots of collaborative work is done.

LEADER ALERT

Bad Professional Development Will Haunt You Remember that what looks like a simple new-principal orientation can be a culture-builder or a buster. Make sure the values and beliefs you model are ones you would be happy to see everyone in the organization use. If you provide "sit and git" training, new principals are likely to take the same approach to professional development with their staff. Specialists will lecture teachers and teachers will "talk at" their students. If this mediocre pattern happens in school after school, you run the risk of creating a district culture that is passive and reactive and doesn't encourage critical thinking, sense-making, or problem solving.

TIPS ON HIGH-QUALITY ORIENTATIONS

✔ Give new principals time to make sense of their new work and ask questions.

✔ Immediately establish norms and characteristics of an Accountable Community (see Chapter 3).

✔ Use the voices of experienced principals and individuals in second and third years to help participants keep perspective on the tasks ahead.

✔ Provide time for newcomers to share their plans with one another and receive feedback.

✔ Give new principals time to get to know one another, network, and maybe even find kindred colleagues and exchange promises to call and coach one another.

✔ Be honest about the things the district is struggling with and how they impact principals and their work.

✔ Provide new principals a binder full of district policies and procedures so they know where to look for important information and who to call.

✔ Ensure that new principals leave the orientation with appointments scheduled to review their budget and staffing and with the keys to their school.

✔ Send new principals off from the orientation feeling simultaneously tired and fortified.

Peer Mentoring

Nothing is more reassuring to a new principal than the support of an experienced colleague. This is the person who:

• Provides quick over-the-phone feedback on a strategy for handling the irate mother who is standing in the front office demanding to talk to the principal about her daughter

• Sits beside the novice at her computer the day before the school budgets are due, typing in dollar figures after weeks of conversation about the new principal's priorities for next year and how to allocate the budget to reflect those priorities

• Waves the new principal over to sit with her at district meetings and introduces her to other principals

• Tells the new principal whom to call if she really needs to get something done

The keys to successful mentoring are the relationship between the new principal and her mentor and the latter's understanding of effective mentoring skills. The relationship must be one of trust, confidentiality, and something that exists along the continuum between mutual respect and appreciation and a great friendship. Most important, the experienced principal needs to understand that the goal of mentoring is not to make a clone of herself. The mentor's charge is to empower the new principal and build her skills so that over time, the novice becomes more confident and skillful and can figure out most of the challenges she encounters.

Mentoring is a skill that needs to be taught. Assuming that a strong principal knows how to mentor is unwise. Consider Gloria M's case.

CASE 11.8 **When Mentoring Goes Awry**

After every phone call between Gloria M, a new principal, and her mentor, Gloria feels discouraged. Her mentor has the answer for every problem Gloria raises, but Gloria can't make them work. Today the issue was how her 7th grade Gold teaching team spends its common planning time bickering about things that have nothing to do with teaching and student learning. She's sat in on the meetings. She's tried to gently redirect the conversation but hasn't had much success. Her mentor told her, "You need to stop pussyfooting around. Go in there and tell them what you expect and that they need to shape up." He made it sound so easy. And yet, hanging up the phone, Gloria knows that's not her style and she doesn't think it will get at the root of the problem. Since her mentor told her what to do, she doesn't think she can talk to him about this issue any more unless she's coming back to report on her success. She shakes her head thinking to herself that she may need to dodge her mentor's calls till something improves with the Gold team.

A small investment in training mentors on strategies for building a trusting relationship, offering support, and asking questions that encourage reflection and problem solving can yield significant returns. Strong mentoring programs include regular, facilitated meetings that bring mentors together to talk about their practices, continue to build their skills, and problem solve. Such programs should also include a mechanism for giving mentors feedback on their efforts. Both components support the mentor–new principal relationships and increase the skill of a group of talented principal mentors, thus preparing them for additional leadership roles.

Technical Support by Central Office Staff

It is not unusual for Central Office staff to tell new principals, "Call me if there is anything I can do to help you." Yet new principals often hesitate to call. They assume the budget director or human resources manager is too busy and that such a call would be a bother. Or, worse yet, they decide that the staff member didn't really mean what she said and likely would not be much help. School leaders sometimes perceive that Central Office is setting up hoops for them to jump through. This interpretation leads principals to feel resentful as they comply or to consciously object by ignoring all but the most compelling requests. Neither choice reflects the behavior of sustainable, Accountable Communities.

To help build formal relationships between principals and Central Office staff, a budget officer might visit a new principal's school in August to walk through the school budget and see what questions the new principal has. The personnel director might meet with the new principal to make a plan for finding the best possible chemistry teacher to fill a sudden vacancy. Or someone from the facilities department would walk through the new principal's school and address her concerns about repairs that must be made before students return.

In these mentoring relationships, Central Office staff must understand that the needs of the new principal come first and that their responsibility is to share knowledge and experience and to do everything they can to help. When relationships between principals and Central Office staff are established well, they go a long way towards breaking down the walls between schools and the Central Office. They build morale and provide Central

Office with a direct link to their customers that yields valuable data about the quality of services and how they can be improved. They also build leadership at the district level and create a cadre of Central Office staff members who more deeply understand their role in supporting schools and are committed to that work.

New-Principal Network

A new-principal network provides a safe space to share and interpret war stories and leave with strategies for handling challenges. It is a godsend to first-year principals. Such an environment helps new principals realize that they are not alone in the travails they face and gives them the chance to hear how their colleagues are approaching common issues. When someone who has been a successful principal, and preferably also a senior level Central Office administrator facilitates the network, the group benefits from a seasoned practitioner's perspective.

School culture is a common topic in the fall. Startled by what they perceive as dysfunctional dynamics, new principals will raise concerns about how:

- Adults in their buildings talk to one another.
- The parking lot is empty 15 minutes after school ends.
- Teachers are visibly anxious when the principal visits them in their classrooms.
- The union representative frequently initiates conversations about low morale.

Using a protocol to focus the discussion and prevent it from being a "beef" session, the network facilitators will engage the group in an analysis of this issue and ways to respond. There are a variety of ways to facilitate this conversation. One approach is an adaptation of the "Consultancy Protocol" developed by the National School Reform Faculty.

Most issues that one principal raises are shared by other principals or speak to a theme such as communication or conflict resolution that other principals are struggling with. So though the activity is organized to give specific support to a particular principal, every case ends up supporting many members of the group and giving them strategies to try.

New-principal networks also provide training that is carefully aligned to specific deadlines the novices face. For example, a month or two before principals have to lay out their staffing plan for the next year, the group will meet with human resources staff and experienced principals who are known for their skills in staffing. These visitors will share their strategies and help the new principals think through the process. The goal of new-principal network meetings is always to support members with information and to help them reflect with colleagues.

LEADER ALERT———————————————————————————

Confidentiality in New-Principal Groups Safety and confidentiality are critical to the success of new-principal networks. What is said in the room stays in the room. There is never editorializing on the challenges new principals face. All energy is focused on understanding the issues and problem solving. Having a neutral facilitator for the group who has no responsibility for supervising new principals is an important consideration in building a safe environment.

Common Just-in-Time Training Topics

- Opening of school
- Teacher evaluations: process and timelines
- School budgeting: nuts and bolts and strategy
- Staffing: hiring, managing underperformance
- Parental involvement: committee elections, outreach, and management
- Standardized testing: preparing for and administering
- Closing the school for summer

In most districts, new principals are expected to participate in the professional development organized for all administrators. Any additional professional development should be planned with restraint because of the burden it places on already overwhelmed new principals. Occasionally, it becomes apparent that many new principals are facing the same challenges such as what to do about teacher supervision and evaluation practices, communication skills, time management, and conflict resolution. A focused training on one of these topics may temporarily take new principals away from their work in schools but will greatly enhance their long-term effectiveness.

Collecting data from new principals and doing a cost-benefit analysis helps in planning targeted professional development. If new principals are spending hours writing teacher evaluations and the quality of their efforts doesn't meet the standard, the data warrant offering training on the topic. These sessions are most beneficial if the new principals get to practice the concepts being taught in response to real situations they face in their schools. Role-playing the difficult conversation a new principal needs to have with a teacher who refuses to participate in grade level team meetings and has filed two specious grievances about the principal is immediately applicable and therefore valuable. The opportunity to practice and get feedback from training facilitators and other new principal participants helps solidify new management skills.

Supervision of New Principals

What Not to Do   Twice a month, without warning, Henry's supervisor visits the school to review his paperwork. She looks through his records and reports and peppers him with questions, then departs. They have never visited a classroom together. There is never an opportunity for Henry to ask questions about how to handle the lack of academic rigor he's seen throughout the school. The visits are so stressful Henry is beginning to think he should spend his days in the office working on reports so he'll be ready for the next inspection. He worries that the job isn't really about leading teaching and learning and that he should have remained a curriculum coordinator. At least in that job he knew he could have a positive impact on the quality of instruction. All he seems to do now is administrivia.

Many new principals are hired on a one-year contract. They come into the job feeling that they have a lot to prove and that the stakes are high. They know a decision will be made about their competence within six to eight months. How their supervision and evaluation is handled will send new principals a strong message about what the district values, what it expects from its principals, and how they will be supported. Monthly supervisory visits that balance classroom observations with time for the new principal and the supervisor to ask questions of one another and time to solve knotty problems suggest to the new principal that she and her supervisor are partners. The supervisor's expectations are not overwhelming because she has been clear about them and is helping the principal develop her skills in priority areas. This approach reinforces a culture of excellence and mutual accountability. The focus is on supervision that supports the new principal in meeting the leadership standards. Evaluation is a tool for assessing a principal's skills and identifying areas of strength and opportunities for growth.

One major sign of a healthy supervisory relationship is the new principal's comfort in calling on her supervisor for support, strategic advice on responding to a crisis, or feedback on a change before she implements it in the school. Supervision can be punitive and force new principals to act defensively, or it can be supportive and encourage growth. Adults, like children, need to feel safe in order to learn; districts with a healthy culture assume that novices will make mistakes and learn from them.

Evaluation of New Principals

What Not to Do   On his first supervisory visit, Dr. Ramirez, the assistant superintendent, found Mrs. C trying to shoo students into their classrooms ten minutes after the period had started. He was concerned by the sheer number of middle schoolers in the hallway and the fact that there seemed to be no plan for getting them into classrooms before the tardy bell, but decided it was probably beginning-of-the-school-year kinks. Out loud he said

"Wow, it's hard to get these kids into class" to make Mrs. C feel at ease. What he was really wondering was, "What are the expectations for getting to class on time?"

On his second visit, six weeks later, Dr. Ramirez and Mrs. C visited classrooms. There were still too many students milling in the hall, but it was an improvement. On this visit he noticed how loose classroom management was and the undemanding questions teachers asked of the students who actually made it to class. The level of rigor in all the classrooms was low, but the principal seemed unconcerned and even unaware of this dynamic. Dr. Ramirez focused the post-visit conversation on getting students out of the halls and into class. It seemed the more immediate and manageable target.

To assess how math curriculum implementation was proceeding, Dr. Ramirez and Mrs. C spent the third visit on a walkthrough of math classes. During the debriefing, Dr. Ramirez was surprised that Mrs. C seemed unfamiliar with the student-centered pedagogy required by the new instructional materials even though she had just attended 15 hours of math training. He tried to refer back to the training as he outlined some key indicators of problems Mrs. C should look for in her next drop-in visits. Later Dr. Ramirez realized that he hadn't talked explicitly about his concerns about classroom management, the low-level of academic rigor, observations in math classrooms, and specific steps he wanted Mrs. C to take.

For substantive and symbolic reasons, all new principals should be evaluated in their first year. The evaluation is an opportunity to reexamine the district's leadership competencies and provide a constructive and honest assessment of strengths and areas for development. If the new principals are performing well, the evaluator can identify their successes and help them set goals. If the novice leaders have struggled but demonstrated adequate growth, the evaluator can focus them on the specific steps they need to take to build their skills. When individuals are not meeting standard and have shown little growth over the course of the year, the district has the opportunity to make a timely decision about the future. These decisions are never easy, but putting them off makes them harder and models the bad practice of avoiding the hardest work.

Evaluating a new principal in her first year sends several clear messages:

- You are a valued employee who deserves my attention, an honest assessment of your skills, and feedback.
- Evaluation is an important job responsibility of managers.
- We believe in standards and accountability.

Because all new principals are given the responsibility of evaluating teachers, it is critical that they have a clear sense of the district's commitment to the evaluation process. Otherwise, the time-consuming and challenging task of teacher evaluation may slip to the bottom of a long "to do list."

Note that in this section we have not emphasized focusing new principals on instructional improvement. New principals care deeply about instruction, and many attempt to focus on it. Yet the struggles that new principals report most often tend to be problems of adult interpersonal interactions, school structure, and school culture. Addressing each of these issues is a step to building a culture focused on instructional improvement.

First-Year Challenges—Reviewing Our Case Studies

To ground these ideas about supporting new principals, let's look in on our four new principals from the beginning of the chapter—Steve, Maria, Isabel, and Alvin—to see how they are doing.

CASE 11.1 **Steve (continued)**

Steve is thrilled about his new position. He has whipped the facility into shape and has the custodian on his side. The floors sparkle, and the lunchroom is under control. Steve hasn't missed a deadline from the Central Office yet. He is diligent about getting his paperwork done, and he hasn't heard a word from a Central Office administrator. Steve had a cookout for all his teachers the first week of school, and people seemed to enjoy it. In terms of teachers' work, Steve inherited a schedule with common planning time for teachers. He's not clear how that time is being used. Several teachers have asked him if they might stop meeting together so they can have more time for their individual preparation and paper correcting, and Steve is tempted to buy a little good will by going along with their request. Steve is visible in the halls but spends little time in classrooms. He prides himself on stopping into every room for 2 minutes at the beginning of the day to greet the students and teachers. Sitting at his desk at midday, Steve looks at the pile of mid-year formative assessments the teachers administered in reading as mandated by the district. He feels churning in his stomach as he wonders what in the world he is supposed to do with all that information.

CASE 11.2 **Maria (continued)**

Maria is in her office, head down at her computer making colored charts and graphs of her school's mid-year student formative assessment results. She can immediately see trends in students' comprehension and vocabulary skills in grades 6-8. Maria develops an outline for how all teachers, regardless of the content they teach can focus their common planning time on strategies to support students in these areas. She smiles, feeling confident that if teachers follow this plan they will see real results by the end-of-year assessment.

Maria hears rustling on the other side of her closed door and looks up in time to see a slip of folded paper slide under the door. She gets up and walks across the room, picks up the paper and sighs at the note from a teacher who has gone to the union to grieve how Maria conducts her classroom visits. This is the fifth grievance Maria has received since September. As she walks back to her graphs she wonders, "Why can't the teachers just do what I ask? I know what I'm doing."

CASE 11.3 **Isabel (continued)**

Isabel is standing in the hallway with her hands full of attendance folders. She has just collected them from the teachers, something she does every day as a way to connect with the teachers and students. Several teachers have raised other issues with Isabel today during her visits. She has added five things to her "to do list" that she needs to address and get back to teachers about. Looking at the list she is discouraged by how the list keeps growing and how few things she has been able to mark off as done. Reviewing the mid-year formative assessment data has been on her list for two weeks, and she still hasn't gotten to it. It's just two weeks after the holiday vacation, and Isabel is already starting to feel the anxiety that was haunting her in the fall and keeping her up at night. She had thought working through the vacation would get her caught up and ahead of the game. She misses her teacher colleagues from her old school. When she took over for her old principal, the teachers all chipped in to help her. None of the teachers at her new school do that, so Isabel is trying to do it all herself. Isabel misses the chats she used to have with her old colleagues. In this new school when she walks into the teachers' room, conversation stops. Isabel trudges back to her office, trying to decide which item on her list she should tackle. As she walks into the office, she sees the parent who visits her twice a week to register complaints about every aspect of her daughter's experience in the school. "There goes my 'to do list,'" Isabel mutters under her breath.

CASE 11.4 **Alvin (continued)**

As you might have guessed, six months into the school year Alvin is leading Washington High School, the big troubled high school rather than Park Street, the small high school for which he applied. He is sitting in a common planning time (CPT) meeting with his English teachers. He is quietly observing as the teachers talk about how long it's taking to get through the required reading books. He marvels at how anyone can spend two months reading Sandra Cisneros' *House on Mango Street*. Flipping through the book he thinks to himself, "The book is only 128 pages long." During the summer Alvin labored over the schedule to make sure students were properly scheduled on the first day of school and that all departments had common planning time (CPT) weekly. Early in the year it became clear that teachers didn't know how to use common planning time well. Therefore Alvin is focusing school professional development on how to structure CPT and specific roles and strategies for teachers. It's too late now, but for next year he wants a clear calendar of the kinds of work teachers are expected to do in CPT. For example, it's January and everyone should be looking at the mid-year assessment data and planning instruction based on results. From his visits to CPT this week, Alvin knows that less than half of the teams are doing what he asked them to do. Sitting with the English teachers, Alvin tries to reassure himself by remembering that in September he couldn't have sat through a CPT meeting. He would have been interrupted by a discipline issue. He spent all summer working with a team of teachers and administrators to develop a code of conduct and discipline policy to address what had been described to him as an out-of-control situation. The fall was spent implementing the policy and pushing administrators and teachers to assume their part of the responsibility. In his head, Alvin runs through the long list of things he must do before his day ends, wondering if he will get home in time to put his two young sons to bed. It's Thursday, and he hasn't seen them awake yet this week.

The challenges our new principals are facing are not entirely surprising given the knowledge, skills, and experience they each brought to the position.

- Steven has bumped up against his limited knowledge of curriculum, instruction, and assessment.
- Maria is distancing herself from her staff, and her staff is making their unhappiness known through union grievances.
- Isabel is trying to keep her head above water as she struggles to keep up with all the demands of the job without having built an infrastructure to support her.
- Alvin is trying to build teacher collaboration, having addressed the immediate impediments to teaching and learning, but the foundation for collaboration has not yet been laid.

Consider our program for new-principal support. Which components might be most helpful to each new principal given his or her specific challenges?

Mapping Supports to New Principals' Needs

Steve

Need: Orientation to the formative assessments being used and how to ana-

lyze the student data to guide instruction
Support: District assessment department technical assistance, the district curriculum specialist, or his mentor

Maria

Need: Supportive ways to reach out to her staff
Support: Mentor, new principal network, training on communication skills

Isabel

Need: Learning to prioritize, manage her time, and delegate her tasks so that all her efforts are driven by her vision for her school and for student and learning
Support: Mentor

Alvin

Need: Building capacity among the teachers, setting a reasonable pace for change, work/life balance
Support: Mentor, network, professional development on leading a change process

It is worth noting that Steve and Maria's skills perfectly complement one another. Steve could teach Maria his strategies for building community; Maria could walk Steve through the assessments and help him with the analysis as well as the instructional implications. If they had gotten to know one another through the summer orientation and monthly meetings, they could begin to help one another. That level of mutual support among new principals is a sterling example of what happens in accountable districts where teams and individual adults support one another.

At the end of their first year in the principalship, each of these new principals is still standing. They are all excited about the breather the summer will provide them and are thinking about what they will do differently next year. Isabel is sleeping through the night and has identified some teachers with great leadership potential whom she is nurturing. Steve is slowly building his understanding of the assessments and what they tell him about instruction. Alvin is celebrating that by the end of the year his English team's common planning time was going well, and the team was sharing lessons for feedback. Maria has suffered the most out of the group. She finished the year with her office door open to her staff and having mediated several of the grievances, but she was exhausted and feeling less sure of herself that she was when she started. She continually reminds herself of her mentor's comment; "We can't do it without the teachers, so we have to make sure we do it with them."

A strong principal induction system builds on the work of principals in their first year and spans the second, and sometimes the third year of a principal's career. The needs of new principals evolve over the first three years. As they learn new skills and apply them, the next challenges they face are more sophisticated and push them and their schools further toward improving instruction. The generalized need for help in the first year becomes more specific in the second year as the principals identify a couple of key issues that need to be addressed to leverage significant improvement in their schools. By providing targeted technical support and consultation in these identified areas, districts can accelerate the rate of principal learning and school improvement. The goals of all of these efforts are to support new principals; to ensure their success; and to create a sustainable, Accountable Community among them and across the district.

Summary

Districts committed to raising student achievement make an equally strong commitment to finding and developing skilled school leaders. They identify competencies for practice and use those competencies to shape supervision, evaluation, and professional development. They design and implement comprehensive recruitment and preparation programs meant to motivate the best possible candidates from a range of feeder pools to apply for principalships. Hiring and placement processes focus on carefully matching new principals' skills to schools' needs. Finally, the district demonstrates its commitment to principals' success and ongoing learning through a variety of targeted supports including training, mentoring, and job-alike networks. By modeling best practices of support and accountability, the district provides a framework for principals to use in their work with teachers and a vision for the kind of community that nurtures growth and demands high performance.

12 Responding to Behaviors that Undermine Learning

All supervisors eventually face the challenge of responding to unmet expectations, broken promises, or inappropriate behavior in the workplace. The frequency and severity of issues that undermine a community's ability to help students are variables that depend on the size of the school, its history, and its culture. However, the stress and distraction that result from attempting to ignore such issues are constants.

In this chapter, we offer examples of oral and written communication to help supervisors respond clearly, efficiently, and respectfully to unprofessional behavior. Because we are focused on tapping the power of pooled intelligence and shared accountability, our examples are about its absence: violation of policies or norms that affect a group's work, poor collaboration, and the failure to implement collegial agreements about improvements. However, the approaches and models described could be used for any identified gap between the performance needed to help students learn or be safe and a staff member's present performance.

Ultimately, supervisors seek a willing, thoughtful, and permanent shift in behavior from inappropriate or ineffective to appropriate, effective, and productive. Approaches to a performance problem can legitimately include initiating the steps of progressive discipline, using the procedures of the normal evaluation cycle, or employing some combination of the two that simultaneously meets contractual obligations and individual development needs.

Typically supervisors begin with progressive discipline in the face of clear failures to follow well-articulated policies or expectations of the district: attendance requirements, reporting requirements, or personal use of district materials or facilities ("conduct unbecoming a teacher"). When concerns are qualitative and therefore subject to multiple interpretations, supervisors are more likely to start with activities that are part of the district's evaluation cycle such as observations, conferences, coaching, or data analysis. Keep in mind that starting with evaluation procedures does not preclude the use of progressive discipline if the situation later justifies it. Nor does beginning with progressive discipline take away a supervisor's right and opportunity to help an individual change through successive rounds of observation and feedback.

Introduction to Zones of Response

If responses to a performance concern can legitimately vary, then what guides a supervisor's choice of method and tools? Skillful leaders assess the severity of the problem and look for evidence of prior clear communication about the expectations for appropriate behavior. They make sure they know contractual and legal requirements related to the problem and get advice from counsel. Finally, they appraise the staff member's demonstrated ability to understand the problem and take independent action to resolve it. We label this initial decision-making process *matching* because leaders sort through their options for the one that best matches the performance problem and the employee.[1] To clarify the different matching options for supervisors, we began to think of two general types of response, each with its own characteristics. To make the image graphic, we associated the two response types with the colors used in managing traffic: green for less severe problems and red for problems that require an immediate cessation of the offending behavior and a higher level of intervention.

In the green zone are a range of responses to problems mutually recognized and acknowledged by supervisor and staff member and for matters that do not involve a mandated written communication. They are not for issues of student safety, potential misconduct, insubordination, or the like. The zone is dubbed *green* because the characteristic exchanges are collegial and collaborative. The function of the exchange is to close a performance gap quickly and efficiently, and the intended message is "*keep going*, but fine-tune or extend your practice." The supervisor names the problem and cites the data that illustrate it. The parties acknowledge that the teacher has the necessary expertise to work on the problem, is expected to be the primary decision maker about the best ways to resolve it, and will be accountable for improvements without further pointed directives and monitoring. The supervisor assumes no formal responsibility for follow-up. Any further exchanges about the issue are generally collaborative and inquiry based rather than directive. We hope that most conversations about instruction, professional development plans, and even interactions around minor breeches of policy or procedure would fit in this zone, but we have worked in schools long enough to know that such exchanges are not the appropriate response to every problem a supervisor encounters.

---

[1] The term is borrowed with thanks from Jon Saphier who originally used it to label the process that a teacher uses in selecting strategies from a repertoire by taking account of student needs, curriculum goals, time of day and year, etc.

Some performance issues require a supervisor to do more than engage in a supportive, problem-solving conversation. Therefore leaders need a range of red-zone responses that say in essence "*Stop* doing X and start doing Y." The compliance, targeted development, or assignment to formal assistance responses are all characterized by variations of that stop-start message. The supervisor signals the severity of the concern, uses his or her authority to make judgments about performance, collaborates on a plan to resolve the performance gap, and takes responsibility for monitoring and follow-up. Each type of intervention we will consider has a particular function and a distinguishing tool or mode of communication and documentation. Compliance responses are appropriate when:

- Careful, respectful green-zone exchanges have not worked.

- Behavior indicates that an individual cannot be trusted to follow policy guidelines or keep school-wide agreements.

- Violations of contracts, policies, or regulations require that an individual be officially notified and disciplined.

Compliance responses are characterized by a straightforward and, if necessary, escalating, demand that the person meet what are usually clear, agreed-upon, concrete conditions of employment. The key tool is the summary memo.

Targeted development is a red-zone response designed to make sure inefficient or inappropriate performance stops and that the individual acquires the necessary competencies to perform effectively. Development-oriented responses are appropriate when evaluation has identified specific, well-defined performance problems that cannot be rectified by compliance alone. These problems more commonly involve deficiencies in instruction than policy transgressions. Perhaps a teacher's work does not meet standard in a particular area or an individual has resisted implementing a specific program or set of strategies. Targeted Development offers a short-term, middle-ground intervention between unmonitored recommendations attached to the end of an evaluation and a full assistance plan consistent with district contract agreements. The supervisor assumes that the individual does not yet have the knowledge or skills to make the change without help and commits to providing that help and assessing its effects. The goal is to engage the individual in his or her own improvement in order to achieve rapid and sustained change. The key tool for this kind of response is the MiniPlan[SM]—or what some states and districts might call the pre-Assistance or Awareness plan.

In contrast, responses that fall into the Assignment to Formal Assistance category are usually dictated by evaluation agreement or contract. They are good matches when an individual's performance is below standard in several areas and when earlier, less stringent and less formal efforts have failed. A planning tool is often specified, and the supervisor may have to employ a team of people with the specific expertise to help the staff member change. Table 12.1 provides an overview of the different responses that we will examine in greater detail.

TABLE 12.1 Overview of Zones of Response

	Function/Audience	Characteristics of Interaction	Key Tools
GREEN ZONE (collaborative interaction)	To promote awareness, reflection, self-assessment leading to self-directed change. Teachers who are engaged learners.	Communication based on data and questions, non-judgmental suggestions. Teacher decides when/if to implement and follow-up. Low accountability.	Data Collegial conferences Summaries of next steps
RED ZONE Compliance	To mandate technical compliance with policies or procedures. Staff who need to be disciplined to adhere to expectations	Administrator driven. No staff choice. Escalated sequence of intervention. Recommendations designed with clear accountability measures. May involve steps of progressive discipline	Data Meetings to clarify expectations Summary memos
Targeted Development	To engage teachers in taking responsibility for and fixing a specific aspect of performance that is currently substandard. Mediocre performers who are willing to engage in their own improvement beyond compliance.	Administrator identifies standard not met and the data that have led to that rating. Teacher and administrator develop goals, select action steps, decide on data to collect, and identify indicators for success. Administrator determines whether standard has been met and next steps.	Data MiniPlan^{SM}
Assignment to Formal Assistance	To remediate performance using district-negotiated policies. Teachers with serious, unresolved problems.	Administrator driven with involvement of appropriate support systems and personnel. Teacher may have some role in helping to design the plan. High accountability. Failure to show progress may result in dismissal.	Data Contractually designated forms and procedures Written feedback

Using Green-Zone Responses

The green zone is a good starting point for communication to improve performance when:

- The teacher is able to respond thoughtfully to positive or negative data.

- The problem under discussion does not involve a contract violation or "conduct unbecoming a teacher."

- The teacher can contribute ideas and options for action to the conversation.

These responses are a good match for skilled, self-directed learners who may simply need help in defining an issue before they fix it. However, the green zone is frequently misused in dealing with low performance. Many observations and final evaluations merely hint that the performance is not satisfactory through vague, gentle suggestions that have no reference to standards and data and no means of monitoring progress and holding the learner accountable. Consider the following examples taken from evaluation documents and adapted to fit some of our Chapter 9 profiles:

"Cary has made a good start and is settling into the department. It is suggested that he seek more assistance from his colleagues."

"Mrs. Knowital should continue to develop more rapport with her students."

"Mr. S might reorganize his teaching to include more opportunities for students to collaborate."

"Ms. Block should work to improve her collaboration with her colleagues."

With little data as a foundation to support the claims of poor practice, these inexplicit suggestions are unlikely to improve mediocre teaching or poor collaboration because:

- In the "collaborative green zone," the teacher decides whether to pursue an idea, and there is no accountability for implementation.

- Conditional language rarely defines steps to address gaps in performance systematically. It requires a reflective practitioner to interpret what has to be done and implement the changes.

- Suggestions often contain inexplicit language such as "continuing and seeking" that does not provide embedded expectations for implementation.

- Some of the suggestions can easily become isolated, "fill in the blank" activities, not clearly aligned with achieving district standards.

The Skillful Leader II

Most "continue" or "needs to" suggestions are really overly nuanced, softened reminders to improve something that has been weakly implemented. Adding detailed criteria on what would constitute quality continuation helps to make them more concrete: for example, "The teacher should continue to improve her planning by listing the key questions in her lesson plans and citing clear assessment strategies."

Collaborative interaction is meant to describe the characteristics of informal conversation about performance as opposed to formal, written feedback. However, the response to behavior that is not yet effective should not be an informal, open-ended chat with no clear goals. This is a professional, problem-solving exchange that begins with an examination of evidence about how well students are learning or about how well an individual is doing at meeting performance standards. One organizing protocol to focus conversation is to name the relevant teacher performance standard, cite the available data, ask a question to clarify the meaning of the data, and, based on the response, ask additional, nonjudgmental questions or make a suggestion. The same steps can be used to shape initial conferences with poor performers. They benefit from an opportunity to reflect on data and assess their own performance in relation to clearly defined standards and student outcomes.

1. **Frame the problem.** "One of the standards we are focusing on this year is Contribution to Professional Community. I heard you say that…"

2. **Cite data (and source if needed).** "During the team meeting that I attended, you were quiet during the discussion on teaching students strategies for answering open-ended questions."

3. **Ask a nonjudgmental question or make a suggestion.** How do you decide when to get involved in team discussions? Or "What was going through your mind at the time? Or "You have much to offer your team; could you contribute, perhaps by offering to review the materials you've collected even if you are not yet ready to speak out routinely at meetings?"

Presenting the relevant data about the effects of choices without judgment gives the individual a chance to respond and add information. The quality of the exchange depends on whether trust has been built so that the teacher views the presentation as a genuine invitation for reflection, not a coy "gotcha" move. The steps identified by the joint analysis can be recorded and become written agreements for follow-up. "At the conference I communicated my observation that Ms. Block offered no ideas during the discussion on open-ended questions. Ms. Block said that she has a tendency to hold back because she thinks her contributions never make a difference. She decided that she would make an increased effort to contribute to her team by going over the research and sample materials she has personally collected and later by providing back-up information for the approaches members have agreed to try." The decision the teacher made has been noted. Although the evaluator has made no commitment to monitor that decision, putting it in writing raises the level of importance attached to the standard and the data about the initial concern. It increases the likelihood that the teacher will respond. Leaders pondering this written summary, however, will have little confidence that behavior will change for resistant teachers or those who need targeted professional development. For these people, we usually need to escalate the response to the red zone.

Using Red-Zone Responses

In confronting personnel with profiles such as those described in Chapter 9, skillful leaders might start with a collaborative, invitational response. However, if improvement is not relatively rapid or cannot be sustained, responses need to come from one of the red-zone options. All three of these approaches are characterized by reduced teacher choice and increased supervisor direction. These responses also require formal documentation, typically for any of the following:

- Persistent behavior patterns that have not improved after feedback such as:
  - Failure to attend meetings regularly and punctually.
  - Failure to engage and actively participate with colleagues, as evidenced by not volunteering to take on tasks, not offering ideas, or not helping to clarify problems and summarize agreements.
  - Failure to implement collaboratively determined agreements about instruction and actively pursue shared goals for student learning.
  - Routine violation of adopted norms of interaction such as frequent put downs and off task comments during meetings.
- Frequent missed deadlines, failure to meet paperwork requirements, missed duties, poor attendance, or problems with punctuality.
- Patterns of toxic interaction including sarcasm, ad hominem attacks, bullying, repeated outbursts of ungoverned temper that disrupt work, misleading of team members or misrepresentation of information, and manipulation through tears and drama. Teams cannot be expected to tolerate or discipline egregious behavior of members.

We begin by considering the most straightforward of the red-zone responses, the demand for compliance.

Responding When the Goal Is Compliance

Supervisors have generally used a compliance-oriented response to handle concerns such as missing paperwork, misuse of materials, tardiness, poor attendance, or failure to carry out assigned duties. Administrators record evidence to prove infractions and apply the steps of progressive discipline rather than those of observation and evaluation to correct non-compliance. As its name implies, compliance intervention involves using one's assigned authority to direct people to meet their professional responsibility. To support our purpose of confronting conditions that undermine learning, we are highlighting responsibilities to one's professional community.

To be effective, the accountability requirements and methods of follow-up should be clearly spelled out in any communication requiring compliance. Soft follow-up suggestions that include little or no demand for accountability rarely change performance. In the deadline-driven spring, evaluators sometimes forget that they need to go beyond merely using the language of compliance in their recommendations or prescriptions to address a particular concern. Consider this sample recommendation taken from a performance evaluation:

> Due to the complexity of some personal responsibilities, Ms. F has not been able to attend SLC meetings. This has been an ongoing discussion, and Ms. F has expressed frustration with trying to maintain regular attendance. She must improve her attendance and punctuality next year.

The word *must* signals a demand for compliance. But what does *improve* mean? Must Ms. F attend all meetings? Some meetings? A few more than she did last year? How will her attendance and punctuality be monitored? What if nothing changes? What if she is still "frustrated?" Skeptical readers realize this flabby directive is not likely to bring about any discernable change. Or examine this directive: "You need to improve your engagement and participation with your team." If you were the recipient, would you know what to do and how you would show that you have complied with the mandate? What is meant by engagement? What steps will increase participation? What will success look like? What data will be collected for assessing progress? Again we have little confidence that team contribution will improve.

"Happy ending" summary paragraphs are also problematic. They sandwich weak recommendations between layers of generic praise and further dilute the likelihood of behavior change. Patterson describes the approach: "To soften the violent blow, you first say something complimentary, next you bring up the problem, and then you close with something complimentary again" (2005 86). Our real example looks like this.

> The teacher manages her classes well and creates a nice climate for learning. She is working hard on behalf of her students. Her active participa-

tion in course work informs her excellent planning. One area for growth: she must enhance her collaboration with her colleagues. Overall, I am pleased by her performance.

Remember the principle of learning that says the first and last items in a sequence are the ones that will be remembered. We are not convinced that the softball recommendation buried in this paragraph would elicit any attention from the teacher. What, for instance, does *enhance* mean? The teacher readily understands that that this is not serious area for improvement.

LEADER ALERT

Respond to Community-Damaging Behavior

Immediately Collecting data to back up a demand that an individual meet expectations for collaboration is challenging. Most of the behavior that shuts down effective collaboration goes underground when an administrator is present. Therefore, if leaders notice even one example of community-damaging behavior, for example at a faculty meeting, a quick, individual oral follow-up "I noticed..." is in order. Do not wait to communicate expectations about change in a specific behavior until you have collected volumes of data about a pattern. You want an individual to have the opportunity to change. If you are a new administrator, marginal collaborators will test the limits early in your tenure. Notice and respond early so that there are no secrets about standards of performance (see Legal Note 12.1). Waiting to communicate gives rise to legitimate claims of withholding information and does nothing to induce a willing, thoughtful, and permanent shift in behavior from inappropriate or ineffective to appropriate, effective, and productive.

Using a Three-Step Process

Ken Chapman, an experienced principal and longtime consultant for Research for Better Teaching, recommends a three-step strategy for dealing with compliance problems. His approach allows a leader to address substandard professional behavior at a relatively non-threatening level and then escalate the response if an initial verbal interaction does result in the necessary change. To help make the process concrete, we will outline the steps and illustrate how those steps might be applied to three different performance concerns: not adhering to contract provisions and administrative policies, failure to implement school-wide agreements about common instructional practices, and unprofessional behavior characterized by a violation of group norms. As you review the steps that follow and the model communications, keep the following essentials in mind:

- Before you begin to confront an unmet expectation, decide whether you may eventually need to use the evidence of interactions as part of a performance evaluation. If you have any indicators that the problem may not be resolved immediately or that the individual may backslide into old, unproductive habits, exercise the option to put a record of your interactions in writing at every stage.

- Make sure that your response is appropriate for the severity of the problem. Nothing precludes the administrator from skipping earlier stages and moving directly to Step 3 if the problem at hand merits that approach.

- Written records of interactions can be placed in two different kinds of files: an unofficial memory aid file you keep in your office to help you recall what has happened and what informal agreements have been made, or the official personnel file. There are usually a number of procedural requirements governing how items may be placed in an official personnel file. Most contracts, for example, require that teachers sign and date any material that is included in a personnel file to indicate they have seen it. Know and follow those requirements carefully.

First Meeting: Communicate a Concern and Collect Data

The purpose of this first step is to make the school or school district's policies and expectations absolutely clear, to be as specific as possible about the supervisor's concern(s), and to uncover any confusions or misconceptions the staff member may have about how to meet those expectations. Minimize power struggles by focusing on the policy or performance standard that is most relevant to the concern. At this step the problem can be stated as facts or as a perception that may or may not be accurate but has arisen from certain actions the individual has taken. Avoid beginning with idle chat or a series of social niceties that will later make the staff member feel that he or she was manipulated. Be clear and straightforward in establishing why you are together and what the goal is. You might say something like "The purpose of this meeting is to make sure you are aware of a (concern that I have), (a potential problem), (a perception), to get some additional data about what is happening and why from you, and to make sure that the school (or district's) expectations are clear." You do not need to create a formal document for a personnel file at this stage, but it always wise to draft a short summary email or a dated set of meeting notes that provide a record of what you and the staff member discussed and what you agreed to do as next steps. You may later want to use this meeting as part of evidence for further action. At a minimum you need a record in the files that you use to support your own memory that you spoke to teacher X about your concerns and that you communicated your expectations.

MODELS FOR FIRST MEETING

Concern A: Indirect information suggesting that someone may not be adhering to an administrative policy

"It has come to my attention that you may have been leaving school earlier than the contract permits on grade level curriculum workshop days. In case this is true, I want to clarify the school committee policy and contract provisions that govern end times on those days."

Note that the teacher may deny the policy breech. Remember, you do not claim firsthand knowledge that it has occurred but are trying to be sure that there are no misunderstandings and that requirements are clear. Remind the individual that this is not presently part of any record or part of their evaluation. The conversation is about "If ... then."

Concern B: Evidence that the individual is not complying with a published school agreement about instructional practice

"In three walks through your classroom, I have not seen the learning goal and curriculum standard posted on your board. As you know, we made a school-wide agreement to do so (cite common agreement) because it helps our students to have more focus on what they are learning. What steps will you be taking to address this gap?" (Note that you are inviting the teacher to make a commitment.)

Concern C: Direct observation that the person is not adhering to supervisor expectations for professional behavior and is violating an established group norm

"During the Nov. 11th release-day workshop on benchmark assessments, I noticed that you: were 20 minutes late in the morning without any explanation, took cell phone calls at least four different times despite our policy that personal calls should take place only at breaks, did not sit with your team initially until I asked you to move, and did not join your team for lunch even though you had all agreed to having a working lunch and ending early. As a result, your team did not benefit from your full participation and contribution to this important topic and did not get the message that you were ready to carry your share of the work. We need every member of the community fully intellectually engaged with the design of these assessments and ready to use them effectively next semester. How can I assist you in honoring the team norm of "everyone present, engaged, and contributing at all times?"

Note that in a case such as this, the individual may claim the behavior was the result of a personal crisis. In that case, the conversation broadens to include how one communicates with a team in the rare instance that s/he cannot (temporarily) help with the work.

The first meeting of the three-step process is built on the positive presupposition that the staff member is a person of good will and good intent who, having been made aware of a problem, will fix it by stopping the inappropriate behavior and starting the requested behavior. Thus the first meeting ends with a combination of a summary of the expectation and an inquiry about how the teacher can be supported or what the teacher plans to do. Because the supervisor is responsible for making sure policies are carried out, there is an unspoken understanding that s/he will look for evidence that problem is solved satisfactorily and will not happen again. Both parties generally behave as if they assume there will be no further issue. Sometimes that assumption is justified. The communication is clear; the matter is resolved; and no further action is necessary. However, in cases where the behavior has been longstanding and unchecked, where the individual is not particularly self-aware, or where no one believes that a supervisor is serious, step two may be necessary.

LEADER ALERT

Stop Nit Picking Do not squander your credibility on minor adjustments, busywork, and tidiness, often referred to as "nit picking." Make sure your requests to honor agreements focus first on practices that are backed by research and can be clearly linked to student learning gains. If you have done a good job of offering the research on how shared objectives and standards affect student learning, for example, then it is easier to counter complaints that you are being controlling about something trivial. Expect to hear "Whatever happened to creativity?" at some point and plan ahead about how to link creativity to the requested action.

Second Meeting: Formalize Assessment

If there is no improvement after a reasonable period of time, conduct a second meeting.[2] Restate the standard and your concern, cite the data, and indicate that you will be assessing progress formally. Tell the teacher what kind of data you will be collecting and what data you would like him or her to provide you as evidence for improvement. Focus the data on the behavior and the effects on the culture. Be as specific as you can.

After the second meeting to communicate the concern and the formal monitoring to be instituted, write a detailed summary that documents the interaction with the teacher. Send the individual the summary, and ask him/her to sign and date the summary to indicate that it has been received and read. Here you must make a decision about where to house the sum-

---

[2]Some matters are either concrete enough (punctuality) or easy enough to fix quickly (no use of videos on Friday afternoon) that change should be immediate. If a teacher is learning to master a new technique or internalize a new routine, the administrator may allow 4 to 6 weeks for compliance to be complete.

MODELS FOR SECOND MEETING

Concern A: Not meeting an administrative policy

"I met with you three weeks ago and reminded you of our school expectation regarding full attendance at team meetings, workshop sessions, and curriculum days. By asking why your name was not on the sign-in sheet,[3] I learned you were 15 minutes late for a period 6 team meeting on 11/20. I also have a note from Mrs. D (the school secretary) that you asked her to let me know you had to leave the curriculum session a half hour early yesterday. In both cases you were present only two-thirds of the time. That is not acceptable. I will now be asking team leaders to have members initial the attendance logs at the end of meetings as well as signing in at the beginning. I am also requiring you to put any request to deviate from contract hours in writing to me and to obtain a written okay from me before you modify your leaving time in any way."

Concern B: Not complying with a published school agreement about instructional practice

"We met a few weeks ago about your apparent failure to comply with our school-wide agreement to communicate learning goals and standards orally and in writing every day. I have seen only one adherence to this agreement on 2/18. On my other visits (1/20, 2/05, 3/05) there was no posted evidence of lesson goals or relevant standards, that information was not in your plan book, and you had not communicated the information orally to students because you 'didn't think you had to tell them again' after going over the goals at the start of the week. Students need the communication to help them understand what they are to accomplish at each lesson and how ideas go together. I expect you to begin posting and communicating goals next Monday and to be consistent in this behavior every day. Please design some kind of log, visual, or check-off that will help you remember and let me see it by the end of the week. I will also visit randomly to monitor the regularity of this communication."

Concern C: Not meeting expectations for professional behavior by violating group norms

"When I dropped by your March 5th team meeting, I observed that you were not focused on the design work. Instead you were reading the sports pages and occasionally looking at your PDA. When you noticed my presence and put away the paper, you had to look on with a colleague because you had not brought any of the materials the team was using with you. At the start of the year, you signed off on the team norms that include 'everyone present, engaged, and contributing at all times.' We have discussed the message that off-task behavior sends and your obligation to be a contributing member of your team. I am asking you to behave in ways that demonstrate you understand and honor that norm. Please let me know what steps you are taking to meet that expectation and ways I, or others, might support you in staying focused and on task. Plan to provide evidence of your contribution to the assessments that shows how you have been honoring that norm when we meet in three weeks."

---

[3]If you have had a history of attendance issues, plan ahead to collect data on attendance regularly for all groups so that you can avoid charges of individual harassment.

LEGAL NOTE 12.1

Confidentiality and Notice

Never guarantee confidentiality to an informant unless you are certain that you can provide other direct supporting evidence. You may be able to withhold the identity of the informant who provided you with the information initially, but if the case proceeds to the discovery phase of litigation, you will not be able to prove your claims without persuasive testimonial and/or physical evidence. In the context of evaluating employee performance, most contracts and evaluation procedures require that all personnel action must be based on documented information that has been communicated with the employee involved. Good practice suggests that this be at the earliest point at which the supervisor begins to think that s/he may rely upon it as part of the data used to reach the factual claims made in an unsatisfactory evaluation report or as the basis for disciplinary action.

LEADER ALERT

Do not personalize the request for compliance. Don't say "Its important to me that..." or " I want you to..." Keep the focus on standards as an external reference, not on what you, the supervisor, want.[4] Emphasize that the concern is about patterns of behavior, not single events except for cases of "conduct unbecoming." Whatever the initial problem, focus on the teacher's failure to alter behavior in spite of feedback. Leaders are looking for indicators that an individual has learned as a result of clear feedback and support for change.

mary. If you have followed procedures required to put something into the personnel file, you can always choose that more formal and high-intensity step. Or, if you think the progress is being made, you may elect a more moderate approach and place the summary in your personal memory aid file to help you keep track of what you have talked about and accomplished so far. Whichever course you choose, make sure the teacher has seen the document.

Third Meeting: Conference and Document

If the problem has not been satisfactorily resolved by a complete change to the requested behavior, conduct a third meeting and write it up for the personnel file. The third conference is directive with no remaining semblance of invitation or inquiry. Over time, you have collected data about problematic patterns of behavior that have not been changed in spite of the clear feedback the individual has received. You refer to the records from your memory aid or "Meeting Notes" file and escalate the communication in order to eliminate all competing interpretations about compliance. During this third conference you:

- Reframe the concern more emphatically as a serious problem, i.e., a gap in performance on an identified district standard over time.
- Elaborate on your explanation of the negative impact on students or colleagues that is a consequence of the individual's action. Cite any available data that support the explanation.
- Note an additional problem: the failure to comply after two distinct requests to do so.

Put together a short, three-part follow-up memo that should include the following elements:

[4]Standards include: state standards; local district contractual policies; and school-identified curriculum priorities, agreements, and norms.

1. **What you communicated in the conference.** Summarize information that was presented and, if necessary, identify the information as hearsay *as long as it can be supported by other direct evidence.*[5] You can use information passed to you orally or in writing by someone who wishes to remain anonymous, but you might need to word this in terms of general patterns to avoid breaching confidentiality.

2. **The individual's response.** Quote when appropriate. Summarize the information provided by the teacher and include any post-conference written responses by the teacher.

3. **A restatement of the standard** and the required expectations for future behavior. If the information is factual and easily documented, then you can identify what might happen as a result of this incident or what the staff member can expect should it happen again.

If the information is not easily documented or the staff member has denied the situation as an incorrect representation of what happened, then you state the standards and expectations around this behavior and identify what would happen should this behavior ever occur (being careful to use words that maintain the behavior is only an allegation).

Note: Include a sign off using the exact language of your contract, usually located on the final page of evaluation document. "I have read..." language does not signify agreement.

MODELS FOR THIRD MEETING AND DOCUMENTATION

Concern A: Not meeting an administrative policy

"On January 30, we had a third meeting to discuss your repeated failure to adhere to the attendance criteria under Standard 6 Professional Responsibilities. When we met on this issue November 29th, you stated that you understood and would adhere to the attendance policy and standard although you did not agree that they were necessary. Sign-in sheets for December and the first three weeks of January show that you were more than 10 minutes late to three team meetings, did not initial that you were present at the end of one meeting, and asked me to leave 30 minutes early on Jan 12th. Your pattern of not being on time and available for a full work session adversely impacts the efficiency of the team as it tries to solve student learning problems. At the January 30th meeting you told me, 'You are nitpicking and out to get me, and we need to cut down on the number of meetings.' I told you that I expect you to adhere to the attendance policy and that if you had a competing obligation that might interfere with your attendance, to please check with me first. If you continue the pattern of lateness and early leaving, your evaluation will indicate that your performance does not meet Standard 6 Professional Responsibilities."

---

[5]There is much misunderstanding about hearsay evidence. In legal circles, *hearsay* means A says something to B, B makes a statement to C, and C testifies or reports information.

Concern B: Not complying with a published school agreement about instructional practice

"On March 31, we had our third meeting regarding your repeated failure to honor a collectively determined, school-wide agreement to post learning goals and standards for students every day. I told you that this behavior undermines our joint commitment to standardize some of our practices in order to develop more clarity and consistency for students. I further indicated that on at least three occasions (3/12, 3/22, 3/24) since our last discussion of this problem I did not see evidence of this practice.

You stated that 'I communicate orally and feel that it is unnecessary and redundant to post them.' Failure to post lesson goals daily creates a potential learning problem because students are not clear about the purpose of activities, have few guidelines with which to assess their own progress, and are less likely to be fully engaged. Your unwillingness to uphold collegial agreements to which you subscribed in September undermines team trust. I expect you to conform to this school-wide agreement and will be closely monitoring your compliance. Should you continue to fail to implement this collective agreement, you will not meet Standard 6 Professional Collaboration."

Concern C: Not meeting expectations for professional behavior by violating group norms

"This memo is to summarize our meeting of April 11th during which we discussed your ongoing difficulty with violations of your team norm of 'everyone present, engaged, and contributing at all times.' This was our third meeting on this problem. We discussed the fact that you have stopped correcting papers and reading during meetings. However your focus is still inadequate. During my 20-minute visits to design team sessions on March 12 and 26, you conducted 2- or 3-minute long, whispered off-task conversations several times or you stared into space while other members were revising assessments that your students will need to take next year. On April 1, you left the meeting for 20 minutes without telling anyone where you were going while others were working on comparing student responses and came back with food for yourself only. You told me, 'I find it difficult to sit through boring meetings, and I am not enjoying this assessment stuff. It's a waste of time.' I told you that this behavior sends a negative message regarding your investment in and commitment to improving students' learning. Because you are not fully focused and contributing, others on your team are being forced to pick up part of your share of the assessment design work. The team's need to regain your attention on a regular basis wastes time and effort and is beginning to cause resentment. I expect you to follow and visibly practice the norms of effective collaboration that you and your team members agreed to in October over the next six weeks. Failure to honor this norm will indicate that you do not meet Standard 6 in Professional Responsibilities."

The key to supervisory responses designed to produce compliance is clear communication about what to stop doing and what to start doing. If an individual cannot or does not comply with repeatedly communicated instructions, this behavior signals a failure to respond to written feedback as well as a failure to meet the standards that describe professional responsibilities and professional interactions. Records of the escalated communication can then be used to support a below-standard rating in a summative evaluation or in the case of serious problems such as abusive behavior in groups or bullying, to support assistance plans or moving an individual from a non-evaluation year in a cycle to an evaluation year.

Limitations of Compliance

In compliance-oriented interventions, administrators exercise their authority to mandate adherence to certain policies and practices or to demand cessation of detrimental behavior. Monitoring compliance is clear-cut as evaluators check off the presence or absence of identified behavior. Failure to comply can result in a charge of insubordination, in progressive discipline, or, at its most extreme, dismissal. As leaders, however, we want to create conditions that support learning, not just short-term compliance with mandates. Even when there is modest improvement through compliance, teachers often exhibit patterns of "backsliding" or returning to the original poor pattern of performance once supervisory attention is withdrawn.

Responding When the Goal Is Development

Many problems cannot be solved by compliance alone. Matching the response to a performance problem appropriately may mean that leaders need to begin with or move to Targeted Development or Assignment to Full Assistance.

Targeting Development Using a MiniPlan^{SM}

Most supervision and evaluation systems contain provisions that enable an administrator to monitor the work of beginning teachers and respond rapidly if there are problems. However the same flexibility and timeliness is not always available when tenured teachers struggle. Administrators frequently tell us how cumbersome and unresponsive the assistance timelines and processes of formal evaluation systems can be when a teacher needs immediate help. Next year's students might possibly benefit from the teacher's being placed in the Formal Assistance track of an evaluation system, but this year's students will languish. Because of the high level of investment required of evaluators, full assistance plans are rarely employed. Our surveys indicate that less than 2 percent of teachers are placed in formal assistance and go through a process of formal improvement planning. When the process is used, it is often in cases of documentation for dismissal. A small number of districts have Peer Assistance and Review (PAR) programs that partially fill this gap, but even these districts have large number of low-performing teachers who are never identified for assistance.[6] In places that do not have short-term improvement provision, creating a MiniPlan[SM] can help.

A MiniPlan[SM] is a small-scale, on-the-spot way to target improvement in one particular area of performance or in a standard about which an evaluator has significant concern. It is a way of organizing effort to provide help without having to go through the full-blown procedures of formal assistance. MiniPlans[SM] are structured so that administrators must clearly define the problem(s) first before any solutions are proposed and provide time for teachers to respond to those problems before proceeding to developing joint solutions. They can be vehicles for communicating clearly about gaps in performance, providing realistic improvement targets with support, and enlisting teachers to own their improvement.

LEADER ALERT

MiniPlans,[SM] Past Practice, and Contractual Obligations Almost all districts have some contractually negotiated improvement plans that may resemble the MiniPlan.[SM] You need to be clear that you are not creating a new vehicle that needs to be bargained. Do not announce a change in practice by referring to MiniPlans.[SM] You are simply implementing higher quality practices associated with making recommendations, allowed in all evaluation instruments. Keep in mind the MiniPlan[SM] process asks teachers to be participants in their own improvement. If an individual refuses to be actively involved then the next step is likely to be assignment to a full assistance plan. If you have any doubt about how to deal with a staff member's behavior, check with your personnel office and/or labor attorney.

Enlisting Ownership for the MiniPlanning Process

We have found that a major factor in achieving sustained change in performance is teachers' willingness to accept responsibility for problems and to become engaged participants in designing and carrying out a change strategy. When the goal is to help individuals learn new behaviors, leaders need to pay attention to the forces that impact motivation and work to enlist ownership. Strategies for enlisting ownership include the following:

- **Persuade individuals that there is some risk in change but a higher risk in not changing.** Robert Evans in *The Human Side of School*

---

[6]In our Skillful Leader training, estimates of underperforming teachers range up to 50 percent in some districts. Virtually none are covered with intensive intervention structures. In two Skillful Leader Training districts with performance evaluations that have middle categories of judgment such as "Meets Standards with Reservations," administrators have found the MiniPlan[SM] to be a small-scale structure to meet the needs of these middle performing teachers.

Change summarizes the communication challenge.[7] "The leader must convey two essential, contrasting messages. The first is 'this is very serious, the risks of inaction are very real and we must change.' The second is 'I value you, and I will help you get where we need to go'" (57).

- **Balance communicating the data and the gaps with reducing the threat level.** Patterson et al. caution: "At the very first sign of fear, you have to diagnose. Are others feeling disrespected? Or do they believe you're at cross-purposes? Or both? Then you have to find a way to let others know that you respect them and that you're not going to trample all over their wishes" (2005 92).

- **If the teacher is resistant, try to surface reasons for resistance, attribute good intentions, and don't take reactions personally.** We often react defensively to teacher responses. Evans (1997) explains that "Their natural aversion to change is intensified by three factors: their stage of life, their stage of career and what demographers would call their 'cohort factor' their unique composition as a group and their unique historical context in which they have worked." We need to get behind the responses.

- **Distinguish between the "tents."** There is a difference between the content of a person's behavior and the intent. Describe the behavior but do nor interpret or judge. Always assume good intent.

- **Establish mutual purpose.** Before detailing problems, affirm common purpose: your goal is to solve problems and make things better for both of you. Try to find what is important to them—not just to you (Patterson 2005 96).

- **Invite the teacher to tell his or her story.** Even as you communicate data and the problems, invite the teacher to tell you what you do not know.

- **Communicate clearly that your overarching goal is to support adaptive change rather than technical compliance.** Acknowledge that you cannot force "changes of heart" (Heifetz and Linsky).

- **Focus on consequences of behavior.** "Your primary job is to [make the invisible visible by helping] others see consequences they aren't seeing (or remembering) on their own" (Patterson 2005 127). This means helping the teacher to connect the identified performance gaps with their impact on students or colleagues.

MiniPlan[SM] Process

The nature of the performance gaps to be addressed may vary as will the resources supervisors and teacher can tap into for expertise and support.

---

[7]Evans introduces an interesting concept about balancing effort. "Unfreezing is a matter of lessening one kind of anxiety, the fear of trying, but first of mobilizing another kind of anxiety, the fear of not trying. Unless something increases the cost of preserving the status quo, the conservative impulse and the cumulative impact of culture and past learning are too strong to prevent innovation.... The change agent must make clear his caring and support, his commitment to working with people to take the difficult steps toward new learning" (57).

However the process and components of the plan remain the same. To respond to a performance concern by targeting an area for development with a MiniPlan,[SM] the evaluator must:

- Identify the standard(s) that has not been met
- Define the problem using relevant data

Identification of the standard at issue is non-negotiable and determined only by the evaluator. All subsequent statements of the performance problem and activities to solve it must be logically aligned to the identified standard. Problem statements are developed by the evaluator and communicated to the teacher. They are also non-negotiable. Write a one- or two-sentence statement that names the gap between the desired performance to meet standard and the present performance. Cite the data that support the assessment of present performance. End with a statement of actual (if observed) or likely impact on student learning if the performance problem is not solved. The last piece establishes the relevance of the concern beyond mere compliance with authority.

Once the problem or gap in performance is clearly defined, the teacher and evaluator should collaborate as much as possible to:

- Select and develop goals
- Select action steps
- Determine data to be collected
- Agree on indicators for success

The goal-setting step is critical to enlist ownership and create a sense of responsibility. It is likely to involve several drafts. Work together to break the problem down into a set of specific, measurable outcomes that, if achieved, would enable the individual to meet the performance standard. Next, identify three to five action steps that specify who is responsible and when actions will be completed. For teachers to have any sense of commitment to the work expected of them, they must be involved in designing the ways in which they will improve their performance. A MiniPlan[SM] may include some compliance-type actions such as "at least four classes a week will end with a summary that asks students to produce something" to help an individual get started and show that s/he is exerting appropriate effort. However, the purpose of the plan is to help teachers develop the capacity to meet a standard independently, not to follow a highly prescribed set of steps outlined by a person in authority. Joint work on the data step is equally critical. Data collected or produced by the teacher should show both what the teacher did and how well students learned. If the goal involves teamwork or collaboration, the data should capture the effect that the teachers' work has had on the success of his or her team. Together decide what evidence might best illustrate that a teacher has improved his or her instruction or collaboration. Evidence might, for example, include pre-post student essays, learning logs, creation of and results on new pre-assessments, or end-of-class summaries. In order to increase ownership and responsibility, the teacher should be responsible for formulating and collecting much of the data. Finally, both parties should agree in advance on what criteria would indicate satisfactory progress toward the goal. Indicators should focus on changes in performance and impact rather than on checking off items on a list of "things the supervisor told me to do."

Ultimately the evaluator must determine whether improvement is sufficient for a rating of meets standards. On an agreed-upon timetable, the evaluator assesses whether the teacher meets the goal and thus can rejoin the regular supervisory cycle or still needs more progress. If the latter is the case, then a decision must be made to revise and continue the MiniPlan^SM the following year or refer the individual to the contractually designated formal assistance process.

TIPS ON PREPARING FOR THE MINIPLAN^SM CONFERENCE

✔ **Write out the conference objective(s).** You can read these to the teacher or put them on an agenda. Make sure the conference outcomes are ones you can control. For example you might say, "The objectives of this conference are to clearly communicate some gaps in performance, listen to your thoughts, and invite you to be a participant in your improvement." You would not say, "The objective of this conference is to have you leave feeling good about our opportunity to work together to help you improve" because you cannot control that outcome!

✔ **Anticipate possible negative responses.** Anticipating teacher reactions allows you to be more confident if the teacher tries to divert you from the intended message. Typical distraction strategies might include seeking sympathy and pity, saying yes to anything the person in authority offers, sidetracking and interrupting, or attacking the evaluator's credibility or integrity. Think about how to restate your key message calmly and with assurances that the individual will have support as s/he goes about making the important changes.

✔ **Figure out where and how you can invite the teacher to participate in the planning.** The evaluator's role is to clearly define gaps between present and necessary performance but also to enlist the teacher's active participation in designing ways to close that gap whenever possible. If the teacher refuses to participate in the formulation of the MiniPlan^SM, write and implement the plan anyway.

✔ **Keep the length of initial conference short (30 minutes).** Focus on communicating data and problems and inviting the teacher to respond by participating in goal setting. Extend the meeting into problem solving only if the teacher agrees to engage with the process.

✔ **Structure the message.** Decide how directive you will be initially and how you will escalate communication about the seriousness of the problem, if necessary.

At the end of the meeting, ask the teacher to summarize what s/he has heard and to state his or her willingness to participate in subsequent planning. Set a date and time to meet again. Avoid the urge to create a happy ending by downplaying the seriousness of the issue, but do end with statement of confidence and support such as "I have real confidence that you can address these concerns. Please let me know if there are any impediments I can help you with." Write up a conference summary focusing on the teacher's willingness to engage in planning.

To illustrate an example of a MiniPlan[SM], we return to the case of Shirley Temple Block cited in Chapter 9. Shirley actively undermines her team and reduces the group's capacity to carry out protocols intended to help teachers analyze errors and design re-teaching experiences for students who are below standard. Using Compliance Intervention is a poor match; mandating behavior is not likely to produce high-quality participation. Shirley needs to change the way she thinks about her job and her responsibilities to her team in addition to changing her behaviors. Thus a better intervention might be the development-oriented MiniPlan[SM]. The following example is tailored to Shirley's case but can also serve as a model for any professional development intervention.

MODEL MINIPLAN[SM] FOR SHIRLEY BLOCK FEBRUARY 26, 2008

Standard to be Improved—Contribution to Community: "Teachers are members of learning communities. Accomplished teachers contribute to the effectiveness of the entire school by working collaboratively with other professionals on instructional policy, curriculum development, and staff development" (National Board Certification Core Proposition 4 www.nbpts.org).

Problem: Shirley Block does not meet Standard 6 Contribution to Community because she does not contribute to the effectiveness of her grade level team. During grade level and curriculum meetings, Ms. Block behaves in ways that undermine the group's ability to agree upon and implement instructional changes that would help struggling students. Non-contributing behaviors include dismissive responses to colleague's ideas, labeling any proposal for change as unworkable without offering alternatives, using non-verbal communication to indicate displeasure and disapproval when team members suggest giving students extra time or support (see memos dated 12/1 and 2/5), and informing team members that she has "too many other pressing concerns" to be able to take her turn at leading the bi-monthly error analysis sessions. As a result, the team cannot operate efficiently to support student learning.

Goal: Ms. Block has agreed that she will participate positively and substantively in her team's problem-solving and error analysis sessions, increase the number of proactive as opposed to reactive contributions that she makes during problem-solving, and assume her fair share of leadership responsibilities within the team. She has agreed to the following jointly developed action steps.

Action Step 1: Ms. Block will monitor her verbal interactions in order to understand what events trigger an automatic negative response. She will start a journal listing both the specific incidents when she is able to resist making a negative comment and the incidents when she makes a positive, proactive contribution to the team (by March 1).

Data Collected and Processed: The journal will be presented to the principal every four weeks.

Indicators of Success: Three or four dated entries per month with concrete examples of supportive action, and oral or written reflection on how those contributions have helped the team make progress on their goal of improving student performance.

Action Step 2: Principal observes team meeting (by March 15) and analyzes findings with Ms. Block.

Data Collected/Processed: Principal collects data on entire team, including Ms. Block's interactions with and contributions to the team.

Indicators of Success: Examples of positive, proactive contributions to problem-solving; reduction in the number of non-verbal signals of displeasure or disapproval; offers of support for initiatives when appropriate; and evidence of the four P's, pausing, paraphrasing, probing for specificity, and putting ideas on the table (Garmston and Wellman).

Action Step 3: Ms. Block will assume and effectively carry out her share of the rotating leadership roles—including facilitator, recorder, and norm checker—that the team has agreed to have in place at all meetings this year (by April 14).

Data Collected and Processed: After carrying out each responsibility, Ms. Block will ask a colleague or two for feedback, self-assess performance, and then be prepared to summarize "how I did, what I learned, how I could improve."

Indicators of Success: All leadership obligations that arise during the normal rotation of tasks will be carried out using guidelines established by the team. Ms. Block will record what she has learned from the experience in her journal and set goals for further growth.

Summary Assessment (written after implemention): June 4, 2008 Principal and teacher met June 1 to assess the data and indicators, and the principal determined that Ms. Block has not yet met the standard. The teacher agreed to continue working on the plan for the fall semester. Progress will be assessed by November 1, and if the teacher has not yet met standard, she will be placed on the (Tier 3) Improvement Plan at midyear.

The MiniPlan^{SM} is a response to ineffective or inefficient behavior that is designed to enlist ownership for focused, concrete improvement that goes beyond simple compliance with mandated procedures. It can be an alternative or a precursor to placing a teacher into the formal assistance category of an evaluation system and a way to assess whether the teacher, with feedback and structure, can take charge of his or her own improvement. The ongoing process of planning, implementing, reflecting on the data collected, and making additional plans can be a good match for individuals who already have a reasonable skill base but have become stuck in unproductive patterns. For such individuals, the process increases the likelihood that the changes in performance will be self-sustaining and ongoing.

The Skillful Leader II

Remediation Plans

"Remediation plans establish a pattern of progressive discipline and demonstrate that teachers have received due process. By establishing clear expectations and criteria for assessing improvements in performance, a district enhances its chances of sustaining a subsequent action to dismiss a teacher. Of course, these provisions also require a district to follow the procedures set forth in the remediation plan and fulfill its part of the bargain. This could create grounds for overturning a dismissal action if an arbitrator determined that the district did not meet its obligations." Source: Ballou Teacher Contracts in Massachusetts 2000, Pioneer Institute for Public Policy.

Responding with Assignment to Formal Assistance

Time-starved and hassle-shy supervisors rarely identify teachers for formal improvement plans even though such plans are usually intended to clarify expectations and help struggling teachers make changes. Those teachers who do get placed in the formal assistance category of an evaluation system are typically low performers who have not been able or willing to make changes in response to previous supervisory requests and guidelines. Because performance issues are usually so dire, the plans (variously labeled remediation, improvement, or assistance) tend to become as much documentation for dismissal as "improvement" initiatives.

When is formal assistance the most appropriate route to confronting unmet expectations, violated agreements, and unprofessional behavior? We think the skillful use of compliance and development-oriented interventions (the MiniPlan^{SM}) can help mediocre performers improve in the specific, carefully defined areas those approaches address. But remember that mediocrity is not a fixed state. The more intelligent and capable the rest of the organization becomes, the worse the mediocre performance looks. If a teacher has failed to improve under favorable conditions, s/he may in fact be worse than mediocre. We might think of the MiniPlan^{SM} as a situational test. With feedback, support, resources, and some measure of accountability, it tests whether the teacher can improve. Sometimes because of capacity or motivation, sufficient improvement does not occur. At that point the contractually designated or district-sanctioned formal improvement plan is needed to send a clear signal to the teacher that s/he must improve or face possible termination. Documented earlier efforts ranging from conference summaries to a MiniPlan^{SM} then become part of the evidence to show that the teacher has been offered opportunities to improve and support for improvement. Our hope is always that the teacher can and will improve to the point where s/he is providing high-quality instruction for students and is a contributing member of a professional community. However, we have expanded the meaning of a satisfactory result to include departure—either voluntarily or through dismissal—if students are not receiving the teaching they need in order to achieve at high levels. Referral to formal assistance requires thorough knowledge of evaluation regulations, contract provisions, and district policies. Following the correct procedures is critical because this type of red-zone response requires the most extensive documentation and carries the greatest potential for procedural slip-ups that could sidetrack a case. Readers wishing to have more detail about strategies for dealing with Formal Assistance plans should consult *The Skillful Leader I: Confronting Mediocre Teaching*.

Summary

This chapter offers a framework for leaders to use in thinking about how they respond to unprofessional or ineffective behavior. The strategies we describe are intended to help supervisors respond clearly, efficiently, and respectfully with a demand for improvement. The models demonstrate the ways in which different types of responses can be used to address behavior that undermines the work of professional communities.

13 Influencing Contracts and Collective Bargaining

We end this book as we began it—with a closer look at institutional conditions worth changing, and the capacities we need to make such changes. Skillful leaders and high-functioning professional communities need three essential capacities to take on the messy problem of institutionalized mediocrity: Conviction, Competence and Control. Most of the strategies in this book are designed to help address the first two. Even when they are motivated by powerful convictions and competently equipped with the requisite knowledge and skills, however, teachers and leaders can be blocked from taking important steps to help students. Hardworking, accountable professional communities can be prevented from implementing carefully crafted plans. Contract provisions, bargained agreements about supervision and evaluation, and practices established by precedent or informal understanding all become impediments to improving achievement if they are outdated, misused, or misunderstood. When we are taking on the messy problem of institutionalized mediocrity, these factors all affect our third capacity, Control.

At the school level, Control refers to the processes, structures, and resources people need to do their work. At the institutional level, Control is affected by a hodgepodge of laws, regulations, and contracts that directly or indirectly affect opportunities to improve student and adult learning such as:

- The length of the duty day
- The number, frequency, and duration of meetings teachers may be asked to attend
- Whether someone can be required to attend training
- Whether an individual with seniority and poor evaluations can bump a person with less seniority and excellent reviews out of a job
- Whether information about the results of instruction can be included as part of employee evaluation

To escape from the limitations of bureaucratic regulations and to have the ability to make independent decisions about working conditions, staffing, and professional development are often-cited reasons for creating charter schools. But relatively few public school educators choose that route. Most must seek to influence Control by working within or around the present system.

In this chapter we sample opportunities to shape the legally governed aspects of leaders' work by looking at three categories: (1) influencing negotiated work conditions, (2) influencing performance standards and criteria, and (3) influencing systems that affect teaching quality. Under work conditions, we will consider the effects of collective bargaining. As part of standards and criteria we will examine the role of student performance data.

Influencing Negotiated Work Conditions

A growing body of literature[1] is highly critical of the impact public sector collective bargaining laws and locally negotiated contracts have had on efforts to reform and improve public education. Limitations cited include:

- The inability to use time flexibly to support collaboration or to modify the length of the duty day

- Restrictions on staffing that block districts' attempts to place the most skilled teachers with the most needy students

- Seniority and transfer provisions that make it extremely difficult to fill vacancies, distribute leadership opportunities, or retain high-quality new teachers

Contract language that hinders reform efforts is most commonly found in the clauses that fall under the general heading of restrictive work rules. For example, a provision such as "there can be only one required faculty meeting per month, which shall not exceed 60 minutes immediately following the dismissal of pupils" illustrates how efforts to create high-functioning communities with shared goals might be undermined. The fact that many contracts allow for department meetings at the secondary level but few contemplate or even allow for grade level team meetings at the elementary level is another example. It is easy to blame unions for such provisions, but unions did not deliberately set out to have an adverse impact upon education reform. Becoming an obstacle to changing practices in public schools was an unintended consequence of well-meaning social policy and legitimate union objectives.

---

[1]For a sampling of what is being said, see *Teacher Contracts: Restoring the Balance*, 3 vols. (2005-2007); *A Better Bargain*, (2006); and *Collective Bargaining in Education: Negotiating Change in Today's Schools*, (2006).

Prior to collective bargaining in public education, the primary forces that regulated what happened in schools were state laws and regulations, local politics, and economic constraints. Starting in the early 1960s teacher organizations successfully lobbied for the passage of public sector collective bargaining laws patterned after the type of private sector industrial models that developed in factory environments in the late 19th and early 20th centuries. The goal of teacher unions was to improve the lot of their membership through advocacy for uniform working conditions. However, the underlying assumption that a parallel could be drawn between teachers and factory workers was false. All roles in schools except for those of administrators are not exactly the same. Moreover, factory workers were not expected to exercise the kind of independent professional judgment in performing their work that teachers are required to do almost every minute of every workday.

Collective bargaining laws require employers to negotiate in "good faith" with unions representing their employees over wages, hours, and other terms and conditions of employment. Over the years, the term *conditions of employment* has been defined and interpreted by courts, arbitrators, and administrative agencies to include almost anything and everything in the workplace setting. Topics have ranged from obvious subjects such as health insurance and layoffs to decisions by school boards to raise the price of faculty lunches and to regulate how employees can be supervised and evaluated. There are dramatic differences between what state laws and cases have determined to be mandatory subjects for collective bargaining from state to state. Class size and/or teacher evaluation may be mandatory subjects in one jurisdiction, such as Massachusetts, while they need not be negotiated at all in a state such as Texas. Even the language of "No Child Left Behind" with its myriad of mandates and lofty goals puts the brakes on improvement when its requirements run up against the constraints imposed by state collective bargaining laws and local collective bargaining agreements.

(d) CONSTRUCTION – Nothing in this section shall be construed to alter or otherwise affect the rights, remedies, and procedures afforded school or school district employees under Federal, State or local laws (including applicable regulations or court orders) or **under the terms of collective bargaining agreements, memoranda of understanding, or other agreements between such employees and their employers.** [emphasis added][2]

This deference to the collective bargaining process should remind administrators, especially principals, of the importance of knowing and understanding the provisions of local collective bargaining agreements.

School districts sometimes fail to help local school leaders get the control they need because they do not invest adequate time and attention to training and to checking that administrators understand their obligations, how to carry them out, and what to do when they wish to institute a change in a condition that has been affected by collective bargaining. Early in your administrative career, make it a point to learn about your state's public

[2]See: Pub. Law 107-110 (Jan. 8, 2002).

employee collective bargaining law. Then be sure to consult with your school district's labor counsel and Human Resources Director or Superintendent before you undertake to make changes in anything that is a lawful subject for collective bargaining in your state. Consider Case 13.1 as a cautionary tale.

CASE 13.1 **Making Unilateral Changes to Evaluation Procedures**

Principal Antonia Walker goes off to a workshop on teacher evaluation during which the presenter introduces a new technique called the "walkthrough," a brief unannounced visit to a classroom to gather data to be used along with other sources of information in writing up an observation report. Principal Walker agrees wholeheartedly with the presenter's assertion that a half dozen walkthroughs can often reveal a more accurate picture of what really goes on in the classroom on a daily basis than pre-announced visits. The next day she vows to put the idea into practice and to provide written feedback on what she sees. Imagine her surprise when she receives a grievance after the first series of walkthroughs are written up in an observation report. The grievance alleges that the practice of walkthroughs violates the contract language that requires that all observations of classroom performance must last for a full instructional period and must be preceded by a pre-conference and followed by a post-conference within five school days! Two weeks later, Dr. Walker receives notice of a "prohibitive labor practice charge" that has been filed with the state's labor relations agency. The charge alleges that she has unilaterally changed a previously established term and condition of employment by implementing a new evaluation practice without first formally notifying the union and bargaining over the impact of the change. Twelve months later, the labor board issues a cease and desist order that compels Dr. Walker and her whole school system to stop walkthroughs and to purge all information gathered during the time walkthroughs were used from the personnel files of all employees who were subjected to a walkthrough.

Case 13.1 is a cautionary tale because the implications of independent action taken by a well-meaning, but ill-informed, administrator can spread beyond the single school in which the action occurs. It is a scenario that can repeat itself over and over again if the union wants to stop the unilateral implementation of any change in the workplace that it alleges to be a change in working conditions. Skillful leaders regularly include workshops and reading on public sector labor relations as a part of their own professional development activities. Professional organizations such as the American Association of School Personnel Administrators and the Education Law Association offer a low-cost and convenient way to keep your knowledge base up-to-date.[3] See if your state has published a guide to its public sector collective bargaining law and contact your school district's counsel for some recommended readings that apply in your jurisdiction.[4]

In places where collective bargaining severely limits district autonomy, skillful union and management leaders seek to bring about changes in work conditions that they believe will have a positive change on student learning with a combination of different approaches that include:

- Collaborative awareness and study sessions that involve union and management members in genuine review of available research, options for action, experiences of other districts, and student achievement data long before any formal negotiation begins

- Collaborative union-management steering or implementation committees that review and evaluate how well certain current policies, procedures, and practices affecting work conditions are serving both students and teachers

- Focused, annual training and inter-rater reliability sessions for administrators that help to make sure that they are able to implement contract provisions fairly and effectively and that their actions do not undermine other efforts to build good working labor-management relationships

- Involvement of teacher members of leadership teams, steering committees, and study groups in presenting about, providing information on, or collecting teacher concerns about proposed changes in conditions

- Administrative team discussions that ask members to identify where or how present bargained restrictions on working conditions are having a negative impact on student learning and to think about a series of gradual steps to build trust and credibility for proposed changes

- Providing samples of new language and needed changes in legislation through involvement with state legislators and local political leadership

As the work of leaders from the Montgomery County (MD) Education Association (MCEA) (such as Bonnie Cullison and her predecessor Mark Simon) illustrates, unions can be powerful forces for change as well when they are partnered with far-sighted district leaders. Finding common ground on negotiated work conditions takes time, effort, and a compelling vision, but it is possible and exciting. Language from the most recent contract between the Montgomery County Public Schools (MCPS) and MCEA, for example, illustrates that the two value and intend to support collaboration as a critical condition of teachers' work. A contract article agrees to "maintain and expand the use of the Labor-Management Collaboration

---

[3]www.aaspa.org and www.educationlaw.org
[4]See: http://www.mass.gov/lrc/gb_toc.htm

Committee" whose overall charge goes beyond the task of "interpreting and administering the agreement" to include these provisions[5]:

- Encouraging individuals, offices, and committees to collaborate
- Creating an organizational expectation for collaboration
- Recommending supports and resources to sustain collaboration
- Serving as a coordinating body and as a resource to facilitate the use of collaboration throughout MCPS
- Reviewing and assessing the effectiveness of collaboration between MCPS and MCEA
- Establishing a process by which school-based collaborative decision-making teams could request contract waivers

This and similar examples of language affecting working conditions such as provisions that enable the district to complete its staffing sooner or to provide incentives that keep high-performing teachers in high-need schools are the result of more than ten years of carefully built understandings of what it will take for the district to meet its goals for students. The task has been difficult. However, rather than throwing up their hands and berating the laws that require them to bargain, these educators on both sides of the table have attempted to influence the content of bargaining in ways that benefit students as well as teachers.

Influencing Performance Standards and Criteria

Evaluation systems use a variety of terms to label the important components of a teacher or specialist's practice, including: propositions, components, elements, domains, principles, descriptors, indicators, standards, and criteria. Here we will use *standards* and *criteria*. By *standard* we mean a statement that identifies a broad category of performance essential for all teachers to master and use such as "Teachers know the subjects they teach and how to teach them to students."[6] By *criteria* we mean sub-categories that name and explain specific attributes of the standard. Criteria attempt to make the abstract standard more concrete. The actual terminology used for the performance expectation part of an evaluation system is less important than the underlying schema and the clarity of the content. A lawfully sound evalua-

[5]Source, *Agreement between Montgomery County Education Association And Board of Education of Montgomery County, Rockville Maryland for the School Years 2008 – 2010.*
[6]The National Board for Professional Teaching standards calls this statement a core proposition and develops specific subject area standards that elaborate on this core idea. Montgomery County Maryland Public Schools use the same wording as one of their six performance standards. (See www.mcps.k12.md.us/departments/personnel/teachereval/)

tion system must contain well-defined expectations that can be understood by evaluators who are responsible for communicating them to supervisees. It should also contain the indicators that help supervisors and teachers to determine whether—and how well—the articulated expectations have been met.

In our review of evaluation documents, we found great variation in levels of specificity about performance expectations ranging from vague topic labels like "Effective instruction" to categorical rubrics, to instruments with detailed indicators. We also found several problems that occur in the majority of systems and have significant implications for the amount of control a leader has.

1. Districts have spent too much time deciding what standards to adopt and too little time on developing indicators that would show evidence of the standards.
2. Published standards and criteria for professional collaboration are generally weak.
3. The idea that teaching practice should have an impact on student learning is missing entirely because districts are struggling with how to use student results data for teacher evaluation.

Each of these three problems is a potential area of influence for leaders seeking positive change.

Developing Indicators

If employees are to be held accountable for their effectiveness in groups, they must be informed about what the organization and therefore their supervisors expect. Indicators provide the "looks-like" and "sounds-like" examples of a standard or criteria in action. We found few districts that gave "life" to standards and criteria by providing clear examples of what students and teachers might be saying and doing if a standard were to be met. The Montgomery County Public Schools in Maryland and the Catalina Foothills District in Tucson, Arizona, are notable exceptions. Both used the National Board of Professional Teaching Standards as starting points in developing their own expectations for staff performance, and both allocated significant time to developing the indicators that would clarify what specific standards and criteria might look like in action. Montgomery County's indicators are divided into categories of "met" and "not met." Catalina Foothills chose to elaborate on the meaning of criteria by identifying indicators of teacher and student behavior and/or student outcomes that would result if teachers were in fact meeting the standard. Certainly some time was spent adapting the National Board Standards, but more effort was devoted to giving meaning to the standards by involving teachers in defining the indicators for meeting that standard. The following examples are excerpted by permission from the 2005 Teacher Assessment Program developed by the Catalina Foothills School District.

EXAMPLE Indicators to Explain Teacher Performance Standards from Catalina Foothills PS, Tucson, Arizona

Standard: Teachers are committed to students and their learning.
Criteria: Teachers hold students and themselves accountable for student learning.
Indicators: Teachers who hold students and themselves accountable for learning often:

- Analyze achievement data and make instructional decisions based on that data
- Collaborate with others to increase achievement for all students
- Set quantifiable learning outcomes for students
- Produce measurable growth in student achievement on system-wide accountability measures
- Provide prompt and specific feedback to students on their work and progress toward goals

Students served by these teachers:

- Request learning activities that are matched to their needs
- Approach faculty members for advice and assistance
- Can state and explain their learning outcomes
- Produce measurable gains on system-wide accountability measures
- Ask for and use teacher feedback to monitor and adjust learning

In this example, notice how a teacher performance standard can be made more concrete by adding indicators. The process of developing these indicators with teachers not only provides more ownership, it makes explicit what practices are associated with meeting the standard.

Supporting Collaboration

Evaluation language should define the district expectations for both excellent teaching and excellent professional collaboration. There is more to appreciate about a teacher's contributions to student learning than what the supervisor can observe during a single classroom visit. Skills at collectively planning, solving problems, and carrying out grade or department level curricula and assessment are becoming increasingly important for schools that are attempting to raise student achievement.[7] Teachers are jointly contributing hundreds of hours and valuable innovations to their schools' efforts to

[7]An Education Trust study reported in *Gaining Traction Gaining Ground* identified collaboration and cooperation as practices contributing to the effectiveness of new teachers who had had a high impact on struggling high school students. The real challenge comes in developing indicators of those characteristics or practices and finding ways to measure them that will be accepted by unions. (see www.edtrust.org)

close achievement gaps. However, many performance standards acknowledge only attendance at required meetings or "cooperation with the administration and colleagues" as behavior worthy of note.

In the example that follows, notice how the indicators spell out specific practices that could guide teachers in meeting the standard and supervisors in collecting data about collaboration.

EXAMPLE Standards, criteria and indicators to support collaboration from Catalina Foothills PS, Tucson, Arizona

Standard: Teachers are committed to continuous improvement and professional development.

Criteria: Teachers seek the advice of others and draw on current research to improve their practice.

Indicators: For example, these teachers:

- Participate in formal, informal, and peer feedback conversations by analyzing teacher and student behaviors and making appropriate comments, asking appropriate questions, and offering suggestions for improvement

- Modify instruction based on feedback from formal, informal, and peer observations

- Examine student work with colleagues to analyze and adjust instruction

- Analyze the success of efforts undertaken during the professional growth years of the cycle and initiate reflective conversations with peer and supervisory staff

Standard: The teacher exhibits a high degree of professionalism.

Criteria: Teachers contribute to schools' effectiveness by collaborating with other professionals to create strong programs.

Indicators: Teachers who enhance the effectiveness of the whole school are often known to:

- Participate in and /or take a leadership role in working with other teachers and administrators to analyze and construct curriculum and to plan the instructional program

- Engage in dialogue, problem solving, planning, or curricular improvement with other teachers in the same grade level or subject discipline within the school or across the district

- Participate in grade level or department level teams that meet regularly to examine and promote student learning

---

Administrative and union leaders who want to influence contractual language to support adult learning and collaboration should push for indicators that anchor understanding of how to meet the standard.

Using Student Outcomes

Almost all deliberations concerning evaluation standards and criteria involve the question of whether or how to use student data for teacher evaluation, but few districts have figured out ways to use results data effectively. Even states like Tennessee and Pennsylvania that are experimenting with statewide value-added models are not recommending their use for individual teacher evaluation. Teacher unions, understandably, are leery about allowing achievement data to be used in evaluating individual teachers, and many administrators lack the skill or will to push for it. Conviction and competence become increasingly important for both district and union leaders. At least some of the obstacles associated with using student results to make sense of teacher practice come from unchallenged misconceptions and exaggerated claims about implications. The goal is not "firing" a teacher because of poor test scores. The goal is identifying reasonable links between teacher decisions about practice and the effects of those decisions on learners. Most excellent teachers are already making those connections regularly for themselves as they go about planning their next steps.

Skillful leaders need to know what they are already allowed to think about and talk about with teachers but rarely do. For example, can you look at the work produced by a lesson together? Can you conference about how youngsters did on a unit test after you have watched those youngsters in action during a science lab? Do you? Can you ask the teacher to bring the results of her previous diagnostic assessments to a pre-conference? Do you? Most likely your existing evaluation criteria will already allow you to incorporate considerations of student outcomes unless the sources of data that you can rely upon in writing summative evaluation reports is specifically precluded or limited by your existing evaluation procedures and contracts.

In *Linking Teacher Evaluation and Student Learning*, Pam Tucker and Jim Stronge describe four case studies of districts trying different approaches to using student achievement data for evaluation. These approaches are:

1. **Work sample methodology.** Teachers present examples of their work as evidence of student learning. The focus is on documenting growth in learning.

2. **Standards-based models.** These use ten professional standards with emphasis on the student learning standard, "The school professional is responsible for increasing the probability of advancing student achievement."

3. **Student academic goal setting.** The staff focus goals on adding value to student academic progress rather than on their own professional accomplishments.

4. **Value-added assessment systems.** These are based on the Tennessee model that focuses on improvement or gain scores. (For further discussion of value-added methodology see Chapter 8.)

These different methods may offer valuable starting points for collaborative design teams of teachers and administrators to consider in advance of the next round of negotiations or as part of proposed pilot initiatives (94-95). Constantly communicating that student outcome data is only one source of information being considered can help incorporate these and other approaches to measuring student outcomes in your district's evaluation procedures. Requiring student outcome data to justify the contents of a Professional Development Plan (PDP) and/or Professional Improvement Plans (PIP) can be another way to build acceptance for linking information about results to assessment of practice. PDP's are generally associated with the ongoing professional development expected of all teachers to maintain and update their basic teaching credential (i.e., a certificate or license). PIP's are generally used to specify activities aimed at remediating previously identified deficiencies. Both are strengthened and made more pointed by information about how well students are learning as a result of actions taken by the teacher.

Making sure that the teacher performance standards contain appropriate criteria and indicators that will ultimately require teachers and evaluators to talk about the results of teaching is an important step. Language such as Montgomery County's performance criterion "The teacher analyzes student information and results and plans instruction accordingly" can help, but it is only part of the task of meaningful data use. The real challenge is whether leaders on both sides of the table actually make that criterion come alive by incorporating data discussions into their routine practice. As Jim Stronge notes in reflecting on his experiences:

> As for the secret for successfully incorporating any direct measure of student success in teacher assessment, if there is one, it is sustained commitment to the policy and practice from a high level within the educational organization and then hard work to make it happen. Perhaps equally importantly, there must be teacher involvement in the design of the new system, carefully unveiling the system through piloting and other means, and, ultimately, broad-based teacher buy-in to the concept. One way to achieve this latter critical element of teacher support is to provide intensive professional development support... at the Greenville County Public Schools in South Carolina teachers are required to collaboratively develop the data-driven achievement goals with their principal and then must meet with the principal at the end of the year to assess actual student progress. Also, the district has an instructional coach at each of almost 90 schools to work with teachers with embedded professional development on matters like student achievement goal setting, data analysis. (personal communication 2005)

Influencing Choices That Affect Teacher Quality

Every personnel decision, and especially tenure appointments, should meet the standard of "predicted high contribution" to the ultimate goal of maximizing each child's educational potential. Leaders have to do everything legally and morally possible to ensure that every teacher who enters the classroom is the best available every day. The task is enormously challenging. Paying attention to several aspects of control can help.

Using Multiple Sources of Data

One of the most common mistakes we see supervisors and evaluators make is "over-claiming": attempting to make a claim about a teacher's practice or a need for improvement based on one narrow data source or one or two rather flimsy pieces of evidence. It may be accompanied by an inappropriate rush to judgment based on one classroom observation, or it may be the result of a supervisor's recognition that s/he ignored earlier warning signs and now needs to "get evidence" of a problem quickly. Finally, over-claiming may reveal the supervisor's ignorance of rules of evidence or lack of experience in corroborating concerns. Whatever the impetus for the behavior, the failure to use multiple sources of data in assessing teacher performance or defining a performance problem undermines both the individual and the district's credibility.

Because past practice in teacher evaluation has almost always involved little more than the minimum number of observations and conferences, new leaders could find themselves facing union challenges when they ask teachers to provide other data such as lesson plans, student test results, formative assessment records, or sample papers. Newly designed evaluation systems that incorporate multiple data sources to show what a teacher is doing often contain explicit statements to that effect. Some districts like Barrington, Rhode Island, or Montgomery County, Maryland, provide appendixes or supplementary data source lists that suggest places teachers and evaluators can look for evidence of how well a particular performance standard is being met. Even though contract language permits the use of non-classroom data, that permission can be undermined if no one ever uses more than classroom observation in official documents or conferences. Thus opportunities to influence how data is used occur well after the original design phase. District leaders need to ensure that administrators and teachers develop a repertoire of ways to collect and analyze data and that supervisees are given every opportunity to demonstrate that they have met or exceeded district expectations. Skill in data collection and analysis is essential to our two other highlighted areas of influence: assigning performance ratings and making employment decisions using due process and just cause.

Assigning Performance Ratings

There are two key opportunities to influence the use of employee performance ratings: (1) during the design of and negotiations about an evaluation instrument and related procedures and (2) during the ongoing training for implementation and the systematic monitoring of implementation. In reviewing evaluation systems and talking to people who were involved in their design, we found considerable debate about the number of ratings that ought to be available on a scale. Many districts allowed evaluators only two possible ratings: "Meets" (the standard, the criterion, etc.) or "Does not meet" or its less recommended counterpart "Satisfactory" versus "Unsatisfactory." The best instruments had ratings for each standard rather than just a holistic summative rating. Because of the popularity of Charlotte Danielson's Framework, a number of systems used four-scale ratings. There is clear merit in using rubrics to guide conversations and goal setting, but we do not typically recommend rubrics for summative evaluation. Our experience suggests that evaluators often have difficulty collecting appropriate data about and clearly determining distinctions between middle categories in a four-scale rubric. What seems to be particularly helpful is a category that allows evaluators to signal that an individual has critical areas of weakness or a need for improvement in a particular aspect of practice without rating that individual's entire performance as either meeting or not meeting standard. Catalina Foothills School District, for example, uses (1) Meets standards, (2) Meets standards with conditions, (3) Does not meet standards.

Although using system design to influence performance ratings is probably the most straightforward approach, it is also the least available. System redesign or negotiation about evaluation occurs infrequently in most school districts; skillful leaders can wait a long time to influence performance ratings in this way. The more readily available chance to affect ratings comes in the way the school district trains its evaluators to discriminate between areas of performance, collect data effectively, communicate about performance clearly, and maintain their inter-rater reliability. If a district has only two available ratings to give, then administrators need constant practice and fine-tuning in using those ratings fairly and consistently as a group. Skillful organizational leaders monitor how their evaluators determine a "meets standards" rating holistically if the system requires them to do so, back up ratings with data, handle evidence of substandard performance in particular areas, and communicate expectations for improvement. Districts that use narratives or comments, either in place of checklists or to supplement them, provide training in writing rating statements that clearly tell teachers where their current performance needs to improve as well as how to make that improvement. If implementation means that everyone except the most egregiously ineffective teachers "meets standard," then there is no point in having a rating system.

Making Employment Decisions

Earlier we examined the inclusion of explicit references to student outcomes in a district's teacher performance standards and criteria. Before educational leaders can be held accountable for pupil outcomes, however, they must be given the authority to assemble and manage the personnel they believe they need to achieve the results they want. Simply put, principals must be able to select the people they believe to be the best available to carry out the school's mission. This becomes more critical as educational leaders try to develop and protect effective work groups who can engineer meaningful improvements in student outcomes.

The system devised to protect against abuses in the context of employment relationships has saddled public schools with a cumbersome and costly procedure known as *tenure*. One of the many challenges associated with the current educational reform movement has to be a reformation of the tenure process. Ensuring that ineffective employees can be removed with reasonable dispatch and fairness is one of the most important challenges the educational leaders and policy makers now face. In the meantime, leaders must have a clear understanding of what the law does and does not allow them to do when they are attempting to influence the quality of the teaching staff through employment decisions. Two concepts—*due process* and *just cause*—are essential cornerstones of such an understanding.

Understanding Due Process

Schools generally have a tenure system that involves a probationary period of service (usually two to five years) after which removal from one's position requires an employer to prove a legitimate cause for dismissal that is not arbitrary, capricious, or unlawfully discriminatory. The "machine" that regulates this propensity to abuse the inherent power associated with the employer/employee relationship in the public sector is *due process*. It serves to protect individual employees and institutions from dictators, doctrinarians, and psychopaths who have managed to achieve positions of power that might enable them to fire anyone who does not share their views. Such protection helps to ensure that a free exchange of ideas and honest differences of opinion can go on in a democratic society without fear of unlawful retribution when one's employer chooses not to tolerate the existence of a loyal opposition.

As a noted Supreme Court justice once said, "[due process] is the wild card of the judicial process" whenever someone in a position of authority has the capacity to fundamentally disrupt a subordinate's "status quo." *Due process* requires notice and an opportunity to be heard before a supervisor can change an individual's current status. It has its origins in the Enlightenment when western political systems evolved to the point of recognizing the inalienable rights of a free people to life, liberty, and the pursuit of happiness. In modern society, due process in its many forms regulates what government can do to individuals and how it must go about doing it. Thus an inefficient or incompetent public employee can be removed but only through the application of the type of due process that applies to the given circumstance. All levels of government, i.e., federal, state, and local, have added layers and local variations of what due process can mean in your school district.

When district level leadership does not ensure that all members of the organization have the same clear understanding of due process, they increase the likelihood that individuals will take inappropriate actions that then boomerang to limit the options available to other administrators. If district-wide orientation to due process is not currently available, ask for it. Know what due process requires in your district and follow it!

Understanding Just Cause

Most collective bargaining agreements, and some state laws, incorporate the concept of *just cause* (or in some cases "cause" or "good cause"). *Just cause* means that the employer did not act arbitrarily, capriciously, discriminatorily, or make a decision not based upon fact. Just cause clauses date back to the earliest years of collective bargaining in the private sector. They pose a challenge for school leaders since in the early years of public sector bargaining, many school districts accepted the classic National Education Association's (NEA) boiler plate "language" which said that "no teacher will be disciplined, reprimanded, reduced in rank or compensation, or denied any professional advantage without just cause." The phrase "just cause" may not have to appear specifically in a contract for the concept to apply. Unless there is clear and unambiguous language that prevents it, many arbitrators will apply a *just cause* standard because of the seriousness of the discipline and finality of dismissal cases. There are few legal guideposts to help the leader seeking clarification. In one helpful case involving the Needham Education Association and the Needham School Committee (MA), Arbitrator Cox stated that "just cause" is absent unless three requirements are satisfied:[8]

1. The employee committed the offense or was guilty of the shortcoming ascribed to him (i.e., the burden of proof).
2. The misconduct or shortcoming justified the disciplinary measure (i.e., an equitable standard was applied).
3. The procedure was consistent with fundamental fairness.

The Cox definition, although better than none at all, falls far short of giving school officials all the guidance they need in order to determine whether *just cause* exists to discipline a teacher whose performance has been determined to be unsatisfactory or falling short of the school district's performance standards. Most evaluation procedures require some remedial opportunity as part of the just clause standard. Stay in touch with your personnel office, and when a case arises, get information and guidance about both the data to be gathered and the remediation to be offered.

[8]*Needham Education Association and Needham School Committee*, AAA Case No. 1139-2023-83 (Cox 1984).

Summary

Schools need to be run in a way that will best maximize the educational potential of every child rather than in a way that defends and preserves the *status quo* for those who are employed by them. The conviction that every child deserves expert instruction and that every child can learn and the competence to deliver that expert instruction are not the only capacities leaders need. In this chapter we examined some of the legally governed aspects of leader's work that affect the third capacity of adequate control over structures, processes, and resources. We paid particular attention to the requirements of collective bargaining, the importance of adopting clear performance standards and criteria, and the need to understand processes and decisions that affect teacher quality.

Epilogue:
Reasons to Hope

An epilogue often tells readers the fate of characters they have come to know and care about. Would that we could do that here. We wish we had the power to determine the fate of schools poised on the edge of improvement. We yearn to tell children who start each September full of determination and optimism that *this time* a team of teachers will see their capabilities and help them meet demanding academic standards. We want to promise leaders across the country that their efforts will be magnified by the problem-solving power of Accountable Communities throughout their schools. Unfortunately, we cannot yet say that all those goals will be met. However, we can point to five reasons to hope and ideas and trends to monitor as they evolve over the next decade.

1. **Experiments with differentiated budgeting are showing promise in helping schools with large numbers of high-need students.**
   Confronting conditions that undermine student learning requires that policy leaders examine how accurately school budgets reflect the actual needs of student populations. More resources are required to close a learning gap for a child who comes to school four grades behind in reading or without an understanding of fundamental mathematics concepts than for one who arrives performing only six months behind expected benchmarks. Some reformers attribute significant improvements in student achievement to budgetary policies that use weighted funding. Under such policies, school budgets are determined by a formula that assigns each child a funding weight reflecting the severity of his or her learning demands. Experiences in Edmonton, Seattle, and Houston suggest the optimism may be well placed. William Ouchi, an expert on the subject, explains how Seattle allocates money to schools.

   Weights range from 1 to 9.2.... A child with no additional weightings—for example, one from a middle-class home living with both parents, who is a native speaker and has no learning disabilities—takes with him to school a weighting of 1 and funds of only the base amount of $2616. A child from a poor home with one parent and severe learning disabilities, who is not fluent in English, may receive the maximum weighting of $24,067 (87).

Leaders who advocate for differentiated budgets believe that providing appropriate funds coupled with school-based decision-making gives principals and teachers the resources to better address student learning needs. This policy also creates the precondition for holding schools and their leaders accountable for results.

2. **New career lattice and differentiated compensation models may help schools and districts provide rewards and incentives to teachers who are able to help students with the highest levels of need.** As skeptics about past merit pay plans, it is perhaps surprising that we find reasons to hope pay for performance might really impact student learning. Few issues engender more union-school board tension than pay for performance or what has historically been called merit pay. Unions have traditionally advocated strongly for higher pay and benefits for all their members and vigorously fought differentiating teachers' compensation based on their performance or the context in which they work. Unions correctly claim that there have been few examples of successful merit pay programs. Indeed, many initiatives have been plagued by underfunding, poor supervisor skill, or inexplicit criteria. Opponents have also argued that differentiating pay for individuals creates unhealthy competition among teachers and undermines the creation of supportive, high-functioning groups in schools. Communities and school boards, however, have been pushing for pay for performance because of public frustration with perceived limitations of present compensation schemes that include:

- Rewarding only experience or graduate credits, not a teacher's impact on learning
- Failing to reward individuals who work in more challenging schools
- Blocking a system's ability to differentiate pay for difficult-to-fill positions

Finally, there is a perception that few unions are perceived to be active participants in pushing for excellence and supporting interventions with low-performing colleagues.[1]

But despite past disappointments, a Pay for Performance experiment is underway in Denver, Colorado. The Denver Teachers

---

[1]Notable exceptions to this perception are the members of the progressive TURN Exchange (www.turnexchange.net/) who have been active supporters of Peer Assisted Review (PAR) and other partnering initiatives.

Association (DTA) has been a full partner in developing and approving The Denver Professional Compensation System (ProCom). Noting a rejection of an earlier similar plan by 96% of Cincinnati teachers, many urban districts are watching as the Denver program enters its second year of full implementation in 2007. There are early reasons to be hopeful because of the strong union support and its differentiated reward structure. The plan is notable for the following components:

- Market incentives that encompass additional stipends for "hard to staff assignments" and "hard to staff schools"

- A focus on student growth that includes both individual and group incentives to teachers who have a positive impact on student learning

- Incentives for completing additional academic degrees including National Board Certification to enhance teachers' knowledge and skills[2]

It is possible that ProCom has the right mix of reward incentives for teacher behavior, student impact, and team functioning, although we expect they will regularly work to fine-tune the balance.[3] We are especially hopeful about the impact of rewards focused on schools and teams rather than individuals. If districts like Denver can collaborate with their unions to create flexible compensation policies that better reflect the different needs of students and honor the work of staff members who push themselves to reach new levels of achievement, others are likely to follow their lead.

3. **Newly minted teachers expect to work collaboratively and are accustomed to teamwork.** They are ready to provide energy and leadership for professional communities. Twenty years ago, futurists warned American educators that young people would need to learn problem solving and teamwork if they were to survive in the workplace of the 21st century. Many districts paid attention, and a generation of young scholars has prepared in schools and universities that regularly asked them to participate in cooperative learning, study groups, and team projects. In general, we find the novice teachers we interview expect—and hope—to be involved in multiple collaborative efforts at their schools. They do not expect to be left alone to flounder until they teach themselves how to teach. Nor do they expect that they will hoard their own strategies and insights rather than share them with others. Most want to be involved in shaping the school's future. Most also say that they

[2]For further information see ProCom link on www.dpsk12.org/
[3]A report by Benjamin Degrow issued by The Independence Institute in 2007 (www.i2i.org/articles/IP_5_2007.pdf) has recommended that more emphasis be put on student achievment because teachers who earned National Board Certification received the largest compensation, as opposed to teachers who have shown impact on student learning.

would like more feedback and more interactions with coaches and administrators who know how to help them improve. The best and the brightest of these new teachers are unwilling to tolerate toxic cultures. They represent a tremendous resource for school leaders and for veteran teachers who have hungered for collegial interaction but found themselves increasingly isolated.

A smaller but nonetheless noteworthy sample of newly hired, middle-level administrators (assistant principals, deans, department heads, and coordinators), lead teachers, and content coaches has had some positive experience with professional learning groups. These new administrators need to be given permission to mobilize faculty in different ways than their predecessors have done, resources to support their initiatives, and ongoing training and feedback to solidify what they learn by doing. Whenever we see principals sharing responsibility for facilitation, assigning vice-principals to grade level teams and instructional challenges rather than endless cafeteria duty, or arranging coaching for new department heads, we see reason to hope.

4. **Growing attention to the importance of leadership development, distribution, and sustainability may help both novice and veteran principals get the support they need to take on significant obstacles to achievement.** Over the years, researchers and reformers have claimed that good leadership was an essential part of what made a school effective. Waters, Marzano, and McNulty's meta-analysis of leadership studies made the correlation between student achievement and leadership behaviors more concrete. Stanford's recently released report on its three-year School Leadership Study notes the increase in coherent state-level training and preparation programs and the development of innovative local certification programs that immerse prospective candidates in doing the real work of school leadership. Graduates of these programs, the study notes, report a greater sense of confidence in their preparation and skills and are more likely to carry out the behaviors of effective principals than colleagues prepared in more traditional programs (Darling-Hammond, LaPointe, Meyerson, and Orr 9). As researchers help to pinpoint the important knowledge, skills, and personal qualities school leaders need, the old notion may be dying that becoming a principal was "what you did when you wanted to make more money" or the only opportunity to advance in an otherwise egalitarian profession. Happily, we think the perception that leadership positions are "owed" to anyone who puts in time or that they are popularity contests may be fading as well.

The individuals we meet in our graduate courses, coaching, and administrator development sessions are much more likely to treat the principalship as a calling and to understand the complexities of the job than were their predecessors ten years ago. If they have been trained in a program that builds strong, supportive, collegial cohorts, they understand the nature and potential of collaboration and are more likely to pool their knowledge and skills to help their district than to pretend they have all the answers and can manage alone. Like their teacher colleagues, a number of these new principals expected and got a rigorous selection process, one that required them to produce evidence that they already had experience with or knew how to be an instructional leader and to reach out to and mobilize communities. Beyond changing assumptions about the role and changing attitudes about what it takes to truly prepare a good principal, we see the greatest hope in districts' commitment to ongoing leadership training, monitoring, and support. Programs such as Montgomery County's Administrator and Supervisor Professional Growth System offer consulting principals for both novices and veterans in need of help. Boston's School Leadership Institute offers a wide range of programs and support that demonstrates its willingness to invest heavily in future leaders. Central Office or Cluster Office staff in large districts across the country pull principals together to share strategies and conduct walk-throughs that help gather first-hand data about what a principal can do. Superintendents in small and mid-sized districts from Lowell, Massachusetts, to Springfield, Illinois, organize and participate in ongoing training programs, self-assessments, and continuous improvement activities that put the importance of adult learning for all members of an organization at the top of the agenda. Moreover, they inspect what they expect, sending the message that every school deserves an expert leader and increasing the likelihood that the next generation will have a powerful model to follow.

5. **Public schools may be getting better.** As competition and NCLB result in better school leaders, better prepared teachers, bursts of innovation and creative partnerships, the pressure for parents and students to seek outside alternatives may be reduced. In 2000 we wrote that public schools were in danger. We cited critics' assertions that schools could not police themselves, as well as parents' interest in more vouchers and more charter schools, in magnet and choice programs and home schooling rather than in trying to preserve and improve the institutions they had. Alternatives to traditional public schools are still growing. Our traditional concept of "a single monolithic public school system," Ouchi notes, "is rapidly being replaced by a garden in which many choices are blooming" (184). For example, a decade ago we did not envision profit-making "cyber" charter schools like Einstein Academy that provide resources for parents who opt for home schooling or virtual academies and schools without walls. Results from alternatives housed both inside and outside the traditional public schools have been mixed. Charter schools and "small schools" vary greatly in their

effectiveness. Some, like the Gates Manual School in Denver, have failed miserably.[4] Replication has been very difficult, and moving to scale with reform has been disappointing.[5] Why then are we hopeful for public schools?

The combination of new funding sources, led by the Bill and Melinda Gates Foundation, and the pressure of meeting NCLB requirements has helped to spur development of entrepreneurial leaders, innovative schools, and creative partnerships.

- Small public high schools with more intimacy and accountability are springing up in some of our most challenging urban centers from New York to Oakland. Many report increasingly positive student outcomes.

- Alternative public schools such as the Pilot Schools in Boston and Dream Schools in San Francisco are being created with union support. More students are succeeding.

- Single-sex academies and classrooms are now permitted through a change of regulation issued by the Department of Education in late 2006 (www.singlesexschools.org/legal.html). This offers one more possible choice for parents and children.

- New partnerships are being created with public schools to offer new opportunities for students such as Career and Technical Education (CTE), which combines strong academic integration with the learning of marketable skills (www.acteonline.org). Colleges are beginning to partner with high schools to offer accelerated progress for able students. The Bard College High School Early College program offers successful students the possibility of earning an AA degree when they graduate from high school.

Granted, in some cases the rambunctious pursuit of choice becomes disconnected from overall reform strategy. Leaders should be cautious about setting off too many competing options within a district. Expanding choice is not an end in itself. Providing a a greater variety of valid and powerful learning models open to more students and accompanied by rigorous monitoring for quality control is the goal. We are learning from our failures as well as our successes. Taking these experiments together, we see reason to hope that we can fulfill the traditional promise of a free and equal public education for all.

---

[4]See "Bill Gates Get Schooled" *Business Week*, June 26 2006.
[5]Paul Hill describes why school choice has been so difficult to implement and has disappointed its advocates by its slow pace of implementation. (Commentary "Waiting for the Tipping Point: Why School Choice is Proving So Hard" *Education Week* September 5, 2007.)

Bibliography

Airasian, Peter W., and Arlen R. Gullickson. *Teacher Self-Evaluation Tool Kit*. Thousand Oaks, CA: Corwin Press, 1997.

Allen, David. *Assessing Student Learning*. New York: Teacher's College Press, 1998.

Ancess, Jacqueline. *Beating the Odds: High Schools as Communities of Commitment*. New York: Teachers College Press, 1993.

Benner, Aprile D. *The Cost of Teacher Turnover*. Austin, TX: Texas Center for Educational Research, 2000.

Bereiter, Carl, and Marlene Scardamalia. *Surpassing Ourselves: An Inquiry Into the Nature and Implications of Expertise*. Chicago, IL: Open Court, 1993.

Bolton, Dale L. *Selection and Evaluation of Teachers*. Berkeley, CA: McCutchan Publishing, 1973.

Bossidy, Larry, Ram Charan, and Ram Burck. *Execution: The Discipline of Getting Things Done*. New York: Crown Business, 2002.

Boudett, Kathryn Parker, Elizabeth A. City, and Richard J. Murnane, ed. *Data Wise: A Step-by-step Guide to Using Assessment Results to Improve Teaching and Learning*. Cambridge, MA: Harvard Education Publishing Group, 2005.

Brown, Lois Easton, ed. *Powerful Designs for Professional Learning*. Oxford, OH: National Staff Development Council, 2004.

Chauncey, Caroline, ed. *Recruiting, Retaining, and Supporting Highly Qualified Teachers*. Cambridge, MA: Harvard Education Press, 2005.

Cherrington, David J. *Personnel Management*. 2nd ed. Dubuque, IA: William C. Brown Publishers, 1987.

Collins, Jim. *Good to Great*. New York: Harper Collins, 2001.

Collins, Jim. *Why Business Thinking is Not the Answer: Good to Great and the Social Sectors*. Boulder, CO: Jim Collins, 2005.

Conzemius, Anne, and Jan O'Neill. *Building Shared Responsibility for Student Learning*. Alexandria, VA: ASCD, 2001.

Corbett, Dick, Bruce Wilson, and Belinda Williams. *Effort and Excellence in Urban Classrooms: Expecting—and Getting—Success with All Students*. New York: Teachers College Press, 2002.

Crowther, Frank, Stephen Kaagan, Margaret Ferguson, and Leonne Hann. *Developing Teacher Leaders*. Thousand Oaks, CA: Corwin Press, 2002.

Danielson, Charlotte. *Enhancing Professional Practice: A Framework for Teaching*. Alexandria, VA: ASCD, 1996.

Danielson, Charlotte. *Teacher Leadership that Strengthens Professional Practice*. Alexandria, VA: ASCD, 2006.

Darling-Hammond, Linda, and Barnett Berry. "Highly Qualified Teachers for All." *Educational Leadership* (Nov. 2006).

Darling-Hammond, Linda, Marcella L. Bullmaster, and Velma L. Cobb. "Rethinking Teacher Leadership through Professional Development Schools." *The Elementary School Journal* (Sept. 1995): 87-107.

Darling-Hammond, Linda, Michelle LaPointe, Debra Meyerson, and Margaret Orr. *Preparing School Leaders for a Changing World: Lessons from Exemplary Leadership Development Programs*. Stanford, CA: Stanford University, Stanford Educational Leadership Institute, 2007.

Donaldson, Jr., Gordon A. *Cultivating Leadership In Schools: Connecting People, Purpose and Practice*. 2nd ed. New York: Teachers College Press, 2006.

Downey, Carolyn, Betty E. Steffy, Fenwick W. English, Larry E. Frase, and William K. Poston, Jr. *The Three-Minute Classroom Walk-Through: Changing School Supervisory Practice One Teacher at A Time*. Thousand Oaks, CA: Corwin Press, 2004.

Doyle, Michael, and David Straus. *The New Interaction Method: How to Make Meetings Work!* New York: Berkley Books, 1975.

Drago-Stevenson, Eleanor. *Helping Teachers Learn.* Thousand Oaks, CA: Corwin Press, 2004.

Dufour, Richard, Rebecca Dufour, Robert Eaker and Gayle Karhanek. *Whatever It Takes: How Professional Learning Communities Respond When Kids Don't Learn.* Bloomington, IN: National Educational Service, 2004.

Dufour, Richard, and Rober Eaker. *Professional Learning Communities at Work: Best Practices for Enhancing Student Achievement.* Alexandria, VA: ASCD, 1998.

DuFour, Richard, Robert Eaker, and Rebecca DuFour, ed. *On Common Ground: The Power of Professional Learning Communities.* Bloomington, IN: National Educational Service, 2005.

Edmondson, Amy, Richard Bohmer, and Gary Pisano. "Speeding Up Team Learning." *Harvard Business Review on Teams That Succeed.* Boston. MA: Harvard Business School Publishing Corp., 2004. 77-97.

Effron, Marc S. "Knowledge Management Involves Neither Knowledge nor Management." *Leading Organizational Learning: Harnessing the Power of Knowledge.* Ed. Marshall Goldsmith, Howard J. Morgan, and Alexander J. Ogg. San Francisco, CA: Jossey-Bass, 2004. 39-49.

Elmore, Richard. *School Reform from the Inside Out: Policy, Practice, and Performance.* Cambridge, MA: Harvard Education Press, 2005.

Evans, Robert. *The Human Side of School Change.* San Francisco, CA: Jossey-Bass, 1996.

Feiman-Nemser, Sharon. "From Preparation to Practice: Designing a Continuum to Strengthen and Sustain Teaching." *Teachers College Record* (December 2001): 1013-1055.

Garmston, Robert J., and Bruce M. Wellman. *The Adaptive School: A Sourcebook for Developing Collaborative Groups.* Norwood, MA: Christopher-Gordon Publishers, Inc., 1999.

Gladwell, Malcolm. *Blink: The Power of Thinking Without Thinking.* New York, NY: Little, Brown and Co., 2005.

Glaude, Catherine. *Protocols for Professional Learning Conversations: Cultivating the Art and Discipline.* Courtenay, B.C.: Connections Publishing, 2005.

Glickman, Carl D. *Leadership and Learning: How to Help Teachers Succeed.* Alexandria, VA: ASCD, 2002.

Glickman, Carl D., Stephen P. Gordon, and Jovita M. Ross-Gordon. *Supervision and Instructional Leadership: A Developmental Approach.* 6th ed. Boston, MA: Allyn and Bacon, 2003.

Grove, Andrew. *High Output Management.* New York: Vintage Books, 1995.

Haberman, Martin. *Star Teachers of Children in Poverty.* Indianapolis, IN: Kappa Delta Pi, 1995.

Haberman, Martin. *Star Teachers: The Ideology and Best Practice of Effective Teachers of Diverse Children and Youth in Poverty.* Houston. TX: Haberman Educational Foundation, 2005.

Heifetz, Ronald A., and Marty Linsky. *Leadership on the Line: Staying Alive Through the Dangers of Leading.* Boston, MA: Harvard Business School Press, 2002.

Heller, Daniel A. *Teachers Wanted: Attracting and Retaining Good Teachers.* Alexandria, VA: ASCD, 2004.

Hoerr, Thomas R. *The Art of School Leadership.* Alexandria, VA: ASCD, 2005.

Holcomb, Edie L. *Getting Excited About Data: How to Combine People, Passion, and Proof.* Thousand Oaks, CA: Corwin Press, 1999.

Johnson, Susan Moore. *Finders and Keepers: Helping New Teachers Survive and Thrive in Our Schools.* San Francisco, CA: Jossey-Bass, 2004.

Katzenbach, Jon R., and Douglas K. Smith. "The Discipline of Teams." *Harvard Business Review on Teams That Succeed.* Boston, MA: Harvard Business School Publishing Corp., 2004. 1-25.

Katzenmeyer, Marilyn, and Gayle Moller. *Awakening the Sleeping Giant.* Thousand Oaks, CA: Corwin Press, 2001.

Kegan, Robert, and Lisa Laskow Lahey. *How the Way We Talk Can Change the Way We Work.* San Francisco, CA: Jossey-Bass, 2001.

Keller, Bess. "Path to Classroom Not Linked to Teachers' Success." *Education Week* 23 Mar. 2006.

LaFasto, Frank M. J., and Carl Larson. *When Teams Work Best: 6,000 Team Members and Leaders Tell What it Takes to Succeed.* Thousand Oaks, CA: Sage Publications, 2001.

Lambert, Linda. *Building Leadership Capacity in Schools.* Alexandria, VA: ASCD, 1998.

Larson, Carl E., and Frank M. J. LaFasto. *TeamWork: What Must Go Right/What Can Go Wrong.* Newbury Park, CA: Sage Publications, 1989.

Lencioni, Patrick. *The Five Dysfunctions of a Team.* San Francisco, CA: Jossey-Bass, 2002.

Lencioni, Patrick. *Overcoming The Five Dysfunctions of a Team*, San Francisco, CA: Jossey-Bass, 2005.

Levin, Jessica, Meredith Quinn, and Joan Schunck. *Unintended Consequences: The Case for Reforming the Staff Rules in Urban Teachers Union Contracts.* New York: The New Teacher Project, 2005.

Levin, Jessica, and Jennifer Mulhern. *Missed Opportunities: How We Keep High-Quality Teachers Out of Urban Schools.* New York: The New Teacher Project, 2003.

Levy, Paul F. "The Nut Island Effect: When Good Teams Go Wrong." *Harvard Business Review on Teams That Succeed.* Boston, MA: Harvard Business School Publishing Corp., 2004. 167-186.

Lindsey, Randall B., Laraine Roberts, and Franklin Campbell Jones. *The Culturally Proficient School: An Implementation Guide for School Leaders.* Thousand Oaks, CA: Sage Publications, 2005.

Love, Nancy. *Using Data/Getting Results: a Practical guide for School Improvement in Mathematics and Science.* Norwood, MA: Christopher-Gordon Publishers, 2002.

Love, Nancy, Katherine E. Stiles, Kathryn DiRanna, and Susan Mundry. *A Data Coach's Guide to Improving Learning for All Students: Unleashing the Power of Collaborative Inquiry.* Thousand Oaks, CA: Corwin Press, In Press.

Marzano, Robert J. *Transforming Classroom Grading.* Alexandria, VA: ASCD, 2000.

Marzano, Robert J. *What Works In Schools: Translating Research into Action*. Alexandria, VA: ASCD, 2003.

Marzano, Robert J., Debra Pickering, and Jane E. Pollock. *Classroom Instruction That Works: Research-Based Strategies for Increasing Student Achievement*. Alexandria, VA: ASCD, 2001.

Marzano, Robert J., Timothy Waters, and Brian A. McNulty. *School Leadership that Works: From Research to Results*. Alexandria, VA: ASCD and Aurora, CO: McRel, 2005.

Maslow, Abraham. *Motivation and Personality*. 3rd ed. New York: Harper, 1987.

Mathews, Jay. "Radical Changes Pay Off For D.C. Catholic Schools: Once-Dying Campuses Find Success by Borrowing from Indiana's Playbook." *Washington Post* 8 Jan. 2007.

McDonald, Joseph P., Nancy Mohr, Alan Dichter, and Elizabeth C. McDonald. *The Power of Protocols: An Educator's Guide to Better Practice*. New York: Teachers College Press, 2003.

McLaughlin, Milbrey W., and Joan E. Talbert. *Building School Based Teacher Learning Communities: Professional Strategies to Improve Student Achievement*. New York: Teachers College Press, 2006.

McLaughlin, Milbrey W., and Joan E. Talbert. *Professional Communities and the Work of High School Teaching*. Chicago, IL: University of Chicago Press, 2001.

Moller, Gayle, and Marilyn Katzenmeyer. *Every Teacher As a Leader: Realizing the Potential of Teacher Leadership*. San Francisco, CA: Jossey-Bass, 1996.

Munck, Bill, Robert Kegan, Lisa Laskow Lahey, Debra E. Mayerson, Donald Sull, Katherine M. Hudson, and Paul F. Levy. *Harvard Business Review on Culture and Change*. Boston, MA: Harvard Business School Press, 2002.

Murphy, Carlene U., and Dale W. Lick. *Whole-Faculty Study Groups: Creating Student-Based Professional Development*. Thousand Oaks, CA: Corwin Press, 2001.

Nelsen, Jeff, Joe Palumbo, Amalia Cudeiro, and Jan Leight. *The Power of Focus: Lessons Learned in District and School Improvement*. Focus on Results, 2005.

Newmann, Fred M., and Gary G. Wehlage. *Successful School Restructuring*. Madison, WI: Center on Organization and Restructuring of Schools, 1995.

Oberman, Ida et al. *Challenged Schools, Remarkable Results: Three Lessons from California's Highest Achieving High Schools*. San Francisco, CA: Springboard Schools, 2005.

Ouchi, William G. *Making Schools Work*. New York: Simon and Schuster, 2003.

Patterson, Kerry, Joseph Grenny, Ron McMillan, and Al Switzler. *Crucial Confrontations: Tools for Resolving Broken Promises, Violated Expectations and Bad Behavior*. NY: McGraw Hill, 2005.

Patterson, Kerry, Joseph Grenny, Ron McMillan, and Al Switzler. *Crucial Conversations: Tools for Talking When Stakes Are High*. New York: McGraw Hill, 2002.

Patterson, Jerry L., Janice Patterson, and Loucrecia Collins. *Bouncing Back! How Your School Can Succeed in the Face of Diversity*. Larchmont, NY: Eye on Education, 2002.

Perkins, David. *King Arthur's Roundtable: How Collaborative Conversations Create Smart Organizations*. Hoboken, N.J.: John Wiley & Sons, 2003.

Peterson, Kenneth D. *Effective Teacher Hiring: A Guide to Getting the Best*. Alexandria, VA: ASCD, 2002.

Peterson, Kenneth D. *Teacher Evaluation: A Comprehensive Guide to New Directions and Practices*. Thousand Oaks, CA: Corwin Press, 2000.

Pfeffer, Jeffrey, and Robert I. Sutton. "The Smart-Talk Trap." *Harvard Business Review on Organizational Learning*. Boston, MA: Harvard Business School Publishing Company, 2001.

Platt, Alexander D., Caroline E. Tripp, Wayne R. Ogden, and Robert G. Fraser. *The Skillful Leader: Confronting Mediocre Teaching*. Acton, MA: Ready About Press, 2000.

Reeves, Douglas B. *Accountability for Learning: How Teachers and School Leaders Can Take Charge*. Alexandria, VA: ASCD, 2004.

Reeves, Douglas B. *Assessing Educational Leaders: Evaluating Performance for Improved Individual and Organizational Results*. Thousand Oaks, CA: Corwin Press, 2004.

Reeves, Douglas B. *The Leader's Guide to Standards: A Blueprint for Educational Equity and Excellence.* San Francisco, CA: Jossey-Bass, 2002.

Reeves, Douglas B. *The Learning Leader: How to Focus School Improvement for Better Results.* Alexandria, VA: ASCD, 2006.

Resnick, Lauren B., and Megan Williams Hall. "Learning Organizations for Sustainable Education Reform." Conference Draft—Institute for Learning Seminar, May 1998.

Ribas, William B., Jennifer Antos Deane, and Scott Seider. *Instructional Practices That Maximize Student Achievement: for Teachers, by Teachers.* Westwood, MA: Ribas Publications, 2005.

Rosenholtz, Susan J. Teachers *Workplace: The Social Organization of Schools.* New York: Teachers College Press, 1991.

Saphier, Jon. *How to Make Supervision and Evaluation Really Work.* Acton, MA: Research for Better Teaching, 1993.

Saphier, Jon. *John Adams' Promise: How to Have Good Schools for All Our Children, Not Just for Some.* Acton, MA: Research for Better Teaching, 2005.

Saphier, Jon, Susan Freedman, and Barbara Aschheim. *Beyond Mentoring: Comprehensive Induction Programs.* Newton, MA: Teachers 21, 2001.

Saphier, Jon, Mary Ann Haley-Speca, and Robert Gower. *The Skillful Teacher: Building Your Teaching Skills.* 6th ed. Acton, MA: Research for Better Teaching, 2008.

Schein, Edgar H. *Organizational Culture and Leadership.* 2nd ed. San Francisco, CA: Jossey-Bass, 1992.

Schmoker, Mike. *Results: The Key to Continuous School Improvement.* Alexandria, VA: ASCD, 1996.

Schmoker, Mike. *The Results Fieldbook: Practical Strategies from Dramatically Improved Schools.* Alexandria, VA: ASCD, 2001.

Senge, Peter, Nelda H. Cambron McCabe, Timothy Lucas, Art Kleiner, Janice Dutton, and Bryan Smith. *Schools That Learn: A Fifth Discipline Fieldbook for Educators, Parents, and Everyone Who Cares About Education.* New York: Doubleday, 2000.

Sergiovanni, Thomas J. "Building a Community of Hope." *Educational Leadership*. (May, 2004): 33-37.

Sergiovanni, Thomas J. *Strengthening the Heartbeat: Leading and Learning Together in Schools*. San Francisco, CA: Jossey-Bass, 2002.

Sergiovanni, Thomas J., and Robert J. Starratt. *Supervision: A Redefinition*. 7th ed. New York: McGraw-Hill, 2002.

Simmons, John. *Breaking Through: Transforming Urban School Districts*. New York: Teachers College Press, 2006.

Stevenson, Harold W., and James W. Stigler. *The Learning Gap*. New York: Simon and Schuster, 1992.

Stiggens, Richard J. *Student-Involved Classroom Assessment*. Upper Saddle River, NJ: Merrill Prentice Hall, 2001.

Stigler, James W., and James Hiebert. *The Teaching Gap: Best Ideas from the World's Teachers for Improving Education in the Classroom*. New York: The Free Press, 1999.

Stone, Douglas, Bruce Patton, and Sheila Heen. *Difficult Conversations: How to Discuss What Matters Most*. New York: Viking, 1999.

Strong, Richard W., Harvey F. Silver, and Matthew J. Perini. *Teaching What Matters Most*. Alexandria, VA: ASCD, 2001.

Stronge, James H. *Evaluating Teaching: A Guide to Current Thinking and Best Practice*. Thousand Oaks, CA: Corwin Press, 1997.

Stronge, James H. *Qualities of Effective Teachers*. Alexandria, VA: ASCD, 2002.

Stronge, James H., and Pamela D. Tucker. *Handbook on Teacher Evaluation: Assessing and Improving Performance*. Larchmont, NY: Eye on Education, 2003.

Title, David G. *How to Hire a Teacher*. Sacramento, CA: American Association of School Personnel Officers, 1995.

Tucker, Pamela D., and James H. Stronge. *Linking Teacher Evaluation and Student Learning*. Alexandria, VA: ASCD, 2005.

Ulrich, Dave, and Norm Smallwood. "Tangling with Learning Intangibles." *Leading Organizational Learning: Harnessing the Power of Knowledge*. Ed. Marshall Goldsmith, Howard Morgan, and Alexander J. Ogg. San Francisco, CA: Jossey-Bass, 2004. 65-78.

Wagner, Tony. *Making the Grade: Reinventing America's Schools.* New York, NY: Routledge Falmer, 2002.

Walstom, Deborah. *Using DATA to Improve Student Achievement: A Handbook for Collecting, Organizing, Analyzing and Using Data.* Suffolk, VA: Successline, 2002.

Wenger, Etienne, Richard McDermott, and William M. Snyder. *Cultivating Communities of Practice.* Boston, MA: Harvard Business School Press, 2002.

Westheimer, Joel. *Among School Teachers: Community Autonomy and Ideology in Teachers' Work.* New York: Teachers College Press, 1998.

Wiggins, Grant. *Educative Assessment: Designing Assessments to Inform and Improve Student Performance.* San Francisco: Jossey-Bass, 1998.

York-Barr, Jennifer, William Sommers, Gail Ghere, and Jo Montie. *Reflective Practice to Improve Schools.* Thousand Oaks, CA: Corwin Press, 2006.

U.S. Dept. of Education *The Education Innovator* #7 volume 2 (February 23, 2004).

Index

Ready About Consulting™

Skillful Leader Professional Development Opportunities

Ready About Consulting offers a range of institutes, courses, consultation and conference presentations on the topics in this book and on *The Skillful Leader: Confronting Mediocre Teaching* (2000).

For further information:
Web: www.ready-about.com
Email: ReadyAb@aol.com
Voice mail: 978-264-4242

The Skillful Teacher: Building Your Teaching Skills 6th edition • 2008

by Jon Saphier, Mary Ann Haley-Speca, and Robert Gower

This book has become the gold standard text in many colleges and school districts across the country for studying generic pedagogy. Designed for both the novice and the experienced educator. *The Skillful Teacher* is a unique synthesis of the knowledge base on teaching with powerful repertoires for matching teaching strategies to student needs. Designed as a practical guide for practitioners working to broaden their teaching skills, the book combines theory with practice and focuses on 18 critical areas of classroom performance. A must for instructional coaches and mentors!

John Adams' Promise: How to Have Good Schools for All Our Children, Not Just for Some 2005

by Jon Saphier

Curriculum reform, structural reform, funding reform, organization reform—all these 20th-century efforts have failed to make a significant dent in the achievement gap and the performance of disadvantaged students, especially in cities and poor rural areas. What are the most important targets for school improvement?

The Skillful Leader: Confronting Mediocre Teaching 2000

by Alexander D. Platt, Caroline Tripp, Wayne R. Ogden, and Robert G. Fraser

Based on *The Skillful Teacher* framework, this book is targeted to evaluators and supervisors who want a field-tested tool kit of strategies to improve, rather than remove, underperforming teachers. The text includes valuable legal notes and a model contract, case studies, assessment tools, and personal accounts of leaders in action.

Talk Sense: Communicating to Lead and Learn 2007

by Barry Jentz

Barry Jentz shows how leaders can build the requisite trust and credibility for improving organizational performance. Typically, leaders *talk tough* to improve performance; when that doesn't work, they *talk nice* (or vice-versa). By learning to *talk sense*, leaders can succeed in their efforts to improve performance.

Activators: Activity Structures to Engage Students' Thinking Before Instruction 1993

by Jon Saphier and Mary Ann Haley

This book is a collection of classroom-tested, practical activity structures for getting students' minds active and engaged prior to introducing new content or skills. Each structure is designed to elicit what students already know about a topic, to surface misconceptions, and to create cognitive hooks when new material is presented.

Summarizers: Activity Structures to Support Integration and Retention of New Learning 1993

by Jon Saphier and Mary Ann Haley

This book is a collection of classroom-tested, practical activity structures for getting students cognitively active during and after periods of instruction. Each structure provides a framework for guiding students to summarize for themselves what is important, what they have learned, and/or how it fits with what they already know.

How to Bring Vision to School Improvement: Through Core Outcomes, Commitments, and Beliefs 1993

by Jon Saphier and John D'Auria

This practical guide provides a proven step-by-step sequence for generating consensus among parents and staff about some of the valued core outcomes they want for all children. Then it shows how to achieve them through concrete areas in school and family life.

How to Make Supervision and Evaluation Really Work: Supervision and Evaluation in the Context of Strengthening School Culture 1993

by Jon Saphier

This book offers school leaders a carefully integrated approach for transforming often divisive supervision and evaluation systems into a positive force for strengthening school culture. Specific guidelines lead to meaningful, multifaceted teacher evaluation systems.

RESEARCH FOR BETTER TEACHING
One Acton Place • Acton, MA 01720
978.263.9449 *voice* • 978.263.9959 *fax*
www.RBTeach.com *web*